"Linda Thomas and Dwight Hopkins have done it again! This collection puts on full display the interdisciplinary nature, intergenerational wisdom, and intervocational fecundity of black and womanist theologies. From the lecture hall, to the pulpit, to the pew, *Walk Together Children* will inform and inspire the hearts and heads of those who seek to better understand this African American faith tradition."

—Jonathan L. Walton
author of *Watch This! The Ethics and Aesthetics of Black Televangelism*

# Contents

## PART SIX: New Voices in the Black Church

## PART SEVEN: Global Future

# Acknowledgments

THE LOUISVILLE INSTITUTE, a program of the Lily Endowment, sponsored the national conference "Black Theology and Womanist Theology in Dialogue: Which Way Forward for the Church and the Academy?" Thanks goes to James W. Lewis, the executive director. The first drafts of the majority of the papers in this book were prepared for that gathering. Dwight N. Hopkins (The University of Chicago Divinity School) and Linda E. Thomas (Lutheran School of Theology at Chicago [LSTC]) were co-principals of the Louisville Institute grant and were co-organizers of the conference.

Thanks to co-funding from the Lutheran School of Theology at Chicago and co-funders from the University of Chicago: The Divinity School; The Center for the Study of Race, Politics, and Culture; The Office of Community and Government Affairs; The Office of Minority Student Affairs; and Rockefeller Memorial Chapel.

Thanks to Keith Baltimore (Hopkins' research assistant). Each conference speaker was introduced by a graduate student either from the University of Chicago or from the LSTC. In addition, these students handled all airport transportation and all hospitality issues.

We also appreciate specifically the professors at the surrounding schools of the LSTC and the University of Chicago who encouraged their students to attend the five-day conference. Some of these professors made conference attendance a class requirement. The professors include, but are not limited to, JoAnne Terrell, Lee Butler, Pete Pero, Richard Perry, Cheryl Anderson, Jeffery Tribble, Deborah Mullen, Ogbu Kalu, Jose David Rodriquez, David Daniels, Larry Murphy, and Homer Ashby. We are aware of these specific names and apologize for omitting others who did the same with their students. Special appreciation is given to Leah Gaskin Fitchue (the first female president of Payne Theological Seminary), who also introduced a speaker.

We thank all the Chicagoland students, faculty, pastors, professionals, and everyday working class people who circulated through the hallowed halls of the University of Chicago and the LSTC for five days. Similar appreciation goes out to the many who traveled nationally. Some, not all, of the states included: California, Colorado, Wisconsin, New York, Connecticut, Tennessee, Georgia, Maryland, Louisiana, Washington DC, Illinois, Texas, Virginia, Ohio, Missouri, and New Jersey.

And special thanks to Richard Rosengarten (Dean, University of Chicago Divinity School) and James Echols and Kadi Billman (President and Dean, respectively, at the LSTC).

This national conference of pastors, professors, women, men, Protestants, Roman Catholics, heterosexuals, and same gender-loving participants, and youth, middle-aged, and elder attendees was a natural outgrowth of a "Black Theology and Womanist Theology" course co-taught by Linda E. Thomas and Dwight N. Hopkins, alternately at the University of Chicago Divinity School and the LSTC, since 1996–1997. Walk Together Children: Don't You Get Weary. There's A Great Meeting in the Promised Land.

# Introduction

**W**ALK TOGETHER CHILDREN: *Black and Womanist Theologies, Church and Theological Education* draws on the long religious, cultural, and singing history of Blacks in the U.S.A. Through the slavery and emancipation days until now, Black song has both nurtured and enhanced African American life as a collective whole. Communality has always included a variety of existential experiences. Plurality and individuality have been part of the ingenuity of what it meant to be Black in the creation and subsequent development of North America. What has kept this enduring people in a corporate process is their walking together through good times and bad, relying on what W. E. B. Du Bois called their "dogged strength" to keep "from being torn asunder."[1] Somehow and someway they intuited from historical memory or received from transcendental revelation that keeping on long enough on the road would yield ultimate fruit for the journey.

Indeed, the title of this book plays off a singing classic gifted by African Americans to America and the world. "Walk together children / Don't you get weary / There's a great meeting in the Promised Land" is a line from one of the famous Negro Spirituals.[2] The Negro Spirituals are songs created by and representative of the human effort of enslaved

---

1. W. E. B. Du Bois, *The Souls of Black Folk* (New York: New American Library, 1969) 45.

2. See John Lovell Jr., *Black Song: The Forge and the Flame—The Story of How the Afro-American Spiritual Was Hammered Out* (New York: Paragon, 1986) 278. Also William Francis Allen et al., eds., *Slave Songs of the United States: The Classic Anthology* (1887; reprint, New York: Dover, 1995); Miles Mark Fisher, *Negro Slave Songs in the United States* (Secaucus, NJ: Citadel, 1978); R. Nathaniel Dett, ed., *Religious Folk-Songs of the Negro: As Sung at Hampton Institute* (Hampton, VA: Hampton Institute Press, 1927); James Weldon Johnson and J. Rosamond Johnson, *American Negro Spirituals: Two Volumes in One* (1926–1927; reprint, New York: De Capo, 1977); James H. Cone, *The Spirituals and the Blues* (1972; reprint, Maryknoll, NY: Orbis, 1991), and Shane White and Graham White, *The Sounds of Slavery: Discovering African American History through Songs, Sermons, and Speech* (Boston: Beacon, 2005).

1

Africans and African Americans in North America, from 1619 to 1865.[3] Physically chained, Black bodies used song to conjure a "new world" identity out of a mixture of West African language groups.[4] Differences forged into one people. Bakongo, Ndongo, Fante, Ibo, Woloof, Shona, Hausa, and Twi—some of the multiple West African language groups forced across the Atlantic in the white, European Christian, slave trade— had to make common sense out of a common predicament.

What had happened to the diverse local ancestors of the families in each language group during the destabilizing ontology of enslavement? Were African ancestors upset because the living relatives had not performed correctly specific rituals? And what about the Almighty West African High God? Had this God abandoned ebony flesh squeezed between knee caps and elbows on the Middle Passage slave ships from West Africa to North and South Americas and the Caribbean? And how did their identities figure in the contorted anthropology of New World, Atlantic empire modernity of European emerging nations?[5]

3. Dwight N. Hopkins, *Down, Up & Over: Slave Religion and Black Theology* (Minneapolis: Fortress, 1999); Gayraud S. Wilmour, *Black Religion and Black Radicalism: An Interpretation of the Religious History of Afro-American People* (Maryknoll, NY: Orbis, 1983); Tim Hashaw, *The Birth of Black America: The First African Americans and the Pursuit of Freedom at Jamestown* (New York: Carroll & Graff, 2007); and Albert J. Raboteau, *Slave Religion: The Invisible Institution in the Antebellum South* (New York: Oxford University Press, 1978).

4. John Russell Rickford and Russell John Rickford, *Spoken Soul: The Story of Black English* (New York: Wiley, 2000); J. L. Dillard, *Black English: Its History and Usage in the United States* (New York: Random House, 1972); Geneva Smitherman, *Talkin and Testifyin: The Language of Black America* (Detroit: Wayne State University Press, 1977); and Winifred Kellersberger Vass, *The Bantu speaking Heritage of the United States* (Los Angeles: Center for Afro-American Studies, University of California Los Angeles, 1979).

5. Robin Blackburn, *The Making of New World Slavery: From the Baroque to the Modern, 1492–1800* (New York: Verso, 1998); J. H. Elliott, *Empires of the Atlantic World: Britain and Spain in American, 1492–1830* (New Haven: Yale University Press, 2007); and Robin Blackburn, *The Overthrow of Colonial Slavery: 1776–1848* (New York: Verso, 1990). I want to thank James A. Noel (Professor at San Francisco theological Seminary in San Anselmo, California) for both drawing my attention to these texts and for our lively and long conversations about what all of these mean. On African endurance during this period and its meanings, see William St. Clair, *The Door of No Return: The History of Cape Coast Castle and the Atlantic Slave Trade* (New York: Blue Ridge, 2007); Sylviane A. Diouf, *Dreams of Africa in Alabama: The Slave Ship Clotilda and the Story of the Last African Brought to America* (New York: Oxford University Press, 2007); and James T. Campbell, *Middle Passages: African American Journeys to Africa, 1787–2005* (New York: Penguin, 2006).

Yet many survived and sang/moaned across the watery journey from the primordial to the modern.

Thus the Negro Spirituals were singing testimonies of joyful people recreating their collective self-identities out of traumatic time and space. These sacred songs united various language dialects into a Black people, an African American people. Blacks or African Americans or African descendants in the Americas are created phenomena in recent human history.[6]

Moreover, not only did song enhance a new corporate character. Negro Spirituals also indicate how a range of African language speakers and singers converted and integrated white missionary Christianity on slave plantations (pre-1865) into a common West African view of the world and music rhythm. The practical daily life of an Africanized Black people (that is, culture) already understood the world of spirits meshed completely in the rituals of a total way of life. Restated, Negro Spirituals show us how enslaved Black people's everyday spirituality took white missionary Christianity and re-viewed it through an African lens, and used it to fabricate their sacred selves. These wailing and hopeful songs, ebony performed sacred songs, plaintiff and defiant songs, are, indeed, the phenomenology of America and encompass a philosophy of history.

The Spirituals draw us into the raw reality and descriptive discourse of America's primeval origins. The recent creation of Black people (recent in terms of human history) is the phenomenon upon which, to a large degree, the U.S. Constitution is formed. In that 1787 sacred document, Blacks are referred to as three-fifths of a person, are by federal law obligated to be put back into slavery if they ran away, and are given the 1808 date when they would be set free. The Constitution refers to Black people at least three times. A large basis of the U.S. Constitution is slavery—the private property of a few white, wealthy men who founded the United States for their own family profit. And insofar as Negro Spirituals connote a mega view of historical deliverance of the enslaved, lyrics sing a speculative philosophy of history. Insofar as the Spirituals are suspicious of the presuppositions underlying the possibility of slave masters logically and morally crafting history, lyrics sound an analytic philosophy

---

6. See Charles H. Long, "Perspectives for a Study of Afro-American Religion in the United States," in *Significations: Signs, Symbols, and Images in the Interpretation of Religion* (Philadelphia: Fortress, 1986) 173–84.

of history. Simultaneously, the Spirituals contain an appreciation for syncretistic traditions of future time and space. In a sense, one could argue that race, in its positive and negative formations and formulations, is the foundation of knowledge, thus constituting a contemporary (in the "new world" context) epistemology. Both speculative and analytic ways of knowing offered some time and space better than the present.[7] Therefore Spirituals sang of new phenomena (i.e., creations of African Americans and the nation of America), offered a critical philosophy of history, and talked about race as one basis of knowing reality.

Truly this process of adaptation, change, modification, unification, fragmentation, pragmatics, embedded worldview, and future hope define the Negro Spirituals. This erratic flow of new people-new religion is writ large in the words of the Negro Spirituals. "Walk Together Children"—even with your differences of language, shades of color, diverse genders and orientations, jobs, callings, vocations, unique gifts of the spirit, agreements and disagreements. It is a joyful and hopeful imperative to move forward together at this time and in this space. Walk now and not wait. Do it together and not alone. And be as children on two accounts.

Black Americans are literally the blood children descendants of a whole bunch of West African forefathers and foremothers. As these children, remember to walk together now in historical memory of particular traditions good and bad. But also move forward without delay as spiritual children of God—made in God's image and possessing internally the vital force of divine breath. "Don't You Get Weary" differentiates getting physically tired from getting spiritually weary. Negro Spirituals allow for physical tiredness; even positive effort can test the body's endurance. But sacred song here gifts us with a calling of healed spirit and balanced life forces over against the limitations of transcendent weariness. Healing and harmony repair, absorb, or overcome the weary and the worn out.

And if all the vibrant, joyful, pathological, wounded, and creative differences can just move now as offspring living in connection, striving for harmony and balance within the spirit and the external creation, there's a great meeting in the Promised Land. The "meeting" is us—

---

7. See M. C. Lemon, *Philosophy of History: A Guide for Students* (New York: Routledge, 2003); Dermot Moran, *Introduction to Phenomenology* (New York: Routledge, 2004); and Joseph Young and Jana Evans Braziel, eds., *Race and the Foundations of Knowledge* (Chicago: University of Illinois Press, 2006).

the coming together of a "both/and" (rather than an "either/or") West African daily philosophy. The power of this spirit was and is its ability to absorb and utilize those who differ. And the newly created Black selves and the newly created sacred selves used the life of Jesus whose great big arms wrapped around all. This God came for everybody: the half and the whole, the good and the not so good, the churchgoer and those of other ritual practices.

In fact, this Jesus announced in Luke 4:18ff. a road for all of the poor and the painful emotions. This Jesus concluded in Matthew 25:31ff. that denominations, Christianity, and individual piety do not matter to walk into heaven (i.e., the ultimate great meeting in the promised land). The promised land is times and spaces where our individual and collective spiritual and societal harmony and balance grow faster than fragmented emotional selves and harmful social interactions with people and nature. The Negro Spiritual, "Walk Together Children," teaches us something about going down this road.

And the essays in *Walk Together Children* offer a window along this material-spiritual way. Contributors to this anthology hope to name, accept, and live with healthy tensions that prove creative catalysts for a holistic and integrated life. Toward this end, people here represent the talking of women and men. Both together ensure that more resources and perspectives are brought to bear on routine and unexpected conditions of life. They both, united even with differences, show forth better a spirituality of interwoven walking. We harness powers and pain through recognizing the particularities of female and male genders that freely choose a decision for comprehensive living and receive a transcendent something beyond solo walking. Moving in group amplifies and challenges the potential ways of an individual world view and faith.

Indeed, the notion of faith opens another pathway into these essays. For not only are men and women assembled here, but also we have two distinct yet intersecting bodies of knowledge engaged in conversation and critiques over what it means to believe in something more than just what we can see. Black theology (i.e., knowledge created by Black male religious self-reflection) and womanist theology (i.e., knowledge created by Black female critical words and witness) have traveled into a destination of full scholarly disciplines; the former since the mid-1960s and the latter since the early 1980s.[8] Their status has institutionalized in

8. Diana L. Hayes, *And Still We Rise: An Introduction to Black Liberation Theology*

various movements and media within organizations of higher learning in the U.S.A. Black theology and womanist theology struggle to support each other in the American Academy of Religion, the Society of Biblical Literature, the Society for the Study of Black Religion, in courses in schools of theology, seminaries, divinity schools, denominational colleges, conferences, colloquia, publishing, funding, generation grooming, internationalizing discourses, and in imagining dreams without drama.

And essays in this book are written by three leadership sectors of Black and womanist theologies—professors, preachers, and the pew. Theology, broadly defined, signifies a renewed energy and commitment to be honest and reasonable on a journey of faith. It is critical and self-critical thinking about others' and an individual's fundamental ways of being in the world. At root, faith displays itself in, at least, two ways. First, how one spends one's time and feelings (from the moment one goes to sleep at night, through dreaming, to the details of actions performed in day light, until bedtime returns) reveals the priorities of a faith. Second, if we had six months to live, what ways would we choose to walk? Data received in our dreams, intuitions, and daily details coupled with the forced finitude of biologically determinacy will make ultimate visions clear. In a word, we advance beyond spiritual weariness towards clarifying our ultimate life and death visions for ourselves and our children— in our great meeting in the promised land.

This clarification process of faith doing theology (that is, faith seeking understanding through intentionality) occurs, at least, three levels. Professors earn their living thinking critically about the academic discipline of theology all the time (i.e., systematic theology). Preachers receive a charge to shepherd a flock of people in daily full time ministry (i.e., practical theology). And the pew engages the theory of faith talk in their theological wisdom outside of seminary lectures and homiletical pulpits (i.e., folk theology). Still various contributors in this book walk in ambiguous ways in combinations of activist-preacher-pew person or preacher-theoretician or professor-hooper. Actually, hooping is the unique African American form of preaching that is singing.[9]

---

(New York: Paulist, 1996); Stephanie Y. Mitchem, *Introducing Womanist Theology* (Maryknoll, NY: Orbis, 2002); and Dwight N. Hopkins, *Introducing Black Theology of Liberation* (Maryknoll, NY: Orbis, 1999).

9. James Weldon Johnson, *God's Trombones: Seven Negro Sermons in Verse*, rev. ed., Penguin Classics (orig. ed., 1927; New York: Penguin, 2008); William H. Pipes, *Say Amen, Brother! Old-time Negro Preaching: A Study in American Frustration* (Detroit:

In addition to three types of Black and womanist theologies, three generations of Black and womanist scholars and practitioners have presented their voices. In that sense, this collection embodies the accumulated wisdom of the 1966 start of Black theology and the 1980s origin of womanist theology. Inter-generational birthing of offspring and transmission of historical theory enliven the heart of Black and womanist theologies as disciplines. They are scholarly disciplines with archival importance bearing metaphors of meaning. And they are daily practices of spiritualized rituals in material routines. We here suggest integrating theoretical and witnessing dimensions of disciplines. We sing our sacred songs and walk our roads together.

A key component of tri-level inter-generational learning is the holding of hands among three biologically differentiated age groups. In a word, essays are written by young adults (for instance, writers under thirty, with at least two younger than twenty-five when they wrote their chapters), middle aged cohorts (for instance, those recognizing the unselfish power of their peer relations), and elder thinker-leaders (for instance, those who have already produced a legacy of texts and can see most clearly the historical future).

And then we encounter varieties of blended contradictory, and complementary positions throughout the book. Some writers are heterosexual and others are self-identified lesbian and gay. Protestants and Roman Catholic authors contribute. Writers walk together from divinity schools, seminaries, schools of theology, religious studies departments, denominational colleges, and Christian education church sectors. Graduate degrees include Bible, sociology of religion, systematic theology, ethics, interdisciplinary studies, cultural anthropology, musicology, education, pastoral and practical theologies, sociology, congregational ministry, systematic and contemporary studies, and environmental history.

Finally, the seven chapter headings marking the journey of conversations in this book enable women, men, the Black church, and theological educators to walk together. Part One foregrounds two sharp

---

Wayne State University Press, 1992); Henry H. Mitchell, *Black Preaching* (New York: Harper & Row, 1979); Ella Pearson Mitchell, ed., *Those Preachin' Women*, 3 vols. (Valley Forge, PA: Judson, 1985–1996); Cleophus J. LaRue, *The Heart of Black Preaching* (Louisville: Westminster John Knox, 2002); and Valentino Lassiter, *Martin Luther King in the African American Preaching Tradition* (Cleveland: Pilgrim, 2001).

distinctions in Black theology and womanist theology literature. Black theology's normative trademark accents "liberation," while a growing cadre of womanist theologians underscore "survival and quality of life." James H. Cone's *Black Theology and Black Power* and *A Black Theology of Liberation* unapologetically centered, and thereby established as benchmark, "liberation" as the touchstone of all authentic Christian identities in the U.S.A.[10] While not dismissing "liberation," Delores S. Williams's *Sisters in the Wilderness* advanced "survival and quality of life" as more comparable to African American women's realities.[11] While the Black man is out in the public square acting out his revolutionary agenda, Black women have not only struggled, they had to also provide practical survival strategies for a quality of life for themselves and the families' children. And, the truth be told, Black women were doing survival and quality of life as well as being on the public front lines along side African American men. So to create new moves with new angles, gender authorship is somewhat reversed around these two themes in Part One. That is to say, two men speak on "survival and quality of life"—a usual womanist theme; and two women explore some aspects of "liberation"—a core Black (male) theology concern. And the theme is divided between pastor and professor authors.

Part Two juxtaposes directly two themes submerged and surfaced both in higher education and in churches: the question of "Black men and patriarchy." Here too, women take on a second related subset (i.e., "Black men as endangered species"), a topic mainly written about by African American men. Men writers confront squarely Black male patriarchy, a trajectory whose authors overwhelmingly have been and remain African American women. A good mixture of professor, pastor, and practitioner authors exists here as well.

Part Three likewise reverses some themes. For instance, "Jesus Man. Christ Woman" specifically questions the standard church and academy portrayal of Jesus the Christ in an exclusive male gender manner. Here, this section recognizes the historical, biological Jesus as a man with women essayists touching on parts of this latter proposition—that is,

10. Cone, *Black Theology and Black Power* (1969; reprint, Maryknoll, NY: Orbis, 2005); Cone, *A Black Theology of Liberation: Twentieth Anniversary Edition* (1970; reprint, Maryknoll, NY: Orbis, 1990).

11. Williams, *Sisters in the Wilderness: The Challenge of Womanist God-Talk* (Maryknoll, NY: Orbis, 1993).

Jesus' maleness. Then "Christ as Woman" calls on men to engage Christ (i.e., the clear divinity status of Jesus) from a perspective of Christ's womaness.

Part Four debates "Sexuality"—an obsessive and fanatical topic raging in North American society, churches, and schools. Two self-identified same gender-loving scholars, male and female, and two heterosexual scholars, male and female, take on this misunderstood, highly politically charged and creative category of (both hetero- and homo-) sexual orientations.

The final three sections speak to the future of women, men, the Black church, and theological education. Part Five delves directly into this overarching question. Part Six opens new avenues of health for and resuscitation of Black and womanist theologies, including hip hop life styles and rap music, Black environmental liberation theology, and young Black men opting out of patriarchy and into allies for womanists, by yielding male material power.

The "Global Future," Part Seven, claims fundamentally that if women and men, Black theology and womanist theologies, professors and preachers, diverse sexual orientations, various professional generations, multiple age groups, and the Black church and theological education are to survive, thrive, and, in certain instances, indicate a positive pathway for any to see, hear, and walk, then we all have to balance this process in a healing and healthy fashion.

Walk Together Children. Don't You Get Weary. There's a Great Meeting in the Promised Land.

## PART ONE

# Liberation, Survival, and Quality of Life

1

# Movin' on up a Little Higher

*Resolving the Tension between Academic and Pastoral*
*Approaches to Black and Womanist Theologies*

DIANA L. HAYES

WHEN I FIRST SET out on the road to becoming a theologian twenty-five long years ago, I had absolutely no idea what was ahead of me. I was confronted by my fellow classmates, all but a few male, with the assertion that I was either a feminist or seeking a husband. Having no clear idea at that time as to what a feminist was and absolutely no desire to rob the cradle (mine was a very late vocation), I rejected both possibilities and so found myself wondering what I was doing studying theology, especially Catholic theology, and what I planned to do after I had completed my doctorate. I must admit that it was rather terrifying; I had absolutely no idea what the future would hold; I only knew quite simply that this was the continuation of a journey I had been on for most of my life. So, as I had done when, to the shock of family, friends, and myself, I converted from AMEZion to Roman Catholicism less than a year earlier, I put my trust in God and held on for dear life. I've been holding on ever since because, if I have learned anything, it is that once you do take hold of God's hand, you better be prepared for a whirlwind ride!

Today, twenty-five years later, I am still engaged in reflection not just on my own journey but also on that of my brothers and sisters of the Black community, Christian, Muslim and no religion at all, as well. Where have we come from and, equally as important, where are we going as a people, especially a people of faith, when so many of our young people are turning their backs on the Christianity that once sustained us as a people? What are the best ways for us to deal with the many critical issues impacting the Black community today? Ironically and sadly, many would be correct in asserting that the worst thing that ever happened to Black Americans in the twentieth century was the success of the Civil Rights Movement. In less than forty years, we have seen a vibrant Christian (and other religions) community centered on the Black Church in all of its myriad expressions, and focused on education and elevation of the race, become, for too many, a place of hopelessness and despair. What happened to Martin's dream, shared by so many? Is this what Rosa Parks sat down for? I don't think so.

The plight of the Black community, religious and non-religious, male, female, gay and lesbian, wealthy and poor, is at the very core of the issues we will be discussing in this book. What is the meaning of liberation for a people historically oppressed and yet still struggling to survive? Does the meaning of liberation change over time as those seeking it themselves change? What role does or should gender and sexual orientation play in defining that liberation today? What has been and continues to be the impact of western, patriarchal thinking and praxis on the Black community and its leaders, male and female? Is it possible to nurture and sustain Black men, Black women, and Black children in our churches, communities, and a society where they are all still denigrated and defamed? Can we have community without church? Can we have church without community? Human sexuality and the increasingly virulent expressions of homophobia in our churches and communities are time bombs ticking away ready to explode in our midst, shattering families, friendships, ministries, neighborhoods. Where do we go from here in terms of mission and evangelization? Our communities are more diverse than ever and increasingly pluralistic. Whom should we be missioning to; how have the definitions of oppression and marginalization changed and what effect do these changes have on us as scholars and pastors? Are the truly poor to be increasingly shut out as we spiritualize poverty and seek to "increase our territory"? How do we rearticulate and live JESUS's mandate to "go ye therefore and teach all nations" when these nations are in our very back and front yards, in ways that uplift and humanize rather than shut out and demonize?

Most of these questions will be addressed, by me and others, in this book. It is my hope that the book, aimed at bringing together academics and pastors, two entities too often seen in opposition rather than accord, will help us take the necessary steps towards resolving the tensions that do exist, thereby enabling us all to move on up a little higher. For, paradoxically, a theological movement that began literally in the pews and pulpits under the leadership of mostly Black male preachers and in the streets of our cities is today in danger of becoming simply an academic endeavor, discussed and analyzed in academia but lifeless and soulless because it is divorced from the reality of everyday Black life.

We who are scholars often find the weight of the struggle to gain tenure and status in the academic world leaves little or no time for working amongst those who need us the most—our own people, serving as pastoral ministers, working with congregations assessing their needs and concerns and responding to them. Even our work with the young people in our classrooms is often filtered through graduate and teaching assistants among others so that we never truly find entrance into their hopes and dreams and whether they are grounded at all in any form of faith or faith life. We are required too often to make either/or choices when we would rather not, choices that leave us disconnected from the very communities that gave us life and the churches that sustained us in our struggle to become the scholars we are today. Somehow, I strongly believe, that has to change if our theology is going to be truly a "doing" rather than simply a "speaking" and "thinking" about necessary changes for those historically marginalized in this country and around the world.

The issue before us is liberation. What is its meaning and significance for Black and womanist theologies today? What are its historical origins and does it still have meaning in this oh so changed world in which we now live? It has always been my contention that Black Liberation Theology emerged when the first African was brought to these shores in chains. By this, I mean that Black and womanist theologies, in and of themselves, are not new but have existed for as long as persons of African descent have existed in these United States and the Diaspora. Theirs was not, however, an articulated theology because they were an oral, rather than literate, people. Yet they had a theology, an understanding of the Divine that uplifted them and an experience of the Spirit that sustained and strengthened them in whatever circumstances they found themselves just as they had done in the homes from which they were illegitimately torn in West and Central Africa, they have carried in their souls and among the few possessions they were able to retain, faith in a God of justice and righteousness who acknowledged and affirmed their humanity. Theirs was a theology of liberation long before the term was coined by James Cone and Gustavo Gutierrez and their colleagues.

So, what is this theology as it came to be developed through centuries of terror and triumph, as Anthony Pinn suggests?[1] How were the slaves, our foremothers and forefathers, able to literally do the impossible—take the distorted and often slanderous religion forced upon them by greedy pseudo-Christians and transform it into a theology of hope and promise, one that enabled them to persevere through more than 400 years of legal and defacto slavery, segregation, and discrimination?

Black theology is a theology of liberation in the simplest sense because it does two critically important things: It liberates those "doing" the theology, that is, it is a theology of praxis not of passivity. It begins with a particular people, a people oppressed and empowers them to freedom through the grace of a loving God. A liberating theology does more than that however. It also liberates theology itself.

Theology, historically, has been a captive, if you will, of those with a string of letters after their names or a string of titles before them. It wasn't available to the ordinary folk; the People of God had no access. It has been seen as an abstract, "top-down" presentation of God's will for the world God created. It was universal and objective, untouched and untainted by humanity itself. At least that's what they taught us but it is not what our ancestors knew. For them, theology or God-talk, if you will, was quite simple. It was an ongoing dialogue between a people and their God. As we have come to understand and acknowledge today, theology, that is "talk" about God, takes many forms, expressed as song, dance, prayer, sermon, poetry, story, truly everything but a dry, sterile, detached, allegedly objective observation of God's qualities and essence, stuff which didn't really help anyone survive or attain freedom. No. For them, their God-talk, in its deepest sense, is interested conversation between a people and their God as the people attempt to understand God's actions within their lived history. All theology is interested conversation. All theology is contextual—that is, grounded in the very hearts and

---

1. Pinn, *Terror and Triumph: The Nature of Black Religion* (Minneapolis: Fortress, 2003).

minds of those "doing", living, and believing. There is no theology, no God-talk, that is distanced or set apart from the culture, tradition, heritage, and yes, gender, race, sexuality, ethnicity, or class of those engaged in that theologizing.

Thus, what has historically been taught as universal is in reality subjective (personal) and that subjectivity has been revealed in the ways in which Christianity, the major example for African Americans, has been and still too often continues to be distorted to fit the desires and interests of the relatively few wealthy, Western, and white Christians and their self-denying followers, in today's world and in the past to the detriment of just about everyone else. Thus a theology of liberation is one that is consciously aware of its subjectivity, of the personhood of those of, by, and for whom the theology exists. It seeks to be about the elimination rather than the perpetuation of oppression in all of its forms in human life.

Black Liberation Theology, as formally articulated in the late 1960's, took as its subjective foundation, race, and more explicitly, Black humanity. Grounded in the Black historical experience, James H. Cone, Gay Wilmore, J. Deotis Roberts, and other Black ministers sought to uncover the mystery and paradox of Black Christianity.

> There is no truth for and about black people that does not emerge out of the context of their experience. Truth in this sense is black truth, a truth disclosed in the history and culture of black people. This means that there can be no Black Theology, which does not take the black experience as a source for its starting point. Black Theology is a theology of and for black people, an examination of their stories, tales, and sayings. It is an investigation of the mind into the raw materials of our pilgrimage, telling the story of "how we got over."[2]

The question remains, however. Why would a people oppressed, terrorized, and dehumanized for centuries by alleged Christians yet confess Jesus Christ as Lord—the same Jesus they were told affirmed their enslavement and dehumanization?

They did so, arguably, because their experience of the God/human Jesus was radically different from that of their masters. Their Jesus, their God, was a wonder-working God, who opposed injustice in all of its

---

2. James Cone, cited in Diana L. Hayes, "James H. Cone's Hermeneutic of Language and the Development of Black Theology," *Theological Studies* 61 (2000) 609–31.

forms; who saw slavery as an evil to be eradicated; who affirmed the humanity of Black slaves, both male and female, over against the degradation foisted upon them by their brother and sister Christians.

The slaves' experience and therefore understanding of liberation was gradual not immediate although their yearning for freedom was with them from their earliest presence here. Gayraud S. Wilmore speaks of three traditions within the African American experience: survival, elevation, and liberation, stating: "In a sense not true of any other immigrant groups in America, the irreducible problem the Africans brought here was survival."[3] He further elaborates: "The liberation and elevation traditions began with the determination to survive, but they go beyond 'make do' to 'do more'; and from 'do more' to 'freedom now' and 'Black power.' All three traditions have to do with making and keeping life human."[4]

As "the single most important and characteristic perspective of Black faith from 1800 to the Civil Rights Movement,"[5] the liberation tradition was that aspect of Black faith seized on by Black (male) theologians confronted with the slowly waning non-violent movement of Dr. King and the increasingly violence-prone demands of the young bloods (also male) who were proponents of the emerging Black Power Movement. Liberation thus became seen as the essence of Black Liberation Theology.[6]

Black Liberation Theology grounds its interpretation of liberation in Sacred Scripture, both the sermon of Jesus in Luke which presents a vision of liberation that changes one's status in the here and now for the better—sight for the blind, healing for the ill, freedom for captives, a new human reality on earth—and the liberation promised the Hebrew slaves in the Exodus story—freedom from an unjust captivity. Black (male) theologians, looking at the experiences, for the most part, only of Black males (slave and free), thus saw liberation as they did—as flight, revolution, decisive but sometimes self-destructive action that brought about immediate results and promised the end of suffering.

3. Wilmour, *Black Theology and Black Radicalism: An Interpretation of the Religious History of Afro-American People*, 2nd ed. (Maryknoll, NY: Orbis, 1983) 254.

4. Ibid., 270.

5. Ibid., 267.

6. Dwight N. Hopkins, *Introducing Black Liberation Theology* (Maryknoll, NY: Orbis, 2007).

It was and is, first, a liberation shaped by the Black (male) histori-cal experience, stressing first, the socio-political freedom envisioned by the Hebrew slaves and Black slave revolutionaries and, second, a cultural liberation that looked back to Africa to reclaim a cultural heritage for so long denied.[7] God, therefore, is seen as a God of justice, righteousness and vengeance, a God of action who intervenes in Black human history through his Son Jesus sent as Liberator to end the suffering of Black humanity.

This, however, has to be seen as a rather limited and exclusive focus for several reasons. First, the emphasis on revolutionary action is not based on an inclusive reading of the Black historical experience. There are, indeed, times when those who have been enslaved or are unjustly oppressed, must make a bold dash for freedom, liberating themselves from tyranny in all of its oppressive forms. But there are also times when that bold dash may not only be dangerous for those participating but self-defeating for them and others not involved. There are times when the oppressed may find, instead, that it is more preserving of life to "hun-ker down," as Hagar did in the wilderness, comforted and sustained by the knowledge that God is still with them, helping them to survive until the time is right for action. The timing is God's but God's action involves a recognition of the growing ability of the oppressed to work towards their own liberation with God's guidance and grace.

Second, Blacks still suffer from oppression in myriad forms. What's taking God so long and if Jesus's actions set us free once and for all, why are we still enslaved in so many ways? This seeming contradiction should lead us to the realization that while liberation may be the ultimate goal, survival and elevation, seen as quality of life, are still very much a critical part of the lives of everyday Black Americans. Indeed, is this not how we have continued to exist as a people?

Black women, and those dependent on them, did not always have the ability to seek liberation when and where they wanted, either inde-pendently or as a group in the style of the Exodus story or Nat Turner and Denmark Vesey, though they did participate. They had concerns that did not allow them to seek only their own freedom as it would probably open up others—children, the elderly, other slaves male and female—to harsh retribution and possible loss of life. Instead, they had to make,

7. See Diana L. Hayes, *And Still We Rise: An Introduction to Black Liberation Theology* (Mahwah, NJ: Paulist, 1995) 81.

quite often, very different choices for themselves and those they were responsible for. Liberation had to be communal; a goal to be sought after but not always achievable in the time, style, and manner desired. Even when a Black woman did step out on her own path to liberation as envisioned in BLT, it still was not usually the end.

> When Harriet Tubman's escape was successful and she was finally free, she likened the experience to being in heaven. However, the realization dawned that she had left behind her family, the old folks, and others in the bonds of family. She determined to bring them to freedom as well. In Tubman's words, "Oh, how I prayed then, lying all alone on the cold, damp ground. Oh, dear Lord . . . I ain't got no friend but you. Come to my help, for I am in trouble!"[8]

Jacquelyn Grant "highlights that Tubman's freedom was 'trouble' that had to be shared, like the gospel song says, Tubman 'just couldn't keep it to herself.'[9] In setting her course of action, Tubman would move into conflict with the status quo, with the law and custom of the land."[10] But she had to do it if she was truly a Christian.

The Black (male) theological understanding of liberation has other problems as well that I will only briefly mention, not just in the limited form it takes but also the limited persons who seem to qualify for it. Cone asserts that liberation in the U.S. has to be Black liberation because historically it has been Blacks in the U.S. who have been the most marginalized and oppressed simply because of their blackness but also affirms that his understanding of blackness is not physical but ontological. God and Jesus are Black because those historically oppressed in the U.S. are Black.[11] In later writings, Cone expands on this understanding: "to be Black encompasses all who are oppressed whether by reason of sex, race, or class or all who take sides with the oppressed by joining in their struggle for liberation."[12]

8. Stephanie Mitchem quoting Jacquelyn Grant, "Womanist and (Unfinished) Constructions of Salvation," *Journal of Feminist Studies in Religion* 17 (2001) 90.

9. Ibid.

10. Ibid.

11. See James H. Cone, *Black Theology and Black Power* (San Francisco: HarperSanFrancisco, 1989) 213.

12. Haynes, "James H. Cone's Hermeneutic," 616.

Yet this liberation is still grounded in blackness and is seen as God acting in history on the side of the Black oppressed. This makes the Exodus story rather paradoxical for us today because while it certainly results in the freedom of the Hebrew slaves, it also destroys not only the Egyptian nation but the land promised the freed slaves results in the destruction of another people, the Canaanites. The oppressed rather quickly themselves become oppressors. If we adhere to this socio-political understanding of liberation and place it in an Afrocentric context, what then do we do with the assumption that not only the Egyptians, but the Canaanites as well were black, not ontologically but physically. Whose liberation should we identify with, why, and at what cost to ourselves and others?

Delores Williams, in her seminal work *Sisters in the Wilderness*, challenges this understanding of liberation with what she perceives to be a more realistic understanding of Black women's encounter with and experience of God.[13] She calls for new language about liberation; language that is viable for both men and women. I see this interpretation of liberation as not necessarily in opposition to that of Black (male) theologians but as rather a way to render it more inclusive of all who have been oppressed for reasons not just of race but also class, gender, and sexuality. For this is a Black woman's reality; this is her experience—that of a triple and at times quadruple oppression. Womanists such as Williams use language that speaks to Black women, a language not of surrogacy, which has too often been their experience, but of liberation as found in survival and quality of life. Like Black men, Black women also rely on Jesus "to help them survive the forging of a new identity." They use "the socio-political thought and action of (the) African-American woman's world to show Black women their salvation does not depend upon any form of surrogacy made sacred by traditional and orthodox understandings of Jesus' life and death. Rather their salvation is assured by Jesus' life of resistance and by the survival strategies he used to help people survive the death of identity . . ."[14]

> I concluded, then, that the female centered tradition of African-American biblical appropriation could be named the *survival/ quality of life tradition of African American biblical appropriation.*

13. Williams, *Sisters in the Wilderness: The Challenge of Womanist God-Talk* (Maryknoll, NY: Orbis, 1995).

14. Ibid., 164.

> This naming was consistent with the black American community's way of appropriating the Bible so that emphasis is put upon God's response to Black people's situation rather than upon what would appear to be hopeless aspects of African American people's existence in North America. In black consciousness, God's response of survival and quality of life to Hagar is God's response of survival and quality of life to African American women and mothers of slave descent struggling to sustain their families with God's help.[15]

Survival and quality of life are, thus, still a very critical aspect of contemporary Black experience. Liberation, as I have discussed it herein, is insufficient and not always appropriate in and of itself.

It is critically important to emphasize that neither Black women nor Black men should bind themselves to the Cross of Jesus in order to re-enact his sacrifice. That sacrifice was once and for all and our continued existence as a people of the African Diaspora on this earth and in this country particularly despite all that has been done to destroy us is a witness to that sacrifice. Blacks in the United States, especially African Americans whom I distinguish as a specific people forged in the fiery furnace of slavery and its aftermath in the U.S., especially the South, serve today as a permanent, indelible subversive memory that gives the lie to America's vaunted claims of "liberty and justice for all" and to U.S. Christians' assertion that they are Christian even as they continue to aid and abet in the on-going dehumanization and deprivation of persons of African descent and so many others.

Hurricane Katrina and those that followed were a great shock to many in this country who have, whether by reason of skin color, wealth, education, or congenital blindness, been sheltered from the reality that is ongoing poor Black life in this nation. As subversive memory, a memory that shocks by turning reality upside down and inside out, Black Americans, by their very existence, remind this nation and the world that the work of liberation is not yet done, that life for far too many is still a matter of survival, sadly, too often without any quality of life. Our presence, our poverty, the decrepit and deteriorating conditions of predominantly Black schools and the too often poor excuses for education that goes on within them should be a jolt that awakens all of us, of whatever race or ethnicity, to the reality of this nation, a reality that still

15. Ibid., 6.

caters to those with the most, leaving those with little scrabbling in the dust and filth of overcrowded, semi-flooded interstate overpasses for the basic necessities to maintain life.

The womanist understanding of liberation, for it too is a liberation theology, recognizes the reality of Black life in its weakest and most vulnerable form and seeks to lift others up as we all climb to higher ground. It recognizes that there is a time for bold, revolutionary action but also time to grow, develop, and mature so as to be better prepared for that action. Womanists, in seeking to eradicate all forms of oppression, look to their spirit-filled historical experience and recognize the face of God within it. As we look at our crumbling inner cities, abandoned by all but those who, as in Katrina's aftermath, have no way out; as we recognize the existence of a permanent underclass whose face is not only Black but too often female as the covers of major newsweeklies revealed; as we read of the further gutting of programs and resources that benefit the many for the benefit of the few, surely we must ask ourselves, where did we go wrong? How did this happen? What went wrong with Martin's vision of a beloved community made up of all races and ethnicities?

I would say that partly what went wrong was our failure to acknowledge, affirm and utilize the varied gifts and talents of Black women. As we have learned, they were present in all of the major events and movements in Black history but too often relegated to the back rooms and the shadows and other places unworthy of mention. As Dr. King and those working with him should have understood, the Black community survives and thrives only when we recognize the value, worth, and dignity of every human being, regardless of gender, class, creed, or sexuality.

Once we begin to deny the humanity of any of God's creation, we risk losing the humanity of all. The late Rosa Parks, the humble seamstress from Montgomery, Alabama, at her death received an honor given to no other woman and few men, other than Presidents, in this country's history. She is being honored for the great and humble soul that she was. Yet for too long a time her role, her critical role, as the catalyst of the Civil Rights Movement was overlooked, primarily because she was a woman. She modeled without knowing it what it means to be a womanist for she refused to stay in or be moved to what others designated as her place in the world. She sat down and the world stood still. As the folk saying goes: If Rosa Parks had not sat down, Martin Luther King Jr. could not have stood up. This saying is at the heart of what used to be Black self-understanding, the solidarity of Black men and women.

True liberation cannot be limited by any human-made social constructions. If we seek true liberation in its fullest sense, which includes therefore survival and quality of life, we must work to ensure that it is provided for all, including those who formerly and continue to oppress us. Thus, liberation for womanists involves the ability to live and provide for future life, to pass on the skills and traditions, the stories and songs, the words to the prayers, the hope for a better and achievable future. This means that Black women rightly refuse to live their lives simply as surrogates whether coerced (as in slavery) or voluntary (yet in many ways still coerced) today. But like Harriet Tubman, they recognize that freedom is not free but comes with strings attached, promises to keep, and responsibilities to bear. They also realize that these must be shared by all in the community who are able to share them. Black women can no longer stand, if in truth we ever did, with heads bowed, duct tape across our mouths, a broom or computer keyboard in one hand, a frying pan in the other and our men, whether husband, father, uncle, as well as our children on our backs. Rather we must work together, sharing burden and responsibility, sorrow and joy, recognizing that we all have gifts to share in order to rebuild our community.

It is still an ironic truth that the Black church is made up predominantly of Black women. Yet few even today find the doors to leadership within those churches, whether lay or ordained, fully open to them. The majority of students studying for advanced degrees in theology in the U.S. today are women yet still the obstacles remain in place, put there too often by Black men and women who still cannot seem to overcome their own biases against women ministers, elders, deacons, professors, Bishops, and who sometimes use the Bible better than the slave masters did to support these distortions and denials. How can we move forward as a people while ignoring the skills and talents of more than half of our communities? How can we climb when our own actions pull us down?

Womanist theologians and those in solidarity with them seek to rebuild the Black and over time all communities, making them places of restorative rather than destructive life. We know that we cannot do this alone but only with the support, encouragement and working hands of Black men any more than they can achieve true liberation without Black women. Somehow we must reclaim the male/female solidarity that enabled us to survive in this country for over 400 years. Are we really willing to allow that solidarity to be only a thing of the past as we seek individual promotion over communal elevation?

Let me repeat myself: True liberation exists not when just a few take risks and escape a life of oppression and marginalization and never look back. It exists only when all, through the grace of God, are given the means and ability to survive and live lives, not of quiet desperation, but of courageous hope and perseverance even as they continue to climb up the rough side of the mountain, step by step, stone by stone, hands reaching down and others lifting up, till all can stand on the mountain top proclaiming we are all indeed truly free at last!

## 2

# The Children Have Come to Birth

## *A Theological Response for Survival and Quality of Life*

FORREST E. HARRIS

We must remember that liberation is costly. It needs unity. We must hold hands and refuse to be divided. We must be ready. Some of us will not see the day of liberation physically. But those people will have contributed to the struggle. Let us be united, let us be filled with hope, let us be those who respect one another.[1]

—Desmond Tutu

I dream of a church that welcomes the poor and combines prayer with social and political action to eliminate poverty . . . I dream of a church where inclusive language about God is not considered too much to ask. I pray that others who share this dream will work together to make it a reality.[2]

—Annie Powell

THE ABOVE STATEMENTS FROM Annie Powell and Desmond Tutu provide great wisdom for those who remain committed to justice and liberation of the Black poor in America and Africa. The planners of this book have asked me to address the topic "Survival and the Quality of

---

1. See "Liberation Is Costly," in *Singing the Living Tradition* (Boston: Unitarian Universalist Association, 1993) 593.

2. "Hold on to Your Dream: African American Protestant Worship," in *Women at Worship: Interpretations of North American Diversity*, ed. Marjorie Procter-Smith and Janet R. Watson (Louisville: Westminster John Knox, 1993) 43–53.

Life" in response to "the way forward for Black and Womanist Theology and the Church." As people of color in America continuously struggle for holistic liberation, I approach this assigned task deeply feeling and sharing the communal pain for a new world to be born that changes the reality of a generation of Black and brown children whose reality today, as evidenced by disturbing systemic failures and global social crisis, is dying in the womb of human possibilities. The poet Audre Lorde reminds us that Black people were never meant to survive the hard trek of white supremacist powers in North American oppression. Black and Womanist theologians, however, and the communities for whom they write are part of a prophetic dream and tradition that believes no place or no time is beyond the reach of Divine presence, love, justice and power. Thus, as Desmond Tutu says, "let us be united, let us be filled with hope."

Historically, when in crisis Black people have returned to "root experiences" of Black religion and liberation traditions that inspire and inform the way forward to freedom and justice. One such root experience is the liberation movement in the early beginnings of the Black churches in America. As the most important institution in Black civil society, the Black churches' historic role in the survival and quality of life for Black existence in America cannot be overlooked in any effort to achieve liberation for the Black poor. As Allison Calhoun-Brown notes, Black churches have been "free spaces—environments in which people were free to challenge racial inequality as an oppositional civic culture."[3] Among the many challenges Black and Womanist theologians face today is how to channel theological resources to nurture communal commitment in and beyond the Black church for the liberation of the Black poor.

This essay addresses the need for active alliances between Black and Womanist theology with agencies of hope in the Black community, primarily the Black churches toward the survival and quality of life for the civic empowerment of the Black poor. As theologies for liberated life, I can think of nothing more urgent for Black and Womanist theology than the building up of the civic capacity and the unity necessary for the birthing of alternative realities that reconnect Black churches to the unique heritage and liberation tradition that birthed them on American

---

3. Alison Calhoun-Brown, "What a Fellowship: Civil Society, African American Churches and Public Life," in *New Day Begun: African American Churches and Civic culture in Post-Civil Rights America*, vol. 1 (Durham: Duke University Press, 2003) 39–57.

soil. If Black churches are to be viable instruments of spiritual and political liberation, I argue that the way forward for us to is to encourage
honest self-criticism of Black churches and the theologies that seek to
undergird them and to share meaningful dialogue on paramount issues
facing the communities for whom the Black churches and Black and
Womanist theologies exist. Of the multiple crises facing Black communities, the complexity and paramount problems of racism in its many
systemic forms, classism and poverty, sexism and homophobia remain
as the last leg of the Black struggle for holistic liberation.

Root experiences of Black religion ground Black and Womanist
theologies in the prophetic conviction that God mandates justice and the
elimination of all forms of oppression that dehumanize life. The projects
of Black and Womanist theology over the past several decades have exposed the demonic character of imperialistic and hegemonic theologies,
and in profound ways theologically connected Divine concern for liberation and justice to the needs of Black civic life. Black and Womanist
theologies have not only been concerned to unmask the destructive
forces of white supremacy upon people of color but also have provided
theological critique of Black churches as they struggle against the real
possibility of liberation traditions in Black Christian churches dying in
the spiritless materialism and globalization of what Pablo Richard refers
to as "savage forms capitalism."[4]

For the purposes of this essay, I employ a biblical reference from a
scene of crisis in the life of ancient Judah that lifts up rather poignantly
and painfully the crisis Black people face relative to who they are now
and the liberated communities they are straining to become. The reference is found in 2 Kings 19:3: "This is what Hezekiah says: 'This day is a
day of trouble and blasphemy and disgrace, as when children come to
the point of birth and there is no strength to deliver them.'" During the
reign of King Hezekiah, Judah was rendered powerless by the threat of
the Assyrian empire and was threatened with defeat and enslavement.
The metaphor Hezekiah uses to describe Judah's predicament was that
of "a child ready to be born, but there is no strength to bring it forth."
This story of crisis is a post-Exodus and pre-exilic crisis in the life of
Judah. Judah was trapped between the ages—one age of oppression and

4. Pablo Richard, "A Theology of Life: Rebuilding Hope from the Perspective of the
South," in *Spirituality of the Third World*, ed. K. C. Abraham and Bernadette Mbuy-Beye
(Maryknoll, NY: Orbis, 1994) 92–108.

servitude that should have been dead and the other age of a peaceful reign of faithfulness and justice that Judah was too weak to birth. The age that Hezekiah and Judah were powerless to birth was that glorious age spoken of by Second Isaiah: "every valley shall be exalted, and every mountain and hill shall be made low, and the crooked shall be made straight, and the rough places plain, and the glory of the Lord shall be revealed, and all flesh shall see it together, for the mouth of the Lord hath spoken it." It was to be an age of a free people serving the purpose and celebrating the presence of a liberating God of love and justice in the ancient world. But within Judah, power to birth it is not found.

Metaphorically, this story of crisis gives us access to language from the ancient biblical world that enables us to explore dimensions of unimaginable and systemic human suffering as it relates to the Black poor today. At this juncture of Black existence in America, the Black poor are trapped between two worlds—one that oppresses, hurts, and cripples Black life and another world that represents Black hopes and aspirations for a liberated future. "The struggle to end slavery," "the struggle to end legal segregation," and "the struggle to give Black people the right to vote" were seen as opening the door for economic justice and liberation of the Black poor. Yet remaining as the toughest struggle to be won is the social injustice and misery of poverty, the healthy wellbeing of the Black poor and their children, a reality in the womb of a Black future ready to be born. But as Cornel West notes, "the lived experience of coping with a life of horrifying meaninglessness, hopelessness, and most important lovelessness (nihilism)" robs the Black community of the strength to bring it forth. Black children are at the point of birth, ready and ripe to name a new era of justice and wholeness but seemly the unending pathology of racism in America coupled with Black churches messianic institutionalism, Black middle-class complicity with racism, and the monumental collapse and saturation of Black solidarity into what Cornel West describes as market forces of individualism and prosperity have rendered Black life weak and without strength to birth it into reality.[5] Ripe and ready to be born also are multi-forms of justice—gender justice, economic justice, political justice, and civic justice in a nation whose Declaration of Independence promised unhindered access to

---

5. Cornell West's book *Democracy Matters: Winning the Fight against Imperialism* (New York: Penguin, 2004) is a must read for Black churches who take seriously a democratic and prophetic vision of liberation in America.

"life, liberty, and the pursuit of happiness" to all its citizens; yet centuries and decades of failure after failure—the Reconstruction eras, the pre and post Black power era, the era of Black women's voices against triple oppression (female, Black, and poor), an era of Civil Rights followed by a period of social integration, this dream has been deferred or we might say conspired against its birth. Not only has this hope and dream been deferred, but historical consciousness as well as the most recent events in the aftermath of Hurricane Katrina informs us that these matters of justice and equality in this nation have existed on the cutting edge of a sabotage agenda; an agenda that is now a more urgent calling for the attention of Black theologians, religious bodies, and denominations in the country.

Black Baptist denominations for the first time in over fifty years came together in January 2005—the National Baptist Convention, USA, Inc., Progressive National Baptist Convention, Inc., National Baptist Convention of America, Inc., and the National Missionary Baptist Convention of America. They gathered with an acute sense of the need to birth new realities for the transformation of Black life but dispersed after five days without the specificity of an agenda for social justice change. With only a few exceptions, missing from this meeting were the voices of Black and Womanist theologians, social scientist, economist, political and health care professionals with whom the Black churches must be in dialogue to deal with the deepest crisis that threatens the future of Black life in America, and tragically for people of color globally—the quality of health and healthcare, education, public policy change, the overpopulation of Black people in industrial prison complexes and the reversal of poverty trends among people of color. These social conditions are theological matters as much as they are political matters that need the urgent attention of social science analysis and strategies for transformative praxis. These areas represent a whirlpool of social catastrophes that require the unity of a broad range of stakeholders in the Black community, of whom the Black community's most vulnerable at-risk population are Black children and women in poverty, and the potential they represent for a usable and responsible Black future in America. Indeed, these social crises require theological and systemic thinking to help us to see that patterns of poverty link Black people in a myriad of ways to context and wider social and economic systems of oppression.

Theologically, the primary challenge of a way forward for Black and Womanist theologians and the Black churches is to have sustained dialogue about the power inherent in the "root experiences" of Black religion and the theological renewal Black churches need to deliver children ready to be born into a new quality of life and liberation. In this regard, Black and Womanist theologies continue to be a an aggressive advocate against the conservative religiosity of Black churches as much as it has been a knife in the side of racism, sexism, and the imperialistic character of white American Christianity. The question for contemporary Black religious bodies is can they, in their present state, represent the message of liberation in the crisis of a nation that places the lives and future of its most vulnerable citizens at risk of demise, and by doing so, threaten to bring moral and social ruin to the nation itself? Or as Manning Marable puts it, "What is the black church's responsibility to cross the boundaries of race and religion, class and gender, religion and language, to help build an environment of pluralism, mutual respect, and civility?"[6] Are Black church denominational bodies and Islamic orders willing to partner with Black and Womanist theologians for self-critique and self-criticism to discover a way forward for justice and liberation in and for the Black community? New socio-cultural-political forms and resurgent powers of racism, sexism, and classism in the Black community makes self-critique imperative for birthing alternatives for liberation. As pastor-scholar Carlyle Fielding Stewart argues, "prophetic ministry involves not only confronting injustice in society, but equally witnessing against those forces, powers, and principalities which stifle the church from within, thus thwarting the full emergence of [liberation] in the black community."[7]

The question for Black and Womanist theologians is how to bridge what Dale P. Andrews describes as "black folk religion and practical theology" with the liberation goals of civic justice and the moral agency of Black churches?[8] This raises yet another equally important question for

6. Manning Marable, "Black Leadership, Faith and the Struggle for Freedom," in *Black Faith and Public Talk*, ed. Dwight N. Hopkins (Maryknoll, NY: Orbis, 1999) 77–88.

7. See Carlyle Fielding Stewart III, *African-American Church Growth: Twelve Prophetic Principles for Prophetic Ministry* (Nashville: Abingdon, 1994).

8. See Dale P. Andrews, *Practical Black Theology for Black Churches: Bridging Black Theology and African American Folk Religion* (Louisville: Westminster John Knox, 2002), in which he argues that Black theology's otherworldly critique of Black churches is misdiagnosis of the folk tradition of Black religious culture and praxis.

Black and Womanist theologians as well as the Black churches: How is healing to occur in the light of immeasurable human suffering and trauma Blacks have seen from the Atlantic Slave Trade and Middle Passage to the worst mass suicide of Black life in Jonestown, Guyana, to the highest poverty rates as was reality in the Ninth Ward of New Orleans now dispersed around the nation and prison rates of Black people in this nation to the global traumas of genocide in Rwanda and Durfur to starvation in the Africa and the pandemic of HIV and AIDS across Africa and among Black people in America?[9] In light of such trauma and suffering, what knowledges need to be unmasked to enhance theological and political literacy among Black churches, empowering them to speak publicly and prophetically for social justice change? How do we build a Black ecumenical movement, multi-cultural, multi-ethnic, and multi-racial for economic justice?

Indeed, "the children have come to the point of birth," ripe and ready to be born to a quality of life, health, economics, and education; but where in America, Black religious, educational, and social institutions can the strength be found to bring it forth? What should our theological response be for delivery? What is our moral assignment in this crisis? How do we do this with theological integrity, collective communal, and political wisdom? What kind of moral agency of hope are the Black churches called to be to deliver salvation in a crisis where white supremacy has sown seeds of genocide against a responsible and usable future for Black people?

I return to what Hezekiah did in the face of Judah's national crisis, not as a comprehensive strategy for a way forward, but as a starting point for theological and civic renewal of the Black churches in the light of the crisis Black communities are facing today. The chronicler of the story says when Hezekiah heard the defiant threat and insult of the Assyrian king against Judah and Judah's God, Hezekiah resorted to Israel's ancient ritual of lament; he tore his clothes and put on sackcloth and went in the temple of the Lord. Hezekiah's spiritual posture here is clearly one of deep lament: "This day is a day of trouble and blasphemy and disgrace."

9. See Archie Smith's article, "We Need to Press Forward: Black Religion and Jonestown Twenty Years Later," (online: http://archive.psr.edu/page.cfm?l=62&id=96) in which Smith gives an important analysis of the kind of trauma faced by victims of the Jonestown, Guyana, crisis. The reference to the high rates of poverty in the Ninth Ward in New Orleans is taken from media releases regarding the hardest hit areas of Hurricane Katrina.

A theology for birthing a liberating future for the next generation of Black children must begin with our capacity for communal lament, or, as Archie Smith Jr. puts it, "communal lament that is personal and personal lament that is communal."[10] Or as Womanist theologian Emilie M. Townes is correct to say: "without lament and institutional repentance liberation will not follow."[11] There is a growing tendency among the upward and mobile middle-class in the Black community to be complicit with and even tolerate the disgrace of Black poverty. Lamenting Black poverty is distant from their religious sensibilities, emotional and spiritual concerns. I agree with Dale P. Andrews's analysis that we have grossly underestimated "the hegemonic powers of racism and capitalism and the destructive element of individualism upon black religious life" and the resulting chasm between Black poor and the middle class as well between Black theology and Black middle-class churches.[12] Today Black churches are turning in vast numbers "to market spirituality and gospels of prosperity" to avoid the pain of the labor room that leads to new birth and social transformation. As Cornel West notes, "we see many Black people and the churches they attend become eager upwardly mobile aspirants in the nihilistic American game of power and might where there is hardly a mumbling world heard about social justice, resistance to institutional evil, or courage to confront the powers that be."

While middle-class Black churches are turning away from prophetic commitment to social justice, our "day of trouble and disgrace" is turning into tragic and permanent loss of life. The cooptation of the Black middle class into the excesses of capitalism coupled with a persistent racism that acts like what Ralph Ellison describes as "a boil bursting forth from impurities in the bloodstream of democracy," affects all aspects of Black life. Mimicking white religious culture, Black people are recycling racism in new forms of conservatism. But even more so, the near absence of a prophetic commitment to justice in many Black churches, which at one time was the distinctive hallmark of the Black Christianity in America,

10. See Archie Smith and Ursula Pfafflin, "Death and the Maiden: The Complexity of Trauma and Ways of Healing—A Challenge for Pastoral Care and Counseling," in *Human Images and Life-Stories in a Multi-Cultural World*, ed. Ulrike Atkins and Karl Federschmidt (Dusseldorf: The Society for Intercultural Pastoral Care and Counseling, 1996) 13–19.

11. Emilie M. Townes, *Breaking the Fine Rain of Death: African American Health Issues and a Womanist Ethic of Care* (New York: Continuum, 1998) 23–25.

12. See Andrews, *Practical Black Theology for Black Churches*, 10.

is a matter for deep communal lament. The Black church was effective in its early existence because of the circumstances of history; it was effective primarily because it never was free to separate its interior institutional life from liberation in and on behalf of Black life. Today the table has turned and many Black churches are taking comfort at the table of fundamentalist pieties that privatize, depoliticize, and de-radicalize the Christian message of liberation and express publicly little or no interest in broadening the Black community's civic capacity for reconstituting justice on behalf of the poor. Also a cause for deep lament is the growing number of Black churchgoers who increasingly are self-absorbed with glamorous appeals of prosperity and who have little or no commitment to the unglamorous day-to-day work required for liberation and social justice activism. Womanist ethicist Emile Townes sees "lament and repentance" as first steps toward restoration of faithfulness to a God of justice and liberation.[13]

Black and Womanist theology must effectively counter disruptive forces that undermine possibilities of justice and liberation in the Black community. One such force is the inability in the Black community to collectively define its situation and develop sustained coalitions for developing new agendas for social policy formation and assessment in which the institutional presence of the Black church is essential. The Black church has a critical interpretive role to play, both theologically and socio-politically in linking religious faith with responsible involvement in civic crises that circumscribe the lives of the Black poor. This interpretive role cannot be effectively done without the aid of Black and Womanist theology. There are encouraging signs that the unfortunate schism between Black and Womanist theologians and the Black churches is healing, and professional theologians in the academy through various forms of media are taking advantage of opportunities for genuine dialogue in Black churches. Such dialogue is critical. For we need to theologically understand and embody the history of Black religious heritage and the possibilities for liberation. This cannot be accomplished when the voices of professional theologians and the people for whom they write are isolated from each other.

Quality of life for the Black poor is understood concretely to include adequate housing, health and health care, effective education, a living wage, environmental safety, and vibrant communal associations

13. See Townes, *Breaking the Fine Rain of Death*, 25.

supporting the dignity and respectability of Black life. These areas of life are the bases for truth, spirituality, justice, goodness, and the beauty of life. Theologically, this understanding of the quality of life is as Pablo Richard puts it, quoting St. Irenaeus, "The glory of God is every creature fully alive."[14] "Every creature fully alive" implies a spirituality and quality of social and religious life where people have access to viable social, economic, and political well-being, and access to the theological language that sustains it.

The theological language that captions and legitimates a quality of life of liberation is inherent in the word salvation, whose Latin root, *salvus*, means to heal and make whole. In its deepest reality, salvation in the Hebrew language is the goal of shalom that is present when people dwell at peace in all their relationships: with God, with self, with others, and with creation. Liberating perspectives of salvation as wholeness recognize that justice includes not only the "integration of the spiritual (how we relate to God), the mental (who we are as thinking and feeling people), and the physical (who we are bodily and biologically),"[15] but also the negation of the demonic in systems and structures that promote injustices and disproportional suffering in the lives of people of color. As Walter Earl Fluker notes, "the existential state of Black people, nationally and globally, would need to be raised as catastrophic and the disproportional suffering of the poor is juxtaposed to the image of a God of mercy and justice, which in the concept of Orlando Patterson is the theological equivalent to 'natal alienation and eternal namelessness.' As it relates to holistic liberation, salvation is a critical theological issue that must involve civic justice as a response to how the Black poor can be saved from "eternal namelessness and invisibility."[16]

The birth of a liberating community for holistic salvation is not easy; it requires presence in the birthing/labor room of spiritual, material and moral crisis until justice is born. Long standing patterns of poverty and injustice create long-term trauma and in some cases irreparable hurt which can become an integral part of everyday life for the poor.

14. See Richard, "A Theology of Life," 95.

15. Townes, *Breaking the Fine Rain of Death*.

16. Walter Earl Fluker, "Recognition, Respectability, and Loyalty," in *The Black Churches and the Quest for Civility in New Day Begun: African American Churches and Civic Culture in Post-Civil Rights America* (Durham: Duke University Press, 2003) 113–41.

But we must be resolved to stay in the labor room of justice and not be tempted into believing that history is sterile for new births of justice, safety, spiritual and social transformation. We need a theology for birthing children ready to be born in communities of justice and wholeness that saves them from "natal alienation, eternal namelessness, and invisibility." Without the understanding and hope of this liberating salvation, the Black poor will be ultimately and hopelessly locked into violent struggles for survival within the poverty of Black communities where for them "liberation of the oppressed" becomes a vacuous euphemism.

Unfortunately, the identification of liberation with the material success of a few, who themselves have become physically and mentally severed from the suffering masses trivializes the unity essential for liberation praxis. As Emilie Townes notes, "genuine lament makes for the kind of pastoral and prophetic activities we need in response to our crisis."[17] If there is one aspect of the 1960's and 1970's that made Black communities strong for managing their plight was the capacity for corporate lamenting of Black suffering. The sea of Black poverty, which the aftermath of hurricane Katrina only exposed the tip of the iceberg, requires communal power and strength in the Black community for liberation praxis. A statement made by a hurricane Katrina evacuee during an interview expresses profoundly our need to reclaim the prophetic nature of communal power, "Before Katrina," the evacuee said, "I had nothing, and in the aftermath of Katrina I have less . . . we need each other."[18] The traumatization of thousands of displaced women, children, and men in the aftermath of hurricane Katrina presents a formidable theological and political challenge to America society at large and Black churches in particular, requiring them to deeply embrace a holistic ethic of care for justice and liberation. Charitable responses to soften the cultural and social dislocation of victims are not sufficient. Black poverty was a national Federal emergency long before Katrina hit New Orleans and the Gulf Coast. Charitable acts without systemic change fall far short of justice. The prophetic dimensions to this challenge is to see the interplay between personal suffering, political reality, and economic contexts, or

17. Townes, *Breaking the Fine Rain of Death*, 24.

18. This comment was made by a Katrina evacuee during a CNN interview. In response to the evacuee's comment, the CNN interviewer asked "What will you do now?" The evacuee responded, "I do not know; we need each other."

as Archie Smith puts it, "the personal is embedded in the political and the political is embedded in the personal."[19]

In Judah's crisis, Hezekiah summons the prophet Isaiah and went into the sanctuary to inquire of the Lord regarding the fate of Judah. Hezekiah found himself between the vestibule and the altar weeping and praying to the God of Israel. The Assyrian king had insulted the power of Israel's God implying that Judah's God too weak, a nonessential reality in the face of the Assyrian empire. In the face of this threat Hezekiah returned to the temple sanctuary; and so must we. But what about Black church sanctuaries? In the early beginnings of Black religious life in America, church sanctuaries were places of healing, restoration, and transformation; we cannot allow sanctuaries of Black churches to become places for uncritical theological development, ineffective for reflecting upon and improving Black civil society and continue as harbingers of homophobia, sexism, and gender discrimination. They instead must become places of counsel for communal cooperation, where people find the dignity of love, restoration, and liberation for sharing in community with others. Black church sanctuaries must become places where the prophetic commitment to justice is made real in what people need physically, socially, spiritually, and aesthetically for wholeness of life. The sanctuary must be inclusive places of love where God calls people to lifelong conversion of deepening relationship with God and of turning toward one's neighbor with all that love requires—justice, peace, inner and outer liberation in the world. Our sanctuaries must become stations of liberation and justice, places where the Word of God nurtures prophetic and moral imagination that allows Black people to envision what cannot yet be seen, that which nurtures constantly and expands the boundaries, possibilities and purposes of God. During the brutal life of slavery, Jim Crow lynching, racist segregated culture, the Black church sanctuaries served as places for people to lament, grieve, and mourn situations where seemingly "hope unborn had died" while serving as an agent of liberation at the same time.

Black theologians, women and male pastors, Black laity in all their diverse realities and sexual orientations must join together in the birth-

19. The several references to the work of Archie Smith signals my high regard for him as a leading pastoral care scholar who has in his article, "Death and the Maiden" addressed the essential need of a shift from the private lives of individuals to the social and political in pastoral care in response to the needs of the Black poor.

ing/labor room of sacrifice and prophetic hope to deliver children ready and ripe to be born in a new age of liberation. Salvation can occur in our contemporary crisis, if there is a small minority, a group of people, who represent what America and Black existence in this nation is called to be. The question of new birth for us and this nation is the question of whether there is a liberative spiritual presence among Black churches willing to resist the anxiety and threats of conformity (as Hezekiah resisted the Assyrian threat of conformity) to America's idolatry of capitalism, individualism, materialism, and lust for power. A theological response for salvation depends upon the healing, liberating grace and power of God, which can work through the agency of any of us. While this is Black and Womanist theology's enormous challenge, it is also the greatest opportunity for the Black churches. We must appeal to and be available to the liberating gospel of Jesus Christ and respond to God's power express through it to bring forth new life.

As a matter for the record of this book, the way forward for Black and Womanist Theology and the communities they serve warrants nothing less than a national dialogue with many collaborators from various interdisciplinary fields to establish a "social justice credo" that links Black liberating faith with the need of Black people for spiritual and social liberation. This collaborative effort includes agenda setting, public policy formation and implementation, as well as theological assessment of the social realities that impact Black life.[20] This book reflects the continuous effort to bridge academic Black theology and the Black church, a career goal I have pursued as a former pastor and currently as Director of Vanderbilt's Kelly Miller Smith Institute on Black Church Studies and President of American Baptist College in Nashville. In these positions, the attempt has been, and is currently being made to bring together Black preachers, social theorists, economists, ethicists, non-profit organizations, political leaders, theologians, pastors, secondary educators, professors in higher education, church laity, and public health officials for clarifying and defining the parameters of a liberating ministry for Black churches. In this regard, I suggest we reexamine the Social Justice Credo Colombia Professor Manning Marable offers as a guide for our

20. This is something Emilie M. Townes has done in her published work, *Breaking the Fine Rain of Death.*

deliberation. I offer here modest revisions to the Social Justice Credo as proposed by Marable for future dialogue.[21]

## SOCIAL JUSTICE CREDO

- *We must strive for theological education that makes essential the God-human relationship in the world to reveal and sustain a movement of liberation.* We should strive to do theological education in Black churches that pertain to how people of faith can change the world for a communal sharing of gifts and resources given to humanity by God, and show how the gospel, life and ministry of Jesus Christ is commensurate with the goal of liberation and justice.

- *We must strive for quality education for all.* We must develop the civic capacity of the Black community to build and maintain effective alliances among a broad cross section of stakeholders that will work toward a collective goal for reform of public education. We should demand greater funding for our public schools, investment in Black teacher development and teacher salaries, classroom construction, computers, and other materials which make learning possible. We should support anti-racist curriculum and educational programs and reinforcing Black history and culture. We should support the preservation and enrichment of historically Black colleges and universities.

- *We must strive for the emotional, physical, spiritual, intellectual health of Black people.* The quality of life, health and health care involves more than the absence of disease. Black churches should establish educational programs of health awareness that includes spiritual, emotional, intellectual, as well as physical health. More attention must be paid to the political education and literacy of Black clergy in the area of public health and poverty. We must be committed to a society, which allows for the healthy and positive development of children. We must demand quality education, health care, housing, and safety for every child.

- *We must be committed to a social policy agenda, which means investment in human beings. We must strive for a society in which all people have the resources to develop their fullest potential.* This can

---

21. Marable, "Black Leadership, Faith, and the Struggle for Freedom."

only occur when the basic needs of all people are met. At minimum, this includes free and universal health care, childcare, quality education, lifelong access to retraining and vocational learning, and low-cost quality public housing. We must strive for a comprehensive national economic policy, which places the interest of people above profits. We should replace minimum wage with a mandated living wage for the poor. We should demand emergency action by the government, especially in areas of concentrated high unemployment, to create real jobs at living wages.

- *We must strive for justice in the legal system.* The U.S. prison-industrial complex has become a vast warehouse for millions of the Black poor and unemployed. We should be in the forefront of a campaign to call for the abolition of the death penalty, this twentieth-first century's version of lynching.

- *We must strive for civil rights, affirmative action, and compensation for centuries of institutional racism.* We should defend the policies of affirmative action and all equal opportunity legislation to create equal conditions as absolutely essential in attacking racial inequality.

- *We must strive for gender justice and women's rights.* We must support full pay equity and the abolition of job discrimination for Black women. We must support strong measures to protect Black women's lives from domestic violence, sexism, sexual abuse and harassment in Black churches and the wider society.

- *We must strive for an end to homophobia and discrimination against people of different sexual orientations.* We should oppose and reject any arguments or constitutional amendment that exclude or marginalize the contributions of people of different sexual orientations toward the goal of freedom in American society at large and particularly in the African American community.

- *We must strive for liberation for all oppressed people throughout the world.* The struggles of peoples of African decent are inextricably linked to the many diverse struggles of oppressed people and nations across the globe.

- *And finally, we must commit ourselves to strive for a real democracy in the United States.* We must be committed to the fight for the realization of a truly democratic and socially just society.

This Social Justice Credo might very well serve as a guide for clarifying the moral assignment and way forward for Black and Womanist theologians and for the communities for whom they write in the twenty first century. Liberation is costly. It is a costly dream for Black churches. It is a dream that represents the Black church's historic presence in America. As theologians and Black church leaders, we are called forth as human agents of this liberating dream that may cost us everything.

# 3

# Survival and the Quality of Life

*Notes on a "Womanist Hermeneutic
of Identification-Ascertainment"*

JOSIAH U. YOUNG

I TAKE THE THEME "survival and the quality of life" from a short section
of Delores Williams's book *Sisters in the Wilderness*. In the section she
entitles "Survival, Quality of Life and God" she discusses Hagar's conflict
with Sarai as recorded in Genesis 16. Let me recount a bit of that story:
Unaware that God will make her fertile in her old age, Sarai gives her
Egyptian slave, Hagar, to Abram, Sarai's husband, so he can have an heir.
According to the scripture, "when [Hagar] saw she had conceived," she
made her mistress feel uncomfortable (Genesis 16:4). Sarai then says to
Abram "May the wrong done to me be on you. I gave my maid to your
embrace, and when she saw that she had conceived, she looked on me
with contempt. May the Lord judge between you and me!" Abram re-
sponds by saying "your maid is in your hands; do to her as you please"
(Genesis 16:6). Thus empowered, Sarai deals so harshly with her slave
that she flees to the wilderness to escape her mistress's wrath.[1] God's

---

1. In her *Texts of Terror: Literary-Feminist Readings of Biblical Narratives*, Overtures
to Biblical Theology (Philadelphia: Fortress, 1988), Phyllis Trible argues that "maid"
and "slave" do not have the same meaning exactly. The distinction works as follows: In
Genesis 16 Hagar is "identified as . . . a virgin, dependent maid . . . whereas in Genesis 21
. . . she is called a slave woman who serves the master of a second wife" (30). The latter
designation is the "more oppressive" as it makes the point that though Sarah give Hagar
to Abraham as a second wife, she is nonetheless a slave Sarah abused because Hagar
forgot her place (and her non-Semitic bloodline it seems to me—that her "father" is
Ham rather than Shem).

messenger finds Hagar in the wilderness and instructs her to return to Sarai and submit to her. Is this because return and submission will be good for Hagar? Delores Williams raises this question on Hagar's behalf and that of all unfree women: "Did God not know about Sarai's brutal treatment of Hagar?"[2] Why *does* this God—whom African-Americans have worshiped as the great liberator of slaves—instruct a slave to return to slavery? Let's continue with more of the story.

As if to provide an incentive for Hagar to return to Sarai, God promises Hagar that he will "so greatly multiply" her descendants that none will be able to count them (Genesis 16:10). Her unborn son, Ishmael—who is also Abram's son—will become the powerful patriarch of this multitude (Genesis 16:11). Earlier in the book of Genesis, God has promised to make Abram a great patriarch too (Genesis 12:2–3); but what God promises Abram differs from what he promises Hagar. Abram will bless those he will encounter; but Ishmael will "be a wild ass of a man, his hand against every man and every man's hand against him" (Genesis 17:12). No wonder Delores Williams argues that God's promise to Hagar reads more like a "curse than a blessing."[3] Nonetheless, the "fact" that Ishmael will "protect the quality of life he and his mother . . . will later develop in the desert" after Abraham and Sarah have cast them out is positive for Williams.[4] Ishmael will become a masterful hunter. Hagar will find him an Egyptian wife (to uphold his maternal heritage and thus strengthen his identity, I suppose); and nobody will mess with Hagar once Ishmael develops into a mighty warrior. Ishmael, though, won't be able to protect his mother's *name* from the dishonor many Christians will attach to it in contrast to the esteem they will extend to Sarah's name.[5]

---

2. Delores S. Williams, *Sisters in the Wilderness: The Challenge of Womanist God-Talk* (Maryknoll, NY: Orbis, 1993) 21.

3. Ibid., 22. One might say, though, that the reiteration of the promise in Genesis 17:20ff. is not as curse-like.

4. Ibid.

5. To the extent that these derogatory portrayals of Hagar indict Ishmael too, they differ, it seems to me, from the Genesis accounts that suggest that Ishmael, despite being cast out by Sarah, is still seen by Abraham, and even Isaac and Esau, as being part of the family—Abraham's flesh and blood. See Genesis 17:18; 25:9; 28:9; and 1 Chronicles 1:28. While, however, the Scripture indicates that Abraham and his son and his grandson do not disown Ishmael, *God* blesses Isaac after Abraham's death; He does *not* bless Ishmael.

In Galatians 4:27–31, for instance, Paul asserts that Hagar represents the earthly-Jewish Jerusalem—the old covenant below—and thus
slavery. She "bears children for slavery." Sarah, on the other hand, represents the heavenly-Christian Jerusalem—the new covenant "above"—
and thus freedom. She bears children for freedom. According to Paul,
Hagar is to the flesh as Sarah is to the spirit: He thus admonishes the
churches to "Cast out the slave and her son; for the son of the slave shall
not inherit with the son of the free woman."[6]

Commenting on Galatians, Gregory of Nyssa finds something redemptive in Hagar's survival in the wilderness. Let's continue with the
story: Abraham had grown fond of his first-born son, at least Genesis
17:18 suggests as much: At first, he laughs when God informs him that
Sarah, a very old woman, will give birth to a son, Isaac. Then, aware that
Sarah's son will undermine Hagar's, the patriarch cries: "O that Ishmael
might live in thy sight." Anyway, Abraham hosts a great feast "on the day
Isaac was weaned." "Sarah saw the son of Hagar the Egyptian, whom she
had borne to Abraham, playing with her son Isaac." Sarah pulls rank
again as she instructs Abraham to "Cast out this slave woman with *her*
son; for the son of *this* slave woman shall not be heir with *my* son Isaac"
(Genesis 21:10, emphasis added). That is the context for the line Paul
appropriates— "Cast out the slave woman." Sarah's God tells Abraham to
heed his wife since the promise is to be fulfilled through *Isaac*. Abraham
obeys the Lord and casts out the slave woman and her son.

Just when Hagar thought her son would perish from dehydration
out there in the desert, God's messenger, Gregory writes, "unexpectedly
appears, and shows [Hagar] a well of living water, and drawing thence,
she saves Ishmael." Gregory writes that this well prefigures baptism
since it is by "means of living water that salvation comes to him that

6. Paul: "Now this is an allegory: these women are two covenants. One is from
Mount Sinai, bearing children for slavery; she is Hagar. Now Hagar is Mount Sinai in
Arabia; she corresponds to the present Jerusalem, for she is in slavery with her children.
But the Jerusalem above is free, and she is our mother. For it is written, 'Rejoice, O
barren one that dost not bear; / break forth and shout, thou who art not in travail; / for
the desolate hath more children than she who hath a husband.' Now we, brethren, like
Isaac, are children of promise. But as at that time he who was born according to the flesh
persecuted him who was born according to the Spirit, so it is now. But what does the
scripture say? 'Cast out the slave and her son; for the son of the slave shall not inherit
with the son of the free woman.' So brethren, we are not children of the slave but of the
free woman" (Galatians 4:24–31).

was perishing."[7] Ishmael's survival, though, pales beside the quality of life Isaac represents. Recounting Genesis 24, Gregory writes that "Isaac was to be wedded." Squeamish about the Canaanite women he was living among at the time, Abraham directed one of his slaves to journey to Abraham's ancestral homeland to find a wife for Isaac. The slave staked out a well in the fatherland and prayed: "God of my master Abraham, grant me success today, I pray thee, and show steadfast love to my master Abraham" (Genesis 24:12). Abraham's God heard his slave's cry at the well and sent him Rebekah. According to Gregory, the union between Isaac and Rebekah produces "the race of Christ" and "had its beginning and its first covenant in water."[8] Substantiating Paul's claim that Hagar and Sarah typify "two covenants," the old and the new—one analogous to the earthly Jerusalem, the other, to "the Jerusalem above"—Gregory suggests that Rebekah's well supersedes (is better than) the one that revived Ishmael.

Augustine's *City of God* also upholds Paul's Hagar-Sarah allegory.[9] According to Augustine, human history is like an "earthly city" with a higher and a lower part. The lower part is the shadow of the upper part, which, in turn, is the shadow of what Augustine calls "the heavenly city" above—the city of God. Augustine argues that Hagar typifies the shadow of the shadow—the murky image of the upper part—while Sarah typifies the shadow, the murky image, of the heavenly city.[10]

As an allegory, the Hagar-Sarah story points beyond itself to God's beneficent kingdom; but does it challenge the mistress-slave dialectic

7. Gregory of Nyssa, "On the Baptism of Christ," in *Nicene and Post-Nicene Fathers of the Christian Church*, vol. 5, ed. Philip Schaff and Henry Wace (Grand Rapids: Eerdmans, 1979) 520–29.

8. Ibid., 521.

9. Augustine, *The City of God* (New York: Modern Library, 1978) 479.

10. Ibid., 480. Augustine writes: "One portion of the earthly city became an image of the heavenly city, not having a significance of its own, but signifying another city, and therefore serving, or 'being in bondage.' For it was founded not for its own sake, but to prefigure another city; and this shadow of a city was also itself foreshadowed by another preceding figure. For Sarah's handmaid Agar (*sic*), and her son, were an image of this image. And as the shadows were to pass away when the full light came, Sarah, the free woman, who prefigured the free city (which again was also prefigured in another way by that shadow of a city Jerusalem), therefore said, 'Cast out the bond woman and her son; for the son of the bond woman shall not be heir with my son Isaac,' or as the apostle says, 'with the son of the free woman.' In the earthly city, then, we find two things—its own obvious presence, and its symbolic presentation of the heavenly city."

here and now? Neither Paul nor Gregory nor Augustine troubled the status quo much. Could it be that their *theology* reflects the mistresses' investment in *their* survival and good quality of life as much it does the distinction between eternity and time and the tension between two sibling religions? Can we separate the biblical characters' and the theologians' social locations from what they are saying about God? What if the disgruntled slaves—those worse off than the Hagars of history— could speak for themselves? What would they say about survival, quality of life and God?

One of the disturbing implications of the Hagar-Sarah story for me is that Sarah would have blessed Hagar if she had been a proper house slave. In my reading of the story, Hagar is the antithesis of Abraham's house slave Eliezer (Genesis 15:2), who "had charge of all [Abraham] had" (Genesis 24:2). In his *The Curse of Ham: Race and Slavery in Early Judaism, Christianity and Islam,* David Goldenberg discusses a midrash in which "Eliezer is said" to relish "serving Abraham, because as a descendant of Canaan he was doomed to a life of slavery" on account of Noah's curse. For Eliezer to leave Abraham would be like jumping from the fire pan into the fire. He might not survive. His quality of life would surely be wretched. "In the words put in Eliezer's mouth," writes Goldenberg, "A Kushi or a Barbari might enslave me! It is better for me to be a slave in this household and not in some other household."[11] A hermeneutic of suspicion suggests that that the masters are speaking and not the slaves.

Apparently, God's liberation of the oppressed goes only so far in parts of the Bible. That conjecture compels me to ponder our history in the United States and pose another question: Would the Africans enslaved in the New World have become Christians in such great numbers without being coerced by the slave owners? I doubt it; which is not to suggest that our ancestors' biblical values reflected nothing but their thralldom in every conceivable case—that one finds in them no "self-sufficiency of insight" (C. Eric Lincoln) regarding the meaning of the Bible and the Protestant tradition. So I'm not suggesting that our theologies today are *nothing but* legacies of bondage. What I am asserting is that the slave-owners knew that their quality of life as masters and mistresses was hardly an affront to Sarah's (or Paul's) God.

---

11. David M. Goldenberg, *The Curse of Ham: Race and Slavery in Early Judaism, Christianity and Islam* (Princeton: Princeton University Press, 2003) 67–68.

The Founding Fathers saw themselves as the free woman's children because they *were* free. They thought Sarah's God had led them to the Promised Land, North America, much in the same way that YHWH led the Hebrews into Canaan.[12] Because they subscribed to the very same Pauline religion that their masters did, the Christianized slaves also identified with Sarah. Despite their this-worldly status as chattel, they saw themselves as citizens of the heavenly Jerusalem rather than the earthly one—an "eschatological dissonance" that surely helped them survive as it did wonders for their psychic well being. They thought they "prefigured the free city," as Augustine put it. That's why they sang *You got shoes, I got shoes all* God's children *got shoes. When I get to heaven I'm going to put on my shoes and walk all over God's heaven. But* everybody *talking about heaven ain't going there.* Their identification with Sarah is clear.[13] But if Paul's allegory reflects the conflict between mistresses and

12. See Alexander Saxton, *The Rise and Fall of the White Republic* (New York: Verso, 2003) 26. Saxton provides an example of their perspective in writing of John Quincy Adams's veneration of the work of "the nationalist poet and Congregationalist pastor Timothy Dwight." "Grandson of Jonathan Edwards, later the ultra-Federalist president of Yale College," Dwight expressed his Puritan theology in his book *The Conquest of Canaan*. He dedicated the epic text to George Washington "and . . . allegorized Anglo-Americans as children of Israel redeeming a promised land from Indian hordes so devilish that 'wives wade[d] in nuptial, sires in filial, gore'; and even their 'babes . . . by vile affections lur'd, in guilt, and years . . . alike matured.'" According to Dwight, America was godless and thus evil until Sarah's God led the English to set things right.

13. Orlando Patterson, *Slavery and Social Death* (Cambridge: Harvard University Press, 1982) 74–75. Patterson writes: "The slaves found in fundamentalist (*sic*) Christianity paths to the satisfaction of their own needs, creating the strong commitment to Christianity that has persisted to this day. In doing so they created an institutional base that provided *release and relief from the agonies of thralldom, and even offered some room for a sense of dignity before God and before each other* [added]." Patterson then points out that this religion was little different from the masters'. Patterson, in fact, goes so far as to argue that the religions were identical—"the same . . . in all essential doctrinal and cultic aspects." While, he argues, "the spirituals [the Blacks] sang may have had a double meaning with secular implications, it is grossly distorting of the historical facts to claim that they were covertly revolutionary in their intent; and most important of all, it is irresponsible to deny that however well religion may have served the slaves, in the final analysis it did entail a form of accommodation to the system." Patterson goes on to explain the this-worldly implications of Paul's allegory as follows: "Both masters and slaves adhered to Pauline ethical dualism, with its sustained '*eschatological dissonance* [added].' And in exactly the same way that Paul and the early Christians shifted from one pole of their doctrinal dualism to another as occasion and context demanded, so did the masters and the slaves. Thus the masters, among themselves, could find both spiritual and personal dignity and salvation in the ethic of the justified and redeemed sinner. The crucified Jesus as redeemer and liberator from enslavement to sin supported

their slaves more than the difference between this world and the one that's a coming, then, it seems to me, Delores Williams has ascertained the matter truthfully: Our ancestors were more like Hagar than Sarah, the Egyptians and the Canaanites than the people to whom God promised a milk-and-honey land.

That certain of our African-American ancestors did not see that reveals the powerful impact the dominant history had on them. For me, one of the painful examples of that hegemony is the fact that their appeal to the Bible's God as a God of liberation pulled in its train negative assessments of their continent of origin. In much of the theology they have produced, Africa has come across as cursed—Canaan-like.[14] Phillis Wheatley places that problematic in historical perspective.

Wheatley was abducted from Africa in the eighteenth century and arrived in North America on the slave ship *Phillis*. Bostonian John Wheatley bought her. The seven-year-old served the man's wife primarily. Phillis soon displayed a talent for writing verse:

> 'Twas mercy brought me from my *Pagan* land,
> Taught my benighted soul to understand
> That there's a God, that there's a *Saviour* too:
> Once I redemption neither sought nor knew.
> Some view our sable race with scornful eye,
> "Their colour is a diabolic die."
> Remember, *Christians, Negros*, black as *Cain*,
> May be refin'd, and join th' angelic train.

To me, the poem conveys that her extraordinary survival and relatively good quality of life depended on her ability to uphold, eloquently to be sure, her mistress' religion—for where is the evidence in Genesis 4, where we find God's punishment of Cain, that Cain was marked with Black, that is, "Negroid," skin? According to Goldenberg, this Christian claim is based on a misreading of the "midrashic tradition that Cain's face," in reacting to God's curse, "became like an ember," which is not to say that he then turned into a Black man, but that his countenance

---

a proud, free group of people with a highly developed sense of their own dignity and worth. Similarly, the slaves in the silence of their own souls and among themselves *with their own preachers* could find salvation and dignity in this same interpretation of the crucified Lord." Patterson thus suggests to me that both slaves and their masters saw themselves as "Sarah."

14. See Stephen Haynes, *Noah's Curse: The Biblical Justification of American Slavery* (New York: Oxford University Press, 2002) 111.

darkened, in the sense of saddened.[15] And what does refinement mean here? What is angelic? Whatever the answer may be, Phillis Wheatley's soteriology— *"Negros,* black as *Cain,* May be refin'd, and join th' angelic train"—and its intrinsic relation to Euro-American aesthetics won her great acclaim and her freedom in 1773.

One source asserts that "no single writer has contributed more to the founding of African American literature" than Wheatley.[16] This same source also finds that Wheatley undermined the widespread view that Blacks were incapable of rendering "civilized" thoughts in tried and true form. We are to believe that "because Wheatley wrote her poems, exploitative assumptions about the African's 'nature' would never again be so easy to maintain in European and American letters."[17] Why—because she proved to be an exception to the rule? Her good fortune was hardly normative and her worldview was not shared by the Africans in the fields. It seems to me that her poetry confirms rather than undermines "exploitative assumptions" precisely because her take on survival and the quality of life negates Africa as it was (in its alterity). Would she have taken that position if she had known as much about Africa as she had the Bible and Homer? It's not my intention to put her down; I just want to suggest that she was a captive in more ways than one, as many of us have been.

David Walker, a free Black as educated as Wheatley and far less accommodating to the status quo, replicates this problem in his powerful nineteenth-century *Appeal.* For good reason, Walker opposes the tactics of the American Colonization Society that sought to repatriate non-slave Blacks to Africa, to places such as Liberia. Walker thought colonization was a ruse to divest the nation of Blacks who wanted to abolish slavery by any means necessary. In Article IV of the *Appeal,* Walker takes on Henry Clay, an exponent of repatriation: "Does he care a pinch of snuff about Africa—whether it remains a land of pagans and of blood, or of Christians, so long as he gets enough of her sons and daughters to dig up gold and silver for him?"[18] Is Walker suggesting that a Christianized

15. Goldenberg, *The Curse of Ham,* 160–81.

16. Henry Louis Gates and Nellie Y. McKay, editors, *The Norton Anthology of African American Literature* (New York: Norton, 1997) 167.

17. Ibid., 165.

18. David Walker, *Appeal to the Colored Citizens of the World* (New York: Hill & Wang, 1982) 50.

Africa would be more humane than Christianized North America? Why would that be—because such an Africa would be more Christian than "heathen"? And yet Walker claims that North American Christians are without precedent in their mistreatment of their Black slaves:

> O my Master! My Master! I cannot but think upon Christian Americans!!!—What kind of people can they be? Will not those who were burnt up in Sodom and Gomorrah rise up in judgment against Christian Americans with the Bible in their hands, and condemn them? Will not the Scribes and Pharisees of Jerusalem, who had nothing but the laws of Moses and the Prophets to go by, rise up in judgment against them, who, in addition to these have a revelation from Jesus Christ the Son of the living God? In fine, will not the Antediluvians, together with the whole heathen world of antiquity, rise up in judgment against Christian Americans and condemn them? The Christians of Europe and America go to Africa, bring us away, and throw us into the seas, and in other ways murder us, as they would wild beast. The Antediluvians and heathens never dreamed of such barbarities.[19]

What, then, makes pagan Africa so contrary to survival and the quality of life in the good sense? For Walker, the answer is that Africa—as far as he knew—was not Christian, and so did not know the one true God-in-Christ. His assumption seems to be that African people are better off as Anglicized Christians than devotees of their ancestral religions. But can we—will we—ever know that for sure?

What accounts for the assumption itself? I think the answer, to re-iterate, is that many of our ancestors appropriated the religion of their parents' masters, and sometimes in ways that cast *them out* of the hope of heaven—*Everybody talking about heaven ain't going there!*— which is par for the course. As David Goldenberg argues, the Bible means different things to different people "due to different historical circumstances." A given text—reconsider Galatians 4:27–31—acquires nuances over time, which provide "us with a picture of changing views, opinions, and attitudes within and among monotheistic cultures."[20]

Let me go back to David Walker's *Appeal* as it exemplifies Goldenberg's point. Walker indicates how a highly influential, Christianized, non-slave African-American thought about Sarah's God in

19. Ibid., 59.

20. Goldenberg, *The Curse of Ham*, 6

distinction from how many whites thought about him within the same Protestant religion. Walker asserts that Sarah's God will destroy slaveholding American Christians if they fail to set their Black slaves free. Walker writes "that God will dash tyrants, in combination with devils, into atoms, and will bring [the oppressed Blacks] out from [their] wretchedness and miseries under these *Christian people!*[21] He is sure the free woman's—Sarah's—God will liberate African-Americans, eventually. Yet—and I am compelled to repeat this—Sarah's God endorses a certain kind of slavery.

Shortly *after* the Exodus, God instructs Moses to tell his people to enslave a Hebrew bondsman for only six years. The bondsman is to be manumitted in the seventh year, and his wife is to be set free too provided they were enslaved together from the first year. But if in the course of six years, the Hebrew master gives his slave a wife who has children as a result of the union, then the woman and the children are to remain in bondage. The man can go free; but if he stays, out of declared love for his master as well as his family, then the Hebrew patriarch must brand the slave—"bore his ear through with an awl"—to mark his permanent bondage.[22] Another part of the Law stipulates that a Hebrew who canes his male or female slave to death—that is, strikes him or her "with a rod"—is to be punished. "But if the slave survives a day or two," the master "is not to be punished; for the slave is his *money*" (Exodus 21:20–21 [emphasis added]).

I think I understand why Black Christians such as Walker did not identify with Israel's slaves and indentured servants: If African-Americans had thought of themselves as analogous to *Hebrew* underlings—the ones bound to serve their Hebrew masters *after* the Exodus—or if they had identified with the non-Hebrew slaves, they would have undermined their hope that God would one day render them equal to their masters. Still, our ancestors' identification with Israel's elite raises ethical prob-

---

21. Walker, *Appeal to the Colored Citizens of the World*, 71.

22. Exodus 21:1–6: "When you buy a Hebrew slave, he shall serve six years, and in the seventh he shall go out free, for nothing. If he comes in single, he shall go out single; if he comes in married, then his wife shall go out with him. If his master gives him a wife and she bears him sons or daughters, the wife and her children shall be her master's and he shall go out alone. But if the slave plainly says, 'I love my master, my wife, and my children; I will not go out free, then his master shall bring him to the door or the doorpost; and his master shall bore his ear through with an awl; and he shall serve him for life."

lems. One of them is the Hebrews' practice of slavery, to be sure. But the big problem—as Delores Williams points out in her reading of the Exodus "as *holistic story* rather than *event*"—is the way the Hebrews take possession of the Promised Land.[23] Our ancestors sang *O Canaan, we love thee*, for Canaan symbolized freedom, the North—New York, or Canada—but they were not too mindful of the American implications of what Moses, the former Egyptian, tells his birth-people to do to the people of the land for God's sake: "utterly destroy them . . . and show no mercy to them" (Deuteronomy 7:1–2). As Native American theologians have pointed out, the Anglo-Saxton settlers legitimized the taking of the land by appropriating the Bible's violent tale of the conquest of Canaan.[24] Many Indian theologians thus think of the Exodus quite differently "from even black church folk in North America," who are not unlike the settlers in embracing the Exodus saga and its tie to Canaan.[25]

Black and white Christians have surely meant different things by the Exodus and the Promised Land much in the same way that they have meant different things by "Sarah." Appropriated in light of what Dr. W. E. B. Du Bois has called "the problem of the color line," Sarah and the Exodus signify in Black and white both the blessedness of the oppressed *and* the oppressors. In her book *The Curse of Cain: The Violent Legacy of Monotheism*, Regina Schwartz discusses the ambivalence this way: "From one perspective—that of the history of the text—the conquest narrative is only a wild fantasy written by a powerless dispossessed people who dream of wondrous victories over their enemies, of living in a land where milk and honey flow, and of entering that land with the blessing and support of an Almighty Deity." But then there's "the text's political afterlife," which involves "the massive displacement and destruction of

23. Williams, *Sisters in the Wilderness*, 150. Williams's perspective helps Black churches see "the exodus as a chronicle" that culminates in "the genocide of the Canaanites and the taking of their land" rather than the liberating episode that stands apart from what appears to be its goal—the promised land.

24. See, for example, George E. Tinker, *Spirit and Resistance: Political Theology and American Indian Liberation* (Minneapolis: Fortress, 2004) 90. Tinker argues that "the closest analogy to Indian history in the hebrew (sic) scriptures seems to be the experience of the Canaanites, who were dispossessed of their land and annihilated by a foreign invader."

25. Ibid.

other peoples, of laying claim to a land that had belonged to others, and of conducting this bloody conquest under the banner of divine will."[26]

In their captivity, our ancestors were, perhaps, more like the Jews— who may have put the redacted Exodus sources together while in exile[27]— than the Anglo-Saxon Christians, who decimated the native people and used our ancestors "to dig up gold and silver for them."[28] Nonetheless, "God" casts out people in both traditions—in that of the oppressed and that of the oppressor. Black and white Christians have therefore not only meant different things by Sarah but the same thing too as they have cast out one another from the heavenly city. The nation's racism—its commitment to segregation— the color-line problem—has served the Bible's violence well. As James Baldwin argues in his *The Fire Next Time*, "the vision people hold of the world to come is but a reflection, with predictable wishful distortions, of the world in which they live." No wonder, then, that Baldwin holds that White American Protestants have held that Blacks are "the descendants of Ham, and . . . cursed forever," while Black American Protestants have thought of whites as "the descendants of Cain."[29] In many of the biblical theologies of the oppressed and the oppressor, the other has acquired a permanent anti-soteriological stigma, and precisely because the oppressed and the oppressor share the same wheat-versus-tares religion.[30]

They express this religion differently—yes: Consider the distinction between the Africanness of the Sanctified Church and the Anglican comportment of white (and a good many Black) Episcopalians. Yet both churches as a rule view themselves as better than Hagar's children. Today, Christian identity is not as set against the synagogue as it is in

26. Regina Schwartz, *The Curse of Cain: The Violent Legacy of Monotheism* (Chicago: University of Chicago Press, 1997) 57.

27. See Ronald E. Clements, *Exodus*, Cambridge Bible Commentary (Cambridge: Cambridge University Press, 1972) 4.

28. The phrase is from Walker's *Appeal to the Colored Citizens of the World*. He uses it no less than nine times.

29. James Baldwin, *The Fire Next Time* (New York: Vintage, 1993) 40–41.

30. Ibid., 31. Anyway, that is my take on Baldwin's claim that "the principles governing the rites and customs of the churches in which I grew up did not differ from the principles governing the rites and customs of other churches, white. The Principles were Blindness, Loneliness, and Terror, the first principle necessarily and actively cultivated in order to deny the two others. I would love to believe that the principles were Faith, Hope, and Charity, but this is clearly not so for most Christians, or for what we call the Christian world."

Galatians. Christian otherness is now made clear in comparison to wild men, certain Muslims who are at odds with certain Christians and certain Jews alike. As Baldwin put it, God has "come a long way from the dessert—but then so [has] Allah, though in a very different direction. God, going north, and rising on the wings of power, [has] become white, and Allah, out of power, and on the dark side of Heaven, [has] become—for all practical purposes, anyway—black."[31] The Christian Right, which includes an increasing number of African-Americans, acknowledges Ishmael's survival by echoing Paul: *we are not children of the slave but of the free woman.* The moral ambivalence here, of course, again in Black and white, is that some of us—until today—despite the fact that we are the issue of the same Founding Fathers, are not as free, that is, Sarah-like, as others. Tragically, nothing has made that clearer to us today than the sad aftermath of Hurricane Katrina—that horrid transmogrification of Congo Square: that postdiluvian revelation that the problem of the color line is the problem of the twenty-first century. How will this all play out? Who will survive it, and what will their quality of life be?

The good news is we don't have to do theology the way our ancestors did. If we had little choice but to internalize the prejudices of the dominant history, even when we have tried to oppose it because of the role it has played in our oppression, we are much farther up the road now. We can read the Bible more critically than ever before and salvage from it only those aspects that reflect who we are coming to be in this new century.[32] Thanks to the pioneering work of scholar-educators, a whole new generation of scholars has taken the field, and is helping the academy and the church see that it's time to take Delores Williams's imperative to heart. She calls this imperative the "womanist hermeneutic of *identification-ascertainment.*" It advises African-American theologians to call the text unjust when it "supports oppression, exclusion and even death of innocent people."[33]

---

31. Baldwin, *The Fire Next Time*, 46.

32. I'm indebted to William Jones's *Is God a White Racist?* (Boston: Beacon, 1998) for this insight.

33. Williams, *Sisters in the Wilderness*, 150.

# 4

# Speaking in Tongues to a Valley of Dry Bones

Patricia A. Reeberg

---

The hand of the LORD came upon me, and he brought me out of the spirit of the LORD and set me down in the middle of a valley; it was full of bones. He led me all around them, there were very many lying in the valley and they were very dry. He said to me, "Mortal, can these bones live?" I answered, "O Lord GOD, you know." Then he said to me, "Prophesy to these bones, and say to them: O dry bones: I will cause breath to enter you, and you shall live. I will lay sinews on you, and you shall live. I will lay sinews on you, and will cause flesh to come upon you, and cover you with skin, and put breath in you and you shall live, and you shall know that I am the LORD."

So, I prophesied as I had been commanded, and as I prophesied, suddenly there was a noise, a rattling, and the bones came together, bone to its bone. I looked, and there were sinews on them, and flesh had come upon them, and skin had covered them; but there was no breath in them. Then he said to me, "Prophesy to the breath, prophesy mortal, and say to the breath: "Thus says the Lord GOD: Come from the four winds, O breath, and breathe upon these slain, that they may live. I prophesied as he commanded me, and the breath came into them, and they lived, and stood on their feet, a vast multitude.

Then he said to me, "Mortal, these bones are the whole house of Israel. They say, 'our bones are dried up, and our hope is lost: we are cut off completely. (Ezekiel 37:1–4, NRSV)

> When the day of Pentecost had come, they were all together in one place. And suddenly from heaven there came a sound like the rush of a violent wind, and it filled the entire house where they were sitting. Divided tongues, as of fire, appeared among them, and a tongue rested on each of them. All of them were filled with the Holy Spirit and began to speak in other languages, as the Spirit gave them ability. (Acts 2:1–4, NRSV)

I grew up with a strong Black consciousness. When I was in the third grade, part of the American history lesson was the history of slavery in the United States. I just stared at the picture of the slaves dancing and playing the fiddles around the fire. When school was completed I came home and announced that I was no longer a Negro. I was an Indian like my grandmother. I was to be called by my Indian name. When my grandfather arrived home from work, my grandmother informed him of my announcement. My grandfather called me into the living room. Once he understood my point of contention, he explained to me that Africans were kidnapped from their homes and forced to be slaves. I said, "Grand, I am not ashamed that we were slaves, I am shamed because we were happy slaves." That evening my grandfather gave me my first history lesson on Black resistance. He told me the story of a Baptist preacher, Nat Turner. Each week, this man, with a third grade education, who taught himself how to read and write, taught me about Harriet Tubman, Frederick Douglass, African Queens and Kings, and the great African civilizations.

When I was fourteen, I had a major crisis in my life. I received Jesus Christ as my personal Savior. I was constantly challenged to choose between being Black and being a Christian. I would walk into my bedroom that had two posters, one of Huey Newton and the other of Bobby Seale. In the middle was a poster I made with my favorite saying, "If the Chairman is bound up tight, we will hold back the night and there won't be light for days." I could not understand why I could not embrace Jesus and still hold on to Bobby and Huey and Angela. While I was in the middle of working through my conflict of loyalties, my grandfather came to the rescue again. During morning worship, my grandfather, Deacon Samuel Lewis Monroe, the chair of the Deacon Board, came strutting into church (and I mean strutting). He sat down in the first row wearing a "Free Angela Davis" button. For the moment I was released from my conflict because there was no one more Christian than Grand.

The demand for me to make a choice reared its head again when I entered Nyack College. When I was President of the Afro-American Club, I confronted a student of African descent concerning his lack of participation. He proudly told me, "I am not Black, I am a Christian." He then began to witness to me about the sin of racism and the grace of God that would free me from my Blackness, if I would only yield to the will of God. By the time I graduated from Nyack College, the white student body was convinced that I was deceived by a demon, because God would never call a woman to preach. They informed me that I was practicing a counterfeit Christianity because true Christianity was colorless. They also accused me of being a cheat, because no Black person, especially a Black woman contained the intellectual capacity to comprehend Western philosophy, or as a white student said to me, "You only get A's because you are Black and you don't sound Black."

So, I went from an academic structure that demonized emotion, my Blackness, and challenged the authenticity of my relationship with Jesus the Christ to Union Theological Seminary (New York City). At Union, I was introduced to Black theology as an academic discipline. I embraced this new phenomenon with every fiber of my being. Being Black and Christian was no longer a question mark; it was now an exclamation point.

When I graduated from Union, I was ready to impart, to practice, to preach, and to teach Black theology in the context of ministry.

The choice to do ministry in the context of community-based organizations, gave me many opportunities "to do" Liberation Theology. The populations I had the privilege of working with include homeless families, families of prison inmates, women substance abusers, and survivors of family violence. Although I attempted to apply my newly learned theories of Liberation in all the communities where I did ministry, I would have to say that working with survivors of family violence and the women in my four support groups who were taking methadone as a transition to being drug-free, were my most challenging and where Liberation Theology was put to the test.

I was introduced to family violence very young, as a watched someone close to me being beaten by her husband. At that time I did not have a name for it, nor did I understand the dynamics of it. I just knew it was wrong. However, I received my degree in family violence at Bedford Hills Correctional Facility. At Bedford Hills I had the opportunity to meet with a group of women who were incarcerated as a result of fighting back. Their stories and their courage, as well as their devastating experiences gave me a totally new perspective on family violence and made it a priority in my life. From that experience I started the first family violence program in the Bronx. Working with the women who came to the program was the continuation of my education. First, I learned to understand that there are various scenarios of family violence. There is the cycle of violence. This represents intergenerational violence. In this scenario, I encountered women who equated abuse with love. Their mothers were abused and when their mothers were placed in the awkward position of explaining the violent relationship with the batterer, she would tell her daughter, "Daddy loves me." Thus the understanding that if you love me then you will beat me was embraced. (I actually met women at Bedford Hills who said they would demand their men beat them.) Abuse was not only appropriate; it was expected and denoted value.

To address this phenomenon, my first objective was to break the cycle of abuse. This learned acceptance of abuse affected the daughters in the household as well as the sons. As a learned behavior that was acceptable, the sons too would grow up to be abusers. I observed this early in the development of young boys who lived in family violence. Many times the son became his mother protector in the home, however, when the mother moved out, or the batterer moved out, the son would move to the position of "man of the house," and many times that entailed his abusing his mother.

Another intergenerational structure of abuse is found within the family structure. This is almost a peaking order. The adult male in the household abuses the adult female. The adult female abuses the child.

However, abuse is not just between male and female, and the male is not always the abuser. There is elder abuse, when the senior member of the household is subjected to physical, emotional, and financial abuse. There are many ways to administer abuse to an elder, from denying food and medication, to denying heat in the winter. If the elder is totally dependent on the members of the household, then most of them are broken in spirit with going one or two days without food, baths, or even being changed. The vulnerability of elders is only matched by the vulnerability of children.

As a practitioner of Liberation Theology, I struggled with how to apply its theories in the context of family violence. I found it most applicable when exploring the power dynamic in the relationship with the battered woman and on those rare occasions, with the batterers.

The majority of the women I actually worked with who were living in violence when they came to me for assistance believed that they were in control. They possessed the power and the batterer was powerless. In other words, they had the power and the batterer just had brute force controlled by emotions. In this scenario the beating the woman receives is her fault. She did something that caused the beating. It actually goes back to childhood. When a child is beaten, after the beating, the child is asked, "What did you do?" I know it was always asked of me and I know I asked my friends that same question. However, in this situation, the woman has carried this "cause and effect" into her adult life. Thus she is beaten because she did something that merited abuse. The power dynamic enters with the woman's assessment of the situation and concludes with a lesson on controlling her environment. She modifies her behavior to please the batterer and to stop him from becoming violent. She continues to evolve into what will make her man happy and thus she remains in control of the situation.

The application of Liberation Theology is first and foremost the re-learning of the power dynamic. Here is an example. An African American woman came to my office for counseling. She worked for the city of New York as a supervisor. She had an earned masters degree and was working on her doctorate. Her husband was also employed and trying to start his own business. Lora first joined our support group. Later, she began coming to me for private sessions. Lora was not coming to me to stop the abuse she was receiving; she wanted to learn how to stop her husband from hitting her in the face. The bruises on her face was causing her to take days off from work until they healed. Lora explained to me in our second session that the abuse was her fault. She knew what her husband did not like and she did it one of the things that set him off without thinking. He lost control and hit her. I asked her to share a few situations in which she ended up being beaten. In each situation it was something she did that caused the abuse.

Clearly, in her mind, she was in control. My first task was to help her realize that her power was false power. She was not in control of her husband's behavior. My second task was to help her understand that one chooses to be in control and one chooses to be out of control. The third task, which is the most difficult, was to help Lora regain self-esteem and self-love. The fourth task was to hold her hand as she discovered her power. The final task was to provide her a sanctuary, a safe place where she could explore her choices.

The first task usually comes about with a series of questions in which the battered person acknowledges that she is in control. The second task is to show the falsehood of the acknowledgment. With Lora, I asked her how her husband keeps a job if he is so "out of control." How does he keep friends? How many lawsuits have they faced because of his abusive behavior? Lora began to realize that the only person being beaten is she. If her husband can control himself with his boss, with his co-workers, with his friends, and with the waitress at the restaurant, who also burnt his toast, then he is not a slave to his emotions. This means that he beats her because he chooses to beat her. This realization was devastating for Lora. When she heard herself say, "Then he beats me because he wants to. It is not me? It is nothing that I did, did not do, or can do."

It is at the point of discovering that the power you thought you had is taken that you re-discover that power that is innately your own.

It was through teaching Lora, and women like Lora how to re-discover their power that they were able to say "no more." Some of them made the choice to leave their relationships. Some of them stayed in the relationship, but on their own terms.

However, I was not always successful in being the midwife to all the women I encountered. The most difficult women to work with were women in the church. Between their male pastors and fundamentalist sisters, these women took the role of being battered as the ministry of the Suffering Servant. They were chosen to be God's vessel to bring their husbands to God through redemptive suffering. For these women to embrace what I was preaching and teaching would entail the dismantling of their entire belief system. For many of them the cost was too high. The internalization of inferiority perpetuated upon these women at home and reinforced from the pulpit, not to mention the domestic violence committed from the pulpit, had created women who embraced suffering as evidence of being Christ-like. And we all know that the Suffering Servant of the Lord, through all the abuse, through all the sorrow, through all the suffering, through oppression and affliction, "he opened not his mouth."

The application of Liberation Theology in the context of fundamentalism theology and literalistic interpretation of scripture always began with the power of love. Then slowly and delicately, the peeling off of the layers of false doctrines, delusions of grandeur, and the revealing of the bankruptcy of the ideal and martyr status of "being co-Saviors with Christ." Once love is embraced, then the women were open to conversations of how love looks, acts, walks, talks, smells, and behaves. When these women starting falling in love with themselves and with God, they also began claiming their power. Finally, they took their pearls back and hung them around their necks with pride.

The challenge: "The Spirit of the Lord is upon me, because he has anointed me to bring good news to the poor. He has sent me to proclaim release to the captives and recovery of sight to the blind, to let the oppressed go free, to proclaim the year of the Lord's favor" remains, but it comes with a deeper sense of urgency.

Now, twenty-years after graduating from Union Theological Seminary. Twenty-years later, the question for me is "What does Black theology say to people of African descent today? What does Black Theology say to a people without hope?" In other words, "Is there a word of power with the capacity to resurrect hope in the Black community?" It is my struggle with this question that brought me to the two passages of Scripture: Ezekiel 37:1–14, the valley of dry bones and Acts of the Apostles 2:1–4, the imparting of tongues, and the theme or topic of my essay, "Speaking in Tongues to a Valley of Dry Bones."

If we look at the passage in Ezekiel, we find the prophet/preacher is not brought out of a spiritual state by God to receive a message of possibility and hope. The prophet/preacher is not positioned at the top of the mountain and told to look down in the valley. The prophet/preacher is given no position of elevation or otherness, but is placed down in the valley that is full of bones. Once in the valley, God leads the prophet/preacher around the valley. There is a need to see. There is a need to understand. There is a need to connect with the disconnected and existentially grasp the outcome of a people who have lost hope. They dry up and die in their hopelessness!

For me, this valley of bones represents people of African descent living in hopelessness, disconnected from themselves and each other. God is calling for the preacher/prophet and the theologian to come down from the tower of elitism and walk around and see what is really happening to the African American community.

When I envision the present position of African Americans in this country I see a barrage of structural, physical, psychological, political, emotional, and economic violence converging together as one solid force moving us deeper and deeper into the dark valley of the abyss. Dr. Walter Stafford, a professor of Urban Planning and Public Policy at Robert Wagner School, has conducted extensive research work on women of color and poverty, the status of African American males in New York City, women and HIV/AIDS, and the unprecedented increase of Black women populating our prison system. His alarming statistics coupled with the many real stories I have lived while doing ministry in homeless shelters, battered women's programs, methadone clinics, and state prisons, brings to life this passage describing a valley of dry bones and its application to the present condition of African Americans in this country. I would dare to say that both the theologian and the preacher/prophet are standing in the middle of a valley of dry bones. A valley of people who have lost their fluid of hope, the spirit of resiliency, and the capacity to connect to their source of divine power.

The intergenerational suffering has suffocated our spontaneity. The structural oppression has eroded the necessary framework to express our rage constructively, and the systematic undermining of our community has regulated us to basically "living in parenthesis", to use a term coined by Dr. Stafford.

Once the prophet/preacher sees the devastating impact of hopelessness. God asks one question, "Can these bones live?"

It is in this setting of the valley of dry bones that we are also asked the same question, "Can these dry bones live? Can hope be resurrected? Can the tide be turned? Will we lose another generation to poverty, cancer, HIV/AIDS, homicide, suicide, and the modernized concentration camps referred to now as correctional facilities? Can we speak with power to resurrect hope? Can these dry bones live?"

The instruction that God gives to the preacher/prophet and I believe to the theologian as well, is "Speak to the bones!" When the prophet/preacher speaks the word God commanded under the anointing of God, the power of the spoken word is sufficient to mend the brokenness and the incarnation of hope is manifested with the flesh covering reconnected bones. However, this first word is insufficient for there is still no breath in the bodies. It is not sufficient to mend brokenness, there must also be life given, or in this situation, resurrected.

It is not enough to preach on Sunday and teach on Monday. It is not enough to provide an emotional pick-me-up to those who are downtrodden. It is not enough to clothe hungry minds with the latest fashion of theological jargon. It is not enough to bring people to the brink of demonstrative praise. It is not enough to polish the intellect until it shines with brilliancy. God calls us to take a second step. God provides the prophet/preacher with the second stage of liberation ministry. God say, "Prophesy to the breath." The wind, the manifestation of the Holy Spirit, the wind comes forth when the word is proclaimed blowing the life into the bodies and they lived.

This is the same phenomena that happened to the disciples of Jesus on the Day of Pentecost. There was a rushing mighty wind, and the disciples began to speak in tongues as the Spirit of God gave ability.

This is the point where I understand the task before the preacher/prophet and the theologian. We are called to speak in tongues. We are called to speak a new language. The language of emancipation.

I propose that we must create a language of emancipation. This is not to say that we did not have this in our past. Our collective history includes the language of the soul that moves from heart to heart and breast to breast. The language of the drum, speaking to us in the coded message of rhythm and non-audible sounds. The language of slave revolutionaries. A language that was equivalent to speaking in tongues, for the Master could not interpret their message of freedom. The language of an old African dialect that enabled Africans to fly to freedom.

Our call, our commission is to recall the language of the soul, to take back the drums that were confiscated from us when we were kidnapped from our motherland, to rediscover the dialect of the ancients, and to reclaim the revolutionary language of our foremothers and forefathers and use them as resources in the creation of a new tongue. A dynamic tongue created by the infusion of the drum, the lost dialect, the language of revolution, and the language of the soul. A language of family. A language of a movement out of the valley. A language that can interpret to us the systemic structures of oppression and remove us from destruction of the conspiracy. A language with the power to ward off the language that is killing our people. A language of the Spirit.

For it is when we dare to speak to the breath that the Spirit comes from the four winds. When the prophet spoke to the breath, the Bible says, "the breath came into them, and they lived, and stood on their feet." It is at Pentecost that we receive the gift of tongues. The ability to speak a new language created by the Holy Spirit with the word power to move the mountain of oppression, open the prison doors of human captivity and proclaim jubilee.

In this scenario the Black Church becomes our private space. It is the sacred space where we can come home and talk. The Black Church has the responsibility to negotiate the language in an emancipatory role. It is the resource because it maintains the language and the tradition of radical transformation. It is the church that provides the people with an imagination, so that "what is" does not automatically become "what will be."

In this setting, the preacher is the interpreter of tongues and constantly fortifies the language of the church. The theologian provides the theological response to the meaning of life.

Together we can create a catechism of liberation that fortifies, maintains and embellishes the ultimate certitude of the presence of God in our midst.

PART TWO

# Black Men and Patriarchy

# 5

# Patriarchy and the Family

JAMES HENRY HARRIS

## INTRODUCTION: THE MEANING
## AND NATURE OF PATRIARCHY

I WILL SEEK TO link the central issue of respect and recognition for the dignity of each person—the core of human identity—to the subject of patriarchy in the family. I begin in philosophy and ethics with the writings of Charles Taylor and Axel Honneth, while drawing upon James Baldwin and Ralph Ellison. Then I talk about the nature of patriarchy—expanding upon my understanding of the patriarch being as much of a systemic cultural and political archetype as Carl Jung's extravert or Sigmund Freud's egotist. The pandemic presence of patriarchal forms of relationships permeate the social structure, thereby manifesting themselves in every fabric of American life including, but not limited to, the family and the church. Patriarchy is so ingrained in our consciousness that it can be described as a way of controlling one's thinking and acting—learned and reinforced by the family, the church, and other institutions such as schools, businesses, etc. In the language of Jonathan Kozol, there are savage inequalities throughout society's educational system, and Blacks and women bear the brunt of these inequalities. Patriarchy, like other forms of oppression and injustice, is grounded in a purposeful, acculturated and "cognitive decapitation of potential" based on perverted practices of power and powerlessness. For modern Blacks, it is a mimetic practice that may have some link to the authority of the

African tribal leader and the system of chattel slavery in this country symbolized by the deistic autonomy of the slave master. Marimba Ani in her book *Yurugu* suggests that the nature of European culture and religion is patriarchal such that the domination of women is superceded by "the association of 'maleness' with superiority and 'femaleness' with inferiority. Perhaps the earliest European definition of 'self' and 'other' was as male and female."[1]

"'The word 'patriarch' comes from a combination of the Latin word *pater*, 'father' and the Greek verb *archo*, 'to rule.' A patriarch is thus a ruling ancestor who may have been the founding father of a family, a clan, or a nation."[2] The etymology of the term "patriarchy" can be traced to the Greek *patria*, meaning "fatherland." In an ecclesiastical sense, "Patriarchy" refers to a system of society or government headed by fathers or elder males of a particular community. "Patriarchy" is integrally related to the term "patriarch." This latter term stems from the Greek term *patriarche*, which has been used to refer to one of the Old Testament fathers (Abraham, Isaac, and Jacob) since the year 1175. *Patriarche* has its roots in *patriarches* (chief or head of a family), which is rooted in another Greek term, *pater* (father). *Pater* has also been used as an honorific title of certain bishops in early Christian churches in Antioch, Alexandria, and Rome.[3]

Patriarchy is a process of self-affirmation through subordination and domination of others, usually, but not always, females. White male patriarchy dominates the entire society, while Black male patriarchy imitates the white model by domination and subordination of Black women and children. Patriarchy is belief in the power to control. Older Black men were often benevolent patriarchs, who provided for and protected their women and children, unlike the nonbenevolent patriarchs, who internalized the media image of the Black male as "pimp" and playboy, who used and abused women for sexual pleasure and profit. These men changed the focus of patriarchy from its racist roots and placed more emphasis on sexual coercion and domination. The use of women as sexual objects and as proof of masculinity has made Black women the

---

1. Marimba Ani, *Yurugu: An African-Centered Critique of European Cultural Thought and Behavior* (Trenton, NJ: Africa World Press, 1994) 242.

2. See, for example, http://www.westarkchurchofchrist.org/wings/hebrewsglossary .htm or http://wwwstudylight.org/dic/hbd/view.cgi?number=T4857.

3. Ibid.

"hated other" instead of the white man, who is the architect of patriarchy. This shift has naturally been supported by the publishing and entertainment establishment and many Black recording artists have succumbed to the lure of vulgar capitalism by degrading their own mothers, sisters and brothers. Jay-Z's "I'm a Husler" and "I Got 99 Problems and a Bitch Ain't One" along with his song "Dirt Off Your Shoulder," represent this mentality. "If you feeling like a pimp nigga, go and brush your shoulders off. Ladies is pimps too, go and brush our shoulders off ... " But the hip-hop artist Ludacris's song is even more patriarchal. He sings, "Pimpin' All Over the World" with these lyrics:

> The fancy cars
> The women and the caviar
> You know who we are
> Cause we pimpin' all over the world (repeat)
> Sing it Hoes ...

And, "The Whisper Song—Wait" by the Ying Yang Twins is even more misogynistic in its sexist and dominance-oriented lyrics. This new pimp-oriented hierarchy is blatantly expressed in the lyrics of many hip-hop artists. bell hooks, in her book *Salvation*, makes this clear when she writes regarding the nonbenevolent patriarchal male:

> They ruled by coercion and domination. This was the masculinity the pimp embodied; it was represented in movies as glamorous and powerful. And this is the masculinity young black men are increasingly embracing. Misogynist rap and woman-hating hip hop culture continues to encourage black males to hate women, and to see being sexual predators as 'cool' ... Hardcore pimp masculinity did not and does not place value on love ... White male playboys legitimized the rejection of fatherhood, but when this stance was embraced by black males it had disastrous implications for black family life.[4]

Moreover, she also suggests that love and loving relationships in Black families are the critical ingredients necessary to actualize wholeness.

---

4. bell hooks, *Salvation: Black People and Love* (New York: Perennial/HarperCollins, 2001) 139–40.

## IDENTITY, PATRIARCHY AND THE BLACK CHURCH

The rhetorical tradition from Plato, Aristotle, Cicero, Quntillian, to I. A. Richards, Jürgen Habermas, Martin Luther King Jr., Malcom X, and Louis Farrakhan is very patriarchal. This is seen today in the Black Church where most of the people who speak to the masses are male. The pastors and preachers remain overwhelmingly male, while the missionaries, auxiliary presidents, choirs, ushers, and general church membership is overwhelmingly female. This systemic issue is not confined to the church but permeates every social, political, business, and religious institution in our society—from the U.S. Presidency, Supreme Court, U.S. Senate, and the Congress to Main Street U.S.A., universities, theological schools, and local churches. Everyone that I can think of who is a part of this cultural matrix is consciously or unconsciously a part of this structure, and nothing short of a revolution in thought and practice will change it.

I do, however, believe that when it comes to the Black church, the male pastor has to intentionally develop a pedagogical strategy for deconstructing the oppressive beliefs and practices of the church. This will necessitate a confrontation with the sacrosanct notion of democracy that is inherent in the nature of the polity of most Black churches. Majority rule has its place, but has historically been used to exclude women from leadership positions - even when the majority of most Black congregations are women. The internalization of oppression often manifests itself in Black on Black crime, and other forms of self-hatred that can be seen in the church when women don't think other women should be pastors and ministers, deacons or other holders of positions of power and authority. I have had some of the biggest and most contentious church fights associated with the advancement of women in ministry and in the church's political structure. In 1977 or 1978, I licensed the first women to the ministry in Mt. Pleasant Baptist Church in Norfolk, Virginia. This church, organized on the heels of slavery, was steeped in the belief that women were not to preach or serve as members of the diaconate. Against the advice and vote of the deacons, in my own church and in violation of the by-laws of the local Ministers' Conference, I licensed Mrs. Corine Brooks to the gospel ministry nearly thirty years ago. And since then, the licensure of women in that city and region of the state has become *pro forma*.

Moreover, in the Second Baptist Church, Idlewood Avenue, in Richmond, Virginia, I lead the church in restructuring the deacons and

deaconess board by trying to create a new semantics, a new terminological approach to leadership at that level. I combined the male deacons
and the female deaconesses into one univocal entity that I termed "the
diaconate ministry," thereby giving all of the women the opportunity to
become deacons. Only fifty percent of the women were willing to try
this new freedom, this new inclusive leadership paradigm that placed
the women and the men on equal par. The fact that many women did
not leap at the opportunity and some of males were very angered by this
practice of gender equalization did not keep me from forging forward
with the implementation of this idea. Next year will mark the ten-year
anniversary of the diaconate and women deacons, and it promises to be
the first in the history of this particular Black church, which was organized in 1846, to have a female chair of the deacons. After 160 years, we
now have broken the wall of resistance. I am not in a position to gloat,
but I do know that as a male pastor, without my support and advocacy
of parity and fairness, justice and equality in the church, this patriarchal
institution would not change. I staunchly believe that change must take
place at the local church level—one organization, one pastor, one congregation at a time.

I am fascinated by the intriguing thought of Charles Taylor's
*Modern Social Imaginaries,* and his essay on "Multiculturalism and 'The
Politics of Recognition.'" These writings are even more fascinating when
viewed alongside Axel Honneth's *The Struggle for Recognition*, and James
Baldwin's novel *Another Country*, and Ralph Ellison's *Invisible Man*. I
cannot do justice to either Taylor or Honneth in this short essay because I will focus on their implications for identity as it relates to the
African American experience of disrespect characterized by insult and
humiliation vis-à-vis the physical and mental abuse of slavery and the
residual experience of denigration and suffering. Identity, race, recognition and their relationship to invisibility and the ontological struggles
of African Americans are surely beyond the scope and intent of Hegel's
Jena lectures as well as Taylor's and Honneth's privileged disposition and
point of departure; nevertheless, their theories have some practical ap-
plicability and can be carefully appropriated to the experience of African
Americans vis-à-vis the nature of identity and patriarchy. The invisibi-
lization of African American women has been even more blatant and
systematic, and unfortunately African American males have adopted
some of the ways of white folk and applied these concepts and practices

in fostering their own brand of invisibilizing Black women. The Black male preacher cannot escape the guilty verdict!

The struggle for recognition is interconnected with the issue of identity and is reflected in the quest for survival by African Americans whose introduction to modernity was marked by the savage and tortuous journey across the Atlantic from the shores of West Africa to the ports of Richmond, Baltimore, and Charleston, South Carolina. This "Middle Passage" or passageway of hell was designed to obviate one's identity and create an "other" identity from freedom to bondage. The experience of suffering and thrownness (*Geworfenheit*) or being thrown into another world vis-à-vis an interpretation of God and evangelical Christianity enabled African Americans to "establish meaning and identity for themselves as individuals and as a people."[5] This struggle for identity, or what Hegel and Honneth called "The Struggle for Recognition," has had many roadblocks and much opposition often posed by the architects of democracy because eighteenth-century theorists often grounded democracy in the notion of a uniform human nature which bleached out difference. This resistance to invisibility or the "hated other" has fueled the struggle for recognition.

This struggle culminated in the Civil Rights movement of the mid to late twentieth century led by Rosa Parks and Dr. Martin Luther King Jr. After many nonviolent protest marches, debates, and speeches, Dr. King went to Memphis at the request of some local ministers to support the garbage workers quest to be recognized as human beings who deserved decent wages, respect, and safe working conditions. After two workers were killed on the job, King went there to prick the conscience of the city leaders and to lead a nonviolent protest march. The march was sabotaged by paid looters and persons to precipitate violence so the march got out of control and King was heavily criticized by national politicos for fleeing from the scene—especially by the senator from West Virginia, Robert Byrd, who called him a coward and a plethora of other negative names. This type of propaganda caused King to return to Memphis out of love and to set the record straight, and on April 4, 1968, to be murdered at the hands of an assassin's bullet. King's life came to an abrupt

5. Albert J. Raboteau, "The Black Experience in American Evangelicalism: The Meaning of Slavery," in *African-American Religion: Interpretive Essays in History and Culture*, ed. Timothy E. Fulop and Albert J. Raboteau (New York: Routledge, 1997) 92 [90–106].

and untimely end while he was struggling to bring dignity, respect, and recognition to the garbage workers of Memphis, Tennessee.

In this connection, Charles Taylor speaks of respect and dignity as the way we carry ourselves in public space. He states:

> Our "dignity," is our sense of ourselves as commanding (attitudinal) respect. The issue of what one's dignity consists in is no more avoidable than those of why we ought to respect other's rights or what makes a full life, however much a naturalist philosophy might mislead us into thinking of this as another domain of mere "gut" reactions, similar to those of baboons establishing their hierarchy ... The very way we walk, move, gesture, speak is shaped from the earliest moments by our awareness that we appear before others, that we stand in public space, and that this space is potentially one of respect or contempt, of pride or shame.[6]

Charles Taylor correlates one's sense of dignity with the importance of ordinary life and in marching with the garbage workers of Memphis or poor Black people in Selma, Alabama or Jackson, Mississippi, Martin Luther King Jr. was advocating human dignity and calling the nation and the world to respect the poor, Black disenfranchised American because it was the inherently moral, just and right action to take. These "ordinary" citizens deserved respect and dignity. Just because someone's skin was dark or non-white was no ground for inferior treatment in a democracy, where Jefferson wrote that "All men are created equal" in spite of the fact that he had slaves. The language of the constitution is laden with patriarchal tones and semantics. King sought to hold American to her stated and written treatises on noble democratic principles, on the one hand, while embodying the attributes of patriarchy on the other.

In reading Charles Taylor's book *The Ethics of Authenticity*, I am reminded of the character Rufus Scott in James Baldwin's novel, *Another Country*. Baldwin writes:

> The policeman passed him, giving him a look. Rufus turned, pulling up the collar of his leather jacket while the wind nibbled delightfully at him through his summer slacks, and started North on Seventh Avenue. He had been thinking of going downtown and waking up Vivaldo—the only friend he had left in the city, or maybe in the world - but now he decided to walk up as far as

6. Charles Taylor, *Sources of the Self: The Making of the Modern Identity* (Cambridge: Harvard University Press, 1989) 15.

a certain jazz bar and night club and look in. Maybe somebody
would see him and recognize him, maybe one of the guys would
lay enough bread on him for a meal or at least subway fare. At the
same time, he hoped that he would not be recognized.[7]

Rufus is ambivalent about the intersubjective concept of recognition. He wants to be recognized, yet he does not want to be recognized
because he is not sure that this present self is one to be lauded or loathed.
This present identity is on the verge of lostness—languishing in a state
of limbo, unlike the narrator character of Ralph Ellison's *Invisible Man*
who blatantly asserts his invisibility: "I am an invisible man." Ellison goes
on to explicate this invisibility as a social and anthropological reality. He
further states:

> I am invisible, understand, simply because people refuse to see
> me. Like bodiless heads you see sometimes in circus shows, it is
> as though I have been surrounded by mirrors of hard, distorting
> glass. When they approach me they see only my surroundings,
> themselves, or figments of their imagination—indeed, everything
> and anything except me.[8]

Charles Taylor in his chapter, "The Need for Recognition," suggests
that one's identity is intimately connected, or more basically, formed "in
dialogue with others, in agreement or struggle with their recognition of
us."[9] He argues that this modern understanding of identity and recognition is highly correlated with the ideal of authenticity. This becomes an
ontological issue—one's being is correlated with recognition. And according to Ralph Ellison, one's visibility is placed in the hands of the
other. People can act like one does not exist and in effect unrecognize
one out of existence. Moreover, Taylor indicates that two changes, "the
collapse of social hierarchies ... intrinsically linked to inequalities,"[10] and
the modern notion of dignity, "where we talk of the inherent dignity
of human beings, or citizen dignity,"[11] have inevitably preoccupied the
modern mind with identity and recognition. While Taylor may theo-

7. James Baldwin, *Another Country* (New York: Dial, 1962) 34.

8. Ralph Ellison, *Invisible Man*, in *The Norton Anthology of African American
Literature*, ed. Henry Louis Gates and Nellie McKay (New York: Norton, 1997) 1518.

9. Charles Taylor, *The Ethics of Authenticity* (Cambridge: Harvard University Press,
1991) 45–46.

10. Ibid., 46.

11. Ibid.

retically be correct, however, I submit that there has been no collapse of social hierarchies as it relates to African Americans and other people of color, and only in a marginal sense has ordinary nonwhite citizens been accorded dignity in the United States, where democracy is still not equal in spite of Taylor's assertion that "democracy has ushered in a politics of equal recognition, which has taken various forms over the years, and which now has returned in the form of demands for the equal status of cultures and of genders."[12] The quest for equality is an ongoing process by Black males and females.

Everyone needs to experience recognition because it helps to shape their identity and sense of self. Charles Taylor in his article "The Politics of Recognition" makes this point quite explicit. He states:

> The demand for recognition in these later cases is given urgency by the supposed links between recognition and identity, where this latter term designates something like a person's understand-ing of who they are, of their fundamental defining characteristics as a human being. The thesis is that our identity is partly shaped by recognition or its absence, often by the misrecognition of oth-ers, and so a person or group of people can suffer real damage, real distortion, if the people or society around them mirror back to them a confining or demeaning or contemptible picture of themselves. Non-recognition or misrecognition can inflict harm, can be a form of oppression imprisoning someone in a false, dis-torted or reduced mode of being.[13]

This is indeed the nature of patriarchy, slavery and other more subjective forms of oppression in everyday life and work. Recognition is often as important as compensation because it is grounded in honor and appreciation, and the lack of it as Taylor says has the affect of an ontological reduction. Jesse Jackson's slogan to African American Youth "I am somebody" is an attempt to recognize and assert the value of those who are Black—those who are systematically unrecognized, overlooked, and made invisible by those who simply "refuse to see me," to use the language of Ralph Ellison.

## PATRIARCHY AND THE POLITICS

12. Ibid., 47.

13. Charles Taylor, *Multiculturalism and the Politics of Recognition* (Princeton: Princeton University Press, 1992) 25.

## OF RECOGNITION AND DIFFERENCE

The politics of difference as a category of recognition, scoffs at any form of assimilation inasmuch as assimilation is the cardinal sin against the ideal of authenticity! Uniqueness is a constitutive element of this differ-ence, and therefore there is no need for conformity because it is unique-ness itself that now calls for differential treatment. Assimilation, by its nature, *a priorily* obviates the value of difference and thereby privileges one culture, gender, experience or race above another. The politics of dif-ference grows out of the "politics of universal dignity,"[14] which fought for forms of nondiscrimination that were quite "blind" to the ways in which citizens differ. The politics of difference often redefines nondiscrimina-tion as requiring that we make these distinctions the basis of differential treatment.[15] This necessarily gestures toward equal dignity and respect for those whose identity is often subsumed into the universal, thus creat-ing what Ralph Ellison describes as the invisibility of the other or what I like to call the Phantom of the Other. Also, it is in this connection that I find Honneth's explication of Hegel's notion of struggle for recognition as developed in his Jena *Realphilosophie* most helpful in understanding the concept of otherness. Hegel's view of "Spirit" or what Germans term *Geist is* overwhelmingly comprehensive and yet precise.

In reference to Hegel's early lectures, Axel Honneth writes:

> Under the renewed influence of Fichte, he came to view the defin-ing features of Spirit as the ability to be "both itself and the other to itself": Spirit is characterized by self differentiation, in the sense that Spirit is able to make itself an other to itself and, from there, to return to itself ... Thus already at this point the structure of the entire Hegelian project is modeled on the process of the realization of system. If not in its execution then certainly in its idea, Hegel's theory already includes the three major components of logic, philosophic nature, and philosophy of Spirit ...[16]

I am intrigued by the ability of his concept of Spirit to transcend the self and become other without abandoning itself or obviating the other. The capability of the Spirit to extend itself into that which is other than itself is an apt description of my own imagination as to the nature of

14. Ibid., 38.

15. Ibid., 39.

16. Axel Honneth, *The Struggle for Recognition: The Moral Grammar for Social Conflicts* (Cambridge: MIT Press, 1996) 31–32.

Spirit which is that it moves where it wills! This understanding of self enables the self to embrace otherness and creates the possibility of perceiving that self and other are one—alleviating the need of the male self to dominate and control the other.

## PATRIARCHY AND THE BLACK FAMILY

The Black family during slavery often suffered from being an extension of the vulgar capitalist practices that motivated the slave master and drove the economic system of free labor. The control of the slave master manifested itself in breeding men and women as if they were cattle, hogs or horses, fulfilling his own sexual lusts by raping Black female slaves and often planning and arranging who would marry whom. The intent to propagate the productive capacity of the plantation was the driving force behind the masters planned and whimsical behavior, regarding siring children himself or permitting marriage among the slaves. Dwight Hopkins in his book *Down, Up, and Over* explains that the patriarchal privilege of power and evil could only be limited by the restraints of the slave master's imagination. He writes: "In his remembrances, Mr. Jordan expresses the master's power to define the slave family according to his imagination and preferences: 'Whenever he thought' and 'he could choose.'"[17]

The ubiquitous power and presence of the master determined the nature of the Black family and terrorized Black slaves through branding, castration, auctioning, and whipping. Hopkins makes this point regarding the strange correlation between these evil acts and the twisted logic of white Christians with clarity: "Whipping as a form of disciplining the black body—thus refashioning it during the sunup to sundown period—drew its inspiration and justification from the strength of Christianity. As a Christian in good standing, a white person assumed a high moral ground by flogging African American slaves."[18]

The nexus between patriarchy and slavery is inescapable and the fact is that Christianity as practiced by the slaves also reflected the same practices embodied in everyday acts of evil and oppression. Christianity was an extension of the slave master's immoral morality.

17. Dwight N. Hopkins, *Down, Up, and Over: Slave Religion and Black Theology* (Minneapolis: Fortress, 2000) 64.

18. Ibid., 71.

The male presence alone is not enough to help constitute a healthy family. A man in the house who is not loving, but abusive, violent and domineering is more harmful than helpful. Those who argue for male presence without regard to the quality of that presence propagate a patriarchy that scapegoats the single mother. I have learned that patriarchy as a word, concept and practice in the lexicon of language and culture is laden with complexities. The terminological screen for talking about this subject includes identity, oppression, privilege, power, race, sex, class, caste, love, family, etc. This is why we have a tendency to be confounded in our understanding of patriarchy, because we underestimate the complexities and limit our interpretation to race, gender, or class without recognizing the correlation or interface between patriarchy and the making and unmaking of identity. It is so pervasive and pandemic that it often takes on illusive forms that are not only difficult to grasp, but difficult to identify. For example, the society and the family often describe certain male behaviors and practices as masculine and inoffensive, others are seen as effeminate and undesirable. Actions such as crying or reading are feminine while stoic disinterest and cussing are masculine. Also, even skin color is an indicator of a patriarchal system that values lighter complexioned Blacks because their complexion and hair texture are closer to whites. This fact itself shows how white supremacy is the matrix out of which patriarchy emerges and mutates throughout the family, church, theology and culture.

When I was growing up in the sixties, I remember the children who had light skin were favored by the teachers and all of us boys migrated toward the lighter skinned girls because the school culture projected the thesis that lighter skin translated into beauty, academic achievement, and superior school performance. The partial divesture of this mentality was accomplished through slogans in the late sixties like, "Black is Beautiful" or James Brown's song, "Say it Loud, I'm Black and I'm Proud."

I remember the story of our pastor's wife, who grew up in North Carolina in the forties. She tells the story of how she was refused the honor of valedictorian in her school because of her dark complexion, even though she had the highest grade point average. These actions were perpetrated by Black educators against other Blacks who were not as aesthetically appealing, according to the prevailing popular culture mindset. bell hooks calls this "patriarchal color caste" within the Black family and community. I have heard stories similar to this about churches that were color struck, only securing pastors who were light-skinned males. This psychology is also seen among Black males who are only interested in dating and marrying women who are light complexioned with a certain hair texture—although many Blacks today use texturizer and extensions in their hair. Moreover, when I was in seminary in the mid-seventies, all of the professors were male, and ninety-nine percent of the student body was also. Even today, a significant majority of ATS schools are headed by males, and those who occupy the highest academic rank are also male. Again, when I was in elementary school, all of the teachers were female, and the only males in the school were the principal and the custodian.

When I was thirteen years old, my parents put on my shoulders certain responsibilities for the entire family. Was this an abdication of responsibility on their part, and an increasing load on me? Growing up in rural central Virginia as farmers and laborers, my daddy and his brothers had migrated from Vance County, North Carolina, to Virginia in the early 1940s. My father was a strong man, and in my view, very responsible and compassionate; but not any more responsible and compassionate than my mother. But it was clear that my mother adored and acceded certain things to our father, who was indeed the dominant force in our household. This was a positive attribute and does not qualify as patriarchy in any negative sense. Put in a very positive way, it was an example of male responsibility as protector of the family, a provider and a moral example who expressed love toward our mother and all of us.

So in a sense, my father was patriarchal, possessing, however, the critical parental trait of love. Our father's love accommodated the strong arm of protection and authority that his persona embodied as well as that bestowed on him by our mother, who would often intone that "When your daddy comes home, I'm going to tell him of your behavior." This suggested that daddy was the one to punish and placed mother in a subservient, almost child-like role. I have struggled with describing our father as patriarchal because the term is overwhelmingly negative in the literature, and my memories of my father as overwhelmingly positive, loving, and kind helps to complexify my understanding of the concept and practice. I cannot help but question, however, the fact that my mother bore eleven children out of compliance to a system of patriarchy in society that influenced the family structure as well as sexual behavior and the submission of women to the will of the male or father. This submission is often out of love, though sometimes out of fear—both love and fear being strong emotional determinates of behavior.

## PATRIARCHY AND WOMANIST THEOLOGY/LITERATURE

In Nella Larsen's novel *Passing*, there are many indications that patriarchy is a white racist notion. In the novel, the main character is a mulatto, Clair Kendry, whose husband, a white man named John Bellew, was not aware that his wife was Black, passing as white. In a meeting with Claire's friends Irene and Gertrude, who were also passing, John's arrogant, demeaning, and condescending attitude towards Blacks is revealed in classic patriarchal fashion. When his Black wife, who was passing for white, said to her white husband, Jack, "My goodness, Jack! What difference would it make, if, after all these years, you were to find out that I was one or two percent colored?" Bellew put out his hand in a repudiating fling, definite and final. "Oh, no nig," he declared, "Nothing like that with me. I know you're no nigger, so it's all right. You can get as black as you please as far as I'm concerned, since I know you're no nigger. I draw the line at that. No niggers in my family. Never have been and never will be."[19]

This white domination and race hatred on the part of whites is also the constitutive nature of patriarchy—borne out of the notion of domination.

In the novel *Johan's Gourd Vine* by Zora Neale Hurston, patriarchy is seen in the way Lucy's brother, Bud Potts, treats his sister. He takes his bed, a wedding gift, while she is pregnant and about to deliver her fourth child because she and her husband, John, owed him three dollars. He is able to do this because John is out on another of his escapades with another woman. When he surmises that Lucy already knows about his appetite for other women, he confesses, but simultaneously asserts his love for his wife. His interest in other women is attributed to his animal instinct. "What make yuh fool wid scrubs lak Big 'Oman and de res of 'em?" "Dat's the brute-beast in me, but Ah sho aim tuh live clean from dis on if you 'low me one mo' chance.'"[20] Like many other promises, this too is a lie deeply rooted in John Pearson's attitude of dominance and greed and his belief that Lucy, his wife, was indeed his property and her major

19. Nella Larsen, *Quicksand and Passing*, ed. Eborah E. McDowell (New Brunswick, NJ: Rutgers University Press, 1986) 171.

20. Zora Neale Hurston, *Jonah's Gourd Vine*, ed. Henry Louis Gates Jr. (New York: HarperPerrennial, 1990) 88.

pay was to be a mother, or more accurately a "mammy." Delores Williams explains the Black Mammy Memorial Association, which was established after slavery to teach and school Black females in maintaining the antebellum ways and traditions of the Big House. Williams writes, "The assumption could be made that by training black women in the skills of mammying, they would also choose to use these skills to further the well being of the black family, and the black community. By learning how to be mammys, black women (especially those with fieldwork heritages) would learn to be the kind of mothers and nurturers who could organize and manage black households as white households were organized and managed."[21]

The emulation of whites in temperament and behavior was often perceived as a virtue and necessary for acculturation or what the historian Joel Williams describes as "more white." More particularly, "Mammy had to be skillful at exerting authority in the household while being careful not to offend or usurp the power of the main authority figures, the slave master and his wife."[22] During slavery, Black men and women were dominated by white males and females. The slave master's wife was dominated by the same man who dominated the slaves and when it came to the slaves, she was a partner in the domination. She also controlled the Black body as means of economic production as well as a sexual object. She was an active, complicit beneficiary of the system of domination and oppression. And, the Big House was where patriarchy was taught and its skills honed and replicated during and after slavery:

> It was in the area of conditioning ex-slaves to continue to perpetuate and/or to be trained in quality white folk's cultural ideals and values that mammy's skills were so important for the black family. One of the key ideals and values was the sanctity of patriarchalism in the family. The fact that mammy knew how to exert authority in household management while not usurping the power inserted in the patriarchal male head of the household meant that if other ex-slave women could be taught this, the patriarchal acculturation of the black family could continue.[23]

21. Delores S. Williams, *Sisters in the Wilderness: The Challenge of Womanist God-Talk* (Maryknoll, NY: Orbis, 1993) 75.

22. Ibid.

23. Ibid., 77.

Moreover, the Black male after emancipation perpetuated a model of dominance and authority toward women that had been practiced by the white man. And their mammys trained in the way of white folks only had to apply their skills in the Black family. Williams states that, "... the freedmen did not want to perpetuate a model of authority subordinating Black men to Black women." Williams's description of Black male authority after slavery suggests that the development of patriarchal values in the Black family was reinforced by social, legal and economic customs of Black men.[24] These customs were reinforced throughout all levels of society and especially in the Black church.

In Nella Larsen's eloquent novel *Quicksand*, the main character, a cultured and refined woman named Helga Crane, is finally married after numerous proposals to what turns out to be a preacher and the church. Her marriage to the Reverend Mr. Pleasant Green and their move from the "sins and temptations of New York" to "labor in the vineyard of the Lord" in a small Alabama town captures the spirit of patriarchy in the family and in the church. This fashionable woman of the world, steeped in social refinement and cultural elitism, succumbs to what the author refers to as the oppression of marriage. In this text, marriage is a metaphor for patriarchy—a symbol of the hegemony of male domination in the family and in the church. Helga, is a mulatto who struggles with issues of identity—racial, social, and sexual. She is a very urban, cosmopolitan, and fashionable personality, who was restless as a school teacher in a backwater southern town called Anaxos. She moves to Chicago and then to New York's Harlem where she finds work as a receptionist for a "Negro" insurance company. This also enables her to hobnob with the middle class and to dabble in various social circles, which she enjoys. Along the way, she has a few forays into romance but always manages to mask or sublimate her desire even for Dr. Robert Anderson, with whom she was secretly in love. After spending two years in Copenhagen, Denmark, with her aunt and uncle, she returns to New York to attend her friend Anne's wedding. Helga was proposed to in Copenhagen by an artist, Axel Olsen; she refused his marriage proposal. In response to a question about marriage by James Vayle, to whom she had been engaged, Helga makes it clear that marriage and patriarchy are highly correlated. She states, "Marriage, that means children to me. And why add more suffering to the world? Why add any more unwanted, tortured Negroes to

24. Ibid., 78.

America? Why do Negroes have children? Surely it must be sinful. Think of the awfulness of being responsible for the giving of life to creatures doomed to endure such wounds of the flesh, such wounds of the spirit as Negroes have to endure."[25]

Helga felt that marriage had ruined her life. She was a fool. Religion also had failed her. There was no god. It was all an illusion. Marriage to her was immoral.

> The thought of her husband roused in her a deep and contemptuous hatred. At his every approach, she had forcibly to subdue a furious inclination to scream out in protest. Shame, too, swept over her at every thought of her marriage. Marriage. This sacred thing of which Parsons and other Christian folk ranted so sanctimoniously, how immortal—according to their own standards—it could be! But Helga felt also a modicum of pity for him, as for one already abandoned. She meant to leave him. And it was, she had to concede, all of her own doing, this marriage. Nevertheless, she hated him.[26]

In Helga Crane's view, her marriage to Reverend Green and subsequent mothering of a host of children vis-à-vis the church folk's religion were all offensive especially since she didn't believe that their God existed. Helga hated marriage and the church folk because her husband, the preacher, represented the "crowning idiocy" of her life. Her life had become degraded and oppressed all because of the patriarchal nature of her family and the church. The negro's religion, according to Helga, was grounded in illusion—a belief and trust in the White man's God. But her most venomous hatred was reserved for her husband, who kept her in agony and pain, sorrow and weakness through childbearing. She hated him and yet she kept on having children. Larsen shows the reality of a patriarchal system when she ends the novel on this tragic note: "AND HARDLY had she left her bed and become able to walk again without pain, hardly had the children returned from the homes of the neighbors, when she began to have her fifth child."[27]

25. Larsen, *Quicksand and Passing*, 103.
26. Ibid., 134.
27. Ibid., 135.

# 6

## Vanishing into Limbo

### Part II: Black Men as Endangered Species . . . Not

EMILIE M. TOWNES

---

. . . what it means to be a Negro in America can perhaps be suggested by an examination of the myths we perpetuate about him.

Aunt Jemima and Uncle Tom are dead, their places taken by a group of amazingly well-adjusted young men and women, almost as dark, but ferociously literate, well-dressed and scrubbed, who are never laughed at, who are not likely ever to set foot in a cotton or tobacco field or in any but the most modern of kitchens. There are others who remain, in our odd idiom, "underprivileged;" some are bitter and these come to grief; some are unhappy, but, continually presented with the evidence of a better day soon to come, are speedily becoming less so. Most of them care nothing whatever about race. They want only their proper place in the sun and the right to be left alone, like any other citizen of the republic. We may all breath more easily. Before, however, our joy at the demise of Aunt Jemima and Uncle Tom approaches the indecent, we had better ask whence they sprang, how they lived? Into what limbo have they vanished?[1]

as some of you know
> i have used this james baldwin quote to look at aunt jemima
> i now turn to consider uncle tom

---

1. James Baldwin, "Too Many Thousands Gone," in *Notes of a Native Son* (Boston: Beacon, 1955) 27.

in his 1955 essay, "many thousands gone" baldwin explores richard
wright's *native son*
>baldwin is working fiercely to construct what it means to be a
>negro in america
for baldwin, this is visceral
>he is tired of black folk being treated as mere social agendas
>>rather than as flesh and blood
>he notes that dehumanization is never a one way street
>>that the loss of identity
>>>be it stolen, borrowed, denied, or annihilated
>>>>has consequences far beyond those who are
>>>>the immediate victims
that our crimes against ourselves
>echo
>and haunt
>and damn
>and eviscerate us
and it is not enough
>not in 1955
>not in 2005
to think that we can leave our memories
>checked at some dismal door of gerrymandered elections or
>xenophobic nationalism or sycophantic equalities or ill-prepared
>disaster plans that make us terrorists of our own people
so i turn to something i've found to be a powerful element in the
gospel--the power of memory
>yes, memory can fail and fail in spectacularly devastating ways
>>it can leave blanks and fill blanks with mistakes
>>it can be a collaborator with forces that only know sup-
>>pression and denial of life and wholeness
>but memory can also succeed in deep and profound ways
>>it can provide hope in the midst of degradation and
>>strength to continue to put one foot in front of the other
>>in movements for justice
perhaps it may be best to think of memory as a kind of counterhistory
>one that challenges the false generalizations and gross stereo-
>types often found in what passes for "history" in this country
for memories can disrupt our status quo

because they do not rest solely or wholly on objectivity or facts
they materialize from emotions and sight and sounds and touch
and smell

       they come from the deepest part of who we are
       they are dynamic and spark new configurations of
       meaning
       and if used well, they keep us on the potter's wheel so that
       we never rest too comfortably with knowledge that is
          at best
             only partial and never ultimately complete
               and memories can vanish
into limbo (into absolute neglect, into oblivion)
       only to filter back into our lives
as shame or anger or pride or righteousness
you see, the american story *can* be told another way
       such that the voices and lives of those who, traditionally and
       historically, have been left out are now heard with clarity and
       precision
       these voices can then be included into our conversations—not as
       additives—but as resources and co-determiners of actions and
       strategies—*an the moral agents they are*
          but not in crass goals-driven moves, but ones that ac-
          knowledge the intimate humanity of our plurality
          and works with as much precision as possible to name its
          textures
indeed, who or what is naming *any* of us—regardless of color, gender,
age, ability, class, nationality, and on and on
       who or what is making our histories—social and religious—
       denigrating ideological constructions
if we do not ask these questions and more, then we allow others
       real others
       to carve out hollow legacies for the generations yet to come
          for all color of children
and womanist moral thought collapses into a *meaningless* drivel of
hosannas
       or inconsequential theological escape hatches
          that only serve to reify demonic stereotypes in religious
          god-talk

I

uncle tom is a complex figure for a complex topic such as black male as endangered species
    he is an object lesson, i think, in what happens when we create caricatures of each other
    and then present them as object lessons for our inhumanity
i suspect harriet beecher stowe meant well
    when she created topsy—the turbo pickanniny
    and uncle tom—the ultimate suffering black christ figure
but because she did not know any black slaves or former black slaves
    because she did not talk with any former black slaves
    but relied on what white folk told her about the horrors of slavery
she gave us black characters that she thought would help the nation understand the horror of slavery—the immorality of owning another person
    that were easily morphed into caricatures that were then painted in black face for minstrel shows
        where all the darkies were happy
        because the white imagination that donned that black face
            wished this were so
                wanted it to be so
                    needed it to be so
                    doo-da-doo-da-day
what can we discover, then, from a caricature who is presented to us as morally and spiritually superior to the 3 white men who own him
    what can we understand from the young and strong slave in the pre-civil war south
        who is the father of 3 young children
        who is a serious christian
what can we learn from a man who is all this and ends up dead
    choosing to be whipped to death rather than give up the hiding place of 2 black female slaves to a white man who raped black women—and would do it again and again and again
is this the man that sits in the back of our imaginations and memories
    probably not
    for many, if not most of us

tom is old
he is obedient
he is submissive
he does not stick up for himself
he is desexualized
he is the ultimate toadying sycophant
he is not a credit to his race
and his brand of christian piety sets our teeth on edge
but like baldwin's aunt jemima
uncle tom became the creation of the white imagination
you see, stowe's abolitionist novel was made into highly
successful theatrical shows that she had no control over
nearly 500 so-called "tom companies" performed
around the country
stowe could not control what she had loosed
the tom of these minstrel shows is not the tom of the novel
he could not be
for all the faults we can name with stowe's romanticization of slavery in an attempt to destroy it
the tom of stowe's novel made choices and was far
from a shufflin', eye-rolling, mumbler
and so the tom we have on our eyeballs is the tom of the stage
the old man i was taught to despise
and i suspect many of you here in this room were taught
this too

## II

for me, to think through what it means to consider the black male as an
endangered species puts me on full alert
much like what uncle tom does
because it reminds me of something i know all to well:
we do not own the public images of ourselves as black folk in
this country and on this globe
and when we do not own the public production of our lives
we can be and often are controlled by forces beyond our making
and shaping
this makes us vulnerable and suspect and wary
and well it should

because although a few of us are doing quite well
>   many more of us are struggling and making it
>   and there are even larger numbers of us who are not seeing any
substantial improvement
>   and things may be getting much worse
into this mix is the troubling reality that eventually these public images
begin to effect how we see ourselves
>   and we have begun to see more and more black folk begin to act
these minstrel show parts
>>   that the elite and often the white script for us
>>>   believe are us
>>>   define as our identities for us
if marketing and imagination can create aunt jemima
>   give her a family
>>   then give her another family when the first one didn't sell
enough pancake mix
>   if marketing and imagination can create her life
>>   and then hire black women to travel the country telling
her story while they did cooking demonstrations on the
ease in which one could now make pancakes
>>   and provide these women an income to feed their families
should we really be so surprised that uncle tom has been hijacked, too
>   and i want to be clear that i'm not talking about turning a young
man into an old man
>>   i actually like old men
what i'm disturbed by is the emasculation that took place when this
character, now caricature
>   moved from printed page
>   to minstrel production
>   to radio shows
>   to movie screen
>   to tv set
>   to real black life
the imagination that is fantastic and hegemonic created a caricature
that bore no resemblance to fact
>   but because this imagination had enough power and persuasion
and money

this caricature of black men became etched out in our lives as
history
           and then as truth
this saga underscores that we must be clear that we live in a culture and
in a theological universe in which uncle tom is not alone
     he is joined by uncle ben
                              rastus
                              sambo
                              uncle remus
                              zip coon
                              jim crow
                              tambo
                              and others who form a deadly fraternity of
                              laughing stock characters
                                        who are deadly because they are per-
                                        ceived to be true
                                        and worse—absolute
this is a moral problem
     when we take black men's lives and turn them into a boondocks
     moment
               where they are relegated to the metaphorical or real back-
               woods of black life and culture
               away from women
               away from children
               away from themselves
this moral problem sits in a larger context of what appears, to this
womanist ethicist's eye, as a mammoth moral threshing floor of evil
     that can use the human-made disaster of gigantic governmental
     ineptitude on almost every level known as hurricane katrina to
     propose cuts[2]
               from Medicaid—$225 billion
                         the last-resort health insurance for the very poor
               from Medicare—$200 billion
                         the health care safety net for the disabled and the
                         elderly

2. "Lawmakers Prepare Plans to Finance Storm Relief," *The New York Times*, 20
September 2005; online: www.nytimes.com/2005/09/21/national/nationalspecial/21
cong.html.

from school lunches for poor children—$6.7 billion
from the safe and drug-free school program—$4.8 billion
    this would eliminate all funding for this program
    and kill it
frankly, it looks like someone is coming for all of us and none of us can
afford the deer in the headlights look any longer
    although we did not create the warped identities that caricature
    black life, we must define for ourselves who we are and what we
    represent

## III

so for me, to think of and assent to such an animalistic and ultimately
essentializing phrase as black men as an endangered species means that
i have given up on the menfolk
    and i simply refuse to do so
        mary and ross townes did not raise me that way
it would mean that i have given up hope
    and turned back the gift of my baptism
    and i cannot with any measure of faithfulness declare that i live
    my life in despair and surrender to human designs of justice
    such that some of need not apply for mercy
i don't think i'm being either irresponsible or clueless or playing with
semantics—words matter
    and we must seriously question the descriptors about us that
    influence those outside of our communities who may not and
    usually don't know the context, history, or *meaning* when we use
    them
        the notion that blackness in this country is an endangered
        species began, in the *public* imagination
        with bill moyers' 64-minute 1986 cartoonish re-working
        of the black matriarch/emasculated male thesis, "the van-
        ishing family: crisis in black america"
moyers' "documentary" was a convoy of black dysfunctionality
that was presented to the american pbs audience as the norm
he set out to prove that the welfare state created poverty and he
used any means necessary to do so
and one of the results—intended or not—is equating black male
life with

      african and asian elephants
      right, fin, and blue whales
      red wolves
      amur, anatolian, and snow leopards
      tigers
      otters
      pandas
      bactrian camels
      the black rhinoceros
      wombats
      spider monkeys
      gorillas
      and the list goes on
i am well aware that there is a systematic and relentless onslaught on
black lives in this country
      the disaster of a plan that unfolded in new orleans in particular
      not only made me stare in horror and then try to find ways that
      i could help
      it also caused an internal head-bob that this *is* what too many
      think of us
          a white man and woman were captioned foraging for food
          a black man was captioned looting
             all three were carrying food, not t.v. sets, gameboys,
             or rims
                what is looting when all the governmental
                mechanisms have broken down and left
                your ass to die?
      and it did not help when a black mayor and black police chief
      then repeated rumor and innuendo as fact about rapes and other
      forms of lawlessness
          *we* are performing the minstrel uncle tom when we do
          this to ourselves
there is too much, brothers and sisters
      there is too much that is deadly and real about what is going on
      in the lives of black men
we cannot repeat threadbare lies about ourselves
      and then expect to liberate anyone from anything

other than that double quarter pounder with cheese that
is clogging our arteries and killing black men day in and
day out
> but many of us eat this because it is the only meal
> we can get and afford
> and can eat in a relatively safe environment

black male health patterns in the u.s. indicate that black men are in the
midst of a health crisis[3]

> black males die of prostate cancer at twice the rate for white men
> more black men die from colorectal and lung cancer than white
> men
> stroke is the 4th leading cause of death
> 2 out of every 4 men with HIV or AIDS are black men
> 1 in 99 black men are living with HIV/AIDS
> white males live an average of 7 1/2 years longer than black
> males
> 40% of black males do no reach the age of 65
> among children age 12–19, 1 in 5 black boys are overweight
> 44% of black men are considered overweight
> 24% are obese

there is no disputing the fact that black men suffer worse health than
any other racial group in america

> the list of whys are not hidden
>> racial discrimination
>> lack of affordable health care
>> poor health education
>> unhealthy choices around diet and exercise
>> poverty
>> jobs that do not carry health insurance
>> insufficient medical and social services designed for black
>> men

and rather than see this as check marks on the endangered species list

> i see this as a call to action for us and to paraphase jawanza kun-
> jufu, we need to declare a state of emergency
>> this is a crisis
>> because if we can name it, we can take steps to deal with it

3. African American Fact Sheet, 27 January 2005 (updated 3 May 2005), www
.michigan.gov.

we do not accept the implicit victim status that i believe
that referring to black men as endangered assigns
this is no sierra club strategy i'm advocating this afternoon
this is one in which we move from allowing someone else to
define for us who we are and what our fate will be
keep in mind, insurance actuaries once predicted that
black folk would die off within 20 years because we could
not survive on our own (read: free) outside of slavery[4]
instead, we stake a claim for our personhood, our dignity, and
the necessity to work on our own behalf to grow black man large
and strong and healthy
it will take health care providers and the black community to deal with
this crisis
one place we must begin this is in the church and in other religious bodies
too often we do not take into the account the effect of religion and faith
on community behavior
although we are returning, slowly, to an earlier model of the
1920's, 30's, and 40's in which health education took place in
churches
we need to continue to encourage our churches or guide our
churches in taking a leadership role in addressing the health care
needs of the males and females in our churches and outside its
doors
community involvement is the church's natural twin in
developing advocacy skills and educational programs that are
consumer-oriented
drawing on community members to design and help implement
these programs
and pointing ourselves to well care as much as ill health care
operating out of a state of emergency in response to a crisis will help us
address the mental health of black men
a subject that is taboo for many of us in this room—male and
female

4. See Emilie M. Townes, *Breaking the Fine Rain of Death: African American Health Issues and a Womanist Ethic of Care* (New York: Continuum, 1998) chap. 3, for an extended treatment of the history of black health and healthcare in the United States.

but when we have a black male youth suicide rate that has increased 146% from 1980 to 1995[5]
>> and these young men are using firearms and stran-
>> gulation to do so
> it is clear that we cannot afford to bow down to a taboo
> that is literally killing our youth and our future
the reasons for this carnage in young black men's lives are not hidden
> the difficulty in finding affordable, respectful, and accessible care
> the scarcity of providers of color and competent providers
> lack of insurance coverage and inadequate means of financing
> care
these are compounded with
> racism
> sexism
> and economic oppression
this is a crisis list we can begin to address
> and no, it will not be easy to do so, but i cannot accept that we
> have the lack of agency that declaring black men an endangered
> species connotes for me
> my father and the other black men who helped raise me fought
> too hard and long to be seen as men and not animals for me ac-
> cept this characterization of black male life
>> regardless of who is saying it

## IV

the prison industrial complex in this country is another major site of
crisis for us when we look at black males in this country
> this growth industry in the black community is obscene
>> from 1980 to 2000, the number of incarcerated black males went
>> from 100,000 to 1.3 million
when *the black commentator* released its survey of the 10 worst places
to be black in the u.s. in july 2005[6]

5. Black Mental Health Alliance, "Souls of Black Men: African American Men Discuss Mental Health"; online: www.communityvoices.org. Youth is ages 15–19 years old. Firearms were used in 72% of suicides. Stragulation was used in 20% of suicides.

6. Bruce Dixon, "Ten Worst Places to Be Black," *Black Commentator* 146, 14 July 2005; online: www.blackcommentator.com/146/146_cover_dixon_ten_worst_pf.html.

they counted the black prisoners and former prisoners and the
communities they came from and are discharged into to come
up with their list
> wisconsin (milwaukee)
> iowa
> texas
> oklahoma
> arizona
> delaware
> nevada
> oregon
> california
> colorado

this litany often begins when we are young
> although black folk make up 10% of the population in san
> francisco
>> 56% of the children (ages 12–18) in juvenile detention are
>> poor and black

the shift in funding prisons rather than education has had a predictable
effect on black men
> 52% of black male high school dropouts have prison records by
> their early 30s
> if current incarceration holds, black men in their early 30s are
> nearly twice as likely to have prison records (22%) than bach-
> elors degrees (12%)[7]

it is important to question why, when we have seen a long decline of
the crime rate, the prison population has grown significantly
> with black males figuring disproportionately in this leap

a history moment is instructive here
> in 1954, the time of the historic *brown v. board of education* deci-
> sion, black folk were about 30% of the prison population[8]

---

7. Justice Policy Institute, "Half of African American Male Dropoouts and 1 in 10
White Male Dropouts Have Prison Records as States Cut School Funds, Prison Filled
with People with Little Education"; online: www.justicepolicy.org/article.php?id=242.

8. Marc Mauer, "The Crisis of the Young African American Male and the Criminal
Justice System," Prepared for the U.S. Commission on Civil Rights, 15–18 April 1999,
Washington, DC) 3. In *Brown v. Board of Education*, the Supreme Court struck down
the "separate but equal" doctrine of *Plessy v. Ferguson* for public education. It ruled
in favor of the plaintiffs, and required the desegregation of schools across America.

this should cause us to raise an eyebrow because even
then, this was substantially higher than the our numbers
in the general population
from slavery to the prison industrial complex
black folk have lived within the panopticon and have
been watched by folk who demonstrate a meticulousness
illiteracy about us
those who control the gaze of the panopticon say that black violent
crime has been rising—it has not
that black young men are superpredators
they are not—what changed was access to firearms that is
linked with the drug trade
i would wager a fair number of black men in this room have
experienced some version of driving while black
this kind of discretionary law enforcement harassment
leads to black males acquiring a criminal record more
rapidly than whites
that then has the daunting trickle down effect of a
greater chance of receiving a prison sentence
those who control the gaze of the panopticon refuse to acknowledge
the impact of race and class[9]
although black males engage in serious violent offences at a
higher rate than white males, the actual 5:4 ratio is much smaller
than what public imagination and media conjures
and even less so between lower class males (7:6)
offenses by black males are much more likely to lead to arrest
than those of whites
and while there is no extraordinary difference in the degree to
which black and white males become involved in offending at
some point
black males are nearly twice as likely to continue
offending into their 20s

---

This ruling did not segregation in other public areas, such as restaurants and restrooms,
nor did it require desegregation of public schools by a specific time. It did, however,
declare the permissive or mandatory segregation that existed in twenty-one states
unconstitutional.

9. Ibid., 6

but this is erased if young black males are employed or living in stable relationships
the rise of critical race theory has helped us understand, on new levels,
the racial biases of the criminal justice system
and the war on drugs has proven to be an extremely racist war in
the lives of black folk
congressional mandatory sentencing legislation passed
in 1986 and 1988 has a whacked color coding system in
which a major dealer in powder cocaine who is caught
with 499 grams will receive at most 1 year in federal
prison
while someone possessing just 5 grams of crack
will receive a mandatory 5 years in prison
what does it say to us, then, that 86% of those charged
with crack trafficking in the federal penal system were
black, but only 30% of those charged with powder cocaine
offenses?[10]
although i have just skimmed the surface
to move from endangered to crisis to action means that we work
to eradicate draconian and racist mandatory sentencing policies
this includes "safety valve" provisions that give judges
wider discretion for offenders who have limited criminal
history and no involvement with violence
who can then divert drug offenders facing mandatory prison terms into long-term residential treatment programs that have a lower recidivism rate
than prison
eliminate or equalize the penalties for crack and powder
cocaine
increase funding for indigent defense and sentencing
advocacy
expand the use of alternative sentencing and monitor
these programs to assess racial balance
increase community-based mentoring and counseling
programs for young and first-time offenders who are now
stigmatized

10. United States Sentencing Commission, *1996 Sourcebook of Federal Sentencing Statistics*, Table 29.

> develop community policing as a viable and necessary
> approach to crime

we become active participants in creating a genuine justice system
while holding ourselves accountable to each other to create safer communities where they are needed
black religious folk can and must be involved in addressing this

> it is ridiculous to think that we can accomplish the transforma-
> tion i am pointing to through faith-based initiatives alone
> we must be vocal and relentless advocates for destroying bad
> public policies that have a heavy hand in growing the prison
> industrial complex like baby huey
> we must declare that it is a naked butt strategy to think that
> we can solve the problem of racially selective mass imprison-
> ment with "a million individual solutions, by several hundred
> thousand family solutions, or by ten thousand black church and
> small business solutions"[11]

## V

there is a fundamental link between education and incarceration that i
alluded to earlier

> between the 1950s and 1980 when the share of state and local
> spending on colleges and universities doubled and the share of
> spending on corrections remained almost the same
> > the prison population changed little
> but the prison and jail population quadrupled between 1980
> and 2000 as the cost of expanding the prison industrial complex
> grew by 104% while the cost of higher education dropped by
> 21%[12]

i do not think that it is coincidence that in 2003 alone

> 21 states were considering cutting funding for k-12 education
> > 16 states raised college tuition by more than 10%
> > 6 states raised tuition in mid-year
> while leading up to 2003, from 1977 to 1999, total state and local
> expenditures on corrections rose 946%

11. Dixon, "Ten Worst."

12. Justice Policy Institute, "Cellblocks or Classrooms?—National Summary"; online: www.justicepolicy.org/article.php?id=2.

this was 2.5 times the increase in spending on all levels of
education (370%)

it is not surprising i think, that in august of 2003, the justice department reported the nation's prison and jail populations grew
by 3.7% between 2001 and 2002

3 times the growth of the previous year[13]

because we can name what is happening and develop strategies to address it

this moves from endangered to crisis to action

we need education not more incarceration

when the facts reveal that a substantial proportion of prison
inmates are uneducated and undereducated

and educational opportunities in prison are declining

when 68% of prison inmates have not received their high school
diploma

when the percentage of prisoners taking educational programs

while incarcerated is declining as the prison population grows

there is something drastically wrong when black men make up 41% of
the inmates in federal, state, and local prisons but only 4% of all students in u.s. higher education

the roots go back to inferior public grade school education

the absence of black men as role models

lower expectations from teachers and other adults

low self-esteem

low aspirations

dropping out of high school

can we hear ourselves in the solution to this

if we do not assume total responsibility for the destiny of our
children

who can we expect to do so

endangered, no
crisis, yes
victims, no
active agents yes

13. Ibid.

## VI

it is small wonder
    that we have tried our best to vanish uncle tom into limbo
        into a gross marginal space
to recognize how he was morphed into an object of mockery and jig-
dancing rather than a radicalizing witness to the evils of systematic oppression is a bitter pill to swallow in postmodern black america
    because he is not an absolutely valiant character
        the flaws in what stowe tried to do are instructive for us
        today
        as we seek state the realities of black male identities
the complex sociocultural matrix of u.s. society
    and the intracommunal dynamics of african american
    communities
    make him a painful reminder of not only slavery
    but the very commodification of identities
        that has become our stock and trade on a global scale
even in the communities of resistance that seek genuine diversity and
equality
uncle tom and his kin
        aunt jemima
        mandy the maid
        preacher brown
        deacon jones
        the Gold Dust Twins
        and ol' Mammy
            rise up as haunting spectered caricatures of black
            life
    created to buy and sell not only products
    but to siphon off our lives
        through a sea of big lips, large grins, rolling eyes
how many more tragedies and unnatural disasters like hurricane
katrina do we need to point to what happens to the poor and darker
skinned in this country?
how do we grasp a-hold of our identity and truly name ourselves
    instead of constantly looking into some strategically placed fun-
    house mirror of distortions and innuendos and mass marketing

that smacks its lips and rolls its eyes while chanting
"mmmm mmmm good"
i have offered the outlines of some solutions this afternoon
because when black identity is property
that can be owned by someone else
defined by someone else
created by someone else
shaped by someone else
and marketed by someone else
we are chattel now dressed in postmodern silks and linens
our buckboards and dusty trails have been exchanged
for one-legged stools by the one way revolving door of
academia and boardrooms
we are told that these canting stools are truly seats
at the table
but when we speak, we are not heard
when we holler, they do not listen
we are often left standing on
some malformed gold dust twins soap box
with auction blocks as our foot stools
and the hangman's noose as our lullabies to rock us
into the ultimate deep sleep
we cannot simply banish uncle tom into limbo
he is here in
Baldwin's *Just Above My Head*
Wilson's "Ma Rainey's Black Bottom" and "Radio Golf"
Hughes' *Simple Explains it All*
Wideman's *Brothers and Keepers*
Ellis' *Platitudes*
Harris' *Just As I Am*
he is in our imaginations and our psyches
and we are his kinfolk
*all* of us
and we must deal with him
we must name ourselves
with precise righteousness
and ornery love
blending justice and truth

relentless faith and moral sass
    to shape and name and create
        an identity
            that is forged on the hope found in those who are
            still here . . . regardless
won't you join me?

# 7

# Black Males as an Endangered Species

## *Peril* and *Promise*

## INTRODUCTION

The question of social location informs much of what I have to say about the place of Black males in the church and academy. In locating myself among this distinguished group of theological and religious scholars, I surmised that I was probably asked to join the conversation because of my experience in higher education at the undergraduate and graduate levels at predominately white institutions. In each instance, I served as a professor or in a director, assistant dean, or dean's role where also added to the job title was "for OR with minorities." Along with classroom teaching, my administrative tasks included serving on curriculum committees, directing summer orientation programs, and sometimes placing students on "probation" encouraging needed tutoring/advising. In all cases, I interacted with many students of color—both male and female.

In my current role I direct the doctoral fellowship programs at The Fund for Theological Education. The program seeks to support racial and ethnic women and men who have accepted a call to teaching and scholarship. This support takes the form of a financial stipend, mentoring, and professional development opportunities for graduate students so that they are *retained in their programs* and *complete their dissertations*. This program remains intact during a time when according to the latest reports: (1) financial support has decreased overall for minority graduates students and (2) shifts in program descriptors to "low income" or "first generation" make it difficult these days to find fellowship support. This difficulty alone will have impacts on the number of minority students in graduate study.[1] Upon graduation students are then available to serve on the faculties of colleges, universities, and seminaries increasing faculty diversity. Since 1999, The Fund for Theological Education (FTE) has awarded 54 dissertation fellowships to African Americans and 30 or 55 percent have completed the PhD degree with 24 of them having secured teaching positions. I might add that in addition to receiving the PhD/ThD over seventy percent of our fellowship recipients are ordained and plan to make important contributions to their faith communities as both scholars and ministers.

On the other hand, I may have just as easily been asked to comment because I am the daughter of a Baptist minister—my father served as pastor of a church in Atlanta for over 30 years while also a professor and chair of religion and philosophy at Morehouse College—called to that position by Dr. Benjamin Elijah Mays. He was also among the first appointed to the faculty of the Interdenominational Theological Center and served there for a number of years. *Several men of Morehouse including Dr. Robert Franklin, Dr. Vincent Wimbush, Dr. Darryl Trulear, Dr. Josiah Young, Dr. Aaron Parker and others now teaching in the academy were his students.* For a very long time, my father was the only African American pastor with a doctoral degree (ThD from Pacific School of Religion) in the city of Atlanta. I knew Howard Thurman because he and my father were very good friends since my father's student days at Morehouse College working with him at Howard University and later living with Thurman and his wife during a portion of his graduate study in California. In fact, Thurman and his wife, Sue Bailey Thurman, claimed responsibility for introducing my parents. And I knew the Ebenezer Baptist Church community in Atlanta because as a young child my grandfather served as a trustee there and my father and Dr. Martin Luther King Sr. were contemporaries—serving churches two blocks from each other. And yes, some of you know that I also married a Baptist minister and theological ethicist who now teaches leadership studies, religion and ethics at Morehouse College.

1. *Diversity & the Ph.D.: A Review of Efforts to Broaden Race & Ethnicity in U.S. Doctoral Education* (Princeton: Woodrow Wilson Foundation, 2005) 5–9.

Finally, my social location is defined by my status as a mother. On any day at any time I can talk about my role as a Black mother—a mother of two sons. And I must tell you that because I am African-American, I struggle daily with the image of pathology and defeat that is assumed to be the legacy of the relationship I have with my sons.[2] I am trying to raise them to have respect for themselves and others; to support their community and give back; and to have hopes and dreams for a future—any future. Everyday I pray for their safety and hope each one will come back home well—simply alive.

It is hard some days for many of us *not* to grow indifferent to the violence, crime, and death all around us in our communities. But indifference is not an option for a great number of us directly impacted in some way by this violence and death—our fathers, husbands, brothers, friends—I lost a brother, who like Nathan McCall in *Makes Me Want to Holler* . . . "didn't fit the convenient theories."[3] My brother didn't come from a broken family, there were many books in my home, and my parents' feet hit the floor everyday to go to work and provide for the basic needs and some desires of our family. They were examples of hard working, Christian folks. As a Black mother, instead of indifference, I continue to be outraged, shocked, and overwhelmed.

In a church parking lot, on a school playground, in the stands at a football game, in a supermarket pushing my shopping cart casually down the aisle where the "real food" is located according to my boys, I can begin a conversation with a stranger or friend about any subject and wind up talking about my sons or the plight of Black boys. *Name a subject*: the war in Iraq, Hurricane Katrina, SAT scores, sports, rap music; I can turn that conversation in such a way that we end up talking about the fears and hopes—the peril and the promise for African American boys—our sons.

## TWO STORIES OF PERIL AND PROMISE

We could host a focus group with any group of African American male adolescents where we might ask the simple question, *What does this*

2. Marita Golden, *Saving Our Sons: Raising Black Children in a Turbulent World* (New York: Doubleday, 1999) 42.

3. Nathan McCall, *Makes Me Wanna Holler* (New York: Random House, 1994) 402.

*phrase "Black Males as an Endangered species" bring to mind?* and we are likely get a litany of descriptions that include:

> Drugs and violence
> "Church is not for me"
> Disrespected
> "My family doesn't understand"
> I don't know where my father is
> School is boring
> Racial profiling
> Poverty
> Isolation
> Fear
> Hassled by police *and the list goes on . . .*

*The negative caricature of Black men looms large and has a long and torturous history in the Euro-Western world.* The fact is that the prevailing images and stereotypes of Black males are negative and emblematic of a larger society that has relegated them to objects. Nonetheless, *I would like to suggest that there are two stories here.* One *is* the deafening story of peril, but the other is the more muted story of promise. One story includes all the negative descriptors we just mentioned and the other holds out hope for the future.

### The Black Male in Crisis

The *first* story is the "Black male in crisis" story. Ronald B. Mincy, professor of social work at Columbia University and author of several studies on the plight of Black males suggests: "There's something very different happening with young black men and its something we can no longer ignore."[4] *And the data appears to substantiate this warning.*

I have chosen a few indicators for our review:

- **Criminal Justice System:** "From the late 1980s to the present, the number one-cause of death for Black males between the ages of 15 and 34 has been homicide."[5] The chance of being a homicide victim

4. Erik Eckholm, "Plight Deepens for Black Men, Studies Warn," *The New York Times*, 20 March 2006.

5. Le'Roy E. Reese, "The Impact of American Social Systems on African American Men," in *Brothers of the Academy: Up and Coming Black Scholars Earning Our Way in Higher Education*, ed. Lee Jones (Sterling, VA: Stylus, 2000) 192 [191–96].

is 1 in 30 for Black males and 1 in 179 for white males.[6] *What must it be like to be a young, gifted, and Black male today where your life can be causally taken by someone your own age and where you are unable to realize dreams and aspirations for the future?*

"While African Americans are 13 percent of the U.S. population, black males are over 40 percent of all juvenile and adult male prison populations."[7] Approximately 30 percent of Black men between the ages of 20 and 30 are currently involved with the corrections and court system. Further research reveals that these young men are either incarcerated, on parole, on probation, or involved in some other supervised-care by the courts.[8] In addition, Blacks are four times more likely to be sentenced to death than whites and they are less likely to get probation.[9]

- With respect to **health and healthcare systems,** African Americans are twice as likely to die as whites from disease, accidents/injuries, and homicide.[10] African Americans lead in numbers disproportionate to their population in disease categories including diabetes, heart disease, cancers (including breast, colon, and prostate), and AIDS (in the age group 25–34, it is the leading cause of death). African American men have a shorter life span than all other men despite racial/ethnic group, although Black males are now living longer than in previous years. They are at the same time less likely to seek medical care when needed or to have health insurance. But there is also evidence to suggest that even when they do seek care, their sickness and disease is less likely to be treated as aggressively as others contributing to this high level of disease and mortality.[11]

- There is some good news on the **education** front. More African Americans are graduating from high school and going on to college. However, evidence suggests we still lag behind proportionally in formal education. When African Americans do go to college,

6. Centers for Disease Control and Prevention, *Men's Health Network*, Fact Sheets, 2003.

7. Reese, "The Impact of American Social Systems," 192.

8. Ibid.

9. Lee A. Daniels, ed., *The State of Black America, 2005* (Washington, DC: National Urban League, 2005).

10. Ibid.

11. Reese, "The Impact of American Social Systems," 192.

there is a wide female-to-male disparity. Go on any historically Black campus where the disparity is most dramatic—the female-to-male ratio is 5–to–1.

In the 1990s, the number of African American, Hispanic, Asian American, and American Indian undergraduate students increased by approximately 45 percent (2.5 million to 3.6 million) composing 28 percent of all undergraduate students in 1999 compared to 21 percent in 1990. In 2000, these groups accounted for 22 percent of the bachelor degrees earned compared to 14 percent in 1991 among four year institutions.

At the same time while there is some recognition of the educational value of student and faculty diversity as a critical resource for optimizing teaching and learning, yet the abandonment of race-sensitive admissions and hiring policies at this critical juncture all but undercuts the earlier progress of the 1960s and 1970s on university campuses. This is particularly alarming since most students of color remain underrepresented in higher education.

And even though some Blacks are enjoying middle class status, the National Urban League reported recently that Black unemployment remained stagnant at 10.8 percent while white unemployment decreased to 4.7 percent making Black unemployment 2.3 times more than whites.[12] Golden suggests that the "trickle-down effect of misery fills street corners in the Black community with men who have never held a legitimate job. Work is available, but not enough for black men who are unable to fill out a job application form, even after graduating from high school . . ."[13]

These are very broad areas that more than adequately paint a picture of the 21st century African American male context. *But, this picture needs a few cautionary notes:*

1. This story is not complete unless we are aware of the historical context and the cultural scripts that Black males (and Black females) have been forced to follow.

2. The problems among (African American males) are far more difficult and complex than something we can solve through jobs alone,

---

12. Daniels, ed., *The State of Black America, 2005.*
13. Golden, *Saving Our Sons,* 15.

building recreations centers, supporting social programs or hiring more policemen.[14]

3. To be a Black male is to be heir to a set of anxieties beginning with the question of self-identity.[15]

4. And finally, the theories associated with background and status (poverty, lack of education, shattered home life) do not always tell the complete story.

*We must work on a different story.*

## The Black Male and Hope

That said, there is a *second* story—there is the story of hope. But you will rarely find this story on the front pages of the newspapers or news magazines.

- **Health Care**—Beyond statistical analyses and the popular media there are some successful stories. One morning while getting ready for work, I flipped on a morning show to discover three African American males discussing their childhood days in Newark, their decision to go to college/medical school; and finally the "pact" they had between them to help each other achieve the goal of becoming doctors. When one didn't have money the other two would pool their resources; when one had to rebound from bad decisions, the others would provide brotherly support. What I later discovered was that these young men after graduating from medical school elected to remain and locate their practices in Newark; they wrote a book about their story to encourage others; and later formed a foundation to "give back" to their community concerned about the health care in their neighborhood. I went quickly to by the bookstore to purchase, The PACT by Drs. Sampson Davis, George Jenkins, and Rameck Hunt for my sons who were already familiar with Drs. Ben Carson (the world renowned pediatric neurosurgeon) and Dr. David Satcher (former U.S. surgeon general). Both Carson and Satcher also came from humble backgrounds and dedicated their lives to promoting good health care among African Americans.

14. McCall, *Makes Me Wanna Hollar*, 402.

15. Henry Louis Gates Jr., *Thirteen Ways of Looking at a Black Man* (New York: Random House, 1997).

- **Education**—Under the leadership of President Freeman A. Hrabowski, III at the University of Maryland, the Meyerhoff Scholars Program was established. While the underrepresentation of African Americans in science and engineering has remained a challenge, this program seeks to expand the pool by creating an environment of support from pre-orientation in the summer through to graduation. This is a nationally known program that works and has built much of its success around grounding students in the first year of their programs: providing academic support; faculty mentoring; and creating an environment of support on the campus for students. Today, the Meyerholf Program boasts that it is one of the nation's leading producers of minority graduates who also go on to post graduate study.

- **Churches and Prison Ministry:** A growing number of churches have created prison ministries that have become core programs of the church's outreach. At one church in Atlanta for example, the prison ministry invites ex -prisoners into the church for workshops that seek to "re-introduce them" to the job world and to family life. Sustained counseling is needed as part of this critical intervention. Efforts like these must become the norm.

## WHAT HAPPENED? WHERE IS THE CHURCH? WHERE IS THE ACADEMY?

### *The Church*

First the church—I have two insights I want to share:

According to one recent article in the *Atlanta Journal Constitution* titled "No Balm in the Pews for Black Males' Pain?":

> The same thing that has happened to thousands, of African American men who now file into coffee shops or bowling alleys or baseball stadiums on Sundays instead of heading to church, or who lose themselves in the haze of mowing the lawn and waxing their cars. Somewhere along the way, for us, for me, the church— the collective of Black churches of the Christian faith, regardless of denomination—lost its meaning, its relevance. It seems to have no discernible message for what ails the 21st -century Black male soul.[16]

16. "No Balm in the Pews for Black Males' Pain," *Atlanta Journal Constitution*, 24 July 2005, B4–5.

With largely women in the pews, the Black church writ-large seems to have no answer for those Black males in crisis and no anecdote for the forces pushing and pulling these men further down paths of destruction and alienation. There seems no plan to bring them into the fold for spiritual nourishment or to help prop them up on every leaning side. The author goes on to say the Black church "seems to have turned inward. It seems to exist for the perpetuation of itself—for the erecting of grandiose temples of brick and mortar . . ."[17]

In addition to this scathing critique, many Black churches have adopted a fundamentalist faith perspective and are essentially concerned with helping individuals develop a spiritual relationship with God and achieve personal salvation. It sees the incidents of crime and violence, HIV/AIDS, etc. as moral and personal failures—the young people can pull themselves up and live better lives. We did it—and our ancestors after all came out of the horrors of slavery and segregation!! This perspective was also evident during the Civil Rights Movement and Martin Luther King Jr.'s quest for social justice and political rights. Not all Black churches agreed with the movement and not all Black churches followed the movement. We know, however, since the rise of the Black Theology movement and its successors, there has been a critique of the theological issues associated with personal piety and self-reliance as viable strategies for social and moral transformation.

## The Academy

Recently, I reread Dr. James Cone's account of his decision to attend graduate school and enter the academy as a scholar and researcher. I am always glad when he "looks back and wonders" and "tells his story" before a group of graduate students because it underscores for them the important step they have taken in accepting a call to the academy. Some things have not changed since his earlier account of navigating the doctoral process and beginning his teaching career. As the numbers of African American males decline or remain stagnant in the academy, they face many of the same challenges Dr. Cone faced including: maintaining self-identity, issues of socialization, persistent racism, and isolation.[18] Yet, the presence of each new African American male (and female) scholar is a

---

17. Ibid.

18. Jones and Akbar, in *Brothers of the Academy*, discuss the ongoing challenges of African American men completing doctoral programs and advancing in the academy.

testament to their endurance and we must do all we can to increase their numbers so they can offer some of the visionary and scholarship leadership needed to live up to the promise—beyond entertainers and athletes our society has deemed the purveyors of this promise.

This leads me to return to my own social location as academician, administrator, daughter of the church, and Black mother by suggesting that the stories of peril and promise are not separate, but interlocking narratives in a larger historical dramatic sequence. In fact, I would argue that the church and academy are caught on the axis of these stories of peril and promise. On one hand, as we reach out to African American males, but on the other the larger socio-historical narrative is weighted against their life chances. Simply put, both the church and the academy must work harder and more strategically because we are running out of time if we desire to save and shape the next generation of African American males. Last summer's FTE's conference theme was: *Bridging the Gap between the Academy and the Church*. We struggled to understand the origins of the disconnect, and the students pressed the scholars to talk about how they made their scholarly work real and meaningful for everyday church folks. I hope those in the academy press forward in new ways to bridge these gaps and vice versa—we all know some progressive pastors and scholar-practitioners—but we do not have enough of them. Not enough of them to ask the critical questions, conduct the research, provide theological reflection, and struggle toward the needed solutions. This anti-intellectualism in our culture is pervasive but we must do everything we can to encourage excellent writing, excellent research, and excellent scholarship that supports this agenda.

Second, there is a question of capacity—and I want to devote my last comments specifically to churches. From a public policy perspective our society has relied on the criminal justice system and social service efforts to solve the "at risk" Black male issue with *more* policemen and *more* prisons.[19] Yet this issue still appears intractable. I believe most us feel that churches are not equipped to provide the kinds of services and support that African American males need—those caught in the clutches of complex systems of injustice and social misery—much of what was discussed here.

19. Walter Earl Fluker, "Raising Up Sons and Daughters unto Abraham: The Capacity of African Churches to Provide Services and Support to At-Risk and Gang-Related Youth," Ford Foundation Project, 1999.

## Growing Church Capacity

Do churches have the capacity to provide services and support to at-risk young Black males? In 1996 I served as a project manager for a small pilot study funded by the Ford Foundation. A one-year preliminary study of eighty-six churches in seven cities was designed. The purpose of the pilot study was to determine the extent to which services and support to at-risk youth and gang related youth were being offered through African American churches. Not nearly enough research is available that details the extent of Black church involvement with at-risk youth—with most of it directly related to youth related church activities including singing in the choir, rallies, revivals, etc. And one might even believe that the location alone would suggest that churches were uniquely positioned to make a difference in the lives of young people. This glaring absence in the literature made a preliminary study like this important. The hope was to unveil models and strategies that might serve as resources for churches struggling to provide services and support. And in addition, the research would also uncover some of the constraints and barriers in providing these services.

The study sought to measure five types of capacity: *strategic, theological, managerial, congregational resource support, and leadership.* In addition to the survey instrument, focus groups were also held with church leaders who were direct providers of the services. What the study found was that the Black church indeed was uniquely positioned to offer services and support for youth in urban centers but these services were limited. These churches can and do respond to the needs of the communities they serve and can create safe, spiritually nurturing, and affirming environments for youth in crisis but this support is more directly related to their own outreach and mission goals. The report also found that most of the churches are "developing very narrow religiously focused youth ministries in the absence of external social support and resources for leadership development."[20]

Other recent findings by Dr. R. Drew Smith, scholar-in-residence at Morehouse College in a 2003 study entitled "Beyond the Boundaries: Low Income Residents, Faith Based Organizations and Neighborhood Coalition Building," funded by the Annie Casey Foundation reported similar results. While the churches in this four-city study have significant

20. Ibid.

institutional presence in their communities and provide some social and spiritual uplift—the overall conclusion was that churches have limited impact on the everyday lives of poor families in the surrounding areas of the church. While physical presence is important; strategic impacts are limited due largely to capacity issues of churches including administrative and cultural readiness among others.[21]

Finally, as both reports conclude, the strategic impact of churches will only be realized when congregations "build broad coalitions with residents, other faith-based organizations, and community groups."[22]  Vital coalitions build on the prominent position that churches hold in the community and the cultural expertise, managerial, and administrative expertise of community groups providing a more comprehensive model. Big Brothers and Big Sisters, 100 Black Men, and the Boys and Girls Clubs are all well-known and established organizations and examples of organizations that might partner with churches to provide services. These coalitions do help build a broader and more systematic impact on Black males that can ultimately influence public and private responses.

As a means of initiating contact and collaboration with the agencies named above, I also recommend that a major conference between churches, the academy and secular youth serving agencies be held which provides a forum for discussion, exchange of approaches and models for churches and the academy that provide support and service to youth populations. A final recommendation is that there be a close look at the ways in which Historically Black Colleges and Universities (HBCUs) might provide both resources and sites of training for a broad, comprehensive effort.

In summary, there are two stories, one of peril, one of hope. How these stories continue to intertwine with each other will depend largely on the ways in which we dream together with these young men and not commit the sins that we so easily identify in others: indifference, negligence, and hopelessness.

21. R. Drew Smith, "Beyond the Boundaries: Low-Income Residents, Faith-Based Organizations, and Neighborhood Coalition Building," Annie E. Casey Project Report, 2–3; online: http://www.morehouse.edu/centers/leadershipcenter/fcuf/reports/BTB Report2003.pdf.

22. Ibid.

# 8

# A Woman's Work, A Man's World

*Critiquing and Challenging Patriarchy in the Black Family*[1]

ALTON B. POLLARD III

It's a man's world. But it would be nothing, nothing without a woman.

—James Brown, 1966

## DISAPPEARING ACTS (A PARABLE)

IT WAS NOT LONG after the terrible phenomenon of the Great Divide, when antagonisms of gender and generation and sexuality and color and class and custom and religion and region and dual heritage and more had been made manifest, and the Black nation no longer cared for each other so much, that the impossible happened. In all the annals of transatlantic history nothing—not four hundred years of enslavement, violence, rape, domestication, breeding, dismemberment, dehumanization, disfranchisement, lynching, emasculation, segregation, discrimination, unemployment, profiling, incarceration, pathology, exploitation, or

---

1. *Author's note:* I offer this improvisational essay as an exercise in engaged scholarship. I was moved and motivated to write in a way that would be accessible to people "on the ground" in their everyday experience, where family dynamics converge in real and critical ways. At the same time, the disciplined demands of the academy are equally acknowledged and addressed here. Living in the tension between narrative and analysis, biography and critique, contemplation and inquiry, is consistent with my values and politics. Each form has become indispensable to my work and to the ever insurgent struggle for a livable future to which all of us are called.

death—had been able to accomplish this. All the Black men vanished. Somehow they simply disappeared.

No one could say precisely why or when or where or how but millions of men of African descent, every single one of them, were gone without a trace. Men who left home for work that morning never arrived. Men who worked the graveyard shift did not come home with the sunrise. Men who dropped off children at daycare and school did not return for pick-up. Men who led subversive lives on mean streets and borrowed time were nowhere to be found. Men who lived under the pain of anonymity were no more. They were not dead. They were not translated to heaven. For no apparent reason, the men just were not there.

That was the good news. The bad news was that, for all their disappearance, many of the women and children who were left behind did not miss the Black men all that much. Not really. In some instances, this meant Black women had to make sacrifices and work additional jobs and shifts or return to school to better prepare themselves vocationally. Black women had to go it alone without the benefit of a second paycheck or additional parental authority in the house. Black women had to make it without the benefit of Black men to be their soul mates, companions, spouses, lovers, intimates, partners, brothers, and friends. Black women had to make their own way, devise a plan, raise the babies, tend to the children, pay the bills, provide shelter, pray their way through, love themselves deeply, care about one another, and create community. No. Many of the women and children who were left behind did not miss the men all that much. Not really. In their absence, Black women did not miss a beat. Sisters kept on doing what they had always been doing—good, bad and otherwise—doing it for and by themselves.

## FATHERHOOD (SIGNS . . .)

We were driving down the South Carolina coast, along highway 17 to be exact, through an assortment of small towns and thoroughfares and unincorporated places. Too quickly, a billboard went by, the message of which I immediately dismissed for believing I had misread it. But new signs continued to flash by, each depicting Black men in a variety of settings, and all repeating the same words: "Santa Claus. Easter Bunny. Tooth Fairy. Daddy." Some time later, I learned that the ads were part of a nationwide campaign sponsored by the National Fatherhood Initiative, an influential Maryland-based nonprofit organization with ties to both political parties. At the heart of the billboard's message was a silent and unsettling interrogation, "What do all these images have in common?" The answer: "Eventually, kids stop believing in things they don't see."

## TOTAL DOMINATION (AND MORE SIGNS)

My car was in a fender-bender last month and in need of some repairs. As I waited at the auto body shop to receive what was certain to be unpleasant news about the estimated cost to fix everything, I walked outside to get some air. Looming overhead was a large billboard, a sign. It read: "Dr. Wellington Boone and Dr. Creflo Dollar invite you to the 'Total Domination Conference.'" Fortunately for me, I was spared the need to have to go and investigate this latest incarnation of domination indoctrination in Black churches and its peculiar appeal to a segment of African American believers; the conference had been held a month earlier.

## NO MORE PATRIARCHY (THE CHALLENGE)

We were bursting with pride. My seventeen-year-old nephew—cool, calm and collected—came down the stairs ready to go with cap and gown draped over his arm. The day of his high school graduation had finally and at last arrived: The incomparable class of 2005. The air was filled with laughter and excitement as we pulled up to the Black college prep high school. The soon-to-be graduates were everywhere—running, hugging, smiling, and kissing—in other words acting crazy, with occasional scenes of quiet reminisce. Dozens of beautiful young Black women and men as well as their families, teachers, and friends stood poised to take the next step, prepared for new challenges, ready to transition on to the world's stage.

The graduation exercises (it was camouflaged Black worship really) opened to "Lift Every Voice and Sing." I skimmed the program's extensive contents as we sang. Each graduate's name was listed along with the college or university they planned to attend in the fall, academic honors conferred, and scholarships received. Some were going to attend institutions of higher learning in other states; others planned to stay close to home. The clear majority was planning to go to historically Black colleges and universities, but a good number were matriculating to state schools.

A few minutes more, a few preliminaries more, and the class salutatorian rose to give the first address of the night. Thoughtful and articulate, his remarks were significant but minor in comparison to the final soaring and tearful tribute he had prepared for his mother. The audience roared its loud approval with wave after wave of applause. The commencement speaker came next, an early 1990s alumnus and local news reporter made good, who delivered a rambling speech. The only moving moment was when he talked about his mother, who steered him through a turbulent adolescence. Diminutive in stature, she sat in the front row of seats smiling, laughing, and crying as her son spoke. The conferral of diplomas came next, followed by the valedictorian's address. Tall, dark, handsome and athletic, the recipient of a full scholarship to a prestigious Ivy League school, the crowd hung on this young man's every word. He closed by thanking his mother and then he thanked God. In the end, all in attendance were deeply moved.

## PREPARATION

I was already thinking about my given assignment for this essay. It was my first time going to a graduation where the leading graduates and featured speakers were all Black males. The paradox was that in a Black community, church, and world immersed in patriarchy, male patriarchs were not mentioned in any of these young men's narratives. And yet, as I looked around me there were many men present who obviously deeply cared.

The portrait of the twenty-first century African American family is turbulent and complex.[2] We cherish our Black mothers for their love, courage, and self-sacrifice. We are fervent, and rightly so, in our reverence for Black motherhood (visions of Proverbs 31 and Victorian notions notwithstanding). But can we say with equal devotion that we are committed to "the survival and wholeness," to the full empowerment, of all Black women everywhere?[3]

Many of our Black fathers are viewed as peripheral at best and effaced at worst. But what is a Black father, after all, if not a patriarch? We

2. "Family," as used in this essay refers to singles, couples, partners, children, marriages, unions, and other intimate bonds of human relatedness that society may or may not officially recognize as such.

3. Alice Walker, *In Search of Our Mothers' Gardens* (New York: Harcourt, Brace, Jovanovich, 1983) xi.

readily denigrate Black men. Are there not also prospects for those Black men yearning to breathe free, who are pro-womanist, anti-homophobic, and anti-sexist?

Otherwise progressive-minded Black women and men routinely practice an exclusionary brand of family politics where same-and-both-gender love is concerned. But can an insurgent practice, a holistic engagement with principalities and powers, take place in Black communities, where the struggle against homophobia and heterosexism—as well as capitalism, sexism, and racism—is waged on every front, as one? The next generation awaits our discerning response. What sacred life ways of Black family and faith will we leave them? What new and inclusive constellations of family will they themselves create?

## REFLECTION

Patriarchy is a difficult word for me(n) to discuss. I am all too familiar with it. I have long sought to make sense of it. I have struggled to resist its perverse power. I have tried to wrest myself from its androcentric, phallocentric, and gynophobic grips. The results thus far have been somewhat less than spectacular. Akin to hip-hop head and journalist Kevin Powell, I am a recovering patriarch.[4] I tremble in the telling, and particularly in an academic setting, where personal confessions are not the norm. Nevertheless, it seems to me that the radical disembodiment of our scholarship has been a disqualifying factor in our efforts as scholars of Black religion to make our work more accessible to as broad a cross-section of the community as possible. Patriarchy does not exist as an abstraction but in fact inhabits real and living Black bodies. Its wounds are piercing. Its impact is demonic. The damage is real and grotesque. This grounding Black feminist-womanist cognition has been central to my own efforts to engage Black familial experiences in ways that are faithful, critical, freeing, holistic and loving.

My beloved father, Alton B. Pollard Jr., is a patriarchal man. My father's father, Alton B. Pollard Sr., was the same. Growing up, I remember my father as a hard working, uniform wearing, blue collar, foundry worker. He was his union's shop steward. He was also a highly respected leader in our church; the oldest and largest Black religious institution in

4. Kevin Powell, "Confessions of a Recovering Misogynist," *Ms Magazine* (Apr/May 2000) 72–77.

the state. He was superintendent of the Sunday school and a member of the board of trustees. He declined repeated invitations to become a deacon, never feeling quite worthy.

To the world outside our family, my dad was a quiet and dignified man. I was terrified of him. He was a steady provider and a stern protector. Seldom a day went by that harsh punishment was not meted out by him in word and in deed. His arms were thick and muscular. His hands were worn and leathered. His face was handsome and chiseled. His physical strength was enormous. His control of his domain never waned. Paradoxically, cleaning and cooking great meals were not foreign to him. He read his Bible for hours on end. God was male and created man for dominion. Women's work was to help men perform their tasks, to obey, and to always assume a subordinate role in relation to a powerful man. An inflexible patriarch, affection and affirmation were alien to him. A strong head of household, our mother was subordinate to him. An ever-present father, he was emotionally absent to us. There is nothing particularly exceptional or even unique about my remembrances except, perhaps, for the lasting terror. In the parlance of patriarchy, my dad was and is a "man's man." With the passage of years he has begun to mellow somewhat. His grandchildren find him more approachable. I am his son. And I love him.

My beloved mother, Lena Laverne Evans, carries a wounded heart. Her mother, Laura Stamps, was barely in her teens when she gave birth to her. My grandmother died early from tuberculosis, the HIV/AIDS of her time; my mother's father was not in her life. Sent to live with one family member or another, her early years are largely a mystery to her three children. By every indication, my mother believed in my father's patriarchy in the early years of their marriage. Early on, she was a patriarchal mother. Despite my father's disapproval, my mother was also part of the working class. Not because we needed the money but because she needed the reprieve. Mostly, she worked part-time as a nurse's aide on the night shift at the county hospital from 11pm to 7am.

In my early days, my mother often spent her free time in lively conversation on the phone, her laughter loud and clear. Like clockwork, our father would come home from work at 4:30 pm, and the phone calls and laughter would stop. My mother and father were together some twenty-seven years but ours was not a happy household. If you can remember the Vietnam War, or know about the Korean conflict today, our home was the domestic equivalent of a "Demilitarized Zone."[5] My mom was a Sunday school teacher and a deaconess. My father could not understand how such an honor was bestowed on her. Mom was not the best cook or house cleaner. I can recall no favorite meals, never a kiss, and no hugs. Nurture was never her strong suit. A grown-woman mother, she was subjugated along with her children. Now requiring extended healthcare, I'm not sure that my mom ever really had the chance to exhale. I am her son. And I love her.

In the world my mother and father grew up in it was especially perilous to be Black. Both my parents are from the alluvial basin of the Mississippi Delta. In the antebellum years, it was routinely said the worst fate that could befall one of the enslaved anywhere was to be sold "downriver" to Mississippi. A century and more later, not much had changed for the better. My parents left the world of Mississippi and its patriarchal white supremacist citizen's councils behind in 1955, scant weeks after the brutal murder of Emmett Till in nearby Money. My father came from a family of eighteen, including his fifteen siblings and parents. The Pollards were sharecroppers, and, to my knowledge, did not own the roof they lived under or the land they lived on.

My mother never was one to divulge much about her own upbringing; even though her experiences surely played a formative role in the way my siblings and I were raised. I think that as a boy who grew up in a Black, patriarchal, working-class household—and in an all white community full of girls my age no less—there was a convergence of issues of race, gender, sexuality, and class. Moreover, it was the height of the civil rights and Black consciousness movements. I was made deeply aware of my gender, and I was acutely aware of the limitations imposed on me by race. Given these interlocking domestic and social realities, I came to a critical stance made manifest in my growing opposition to hierarchal forms, my affirmation of human equality, and reverence of all life. Still, I needed to better understand the complex circumstances that had shaped and influenced my parent's lives, and how this contributed to their unvoiced yet very real love for their children.

5. The Demilitarized Zone, or DMZ, is an unoccupied territory that serves the purpose of keeping opposition forces apart, whether through treaty or international pressure. Interestingly enough, the term now exists in the domain of computer networks as a reference to firewall configurations.

## CRITICAL EXCURSUS

Black feminist scholar Candace Jenkins defines the term patriarchy as "the rule of the father, including the rule of older men over younger men and of fathers over daughters, as well as husbands over wives."[6] I would expand this definition to include all hierarchal structures throughout society and culture, where men are the harbingers and arbiters of power and where women and all who are effectively "feminized" with them—children, young people, the poorest of the poor, the working poor, same-and-both-gender loving persons, and less powerful men—are subjugated by the powerful.

Patriarchy is a system of institutionalized gender roles. It is male privilege. It is male dominance. It is male entitlement. It is violence against women. It is a patent hatred of women. It is the abject fear of women. Many women and far more men have embraced this gendered script as natural. It is an attitude learned in our family of origins and a behavior reinforced and reified in every social institution from churches and schools to the most common aspects of our culture. As an ideology, it is not limited to capitalism or modernism alone. As a way of life, its first allegiance is to the white male elite; its second allegiance is to less powerful white males. It includes but is not limited to physical, spiritual, emotional, cultural, psychological, ideological, and socio-political forms of masculine hegemony. For our purposes, patriarchy foments division, dis-ease, disease, distrust, despair, distress, and death in Black families and Black communities. Its negatives far outweigh any so-called advantages. Yet the pornographic power of patriarchy and its misanthropic companions—sexism, heterosexism, racism, classism, supremacy, homophobia, misogyny, violence and more—continues to hold the Black estate psychically and systemically captive.[7]

6. Candice M. Jenkins, "Queering Black Patriarchy: The Salvific Wish and Masculine Possibility in Alice Walker's *The Color Purple*," *Modern Fiction Studies* 48 (2002) 973 [969–1000]. Also Claudia Lawrence-Webb, Melissa Littlefield, and Joshua N. Okundaye, "African American Intergender Relationships: A Theoretical Exploration of Roles, Patriarchy, and Love," *Journal of Black Studies* 34 (2004) 623–39.

7. For specific resources dealing with sexuality and Black churches see Alton B. Pollard III, "Teaching the Body: Sexuality and the Black Church," in *Loving the Body: Black Religious Studies and the Erotic*, ed. Anthony B. Pinn and Dwight N. Hopkins (New York: Palgrave Macmillan, 2004) 315–46. The entire volume is an indispensable resource.

Four centuries of untold sexist-racist violence and white patriarchal proscription have exacted a devastating toll on the African American family and soul. In the antebellum era, sexual, racial, and economic forces largely dictated Black family and community requisites. The labor-intensive, agrarian economy of the South severely restricted the ability of Africans to control their bodily, temporal, occupational, and communal life, whether enslaved or freed. In the free states of the North, Africa's progeny worked diligently to establish a communal division of labor that recognized or not, invariably mirrored white patriarchy. Black churches were led by male bishops, pastors, evangelists, and deacons. Black newspapers and mutual aid societies were directed and controlled by males. Black male activists critically equated Black liberation with the attainment of "Black Manhood."[8] Through periods of legal emancipation, post-Reconstruction, and Jim Crow segregation Black patriarchal outcomes did not appear to appreciably change. As W. E. B. Du Bois powerfully observed, "the race question is at bottom simply a matter of the ownership of women."[9]

At the same time, the story was far more complicated and nuanced than that. In the crucible of slavery, women were subjected to the slave owners' bidding, men were torn away from their families, and both were bred like animals. When and where possible Black families—in a variety of permutations—sustained themselves, although burdened in ways painful to recount across the generations. Far more than most scholars have appreciated, and most of us care to know, resistance to white patriarchy was a principle means by which Black women, and their men, maintained their inner strength and integrity.

This resistance assumed more forms than can possibly be recounted here, but the historical record is clear that throughout their enslavement and later proscription, large numbers of women and men pursued freedom together and in equality as their most precious goal. The children of Africa were not hesitant to resist white domination even unto dismemberment or death. The plantation may have been the locus of sexual assault, violence, rape, tyranny, forced breeding, and imprisonment, but the proprietary nation was far more complicitous in ensuring

8. See, for instance, the important documentary reader in African American male history: Darlene Clark Hine and Earnestine Jenkins, eds., *A Question of Manhood* (Bloomington: Indiana University Press, 1999).

9. W. E. B. Du Bois, "Opinion of W. E. B. Du Bois," *The Crisis* 23.5 (1922) 199–200.

REALITY
OF WHITE
PATR ORDER

entrenched Black suffering and social death. In service to the patriarchal order, African women's bodies were a resistance to be broken and
African men's bodies remanded to brutal control. In the world that the
white supremacist capitalists made, how was the African American family, church, community, and culture able to endure?

Paula Giddings, Darlene Clark Hines, Angela Davis, Evelyn Brooks
Higginbotham, bell hooks, and Manning Marable are but a few of the
progressive scholars who have well chronicled the history of patriarchy
and the exploitation of Black women, children and men in this land.[10]
What they and other feminists-womanists have rightly argued is that
racist and sexist America proved incapable of offering the uprooted of
Africa a viable model for being human, sexually, socially, or otherwise.
They all underscore the power of white patriarchal culture, the tyranny
of the prevailing social order on Black ancestral life, males as well as
females. They have been equally careful to interrogate generations of
Black men who, consciously or not, privileged the patriarchal with its
attendant system of rewards and compensators.

Black men have given their allegiance to various (and, with the gift
of hindsight, far too narrow) forms of nationalism, from Pan-Africanism
to Afrocentrism, in fierce and noble calls for freedom, but in part as
a conditioned response evoked by white patriarchy. While not always
clearly recognized, for African American men the historic struggle for
liberation ultimately meant the attainment of an oft-stated but unspeci-
fied "Manhood."

Not surprisingly, Black patriarchal society often surpassed white
supremacist patriarchy in its extreme conservatism and oppression of
women.[11] The relative equality of labor once imposed by the brutalities

10. Paula Giddings, *When and Where I Enter: The Impact of Black Women on Race
and Sex in America* (New York: Morrow, 1984); Darlene Clark Hines and Kathleen
Thompson, *A Shining Thread of Hope: The History of Blac Women in America* (New York:
Broadway, 1998); Angela Davis, *Women, Race, and Class* (New York: Vintage, 1983);
Angela Davis, "Reflections on the Black Woman's Role in the Community of Slaves,"
*Black Scholar* 3 (Dec. 1971) 3–14; Evelyn Brooks Higginbotham, *Righteous Discontent:
The Women's Movement in the Black Baptist Church, 1880–1920* (Cambridge: Harvard
University Press, 1993); bell hooks, *Feminist Theory: From Margin to Center* (Boston:
South End, 1984, 2000); and Manning Marable, "Groundings with My Sisters: Patriarchy
and the Exploitation of Black Women," in *Traps: African American Men on Gender
and Sexuality*, ed. Rudolph P. Byrd and Beverly Guy-Sheftall (Bloomington: Indiana
University Press, 2001) 113–52.

11. Marable, "Groundings with My Sisters," 131–42.

of slavery no longer held in post-Reconstruction and twentieth century Black America. Many Black men were threatened by the emergence of social, economic, religious, educational, and political opportunities seized upon by dynamic and progressive-minded Black women. At least since the late nineteenth century, Black and white men alike have been disturbed by what can only be described as a revolutionary transformation in gender role relationships in the public and private spheres. Well into the twenty-first century, men's weeping and gnashing of teeth continues as entrenched forms of institutional sexism are challenged and dismantled on every hand.

Still, this is not the whole of the story. To examine the history of patriarchy in America is to also suggest that Black and white men have not been its sole purveyors. As a Black male, to venture such a critique is not without its own risks. White women have been neither naïve nor passive participants in the racist exploits of patriarchy, often utilizing them to their own advantage. From Susan B. Anthony and Elizabeth Cady Stanton to present-day activists and theorists, white feminists have helped to create a climate where sisterhood with Black women could be called into question (opposition to the Fifteenth Amendment and Black women's suffrage) and where young Black men are viewed with contempt, vilified as the antithesis of privileged white culture (primal and penal hip-hop culture).[12]

There can be no denying that elements of hip-hop culture, similar to the Black church, deserve the most radical challenge and critique we can bring to bear.[13] How much more, then, does this same truth apply to the "white supremacist patriarchal culture" that produces so much of the opposition and the need?[14] Mainstream white feminists who critically

12. One of the most definitive texts on male hip-hop culture at present is Bakari Kitwana, *The Hip-Hop Generation: Young Blacks and the Crisis in African American Culture* (New York: BasicCivitas, 2002). On women and hip-hop culture see Gwendolyn D. Pough, *Check It While I Wreck It: Black Womanhood, Hip-Hop Culture, and the Public Sphere* (Boston: Northeastern University Press, 2004).

13. At the same time, for non-hip-hop "heads" to overlook the very real and constructive dimensions of youth culture and rap and hip-hop critique—and they are many—is to uncritically perpetuate bourgeois values. Some of the best work in this regard is the provocative and detailed study by Imani Perry, *Prophets of the Hood: Politics and Poetics in Hip Hop* (Durham: Duke University Press, 2004).

14. bell hooks is well known for coining the phrase "imperialist white-supremacist capitalist patriarchy" to describe the interlocking political systems that are foundational to the extant social order.

accept and perpetuate expressions of white patriarchy reflect their own "bourgeois" values and "cultured" standards and reveal their own lust for power. Female racists falsely donning the mantle of victim-hood, they do not dismantle the patriarchal apparatus at all. White feminists must end their allegiance to the "bourgeois agenda of the status quo," as bell hooks says, if they would be "useful allies in the struggle."[15]

Regrettably, and for vastly different reasons, the legacy of sexist and racist domination has also led some Black women to be the staunch defenders of a Black patriarchy. Under the constant glare of pathologizing scrutinies, some women have retreated to the relative security of the known patriarchal world. Repeated assaults from white patriarchal society—from institutionalized rape to immoral biblical teachings and institutional glass ceilings—have invalidated Black female bodies, reinforced a social ethic of submission, and embedded Black male domination.

Repeated assaults from within Black patriarchal society—accusations that the emancipation of Black womanhood has come at the expense of Black manhood, that the Black woman has emasculated the Black man, and more—have undermined many a Black woman's emotional, spiritual, physical and social well-being. Throughout the struggle for Black self-determination, African American women have struggled with the meaning of Black masculinity and it relationship to their own gender role (including the contrast of their gender role to that of white females). They have been "kept in their place" in accordance with the God-given "natural order of things." For far too long, it's been a woman's work in a man's presumed world.

At the consumerist level, some women vehemently protect patriarchal thinking, and criticize as selfish, lazy and irresponsible the Black man who does not "bring home the bacon" or the most extravagant "bling-bling."[16] Obviously, some patriarchal men are reliable providers and protectors, but this does not change the fact that the system itself is exploitative and oppressive. It is ironic, in light of the desire to promote group safety, in the historic absence of women's rights or freedom, in the repudiation of mischaracterizations of Black female and male intimate life (including but not limited to sexual differences as in same-and-both-

15. bell hooks, "Sisters of the Yam: Challenging Capitalism & Patriarchy," *Z Magazine* (July/Aug 1995); online: www.zmag.org/ZMag/articles/july95hooks.htm.

16. See, for instance, Terrence Real, *How Can I Get through to You? Reconnecting Men and Women* (New York: Fireside, 2001).

gender love), that some Black women choose to endorse and sustain conventional patriarchal norms.

The same hierarchical system that privileges maleness and whiteness does likewise for heterosexuality. Jenkins describes the heteronormative drive in many Black families as "part of a pattern of Black desire that I call the 'salvific wish.' The salvific wish is best understood as an aspiration, most often but not only middle class and female, to save or rescue the Black community from white racist accusations of sexual and domestic pathology, through conventional bourgeois propriety."[17]

Lesbian and gay scholars and queer theorists have carefully explicated the enormous price that same-and-both-gender-loving women and men pay for participation in Black communal structures, including their families and church.[18] Invoking the authority of religion has been a primary means by which patriarchal Black families seek to maintain the "natural social order." For Black people to talk about gender, race and class and to ignore sexual identity encourages a patently false liberative consciousness. The stigma of deviation that has been attached to African American sexual identity—analogous to male gender pathologies, consumerist class views, and white racial constructs—reflexively shapes the way Black communities express sexual and family values in private and, for certain, in the public sphere.

In Black churches, gay rights are not human rights, but an immoral and decadent kind of "special rights" that endangers the sanctity of marriage and the family. There is only one sexually Authorized Version, one pattern of human loving, in muscular Christianity and Black patriarchal society.[19] That Black lesbian, gay, bisexual, and transgendered persons are made to feel unworthy in their own families and homes is a matter of

---

17. Jenkins, "Queering Black Patriarchy," 973.

18. For examples, see Audre Lorde's classic collection of essays in *Sister Outsider* (Berkeley: Crossing, 1984); E. L. Kornegay, "Queering Black Homophobia: Balck Theology as a Sexual Discourse of Transformation," *Theology and Sexuality* 11 (2004) 29–51; Irene Monroe, "When and Where I Enter, Then the Whole Race Enters with Me: Que(e)rying Exodus," in *Loving the Body: Black Religious Studies and the Erotic*, ed. Anthony B. Pinn and Dwight N. Hopkins (New York: PalgraveMacmillan, 2004) 121–32; and Reginald Glenn Blaxton, "Jesus Wept: Reflections on HIV Dis-ease and the Churches of Black Folk," in *Dangerous Liaisons: Blacks, Gays, and the Struggle for Equality*, ed. Eric Brandt (New York: New Press, 1999) 102–41.

19. While the focus here is on Black Christian churches, no form of institutional religion in African American communities from the Nation of Islam to the Hebrew Israelites is immune to the patriarchal gaze.

imperative concern. To the degree that Black people continue to engage in a kind of existential avoidance, or worse, effacement of gayness, to that extent will we fail to embrace with our whole beings the struggle for self-determination and self-love. The cost to our very souls may well prove to be beyond measure.

## CHALLENGING PATRIARCHY

Considerable attention has been given in this essay to critical examination of the patriarchal matrix in American society as relates to the Black family. In hierarchal order of proximity, past and present, to the poles and prerogatives of societal power they are briefly identified as follows:

1. *White male supremacist capitalism.* White maleness, pro-capitalist, imperialist, socially and culturally constructed as an inalienable right. Rhetorics of inclusion exist but are implemented in the socio-political order only in periods of extreme duress (i.e., abolitionist movement, women's suffrage, civil rights movement, women's rights movement, environmentalist movement, etc.).

2. *White female patriarchy.* White mainstream feminism. Politics and ideas presented as inclusive and in solidarity while strategically maintaining the race and class benefits of patriarchy. A bourgeois white feminism is life-denying to Black children, women, and men.

3. *Black male patriarchy.* Black male superiority. A reactionary impulse made manifest in our politics and culture. Given over to misogyny, violence and related violations. Male aggression and female domesticity is institutionalized as normative to Black family life.

4. *Black female patriarchy.* Black patriarchal male role idealized. Female patriarchs are not uncommon. Often occurs, but not always, in the absence of a male patriarchal figure. Hidden in plain sight, among the most ardent defenders of strict gender roles and expectations.

5. *Black heterosexual patriarchy.* Homophobic and heterosexist. A mood and behavior of deep intolerance. Denigrates and ostracizes gay and bisexual love as unnatural. Not claiming diverse sexualities diminishes capacity for addressing AIDS and victimization in the Black family.

*Is The Domination System*

Truly authentic challenges to patriarchy in the Black family cannot occur without a more complicated interrogation of muscular or masculinized domination in its myriad forms. This includes investigation into the larger structures of domination and the individuals (often white and male but not always) who are hierarchically positioned to perpetuate the extant order.

At the same time, great care must be taken not to view any individual or even social group as a mere monolith. Allies in the struggle against patriarchy exist in all communities, implausible to some as this may seem. For us to consider otherwise is to continue to perpetuate Balkanized if not disingenuous notions of struggle in Black communities and the broader society. With this caveat in mind multiple, adaptable, and textured frames of analysis have been used here to expose patriarchy in Black families. Let us now turn our attention to some specific ways in which African American families can become realms of resistance and sites of liberating self-love.

One of the dominant cultural mythologies of the African American family is that it is "matriarchal." For reasons criminal, pathological, and otherwise African American men are presumed to play no significant role in their families and communities, patriarchal or not. This has especially been the case since Daniel Moynihan's infamous seventy-eight-page report on the Black family in 1965, having gained both popular validity and social currency via print and electronic media bias.[20]

As we have been careful to indicate, the historical record, for better or worse, offers a far more discerning portrait. To be sure, many African American men and some women have erred egregiously on the side of what is impulsive and self-destructive today. Clearly, patriarchal preoccupations and emotional arrest pose a growing threat to our actuarial life chances. The responsibility for our liberation as sexist and homophobic males begins (but does not end) with us. Self-love is our challenge. C. Eric Lincoln expresses the male dilemma well: "No wonder [young African American men] are alienated. They never really knew what our [older African American men's] values were, and when they discovered it they found out that we didn't know either."[21] Notwithstanding the

---

20. Daniel P. Moynihan, *The Negro Family: The Case for National Action*, U.S. Department of Labor, 1965.

21. Cited in Alton B. Pollard III, "Magnificent Manhood: The Transcendent Witness of Howard Thurman," in *Redeeming Men: Men and Masculinities*, ed. Stephen B. Boyd,

coercive and destabilizing forces with which Black men must contend—and many men are in crisis—many others are deeply and constructively involved in Black family and community life.

Lora Bex Lempert, in an important but little-known article, makes a compelling case for the relational phenomenon that occurs in Black families every day known as "other fathers."[22] Analogous to Patricia Hill Collins's well known depiction of "othermothers," under loss of parental involvement and adverse social and economic circumstances Black male family or community members actively and positively assume responsibility as role model, mentor, protector, and provider to children who are not biologically their own.[23]

*Otherfathers* include grandfathers, brothers, uncles, cousins, fictive kin, in-laws, church and community members, and men in social organizations, such as 100 Black Men, Boys & Girls Club, Big Brother and Big Sister, Black fraternal organizations and so on. The relationships may be of relatively short duration or last for many years. They may be of an instrumental and/or caring nature. They may or may not represent traditional patriarchal patterns. As a social safety net, they are typically multiple in number and fulfill distinct purposes. While not always apparent to the wider public *otherfathers* serve a valuable and real function in Black family and community life. At the same time, these socially assumed (as opposed to biologically determined) roles are not capable of unilaterally transforming negative life circumstances, nor should they. However, these men are an affective, cognitive and motivational presence in a frequently inhospitable world.

Further contrary to popular belief, research has long shown that children in single parent or extended family households, no matter the income, have constant and close contact with men who are *otherfathers* even when and where they are not specifically named.[24] A case in point comes from the life of Howard Thurman, African American

---

W. Merle Longwood, and Mark W. Muesse (Louisville: Westminster John Knox, 1996) 231.

22. Lora Bex Lempert, "Other Fathers: An Alternative Perspective on African American Community Caring," in *The Black Family: Essays and Studies*, ed. Robert Staples (Belmont, CA: Wadsworth, 1999) 189–201.

23. Patricia Hill Collins, *Black Feminist Thought: Knowledge, Consciousness, and the Politics of Empowerment* (Boston: Unwin Hyman, 1990), 119.

24. See, for instance, sociologist Carol Stack's classic work *All Our Kin: Strategies for Survival in a Black Community* (New York: Harper & Row, 1974).

mystic exemplar and ancestral griot, who grew up without his biological father a century ago. Thurman's immediate family consisted of his mother and sisters, and especially "Grandma Nancy." But his life was also shaped by the extended family network of church and community. Church members validated his talents and sensitivities and encouraged their cultivation. In the absence of his father, several men served as elder non-patriarchal males for Thurman, from his two stepfathers to "the stranger in the railroad station in Daytona Beach." The most important of these male influences, however, was a cousin and the family physician. Thurman held both men in deep esteem as "my masculine idols."[25]

Such positive images of responsible male participation more accurately reflect the interdependent nature of much of African American family and community life, now and then, without in any manner diminishing the centrality of women.[26] These versatile family accommodations may also reflect something of the West and Central African inheritance, a creative residuum continuing to provide Black families with a range of adaptive strategies by which to navigate adverse societal conditions.[27] In the end, the focal and fontal credit for Thurman's moral, cognitive, and affective well-being rests with his mother and especially his grandmother.

In an important study on the impact of mothers of successful children, sociologist Charles Willie concluded that regardless of whether African American women were single, married, widowed, the poorest of the poor, the working poor, or middle class, they invested in and supported their children's success by nurturing, providing, and holding them to high occupational and educational expectations.[28] Still, the greater the degree of disparity and disprivilege experienced, the harder it is for Black women to create a secure environment and hospitable future for themselves and their posterity. Once again, it is white supremacist pa-

25. Pollard, "Magnificent Manhood," 222–33.

26. Journalist John W. Fountain recently paid tribute to his maternal grandfather, a contemporary *otherfather*, in *True Vine: A Young Black Man's Journey of Faith, Hope, and Charity* (New York: Public Affairs, 2003).

27. While not the focus of this essay, it is the case that too many African Americans do not know and appreciate their African heritage and cannot draw on it as a primary source of possibility, resistance, and critique. Still others suffer from expressly sentimental and romanticized perspectives on the continent.

28. Charles V. Willie, "The Role of Mothers in the Lives of Outstanding Scholars," *Journal of Family Issues* 5 (1984) 291–306.

triarchal capitalism with its vicious and demonic system of poverty and gross inequalities of access—and not African American female headed households—that has always presented the greatest obstacle to the development of young Black women and men.

The identification of *othermothers* and *otherfathers* in Black communities, those women and men who quietly take on responsibilities for the entire community, who provide nurture and support and strength in the most intractable of situations, should give us pause when considering who and how we love in the context of gayness. There is no one among us who does not have gay relatives or friends. For Black heterosexuals to embrace gayness is to embrace our community in its fullness, inside and outside the home.

When and where the presence of gays is not known it is usually not safe and affirming enough to be openly out. And it is precisely in the unknowing that we are especially apt to hurt and, in turn, to receive hurt. If the Black family is the primary terrain upon which Black women and men struggle for agency and control then heterosexuality has long been the great mythic (true and false) unifier. White male patriarchy serves as the backdrop for much of our existential angst but, once again, it is not the entire story. The sad and painful truth is we have internalized the fictitious yet injurious judgments others have made about us as the pretext for violating and oppressing gays in our own families and communities.

The time has come to divest ourselves of patriarchal behaviors that mark us off from each other in counterproductive ways that separate us by gender and sexuality as kith and kin. Gay and straight, we must be forthright in discussing among ourselves without acrimony our gendered and sexual apprehensions and affirmations in relation to each other. Such a call to decentralize Black patriarchy is marvelously and prophetically envisioned by Jenkins to lead to a "more democratic distribution of kinship ties."[29] In this movement beyond a fictive nuclear centrality, the impact of which has nevertheless been severe, "family becomes an extension and inclusion—anyone who preserves life and its callings becomes a member of the family, whose patterns of kinship and resemblance fall into disguise."[30] Such a micro-meso-macro understand-

---

29. Jenkins, "Queering Black Patriarchy," 973. See also Johnetta Betsch Cole and Beverly Guy-Sheftall, *Gender Talk: The Struggle for Women's Equality in African American Communities* (New York: Ballantine, 2003).

30. Jenkins, "Queering Black Patriarchy," 973.

ing of our new relatedness to each other has profound communal and
public advocacy implications as well.[31]

For Black heterosexual men this will mean relinquishing our will
to dominate and investing instead in emotional vulnerability. It means
becoming the men that we long to be, self-assured in our need to no longer dominate and control. For Black heterosexual women this will mean
the recovery of a radical symmetry between genders and with each other
as well. It means becoming revolutionary womanists joined in struggle
with a generation of "new Black men."[32]

For Black same-and-both-gender-loving women and men, the
inspiring potential exists for partners to be openly lovers and heterosexuals to be sister and brother again. It means speaking truth to power
and in love to Black homophobia and heterosexism. It means reclaim-
ing authentic Black community in positive self-love and respect. For
conscious Black family systems it means learning to communicate in
alternative, loving and life-giving ways across the generations. It means
becoming fully present to and for and with our children and our elders,
whose dignity is threatened and sensibilities are assaulted on a daily basis. Companioning together, women and men as equals, as comrades,
lovers and friends, we can unsettle the present, and enter the darkly
radiant future, a self-determined people, embracing our wholeness. We
will not let the principalities and powers of patriarchy come between us
any more. We must dismantle patriarchy. Our ancestors, our children, we
ourselves, deserve no less.

31. So understood, families are part of a broader relational system incorporating
neighborhood, community, civic, and voluntary associations (including religious bodies), state, national, and global entities.

32. Mark Anthony Neal, *New Black Man* (New York: Routledge, 2005); and Dwight
N. Hopkins, *Heart and Head: Black Theology, Past, Present and Future* (New York:
Palgrave, 2002) 91–105.

## PART THREE

# Jesus Man, Christ Woman

# 9

## Forging Community and *Communitas*

### *Toward a De-Masculinization of Christology in Black Churches*

KERI DAY HARRISON

A S AN AFRICAN-AMERICAN FEMALE scholar and minister squarely situated within the academy and Pentecostal Black church (Church of God in Christ or COGIC), I am constantly compelled to reflect upon my vocation and call. My liberative longings for a Black church community called to "love unto freedom" both women and men has claimed me, and this love for all humanity propels me forward to speak truthfully and with integrity in every scholarly pursuit, sermon, and conversation. However, the Black church is still plagued with a number of issues, one issue being its sexist treatment of women who continue to unflinchingly serve the church with a wholehearted fidelity. I experience a liminal existence in the Black church in which I am informally acknowledged and "turned loose" to explore my call as a minister while denied formal recognition of my call and barred from occupying the highest levels of leadership, even at the expense of the church's well-being and growth. Consequently, the Black church[1] is at a crossroads, deciding which path

1. In using the "Black church," I do not seek to negate the plurality of *Black churches*. I do not wish to suggest that the Black church is a monolith or homogenous entity. Rather, I speak of the Black church in order to invoke a historical narrative about racism that necessitated the Black church experience and its subsequent cry for liberation and freedom. This Black church experience and its goal for liberation of all oppressed people is invoked and remembered as the needed standard for the Black church experiences of today.

it will take—will the church remain true to its mission and identity of justice and liberation for all oppressed people or will it retreat and acquiesce to the hypocritical impulses of oppression? Moreover, how will Black scholars in the academy encourage or inhibit an agenda of liberation that forges true community and *communitas, communitas* defined as the intersubjective experience of all members that cause them to think and act liberatively as *one body*? Which way forward will the church and academy choose?

In particular, gender oppression in the Black church has been my unique experience, and this sexism has been bolstered in part by a distorted Christology that emphasizes and divinizes "Jesus as man." Much Christology within the Black church explicates and lifts up the "manhood" or maleness of Jesus, tacitly according maleness a divine status. For example, as a female "minister"[2] in COGIC, I was told that I could not possibly be called to pastor because pastors and apostles were men, picked by Jesus himself who happened to be male also. Moreover, biblical literalists quoted the famous Titus 1:6 passage to me, which posits that a pastor must be the husband of one wife, which unequivocally excludes me from this call. Therefore, the underlying assumption of this conversation was if I could just be male, I could be more like Jesus and his male apostles, which would make me worthy of the pastorate. In other words, maleness secures privilege and power before the presence of God as God determines who will pastor and who will not. If maleness becomes the norm by which one's calling is defined, how then do I define my calling before God as a woman? If maleness accords full humanity, then how is my full humanity affirmed before God as a female?

This experience of gender oppression in the church that I love— a church that has nurtured, sustained, supported, and reminded me of who and whose I was—threw me into cognitive dissonance. I loved my tradition of nurture yet felt violated by this tradition because of its salient ability to preach truth and justice but stop short of this message

2. The title "minister" is defined strictly in male terms within COGIC being applied to men solely, appropriating such titles to women as "missionary," evangelist," or "deaconess." Naming myself as "minister" is not only an act to challenge the institutional interpretation of minister as male but also an act to disclose the ambiguity that surrounds this title in which women are not officially acknowledged as ministers in COGIC but discharge all the duties of a minister. Moreover, churches such as Cathedral of Praise (COGIC) subversively acknowledge women as minister, although COGIC as a denomination does not acknowledge women as ministers.

with its chauvinistic treatment toward women. This experience caused me to reflect upon the type of Christological conceptions that continue to reinforce sexist behaviors and practices within the Black church, thwarting all meaningful, liberative, and life-giving understandings that include the full humanity of both men *and* women. Moreover, this experience compels me to ask what I am required to *do* as a Black scholar in the academy and church to help encourage a more egalitarian vision of gendered relations within the Black church.

## BLACK THEOLOGY AND WOMANIST THEOLOGY: PROBLEMATIZING JESUS AS MAN

While Black theology detailed the liberative effects of Jesus's message and ministry for all oppressed people, Black theology initially did not deal with the problem of sexism within theology and the Black church. In particular, Black theology did not address the problems of emphasizing the manhood or maleness of Jesus, which partly engendered sexist beliefs and behaviors within the Black church and community. The centrality of Jesus's maleness translated into maleness as more divine, reflecting sexist inclinations in doctrine and subsequent practices. Consequently, this relative absence of giving attention to sexist oppression in Black theological analysis caused womanist scholars to raise their voices in a concerted effort in order to disclose and *name* sexism as sin within the Black church.

The naming of sexism as sin underscored the oppressive nature of sexism that not only creates injustice for Black women but also adversely impacts the community as a whole. Sexism not only distorts the identities of women but also obscures the identities of men. Marcia Riggs refers to the adverse effects sexism and patriarchy have upon Black men, forcing men to assume overly masculine roles in order to be viewed as men: "masculinity tends to encourage 'traits of aggressiveness, violence, competitiveness, heterosexuality, cool poses, dominance, sexism, and passivity/indifference . . . When socialization [of black men] into this masculinity occurs, black male identity is contradictory and conflictual . . ."[3] Riggs's analysis suggests that patriarchy and sexism create notions of masculinity which impede men's capacity to mature into empowered *human beings* instead of socially constructed beings. If sexism is both

3. Marcia Riggs, *Plenty Good Room* (Cleveland: Pilgrim, 2003) 50.

violence and violation of women's bodily integrity, humanity, and capacity for full self-hood, sexism is also the distortion of male humanity.[4] Sexism within the Black church distorts *humanity*, which not only
inhibits liberation for women but also obstructs genuine liberation for
men. Naming sexism as oppression of women and men within the Black
church and community engendered an agenda that situated sexism
alongside racism, inaugurating a *holistic talk* of liberation that aimed and
still aims at unshackling the chains placed upon *all* oppressed people.

For Black women, the relationship between oppression and theological images and symbols remains important in defining liberation for
Black women.[5] The symbol of Jesus as man is such a symbol that has
been used to undermine and oppress women, indicating maleness as
more closely associated with the divine. In addition, Jesus's maleness has
symbolized the importance of "divinely ordered male leadership," which
subordinates women to men. As a result of this privileging of maleness,
the man is declared the most perfect human representative of God to the
church and family. This oppression of Black women through privileging
the maleness of Jesus has become an inadequate symbol in affirming the
divine in women when reflecting on their identity and call.

Sojourner Truth, a harbinger of civil rights for Blacks and women,
confronts the problem of prioritizing the maleness of Jesus: "Then that
little man in the black there, he says women can't have as much rights as
men, 'cause Christ wasn't a woman! Where did your Christ come from?
Where did your Christ come from? From God and a woman. Man had
nothing to do with him."[6] Sojourner recognizes that the ontological status of Jesus is an issue of rights and power for men. If Jesus's maleness
was of paramount importance, the role and status of women are judged
by this male norm, subjugating women in family and social structures as
well as ecclesial practices. Jesus's maleness establishes a hierarchal model
of gender relations and secures male privilege and power at the top of
this hierarchy. As a result, women live inside of a male system with a
male Jesus that refuses to affirm the full humanity of women.

4. Rosemary Radford Ruether, *Sexism and God-talk* (Boston: Beacon, 1983) 178.

5. Jacquelyn Grant, *White Women's Christ and Black Women's Jesus* (Atlanta:
Scholars, 1989) 219.

6. Sojourner Truth, "Aint I A Woman," in *Feminism: The Essential Historical Writings*,
ed. Miriam Schneir (New York: Vintage) 94.

However, the particularity of Jesus's maleness can be privileged in a way that is liberative for women and men. Highlighting Jesus's actions of liberation towards men and women causes Jesus maleness to become important and paradigmatic of how men enter into relationships and community with women, taking the full humanity of women into account and affirming their human identity before the divine. Hence, Jesus's maleness can be interpreted in a constructive light, enabling and empowering men to recognize the full divinity and humanity in women as equal members within our human community. As a result, the way in which Jesus embodies his maleness becomes paradigmatic for men's actions, actions defined by mutuality, reciprocity, and solidarity towards women.

Yet, because Jesus's maleness has been used to subordinate women rather than liberate women towards equality and freedom, womanist scholars have raised questions to male theologians (Black and white) concerning the maleness of Jesus. Jacquelyn Grant's *White Women's Christ and Black Women's Jesus* introduces an egalitarian Christology by reviewing the problem of Jesus as man. "Even our sisters, the womanists of the past . . . had some suspicions about the effects of a male image of the divine, for they did challenge the oppressive and distorted use of it in the church's theology. In doing so, they were able to move from a traditional oppressive Christology, with respect to women, to an egalitarian Christology."[7] Grant posits that emphasizing the maleness of Jesus has been insufficient for the liberation of women because this oppressive Christology accords maleness divine status and insures access and maintenance of male group privilege.[8] This focus on the maleness of Jesus has led to the masculinization of Christology or interpreting Jesus as "masculine," which suggests that Jesus is principally defined by socially constructed notions of maleness, making women secondary in notions of divinity and church life. *As a result, the masculinization of Jesus translates into a masculinization of Black churches, which has led to broken and wounded communities that have not promoted full inclusion of women.*

---

7. Jacquelyn Grant, *White Women's Christ and Black Women's Jesus: Feminist Christology and Womanist Response*, American Academy of Religion Academy Series 64 (Atlanta: Scholars, 1989) 219.

8. Ibid., 221.

Moreover, Grant posits that the symbol "Jesus the man" is part of a larger dilemma of masculine language and imagery in the church that has oppressed women.[9] Traditional articulated theologies within the Black church have promoted masculine imagery of God, Jesus, and the Holy Spirit that has vitiated attempts in fashioning new imagery that identifies and affirms women as equally worthy before the divine. Speaking of God as mother and father have been new ways of envisaging the divine for women, but Black churches remain relatively hostile to new language surrounding the divine. As a result, an impasse is experienced in which "traditional believing" men and women in the church are not willing to be more inclusive and concede power while progressive women justifiably remain unwilling to submit to oppressive structures that do not affirm their divine identity. Similarly, an impasse is experienced in the Black church when prioritizing the maleness of Jesus, which has led womanist scholars and practitioners to promote a more equalitarian Christology that commits to prioritizing one aspect of Jesus that is most liberating for all oppressed people: Jesus's *humanity*.

## JESUS AS HUMAN, INCARNATION AS DEPARTURE POINT

Although Grant acknowledges that traditional oppressive Christology still pervades the church, she also offers a prescriptive analysis in how to reinterpret Jesus in light of liberation. This prescriptive analysis focuses on Jesus as *human* as a way to posit a liberation that includes both men and women as equal before the divine. When Jesus as human becomes the norm by which men and women are described, liberative attitudes and actions of equality can emerge within the Black church and Black community, rendering Black churches as *sites of nurture instead of sites of oppression*.

However, the incarnation can be one departure point from which Jesus's humanity can be fully understood. Grant poses some questions: Was Jesus merely a man of Nazareth? Or was it that the incarnation was made manifest in a broader *hu-man* who happened to be male but representing all humanity?[10] From the perspective of Black theology, the incarnation details God's profound and gracious act of solidarity in which

9. Ibid., 219.

10. Ibid., 185.

ⁿⁿ Oology

God deliberately chose to become human in order to not only identify with the suffering of the oppressed but also inaugurate in a liberation that would free the oppressed from their suffering or captivity. Hence, the incarnation reveals God coming into solidarity with the oppressed through Jesus's humanity which groans with all humans in expectation of liberation and deliverance. These incarnational moments disclose one meaning of Jesus as human, coming into solidarity with the oppressed in order to accord humanity equal status and worth before the divine with a promise of liberation. Because the incarnation can be a departure point in constructing an interpretation of Jesus, Jesus's maleness becomes peripheral and less significant. Through the incarnation, Jesus as human becomes the epicenter of Christian reality and resurrects both men and women as equally loved and called before God.

It is important to note that Jesus as human is not advocating an androgynous Jesus. An androgynous Jesus is a Jesus that possesses both feminine and masculine psychological traits, freeing him from the confines of maleness. However, the problem with androgyny is that it presupposes the masculine/feminine binary—it assumes all kind of stereotypical, social traits that have traditionally defined what it means to be woman and man. Moreover, to suggest an androgynous Jesus is to imply that Jesus was limited by the cultural norms of masculinity and femininity. As a result, Jesus as human does not identify with an androgynous Jesus but recognizes that Jesus identifies and accords equal worth to all humanity through his humanness.

Jesus as human also overturns social hierarchy and establishes a new vision of mutual and reciprocal social relations. Jesus as male ensures a social hierarchy that privileges male power at the expense of female powerlessness. However, Jesus's humanity and liberative acts are a "reversal of a male-oriented social order that does not merely turn the hierarchy upside-down but aims at a new social reality characterized by mutuality and reciprocity that overwhelms dominating and hierarchal impulses."[11] Jesus aims towards a new humanity, male and female. Jesus as human (or person) represents a *kenosis* of sexist, patriarchal ways of being and doing,[12] emptying out of society (including church communities) sexist pronouncements that deny Black women their full human-

---

11. Rosemary Radford Ruether, *Sexism and God-talk: Towards a Feminist Theology* (Boston: Beacon, 1983) 178.

12. Ibid.

ity in order to announce a new humanity that dismisses and discards a "hierarchal caste system of privilege and patriarchy."[13]

Jesus as human de-masculinizes Christology and the Black church because it causes both doctrine and institutional practices to affirm the divine in men, women, the poor, the hungry, and the outcast—in short, all marginalized groups. The de-masculinization of Christology within Black churches will hold Jesus's maleness as accidental to Jesus's identity, avoiding equivocation between maleness and Jesus, masculine and the divine. Jesus's humanity will create new possibilities for marginalized people inside the Black church and will produce new visions of egalitarian relations between all of God's children.

## WHERE DO WE GO FROM HERE? THE PROPHETIC WITNESS OF THE BLACK CHURCH AND BLACK ACADEMIA

How will the Black church participate in the de-masculinization of Christology? How will Black churches respond to the cry for equality by the marginalized within its community, one group being women? Moreover, how will Black scholarship stay connected to the Black church in order to remind the church of its prophetic witness to the world, defending "the least of these"?

Foremost, the church and academy must remain committed to dialogue to avoid pathologizing each other. There is proclivity that these two institutions have towards each other: the church sees the academy as liberal, morally loose, and spiritually destitute while the academy sees the church as discriminatory, traditional at the expense of justice, and dogmatic. As a result, these stereotypical ideas often stifle dialogue and action between the church and academy. However, dialogue removes assumptions of the church and academy that often inhibit moments of mutual understanding that make transformation and justice possible.

Black clergy leaders and Black scholars in the church and academy respectively must see themselves as *organically* related to each other. This organic relation between the academy and church is important because isolation, separation, and division have marked relations between these two institutions for far too long. emilie townes describes the profound dilemma between the church and academy:

13. Ibid.

> It is as though we in the academy and we in the church are ships
> passing in the night and we are not even looking for one another
> . . . We must repeat kindergarten and nursery school over again
> and practice sharing. We must reject the deadly dualism we have
> adopted—that you are either a thinker or a doer. The reality is
> most of us are both and all of us need to learn how to do both
> better and more faithfully.[14]

The academy and church are not antithetical to each other but constitute
a larger prophetic witness that faithfully seeks—through thought and
action—to restore justice and peace to the oppressed, downtrodden, ex-
ploited, browbeaten, subjugated, downcast, broken, demoralized, humiliated, dispirited, dispossessed, and dominated. This prophetic voice calls
upon the oppressed to "stand between reality and hope" in order to fight
hopelessness and resignation with a righteous indignation. The reality
of liberation can only be achieved through the *whole*, the whole being
both the academy and the church. Hence, faithful dialogue consecrated
towards justice and liberation must not be seen as charitable—scholars
and clergy leaders must not see their involvement in dialogue and action
as acts of kindness or peripheral to their Christian witness.

Instead, this dialogue must be seen as intrinsic to their Christian
witness—the church and academy stand together to "love thy neighbor
as thyself"[15] which will enable the church to prioritize Jesus as human in
their theological doctrines in efforts to participate in the de-masculinization of Black churches. Both men and women will be fully affirmed
before God in ecclesial thought and practice, birthing greater equality
and equity in churches. This process of de-masculinization can only be
started and maintained when the church and academy see themselves as
organically related to each other, both constituting a prophetic witness
that remains committed to liberation for all.

Second, the church must *re-member* the moral courage of its past.
The Black church can only continue to be a transformational agent if it
re-commits to the type of moral courage needed to challenge oppressive structures. The process of gathering in those liberative attitudes
and actions that have promoted social justice in the Black church and
wider society is an act of remembering the past and *re-membering* the

14. Emile Townes, "On Keeping Faith with the Center," in *Living Stones in the
Household of God* (Minneapolis: Fortress, 2004) 201.

15. Mark 12:33 (KJV).

dismembered parts (faith, truth, hope, love) of moral courage. When moral courage is being embraced and embodied by the Black church— a moral courage that unabashedly stands for equality and wholeness for all people—the Black church will reflect the vision of its earlier, nascent mission: justice. Black clergy leaders will have the moral courage to defy and overturn sexism within their local assemblies at the expense of money and popularity. Moral courage was the greatest virtue the Black church possessed at its formative stage and this courage establishes and drives internal reflection and critique of existing relations within the church and society.

Third, Black religious scholars must continue to ground their work in *experiences*, not abstractions. If the Black community is the starting point of Black and Womanist theology, Black and Womanist theology must include experiences related to Black people's oppression. When Black scholars maintain their presence within the church and speak from multiple Black experiences, Black and Womanist theological scholarship will speak authentically and appreciatively yet self-critically of the church's beliefs and practices as the church seeks to secure social justice for all people. When scholarship remains committed to the real-lived texture of Black experiences (the Black church being only *one* repository of Black experiences), the dilemma of irrelevancy that theory and abstractions engender will not be present. Black scholarship must "make room" for the Black church and its myriad experiences expressed among its members.

Yet, the Black church must be willing to "make room" for Black scholarship. Cone asserts that the church must be committed to nurturing a critical and prophetic theology—the church must embrace the *life of the mind* as it listens to what the spirit is saying.[16] Cone states, "The Black church suffers from a lack of intellectually accomplished and spiritually committed scholars who feel as deeply the need to understand the faith as preachers do to proclaim it."[17] The church must not make one feel like one must choose to be a scholar *or* a preacher. Black and Womanist theological scholarship is about constructing our theological, social, and political conceptions from a liberative theology which plants the spirit of liberation in our hearts, minds, and souls (individually and

16. James H. Cone, "Loving God with Our Heart, Soul, and Mind," in *Blow the Trumpet in Zion* (Minneapolis: Fortress, 2005) 60.

17. Ibid.

communally), creating freedom and life for us all. Partly through Black scholarship, the Black church will recognize the import of egalitarian Christology that affirms the wholeness of both men and women, which enables and empowers the church to commit to equality for all its members. Hence, the Black church must recognize the value of Black scholarship: it provides ways of *understanding* this spirit of liberation that works in our midst to free every captive and restore sight to the blind.

When the church and academy recognize and embrace their symbiotic relationship, traditional oppressive Christology will transform into egalitarian Christology. The humanity of Jesus will become the cornerstone of the Christian witness and call rather than Jesus's maleness or manhood. Jesus as human will be one departure point in grasping the identity and worth of both men and women before the divine, renewing community and *communitas*—the Black church will be able to think, feel, and act in the name of liberation as *one body*. Consequently, the human experience as seen through Jesus's incarnational gesture will stand at the center of the Christian experience, compelling men and women within the church to love greater in order to live life more fully. Moreover, Black religious scholarship must continue to make the church appreciative but self-critical of its own theological postulates and practices, and the church must supply the academy with the heartbeat of inspired, transformational information, being Black people's experiences. The de-masculinization of Christology within the Black church does not answer all problems that plague the church but does suggest, in part, the conditions and possibilities under which transformation can occur, ushering in hope and faith that marches on towards freedom for all—especially the least of these.

## 10

# Christ As Womanist

MICHAEL JOSEPH BROWN

BIBLICAL STUDIES AS AN academic discipline has cultivated an aura of objectivity surrounding its methods and pronouncements.[1] Although most biblical scholars would tell you that such an impression is an overstatement, as an appraisal it is not without some merit. Biblical scholarship in the historical critical mode has always sought to be value neutral. Neutrality, or better disinterestedness, is supposed to be the hallmark of scientific investigation. We cannot be concerned, it is supposed, with the possible implications or outcomes of our work. Such a view is individualistic and imperialist, however. /

All members of the community, wherever they live or whatever they do, make decisions that bear on the welfare of the rest of the community. Biblical scholarship has fostered a great deal of innovation in our understanding of the Bible. This should not be denied. Without it, we might not be in this advantageous position of focusing a critical lens on sacred Scripture. Nevertheless, a misguided notion of neutrality grounded in an Enlightenment conception of the universe has cultivated a pattern of less than benign neglect among biblical scholars. This point was made

1. *Author's note:* I would like to thank the editors, Dwight and Linda, for their gracious invitation to participate. I am humbled that they would invite a biblical scholar to participate in a gathering that is normally confined to theologians, ethicists, pastors, and sociologists of religion. I am also somewhat reticent since I used to occupy these halls at the University of Chicago Divinity School. It feels odd to lecture those who once lectured me. I hope the statement in the Gospels is not universally valid: "no prophet is accepted in the prophet's home town" (Luke 4:24). Finally, and most importantly, I am excited at the prospect of addressing a glaring deficiency in biblical studies.

quite forcefully a few years ago by Daniel Patte, who wrote, "[Biblical scholars] must assume the responsibility for the negative effects upon many people whom our critical studies of the Bible marginalize(d) and help(ed) to oppress, however unintentionally."

Recent biblical scholarship is just beginning to respond to the critiques of marginalized individuals. This is due in large part to the steady growth in the number of women, African Americans, Asians, Hispanics, and others in the guild of biblical studies over the last twenty or so years. This growing internal critique notwithstanding, external constituencies have yet to see in large measure biblical scholars making a concerted effort to incorporate larger ethical concerns into their work. I hope what I say today may contribute to this growing trend.

I would like to revise my topic somewhat. Instead of Christ as woman, I would like to address more specifically the idea of Christ as *womanist*. I do this because I believe it highlights the central concerns of this edited book more directly. More importantly, I do this because I think that to speak of Christ as woman is to include, by necessity, the concerns of various women about which I am not prepared to speak.

In my understanding, there are several salient themes that pervade the womanist theological enterprise. These include: survival, interconnectedness or mutuality, and the exposure of ideology in its various forms. I would like to explore two of these briefly as they appear in selections from the Gospel of Matthew. Of course, some would argue that the privileging of these themes in the Gospel does violence to the overall theological message intended by its writer. This may be true. I would argue, however, that these themes are present nevertheless; and that the purpose behind the author's theological message was to equip his readers and hearers to confront contemporary social situations. Since some of their concerns were not our concerns—and we too read this text in order to confront contemporary social situations—it seems fruitless to impose first-century concerns on twenty-first-century readers. What does seem to be advantageous is to investigate the intersections between our concerns. In other words, what I offer in this womanist reading of Christ in the Gospel of Matthew is, in truth, a brief investigation of the places where early Christian concerns intersect with contemporary African American concerns.

## THE REALITY OF SURVIVAL (MATTHEW 1:1–25)

Traditional biblical scholarship has maintained that Matthew provides this genealogy of Jesus as a means of securing his authenticity as the Davidic messiah. Patterning his style after that found in Genesis 5:1 (LXX), the evangelist lays out what appears to be a complex and comprehensive messianic pedigree. More than that, Matthew wants to make clear to the reader that in outlining the family history of Jesus we are talking about the ongoing influence of the past on the present. Jesus is who he is because of who his ancestors were. We are led to believe that what marks the messiah is a distinguished family history. In earlier days, people might have said that Jesus comes from "people like us."

Matthew identifies Jesus as an heir of David, and thus the Lord's promised messiah. This is odd, however, because in Mark 12:35–37, a gospel Matthew consulted in writing his own, Jesus questions the idea that the messiah must be a descendant of David. We must ask, then, does Matthew have something else in mind by presenting this family history to his readers?

Matthew connects Jesus to the Old Testament covenants made with Abraham and David (see Genesis 12:1–3; 17:1–8; 2 Samuel 7:12–17). The importance of this highlighted when we compare Matthew to Paul, who emphasizes Jesus's connection to Abraham repeatedly but not David, except in Romans 1:3. It raises the question of authenticity or better legitimacy for us as readers. Why would it be important to Matthew that the messiah come from a legitimate and verifiable bloodline?

In the recent past, those involved with social empowerment movements in the African American community were often fond of saying, "We were kings and queens." This was meant to emphasize the honorable, even venerable, bloodline that runs through the veins of contemporary African Americans. We have survived, it presumed, because we came from the best Africa had to offer. Although empowering in many ways, this idea is also very dangerous. It smacks of a social Darwinism ("the survival of the fittest") that only attempts to play the same game white Westerners have been playing on Africans in America for centuries.

One of the widespread justifications for slavery was the superiority of Europeans and their descendants to the Africans whom they enslaved. Many saw it as their religious duty to civilize these so-called uncivilized Africans. Even after the end of slavery, many believed themselves to be superior to their former captives. The ugly history of Jim Crow is a shining example of what happens when one group believes that biology confers superiority. Although it is no longer legal, social Darwinism still exists. Are we as readers to believe that Matthew wants us to accept the idea that what makes Jesus the legitimate messiah is that he comes from the right bloodline?

Matthew is an author full of surprises. He leads his readers toward ideas and ways of thinking that he then shows to be wrong. This becomes evident in his continuation of the genealogy of Jesus. The next four verses challenge the idea that Jesus is the messiah because he comes from a superior bloodline (1:3–6). Matthew includes in his genealogy the names of women. To the reader, the inclusion of females in a Jewish genealogy should be puzzling. An examination of the Old Testament demonstrates clearly that legitimate lineage for the ancient Israelites came through the father.

Matthew makes clear that the birth of Perez and Zerah occurred because of the coupling of Judah and Tamar (1:3; see for background Genesis 38:1–30). This incident should disturb the reader for several reasons. First, Tamar is not an Israelite, at least as far as we can tell. Second, Tamar is not Judah's wife, but his daughter-in-law. Third, the event challenges our idea of how families should operate because the story is full of deception and inappropriate sexual interaction that cannot fit with our idealized model of biblical families, an ideology that attempts to convince some that their lives are not worth living.

Matthew goes on to name Rahab, Ruth, and Bathsheba ("the wife of Uriah") as among the ancestors of Jesus (1:5–6). Although the inclusion of Rahab presents a clear historical problem for the reader, since she belongs to the time of Joshua, Matthew's theological point becomes clearer as we reflect upon the significance of these women. Each one is of questionable social and ethnic background, which highlights the interesting mix of Israelites and foreigners, individuals of unquestioned and questionable backgrounds, in the family history of Jesus. In this sense, what Matthew presents in this genealogy affirms what Kelly Brown Douglas maintained about womanist theology, "Not only has Black women's experience been characterized by their complex and determined struggle for freedom, but most significantly by their ability to survive with dignity in spite of demeaning social-historical circumstances, and their extraordinary commitment to the survival of their families."

Jesus does not descend only from a distinguished bloodline full of kings and queens. He also comes from people who were outsiders, persons of questionable character and practice, according to the prevailing social structures of the day. Even the patriarchs and kings in Jesus's bloodline are not above reproach (e.g., Judah and King David). In fact, the grouping of the generations into sets of fourteen is flawed (1:17). If one counts the number of generations named by Matthew, they actually amount to sets of fourteen, fourteen, and thirteen. Even if we restored King Jehoiakim to his rightful replace in the genealogy, it would give us the needed forty-two names, but only in sets of fourteen, fifteen, and thirteen.

Matthew's genealogy challenges any idea of "the survival of the fittest," with one that more reflects what womanists call a "spirituality of survival." The evangelist's genealogy is not the record of "the survival of the fittest," it is the record of "the survival of the survivors," one that affirms the presence of God in the day-to-day struggle for survival." Matthew highlights this idea forcefully in his account of the events surrounding the birth of Jesus.

Unlike Luke, Matthew does not describe the birth of Jesus. He focuses instead on the events leading up to the birth (1:18–25). Mary's pregnancy calls into question her legitimacy as a wife for Joseph, who is described as a righteous man (1:19). She is in the same dangerous position that threatened Joseph's ancestor, Tamar. Although Joseph's compassion prevents Mary from being put to death for this scandal, his decision to divorce her raises sharply the issue of legitimacy that runs through this family history. The angel's appearance to Joseph helps him see that God's purpose are advanced not only by those considered the "fittest," but also by those who find themselves in the position of needing to survive (1:20–21). In fact, one could say that the salvation of the world depended upon and was advanced by the determination, not to triumph, but to survive.

## THE NECESSITY OF MUTUALITY (MATTHEW 18:23–35)

The parable of the unmerciful slave has long been troublesome for exegetes and theologians alike. It resides in a section of the Gospel concerned with how individuals treat one another, especially in the church. More specifically, it is Jesus's response to Peter's query, "Lord, if my brother sins against me, how often should I forgive?" (18:21)

The idea of a king or official settling accounts often points to an eschatological context, which would imply that what is outlined in this story is redolent of eternal significance. Such an implication challenges our almost nonchalant practice of forgiveness. More importantly, it points to the interconnected and social nature of existence as such.

This story, at its most basic level, is one about the economic experience of indebtedness. As a phenomenon of human existence in antiquity, indebtedness was not a neutral matter. The consequences of indebtedness could include the loss of property, family, earning potential, freedom of movement, status and honor. In short, indebtedness limited an individual's ability to actualize her existence. The remission of debt meant the restoration of an individual's ability to maintain his standing in the social order, and potentially to improve it. Keeping people in debt, therefore, meant the diminishment of an individual's life chances.

Debt is a phenomenon that serves to emphasize the fundamental social nature of all existence as such. In the Roman mind, for example, a debt was created whenever two individuals decided in good faith (*bona fides*) to create a relationship in which one individual gives to another who receives. Social scientists characterize the specific social context in which Greco-Romans accumulated and discharged their debts as one of generalized reciprocity. The commodity involved in the creation of this relationship could be financial, material, or social. Although the presumption underlying this relationship may be the mutual benefit of the persons involved, the constant accumulation of debt undoubtedly meant the social and material superiority of some over others. In addition, the continuation of this superiority over time creates a social situation that is (potentially) unjust. The injustice lies not in the debt itself, which is presumably a transaction of mutual benefit, but in its inability to be discharged successfully.

One of the often-overlooked aspects of this parable is its implication that forgiveness is an act that affects more than just individuals. As a moral practice, it has the potential to influence the nature of justice in human relationships. The parable of the unmerciful slave highlights the idea that life, as we experience it, should be understood as interconnected. The slave who had been forgiven a tremendous sum is subsequently thrown in prison and tortured because of his refusal to forgive another slave for a relatively minor debt. In a traditional ethical approach, it would have been the king's prerogative to forgive the slave's enormous debt. It was also the slave's prerogative not to forgive the debt owed him by a fellow slave. An ethical structure that places primary importance on obligation (and the adjudication of matters between two individuals) would view these two instances as logically separate (e.g., deontological ethics). Each individual had the right to demand or remit payment as he saw fit. The outcome of one should not have had an effect on the outcome of the other. And yet, this is an ethical model that the parable undercuts. Ulrich Luz highlights this when he says, "The kind of behavior that was ordinarily taken for granted becomes intolerable in the light of God's overpowering forgiveness." According to the parable, the remission of the slave's debt should have influenced his subsequent determination of what was just behavior in his dealings with others. It was not a simple matter between two individuals.

The reader recognized the social nature of forgiveness in this parable almost instinctively. Although she may not be able to articulate it initially, she recognizes that there is something unjust in how the forgiven slave interacts with his fellow slave. In the parable, this perspective is represented by other slaves, who were outraged and informed the king of the forgiven slave's actions (18:31). The forgiven slave's behavior subsequent to the king's action had a deleterious effect on his standing and relationships in the community. Likewise, by throwing his fellow slave in prison, he disrupted that slave's ability to maintain his social and material relationships—something the forgiven slave was trying to avoid in his own pleading with the king. In short, the communal ramifications that followed the forgiven slave's actions highlight the larger social context in which the act of forgiveness takes place. By negative example, the reader is led to understand that forgiveness, like indebtedness, is not a private matter between two individuals.

It would be simplistic to read the parable from Matthew 18 and conclude that it can be reduced to some sort of Kantian ethical imperative. In fact, the parable lures the reader away from such a conclusion toward an understanding that ethical actions take place within a wider and richer social context. Another example of such a proposition can be found in the "parable of the unjust steward" (Luke 16:1–9). In this case, the narrative directly challenges conventional moral norms—again around the issue of debt.

According to the parable, a manager is charged with squandering his master's property. The master resolves to dismiss him. As a result, the manager conceives of a plan that will rescue him from destitution. He calls his master's debtors together and instructs them to take their bills and decrease the amount of their debts. The subsequent response strikes the reader as odd. The master praises the manager for his ingenuity: "And his master commended the dishonest manager because he had acted shrewdly" (16:8). In other words, the manager used the indebtedness experienced by others to strengthen his own social (and material) relationships. In remitting their debts to his master, the manager created a relationship to the debtors that mutually enhanced their social situations: "And I tell you, most friends for yourselves by means of dishonest wealth so that when it is gone, they may welcome you into the eternal homes" (16:9).

In Matthew and Luke, the reader is confronted with acts of forgiveness that support the premise that all human beings are socially interconnected, and that oppression, as well as liberation, is only understood properly with a context of mutuality. As Renita Weems makes clear, "[As] human beings we are all mutually connected to each other and dependent upon one another for our emancipation and for our survival." Norms of social interaction that maintain the dominance of some over others, or that liberate some to the detriment of others, are to be renounced as immoral and inconsistent with the divine character.

As a matter of course, obligation, broadly understood, has the potential to limit human freedom and development. When that is perceived as debt, the accumulation of debts, especially over time, perverts the actualization of human existence as such. This constant threat to one's social and material relationships partially determines and steadily influences one's future agency. The parable of the unmerciful slave represents a realization that all persons need release from the chains of obligation that oppress them. Likewise, the parable illustrates how human activity and social institutions are interconnected. Although the parable undermines the traditional Protestant conception of grace, it does signify graciousness in that it demands that responsible human action, whether individual or corporate, include an "adequate awareness of the value of others." As a moral practice, this ethic of mutuality recognizes the ability of an individual's actions to influence the larger social structures and their continuing self-formation that defines the serially ordered experience of events known as society as such. In this specific instance, forgiveness reintroduces the possibility of freedom into the social order.

Its denial only perpetuates injustice and oppression, something that will not be tolerated by God. In short, the parable affirms the fundamental and ontological reality that to be human means to be related to and dependent upon others.

In sum, I believe a womanist reading of the New Testament, particularly the Gospels, holds promise for the future of the church as it struggles with issues of survival and liberation, particularity and universality, inclusiveness, mutuality, and grace. To a large extent, at least from my reading of traditional Protestant theology, structures of oppressiveness that plague the church have been "built in" as a matter of course. Take, for example, the two texts I have highlighted today. To continue to maintain that the New Testament somehow purports to present a messiah that descends from an impeccable pedigree is to say that we can have no meaningful connection to Jesus in that regard. All of us come from family lines that dispute and undercut any supremacist claim that we come from a superior class of people. For ideological reasons, individuals have continued to push the idea that Jesus came from a family line that was above reproach, telling the rest of us by implication that our lives are somehow unworthy. Likewise, troublesome parables like that found in Matthew 18 challenge the mistaken idea that grace is a transaction that occurs solely between the individual and God and thus has no larger social import. More importantly, this traditional concept of grace excuses us from taking seriously the challenge of social justice that the parable highlights. It is not enough that God has forgiven us, we must live and act out that forgiveness in ways that make it meaningful. Without an ethic of mutuality we cannot truly understand how to be the church, whether Black or otherwise, in a world where the masses continue to writhe "silently under a mighty wrong."

# 11

# Christ as a Woman—A Hope for the Church

## J. Alfred Smith Sr.

THE PURPOSE OF THIS chapter is to unpack the notion of "Christ as a Woman—A Hope for the Church." Before proceeding to that task, it is helpful for my argument to foreground my social location. I am the senior pastor of the historic Allen Temple Baptist Church in Oakland, California. I was installed on February 21, 1971. In 1948, I announced my call to preach in the Christian ministry. Past national president of the Progressive National Baptist Convention, and a past president of the American Baptist Churches of the West, I was one of *Ebony Magazine*'s "most influential Black Americans" for two years in a row, and was among the magazine's "Top 15 Greatest Black Preachers of 1993." I have fought for the poor and oppressed my entire adult life as a leader in the Christian ministry. In that sense I, and many other Black churches across the nation whom the mainstream media refuses to recognize, have been doing (and continue to do) Black theology in the church and the community.[1]

Moreover, women preach from the pulpit at Allen Temple. I ordain them as ministers. So we welcome womanist theology because it helps us make sense of Black women's role and leadership in church and society. As a local and national Black Baptist church leader and elder, I welcome the second generation of Black and womanist theologians who continue to demonstrate that faith and the church without scholarship

---

1. See my autobiography, J. Albert Smith Sr., *On the Jericho Road: A Memoir of Racial Justice, Social Action and Prophetic Ministry* (Downers Grove, IL: InterVarsity, 2004).

tend toward empty "hooping."[2] And the academic professors separate from the Black church have a whole lot of learning but no "burning." Yet, younger voices are developing a wholistic approach. For instance, Linda E. Thomas, a second-generation womanist, combines her publications with anthropological research on everyday living, Black church women. And Dwight N. Hopkins was a member of Allen Temple Baptist Church when he taught full-time at Santa Clara University (Santa Clara, California), was an adjunct professor of systematic theology at the Pacific School of Religion (Berkeley, California), and lived in Oakland.

And so, this volume of essays indicates the reality of writing together the head with the heart, the intellect with compassion. The contributors to this anthology love the best scholarship the academy produces and what the prophetic Black church has to offer. In fact, throughout these pages, we find professors who are pastors, preachers, and lay leaders in their churches. And we encounter pastors who are also adjunct and visiting professors in institutions of higher education.

I am deeply indebted to the first generation and second generation of womanist and Black (male) scholars who have stretched my mind and who continue to do so. James H. Cone and his offspring of younger Black theologians, men and women, challenge me to embrace prophetic dimensions of faith in a time when prosperity religion and status quo religion fail to "traverse the chasm between oppression and transformation." Yet, despite these false winds blowing pseudo-religiosity, womanist hope is an active hope in the struggle for resurrected transformed existence.[3]

## HOPE IN CHRISTIANITY

James H. Cone addresses the broader dimension of our theme of hope and Christ when he asserts:

---

2. Hooping is a unique form of Black American preaching where the preacher hums or sings the sermon, especially the ending climax. It is a powerful genre that too often is used by men preachers who have less substance in their homily. Consequently, they rely on the enthusiastic emotional response offered by the congregation to the preacher's hooping. However, the hooping style plus deep theological substance can produce some of the best sermons in America.

3. A. Elaine Brown Crawford, *Hope in the Hollar: A Womanist* (Louisville: Westminster John Knox, 2002) 116.

Christ is the eschatological hope. He is the future of God who stands in judgment upon the world and forces us to give an account of the present. In view of his victory over evil and death, why must human beings suffer and die? Why do we believe as if the present were a fixed reality and not susceptible of radical change? As long as we look at the resurrection of Christ and the expected end, we cannot reconcile ourselves to the things of the present that contradict his presence. It is this eschatological emphasis that black theology affirms.[4]

Cone links together ultimate hope with the resurrected Jesus who serves as the world's accountability authority. Hope for the church, indeed the earth, emerges not from mere human efforts to create a better world or another world. The dimension of hope that empowers human beings to be their best as created in God's image originates from the future beyond the end time. Here, in this cosmic movement or process, Jesus Christ will adjudicate those who have been faithful to clothing the naked, feeding the hungry, providing a balm for the broken hearted, comforting the widow, and bringing good news to the structurally poor. To make it plain, the norm of Christ as Judge par excellence of justice (i.e., future hope) emboldens us to witness and work in the world for saved souls and revolutionary relationships (i.e., present hope).

Jacquelyn Grant emphasizes also a futuristic view in line with my chapter's theme when she helps us to see Jesus as the one who inspires womanist hope and empowerment. Grant was one of the earliest womanist theologians to discuss Black women's hope in her elaboration of the positive dimensions of Christ as divine co-sufferer.[5]

Not only do Black and womanist scholarship inform my christological grasp of hope. Another fundamental source of constructive Christian witness and wisdom of hope are the real women in my everyday life. Therefore whatever I have written on the topic of Christ as a woman is based on the academic influence of the scholarly writings of Black theologians and womanist scholars as well as my beloved mother, Amy Smith, my grandmother, Martha Henry, and my wife of fifty-four years, JoAnna Smith. These powerful women in my life stand tall in their

4. James H. Cone, *A Black Theology of Liberation*, Twentieth Anniversary Edition (Maryknoll, NY: Orbis, 1990) 140.

5. Jacquelyn Grant, *White Women's Christ and Black Women's Jesus: Feminist Christology and Womanist Response*, American Academy of Religion Academy Series 64 (Atlanta: Scholars, 1989) 209–18.

exposing me to critical theological thinking and in allowing the risen Christ to live in their lives. These church women, and the Christ hope they embody, are the salt of the earth and a key ingredient to healthy, non-patriarchal male participation in the Black and womanist theologies dialogue.

## HISTORICAL PATRIARCHAL PROBLEMATIC

Still the dialogue between Black theology and womanist theology cannot disregard the long patriarchal domination in church history. The first five hundred years of Christianity were based on a male dominated clergy; and this gendered hierarchical structure continued into the ninth and tenth centuries. The male clergy, at this time, were the means through which laypersons were recipients of Gods' grace.

However, during the middle of the eleventh century with the religious reforms of Pope Gregory, the supernatural power that resided in the clergy was centered in the priest-controlled Eucharist. Hence some shifting from absolute clergy control and uniform Christian vocation, between 1050 and 1216, enabled new types of religious vocations to emerge. Changes in Gregorian ideology took place between withdrawal from the world to service in the world. The founding of the order of Friars in the early thirteenth century created evangelical preaching and a renunciation of material support. The Friar movement over shadowed the monastic goal of personal salvation through societal withdrawal and many men flocked to the Friars. The major theological, philosophical, and spiritual leaders in the thirteenth century were Franciscans and Dominicans who devoted themselves to caring for the poor with preaching, pastoral care, and the administration of the sacraments, mainly penance and the Eucharist.

These changes had important consequences for women. Women flocked to wandering preachers like Norbert of Xanten and Robert of Arbrissed. These religious leaders established monasteries for the women who did not stay locked up in them but who became bands of traveling female evangelists. Women affected the piety of the thirteenth and fourteenth centuries' devotion to the sacred heart of Jesus, the wounds of Jesus, and a nuptial mysticism that contains spiritual ecstasy and paramystical experiences. Nevertheless, male-dominated church leadership maintained negative stereotypes of women.

Yet the Cistercian monks of the twelfth century could not escape the influence of maternal imagery in their writings. They spoke about abbots, bishops, and the apostles by using maternal imagery. The Cistercian writers were influenced by an affective spirituality that expressed devotion to mother Jesus. Some of the Cistercian monks were Bernard of Clairvaux (1153), Aelred of Rievaul (1167), Guerric of Igny (1157), Isaac of Stella (ca. 1169), Adam of Perseigne (1221), and Helinand of Froidmont (1235), William of St. Thierry (1148; a Black Benedictine who became a Cistercian only late in life), and the Benedictine, Anselm of Canterbury (1109), from whom the Cistercians perhaps borrowed the idea of mother Jesus.[6]

Caroline Walker Bynum, however, explains that these twelfth-century devotional writers did not invent the concept of God or Jesus as mother. She calls attention to the times that God is described as mother in the First Testament. There are three references where God calls herself mother, one who bears Israel in her bosom, and a woman who conceives Israel in her womb. These scriptures are: Isaiah 49:1; Isaiah 49:15; and Isaiah 66:11–13. In Ecclesiasticus, a book in the Apocrypha, the wisdom of God is feminine. "I am the mother of fair love, and of fear, and of knowledge, and of holy hope ... Come over to me, all ye that desire me: and be filled with my fruits" (Ecclesiasticus 24:24–26).

Bynum also points out that although in Matthew 23:37 Jesus is described as a hen gathering her chicks under her wings, God or Jesus as woman or as mother is nonexistent in the Second Testament. Bynum believes that from Anselm to Julian there are three basic stereotypes of mother. They are the generative, the sacrificial, and the nurturing. She says: "The female is generative (the fetus is made of her very matter and sacrificial in her generation [birth pangs]), the female is loving and tender a mother cannot help loving her own child; the female is nurturing (she feeds the child with her own bodily fluids)."[7]

Bynum warns us that there is little evidence that the popularity of feminine and maternal imagery in the high Middle Ages reflects an increased respect for actual women by men. She remarks that the same authors who speak of motherhood or the Virgin Mary with compas-

6. Caroline Walker Bynum, *Jesus as Mother: Studies in the Spirituality of the High Middle Ages* (Berkeley: University of California Press, 1982) 112.

7. Ibid., 131.

sion and nurture also use woman as a symbol of physical or spiritual weakness.[8]

Against this grain of a historical patriarchal problematic, the writings and life of Julian of Norwich inspire me. She was born in 1342 and died in 1416. Coming from a society where women were prevented from teaching and writing, Julian wrote against the mysogyny and mean spirit of her adversaries, similar threats faced by Sojourner Truth. Like Sojourner Truth's "Ain't I a Woman" speech, Julian of Norwich's famous words still have power today. "But God forbid that you should say or assume that I am a teacher, for that is not what I mean, nor did I ever mean it; for I am a woman, ignorant, weak and frail. But I know well that I have received what I say from him who is the supreme teacher … Just because I am a woman, must I therefore believe that I must not tell you about the goodness of God, when I saw at the same time both his goodness and his wish that it should be known."[9]

Through her own sufferings and rich mystical spirituality, Julian wrote about the female nature of Christ's sufferings; and she has a developed and textured theology of the Trinity which is inclusive of the feminine gender. She is controversial in embracing a universalism that speaks of the inclusive nature of God's inexplicable love. On May 8, 1373, when she was sick enough to die, she was given by God a series of visions. Her priest held up a cross before her face and she saw blood streaming down the face of Jesus. When Julian was healed, she concluded that God is our mother as well as our father and that God cannot be angry with us and that no Christian will be lost.

Although Julian of Norwich was at odds with the theology of the church as it relates to the doctrine of salvation, she held to the Trinitarian theology of her church. Sometimes she would call God Father and other times Mother. And she was called mother. Julian was fond of thinking about God and life in categories of three. Julian said: "For our whole life falls into three parts. In the first we exist, in the second we grow, and in the third we are completed. The first is nature. The second is mercy. The third is grace."

Julian went on to draw a set of pioneering trinitarian parallels implicating the relations among human development, divine attributes,

---

8. Ibid., 143–44.

9. Julian of Norwich, *Revelations of Divine Love*, trans. Elizabeth Springer, notes and introduction by A. C. Spearing, Penguin Classics (London: Penguin, 1998) xviii.

and transcendent virtues. That is, all human beings have the capability to progress from existence to growth to completion. Nature determined the first movement of this dynamic. Our existence is natural. In order for us to grow, however, we require intervention or assistance from a higher than human source; this defines the role of mercy. But to move beyond a natural state and even a growth period, we achieve ultimate competition through grace realized by sacred authority. The "father" of the "Trinity," in Julian's writings, seems to correlate with existence and its natural state. His transcendent virtue is power. The mother relates to human growth through mercy and brings wisdom. The Lord, the third person of Julian's Trinity, uses love to actualize grace toward human completion.

Julian then proceeds immediately to take this redefined understanding of mother as the Trinity's second person (i.e., associated with growth, mercy, and wisdom—themselves a trinitarian formulation) and names her mother Christ. Here mother, though related to our essential being, works primarily as the parent of our essential creation. Not only operative at the essential level, Mother's mercy takes on our sensory being. Ultimately Mother Christ models for us the inter-relatedness of apparent opposites or a paradigm for bridging the gap between entities often perceived at odds. Yet Mother Christ brings us hope through mercy and wisdom. Thus we grow.

Resuming her comments, she states:

> And furthermore, I saw that as the second person is mother of our essential being, so that some-well loved person has become mother of our sensory being; for God makes us double, as essential and sensory beings. Our essential being is the higher part, which we have in our Father, God Almighty; and the second person of the Trinity is our mother in nature and in our essential creation in whom we are grounded and rooted, and he is our mother in mercy in taking on our sensory being. And so our mother in whom our parts are kept unparted, works in us in various ways, for in our mother, Christ we profit and grow.[10]

## CHURCH AND ACADEMY TOGETHER

In our Mother, Christ, we can profit and grow as Black theology and womanist theology choose wisely the way forward for the church and

---

10. Ibid., 138.

academy. However, the mainline Black church denominational leaders and the Black theology academy must convene to begin long overdue dialogue over these great issues of gender, sexism, racism, homophobia, and a relevant Christology for a post-modern world.

As a long time pastor who continues to struggle with male clergy peers on the issue of sexism in the parish church and in our denominational and ecumenical church life, I am not as hopeful as I would like to be about the progressive pace of the mainstream church in resolving the injustice of gender. It is sad that the best prepared students in our seminaries are often women students who are overlooked by the pulpit search committees who are in search of pastoral leadership. The majority of Black churches have a long way to go before they will even begin to have dialogue with the Black members of the theological academy. I am pained and to some extent marginalized by strong vocal and visible power pockets of anti-intellectualism in the Black church. As of this writing, I am still beginning to forge a bridge of communication between the church and the academy. /

Among others, one paradigm for implementation has been established by Dwight N. Hopkins and Allen Temple Baptist Church. Hopkins presented lectures at Allen Temple in Oakland, California, prior to publishing them. Hopkins and Linda E. Thomas also help close the gap between the church and the academy by serving as the convocation speakers for the Leadership Institute of the Allen Temple Baptist Church. Jacqueline Grant, on several occasions, has lectured to the women of Allen Temple on womanist theology. The Black church anti-intellectual tendencies need to be corrected with the expansion of similar dialogues with the academy.

We can find how other examples of the mercy and wisdom of Mother Christ can increase the growth of "lectern and pulpit" witnessing together. In keeping with the October 24–27, 2005, Fall revival of Allen Temple Baptist Church of Oakland, California, an ecumenical effort was made to close the gap between the town and the gown. James A. Noel, of the San Francisco Theological Seminary faculty and also the Interim Pastor of Sojourner Truth Presbyterian Church of Richmond, California, secured foundation funding for continuing education lectures with Charles H. Long, retired Professor of the History of Religions at the University of Chicago Divinity School. Long spoke from the theme of "Transformational Preaching." The sponsors for this ecumenical gathering were the American Baptist Seminary of the West, Berkeley, California; San Francisco Theological Seminary of San Anselmo, California; Sojourner Truth Presbyterian Church of Richmond, California; and the Allen Temple Baptist Church of Oakland. The participants came from Southern California as well as Northern California. It is interesting to know that the evening revival preacher was pastor Matthew Johnson of Atlanta, Georgia. Johnson received his PhD in Philosophical Theology from the University of Chicago Divinity School.

## CHRIST AS A DARK WOMAN

Not only does Julian of Norwich's notion of Mother Christ have implications for enhancing academy and church relations and Black and womanist theologies being together. Mother Christ resonates with African American women's lives and literature. *My Soul Is a Witness: African-American Women's Spirituality,* edited by Gloria Wade-Gayles, has a powerful essay written by Johnnetta B. Cole, the former president of Spelman College. This essay was a speech delivered January 9, 1992, in Sisters Chapel at Spelman College for the opening convocation of the Spring semester. The title of the presentation was "Jesus Is a Sister." Cole said:

> Jesus as the sister? Clearly, it was not an outrageous notion to David Driskell to portray the Black Woman as our Lord. And yet we must ask why on first hearing this concept we find it difficult to comprehend, indeed some find it a disturbing notion. The answer, I think, is that the idea of Jesus as a Black woman challenges two deeply rooted bases of power in "western civilization," including American society: that which is white and that which is male. But Jesus sided with, identified with, saved, and was at home with the powerless. And thus how easy it should be for us to see Jesus himself as a Black woman. Let us remember that an enormous effort has been made to distort Christianity so that it stands in the interest of patriarchy and racism.[11]

Cole explains clearly how the revelation of the Mother Christ in the U.S. context and other parts of the world becomes anathema for our ears and eyes because of the power structure. "Western civilizations" historically and today have distorted not only christology, but also pigmentol-

11. Jonetta B. Cole, "Jesus Is a Sister," in *My Soul Is a Witness: African-American Women's Spirituality,* ed. Gloria Wade-Gayles (Boston: Beacon, 1995) 153.

ogy. People of a certain race and of a certain gender had power while the majority population lacked power due to a different pigment texture and gender orientation. Here we see how Mother Christ, Son of God, Son of Man, or the Second Person of the Trinity is not abstract pietistic, religious belief. These are our attempts to give expression to the powerful mystery that is God. But because it is human effort, we bring our human political economy, race, and gender perspectives—we bring the particularities of our power positions to our perspectives of christology.

Unfortunately those in western civilizations have been an elite and small group of people who have monopolized power. These folk have used their context of power to promote a Jesus Christ that looks like them. So when Cole argues for the idea of Jesus as a Black woman, the elite gender and racial group with power probably find that suggestion as comic relief or a touch of insanity.

But Cole goes on to substantiate her claim by drawing on the theological and theoretical authority of one of the founders of womanist theology—Jacquelyn Grant. Instead of accepting an untrue white male portrayal of Jesus, Grant pushes for "a more wholistic theology." "Wholistic" seems to suggest at least two things. One is that a minority population on a global scale (i.e., white, male, western) has enslaved Jesus in a global minority power perspective. Two, by the method of a realistic portrayal of Jesus as a Black woman, Jesus becomes the Savior of humankind (i.e., the overwhelming numbers of the 6 billion global population are women and darker skin peoples). So Mother Christ is a Black woman who speaks for, to, and through the world. And from her dark skin, gendered self, Mother Christ even saves and liberates the minority western, white male brothers. Mother Christ—Black Woman is both particular and universal. Cole, through Grant, teaches us that Black women identified with Jesus because they believed Jesus identified with them. This specific dialectic of identification provides the basis of a cosmic soteriology for all of humanity and creation.

Following in the noble tradition of African American foremothers Sojourner Truth, Jarena Lee, Zilphaw Elaw, Bishop Leontyne Kelly, today's Congresswoman Barbara Lee, and our living womanist theologians, let us also learn about the image of Mother Christ from African women Christian scholars: Anna Mary Mukamwezi Kayonga of Uganda, who uses Genesis 1:27 to write about the equality of the sexes; and Philomena N. Mwawra of Kenya, who details the harmful effects of woman's subordination. Dwight N. Hopkins's seminal work, *Being Human: Race, Culture and Religion*, introduces them to us and to theologian Mercy Amba Oduyoye of Ghana, who, like our own Jacquelyn Grant, says that "Women should not have a monopoly on the servant role. We cannot assign the cross to half of humanity and the resurrection to the other half. Our theology of cross and resurrection must remain together."[12] May the theology of Jesus as a woman resurrected from the grave of patriarchy usher in a new age of gender justice that will bring healing and wholeness to the fragmented and the forlorn.

May men be open to hear with the ear of repentance and restitution the angry voices of women whom we have hurt. May we come closer to Jesus who lives in the faces of the women we meet as we strive to match our deeds with our creeds. May we remember the woman who became the prophetic-priest who anointed Jesus for his death with expensive perfume while disciples under demonic control discussed how the money for the perfume could have been better spent. May the Jesus in men and the Jesus in women hasten the coming of the rule of God on earth as it is in heaven. May the meaning of Jesus as woman and may it's revelation be ever unfolding and ever growing in us.

May the male-female unity of Eden that became paradise lost become paradise gained so that roses will bloom in the desert and lions and lambs will live together in a peace that will put to rest Howard Thurman's search for common good because Martin Luther King Jr.'s beloved community has been actualized. May womanist hope never tire as active hope in the struggle for resurrected transformed existence.

May we who are men see Jesus in the women who touched our lives. My Mama Amy in her passionate prayers became Jesus praying in the Garden of Gethsemane. Grandmother Martha became Jesus when I was failing in reading. She invited me to sit on the front porch next to her. From her rocking chair she taught me to read; the Bible was the textbook. My patient wife JoAnna, who waited for me to grow up into a mature man, is Jesus as a woman. We married when I was nineteen years old. My wife is Jesus as a woman in teaching me to forgive coldhearted church leaders who hurt us just like the Pharisees and the Sadducees hurt Jesus. Joanna is Jesus like a woman in bearing her physical illness with grace and quiet dignity. My daughter, Amy Jones, is Jesus as a woman,

---

12. Oduyoye, quoted in Hopkins, *Being Human: Race, Culture and Religion* (Minneapolis: Fortress, 2005) 116.

who with gentleness and graciousness serves as my backup caregiver for Joanna, my wife and her mother.

The elderly woman on the cane is Jesus when she greets me at the door of the church and says: "Son, I am praying for you. Now, don't you quit son. Keep on Keeping On." Look into your own life and see the many ways that Jesus as a woman touches your life with beauty and purpose.

## 12

# A Womanist Christology

## Jacquelyn Grant

### INTRODUCTORY MATTERS

BECAUSE IT IS IMPORTANT to distinguish Black and White women's experiences, it is also important to note these differences in theological and Christological reflection. To accent the difference between Black and White women's perspective in theology, I maintain that Black women scholars should follow Alice Walker by describing our theological activity as "womanist theology." The term "womanist" refers to Black women's experiences. It accents, as Walker says, our being responsible, in charge, outrageous, courageous, and audacious enough to demand the right to think theologically and to do it independently of both White and Black men and White women.

Black women must do theology out of their tridimensional experience of racism/sexism/classism. To ignore any aspect of this experience is to deny the holistic and integrated reality of Black womanhood. When Black women say that God is on the side of the oppressed, we mean that God is in solidarity with the struggles of those on the under side of humanity.

In a chapter titled "Black Woman: Shaping Feminist Theory," hooks elaborates the interrelationship of the threefold oppressive reality of Black women and shows some of the weaknesses of White feminist theory. Challenging the racist and classist assumption of White feminism, hooks writes: "Racism abounds in the writings of white feminists, reinforcing white supremacy and negating the possibility that women will bond politically across ethnic and racial boundaries. Past feminist refusal to draw attention to and attack racial hierarchy suppressed the link between race and class. Yet class structure in American society has been shaped by the racial politics of white supremacy."[1] This means that Black women, because of oppression determined by race and their subjugation as women, make up a disproportionately high percentage of the poor and working classes. However, the fact that Black women are a subjugated group even within the Black community and the White women's community does not mean that they are alone in their oppression within those communities. In the women's community, poor White women are marginalized; and in the Black community, poor Black men are also discriminated against. This suggests that classism, as well as racism and sexism, has a life of its own. Consequently, simply addressing racism and sexism is inadequate to bring about total liberation.[2] Even though there are dimensions of class which are not directly related to race or sex, classism impacts Black women in a peculiar way which results in the fact that they are most often on the bottom of the social and economic ladder. For Black women doing theology, to ignore classism would mean that their theology is no different from any other bourgeois theology. It would be meaningless to the majority of Black women, who are themselves poor. This means that addressing only issues relevant to middle class women or Blacks will simply not do. The daily struggles of poor Black women must serve as the gauge for the verification of the claims of womanist theology.

Theological investigation into the experiences of Christian Black women reveals that Black women considered the Bible to be a major source for religious validation in their lives. Though Black women's relationship with God preceded their introduction to the Bible, this Bible gave some content to their God-consciousness.[3] The source for Black women's understanding of God has been twofold: first, God's revelation

---

1. bell hooks, *Feminist Theory: From Margin to Center* (Boston: South End, 1984) 3.

2. This is reflected in the fact that the Black movement (Civil Rights/Black Power) has resulted in advancement of only some Blacks, primarily men, creating an emergent Black middle class. Likewise, the women's movement has meant progress for some women, primarily White, resulting in the increased class stratification in the women's community.

3. Cicil Wayne Cone, *Identity Crisis in Black Theology* (Nashville: African Methodist Episcopal Church, 1975), esp. chap. 2.

directly to them, and secondly, God's revelation as witnessed in the Bible and as read and heard in the context of their experience. The understanding of God as creator, sustainer, comforter, and liberator took on life as they agonized over their pain, and celebrated the hope that as God delivered the Israelites, they would be delivered as well. The God of the Old and New Testament became real in the consciousness of oppressed Black women. Though they were politically impotent, they were able to appropriate certain themes of the Bible that spoke to their reality. For example, Jarena Lee, a nineteenth-century Black woman preacher in the African Methodist Episcopal Church constantly emphasized the theme "Life and Liberty" in her sermons, which were always biblically based. This interplay of Scripture and experience was exercised by many other Black women. An ex-slave woman revealed that when her experience negated certain oppressive interpretations of the Bible given by White preachers, she, through engaging the biblical message for herself, rejected them. Consequently, she also dismissed White preachers who distorted the message in order to maintain slavery. Her grandson, Howard Thurman, speaks of her use of the Bible in this way: "'During the days of slavery,' she said, 'the master's minister would occasionally hold services for the slaves. Always the White minister used as his text something from Paul. "Slaves be obedient to them that are your masters . . . , as unto Christ." Then he would go on to show how if we were good and happy slaves, God would bless us. I promised my Maker that if I ever learned to read and if freedom ever came, I would not read that part of the Bible.'"[4] What we see here is perhaps more than a mere rejection of a White preacher's interpretation of the bible, but an exercise in internal critique of the Bible. The Bible must be read and interpreted in the light of Black women's own experience of oppression and God's revelation within that context. Womanists must, like Sojourner, "compare the teachings of the Bible with the witness" in them.[5]

To do Womanist Theology, then, we must read and hear the Bible and engage it within the context of our own experience. This is the only way that it can make sense to people who are oppressed. Black women of the past did not hesitate in doing this and we must do no less.

4. Howard Thurman, *Jesus and the Disinherited* (New York: Abingdon-Cokesbury, 1949) 30–31.

5. Olive Gilbert, *Narrative of Sojourner Truth* (1850; reprinted, Chicago: Johnson, 1970) 83.

## JESUS AND THE BLACK WOMAN

In the experiences of Black people, Jesus was "all things."[6] Chief among these, however, was the belief in Jesus as the divine co-sufferer, who empowers them in situations of oppression. For Christian Black women in the past, Jesus was their central frame of reference. They identified with Jesus because they believed that Jesus identified with them. As Jesus was persecuted and made to suffer undeservedly, so were they. His suffering culminated in the crucifixion. Their crucifixion included rape and babies being sold. But Jesus's suffering was not the suffering of a mere human, for Jesus was understood to be God incarnate. As Harold Carter observed of Black prayers in general, there was no difference made between the persons of the trinity, Jesus, God, or the Holy Spirit. "All of these proper names for God were used interchangeably in prayer language. Thus, Jesus was the one who speaks the world into creation. He was the power behind the Church."[7]

Black women's affirmation of Jesus as God meant that White People were not God. One old slave woman clearly demonstrated this as she prayed: "Dear Masse Jesus, we all uns beg Ooner [you] come make us a call dis yere day. We is nutting but poor Etiopian women and people aint tink much 'bout we. We ain't trust any of dem great high people for come to we church, but do' you is de one great Massa, great too much dan Massa Linkum, you ain't shame to care for we African people."[8]

This slave woman did not hesitate to identify her struggles and pain with those of Jesus. In fact, the common struggle made her know that Jesus would respond to her beck and call. "Come to we, dear Massa Jesus. De sun he hot too much, de road am dat long and boggy (sandy) and we ain't got no buggy for send and fetch Ooner. But Massa, you 'member how you walked dat hard walk up Calvary and ain't weary but tink about we all dat way. We know you ain't weary for to come to we. We pick out de torns, de prickles, de brier, de backslidin' and de quarrel and de sin out of you path so dey shan't hurt Ooner pierce feet no more."[9]

---

6. Harold A. Carter, *The Prayer Tradition of Black People* (Valley Forge, PA: Judson, 1976). Carter, in referring to traditional Black prayer in general, states that Jesus was revealed as one who "was all one needs!" 50.

7. Ibid.

8. Ibid., 49

9. Ibid.

As she is truly among the people at the bottom of humanity, she can make things comfortable for Jesus even though she may have nothing to give him—no water, no food. But she can give tears and love. She continues: "Come to we, dear Masse Jesus. We all uns ain't got no good cool water for give you when you thirsty. You know, Massa, de drought so long, and the well so low, ain't nutting but mud to drink. But we gwine to take de 'munion cup and fill it wid de tear of repentance, and love clean out of we heart. Dat all we hab to gib you, good Massa."[10] For Black women, the role of Jesus unraveled as they encountered him in their experiences as one who empowers the weak. In this vein, Jesus was such a central part of Sojourner Truth's life that all of her sermons made him the starting point. When asked by a preacher if the source of her preaching was the Bible, she responded "No honey, can't preach from de Bible—can't read a letter."[11] The she explained; "When I preaches, I has jest one text to preach from, an' I always preaches from this one. My text is, 'When I found Jesus!'"[12] In this sermon Sojourner Truth recounts the events and struggles of her life from the time her parents were brought from Africa and sold "up an' down, an' hither an' yon . . ."[13] to the time that she met Jesus within the context of her struggles for dignity of Black people and women. Her encounter with Jesus brought such joy that she became overwhelmed with love and praise: "Praise, praise, praise to the Lord! An' I begun to feel such a love in my soul as I never felt before—love to all creatures. An' then, all of a sudden, it stopped, an' I said, Dar's de white folks that that have abused you, an' beat you, an' abused your people—think o'them! But then there came another rush of love through my soul, an' I cried out loud—'Lord, I can love *even de white folks!*'"[14] This love was not a sentimental, passive love. It was a tough, active love that empowered her to fight more fiercely for the freedom of her people. For the rest of her life she continued speaking at abolition and women's rights gatherings, condemning the horrors of oppression.

10. Ibid.

11. Gilbert, *Narrative of Sojourner Truth*, 118.

12. Ibid., 119.

13. Ibid.

14. Ibid., 122.

## BLACK MALE THEOLOGIANS AND JESUS

More than anyone, Black theologians have captured the essence of the significance of Jesus in the lives of Black people, which to an extent includes Black women. They all hold that the Jesus of history is important for understanding who he was and his significance for us today. By and large they have affirmed that this Jesus is the Christ, that is, God incarnate. They have argued that in the light of our experience, Jesus meant freedom.[15] They have maintained that Jesus means freedom from the sociopsychological, psychocultural, economic, and political oppression of Black people. In other words, Jesus is a political messiah.[16] "To free (humans) from bondage was Jesus' own definition of his ministry."[17] This meant that as Jesus identified with the lowly of his day, he now identifies with the lowly of this day, who in the American context are Black People. The identification is so real that Jesus Christ in fact becomes Black. It is important to note that Jesus's blackness is not a result of ideological distortion of a few Black thinkers, but a result of careful Christological investigation. Cone examines the sources of Christology and concludes that Jesus is Black because "Jesus was a Jew." He explains:

> It is on the basis of the soteriological meaning of the particularity of his Jewishness that theology must affirm the Christological significance of Jesus' present blackness. He *is* black because he was a Jew. The affirmation of the Black Christ can be understood when the significance of his past Jewishness is related dialectically to the significance of his present blackness. On the one hand, the Jewishness of Jesus located him in the context of the Exodus, thereby connecting his appearance in Palestine with God's liberation of oppressed Israelites from Egypt. Unless Jesus were truly from Jewish ancestry, it would make little theological sense to say that he is the fulfillment of God's covenant with Israel. But on the other hand, the blackness of Jesus brings out the soteriological meaning of his Jewishness for our contemporary situation when Jesus' person is understood in the context of the cross and resurrection.[18]

15. J. D. Roberts, *A Black Political Theology* (Philadelphia: Westminster, 1974) 138. See esp. chap. 5. See also Noel Erskine, *Decolonizing Theology: A Caribbean Perspective* (Maryknoll, NY: Orbis, 1980) 125.

16. Ibid., 133.

17. Albert Cleage, *The Black Messiah* (New York: Sheed & Ward, 1969) 92.

18. James H. Cone, *God of the Oppressed* (New York: Seabury, 1975) 134.

The condition of Black people today reflects the cross of Jesus. Yet the resurrection brings the hope that liberation from oppression is immanent. The resurrected Black Christ signifies this hope. Cone further argues that this christological title, "The Black Christ" is not validated by its universality, but, in fact, by its particularity. Its significance lies in whether or not the christological title "points to God's universal will to liberate particular oppressed people from inhumanity."[19]

## TRI-DIMENSIONALITY OF THE LEAST

These particular oppressed peoples to whom Cone refers are characterized in Jesus's parable on the Last Judgment as "the least." "The least in America are literally and symbolically present in Black People."[20] This notion of "the least" is attractive because it descriptively locates the condition of Black women. "The least" are those people who have no water to give, but offer what they have, as the old slave woman cited above says in her prayer. Black women's experience in general is such a reality. Their tri-dimensional reality renders their particular situation a complex one. One could say that not only are they the oppressed of the oppressed, but their situation represents "the particular within the particular."

But is this just another situation that takes us deeper into the abyss of theological relativity? I would argue that it is not, because it is the context of Black women's experience where the particular connects up with the universal. By this I mean that in each of the three dynamics of oppression, Black women share in the realty of a broader community. They share race suffering with Black men; with White women and other Third World women, they are victims of sexism; and with poor Blacks and Whites, and other Third World peoples, especially women, they are disproportionately poor. To speak of Black women's tri-dimensional reality, therefore, is not to speak of Black women exclusively, for there is an implied universality that connects them with others.

Likewise, with Jesus Christ, there was an implied universality that made him identify with others—the poor, the woman, the stranger. To affirm Jesus's solidarity with the "least of the people" is not an exercise in romanticized contentment with one's oppressed status in life. For the Resurrection signified that there is more to life than the cross for Jesus

19. Ibid., 135.
20. Ibid., 136.

Christ, for Black women it signifies that their tri-dimensional oppressive existence is not the end, but it merely represents the context in which a particular people struggle to experience hope and liberation. Jesus Christ thus represents a three-fold significance: first he identifies with the "little people," Black women, where they are; secondly, he affirms the basic humanity of these, "the least"; and thirdly, he inspires active hope in the struggle for resurrected, liberated existence.

To locate the Christ in Black people is a radical and necessary step, but an understanding of Black women's reality challenges us to go further. Christ among the least must also mean Christ in the community of Black women. William Eichelberger was able to recognize this as he further particularized the significance of the Blackness of Jesus by locating Christ in Black women's community. He was able to see Christ not only as Black male but also Black female.

> God, in revealing Himself and His attributes from time to time in His creaturely existence, has exercised His freedom to formalize His appearance in a variety of ways. . . . God revealed Himself at a point in the past as Jesus the Christ as Black male. My reasons for affirming the blackness of Jesus of Nazareth are much different from that of the white apologist.
>
> God wanted to identify with that segment of mankind which had suffered most, and is still suffering . . . I am constrained to believe that God in our times had updated His form of revelation to western society. It is my feeling that God is now manifesting Himself, and has been for over 450 years, in the form of the Black American Woman as mother, as wife, as nourisher, sustainer and preserver of life, the Suffering Servant who is despised and rejected by men, a personality of sorrow who is acquainted with grief. The Black Woman has borne our griefs and carried our sorrows. She has been wounded because of American white society's transgressions and bruised by white iniquities. It appears that she may be the instrumentality through whom God will make us whole.[21]

Granted, Eichelberger's categories for God and woman are very traditional. Nevertheless, the significance of his thought is that he was able to conceive of the Divine reality as other than a Black male messianic figure.

---

21. William Eichelberger, "Reflections on the Person and Personality of the Black Messiah," in *The Black Church* 1.2 (1974) 54 [51–63].

## CHALLENGES FOR BLACK WOMEN

Although I have argued that the White feminist analysis of theology and Christology is inadequate for salvific efficacy with respect to Black women, I do contend that it is not totally irrelevant to Black women's needs. I believe that Black women should take seriously the feminist analysis, but they should not allow themselves to be co-opted on behalf of the agendas of White women, for as I have argued, they are often racist unintentionally or by intention.

The first challenge, therefore, is to Black women. Feminists have identified some problems associated with language and symbolism of the church, theology and Christology. They have been able to show that exclusive masculine language and imagery are contributing factors undergirding the oppression of women.

In addressing the present day, Womanists must investigate the relationship between the oppression of women and theological symbolism. Even though Black women have been able to transcend some of the oppressive tendencies of White male (and Black male) articulated theologies, careful study reveals that some traditional symbols are inadequate for us today. The Christ understood as the stranger, the outcast, the hungry, the weak, the poor, makes the traditional male Christ (Black and White) less significant. Even our sisters, the womanists of the past, though they exemplified no problems with the symbols themselves, had some suspicions about the effects of a male image of the divine, for they did challenge the oppressive and distorted use of it in the church's theology. In so doing, they were able to move from a traditional oppressive Christology, with respect to women, to an egalitarian Christology. This kind of equalitarian Christology was operative in Jarena Lee's argument for the right of women to preach. She argued: "the Saviour died for the woman as well as for the man."[22] The crucifixion was for universal salvation, not just for male salvation or, as we may extend the argument, not just for White salvation. Because of this Christ came and died, no less for the woman as for the man, no less for Blacks as for Whites. Lee makes the point of gender universality: "If the man may preach, because the Saviour died for him, why not the woman? Seeing he died for her also.

---

22. Jarena Lee, *Religious Experiences and Journal of Mrs. Jarena Lee: A Preachin' Woman* (1849; reprinted, Nashville: AMEC Sunday School Union/Legacy, 1991) 15–16.

Is he not a whole Saviour, instead of half one? As those who hold it wrong for a woman to preach, would see to make it appear."[23]

Lee correctly perceives that there is an ontological issue at stake. If Jesus Christ were a Savior of men, then it is true that maleness of Christ would be paramount.[24] But if Christ is a Saviour of all, then it is the humanity—the wholeness—of Christ which is significant. Sojourner was aware of the same tendency of some scholars and church leaders to link the maleness of Jesus and the sin of Eve with the status of women and she challenged this notion in her famed speech "Ain't I A Woman?"

> Then that little man in black there, he says women can't have as much rights as men, 'cause Christ wasn't a woman! Where did your Christ come from? Where did your Christ come from? From God and a woman. Man had nothing to do with Him.
>
> If the first woman of God ever made was strong enough to turn the world upside down all alone, these women together ought to be able to turn it back, and get it right side up again! And now they is asking to do it, the men better let them.[25]

I would argue, as suggested by both Lee and Sojourner, that the significance of Christ is not his maleness, but his humanity. The most significant events of Jesus Christ were the life and ministry, the crucifixion and the resurrection. The significance of these events, in one sense, is that in them the absolute becomes concrete. God becomes concrete not only in the man Jesus, for he was crucified, but in the lives of those who will accept the challenges of the risen Savior, the Christ.

For Lee, this meant that women could preach; for Sojourner, it meant that women could possibly save the world; for me, it means today, this Christ, found in the experiences of Black women, is a Black woman. The commitment to struggle not only with symptoms (church structures, structures of society), as Black women have done, but with causes (those beliefs which produce and re-inforce structures) yields deeper theological and christological questions having to do with images and

---

23. Ibid., 16.

24. There is no evidence to suggest that Black women debated the significance of the maleness of Jesus. The fact is that Jesus Christ was a real crucial figure in their lives. Recent feminist scholarship has been important in showing the relation between the maleness of Christ and the oppression of women.

25. Sojourner Truth, "Ain't I a Woman," in *Feminism: The Essential Historical Writings*, ed. Miriam Schneir (New York: Vintage, 1977) 94.

symbolism. Christ challenges us to ask new questions demanded by the context in which we find ourselves.

The second challenge for Black women is that we must explore more deeply the question of what Christ means in a society in which class distinctions are increasing. If Christ is among "the least," then who are they? Because our foreparents were essentially poor by virtue of their race, there was no real need for them to address classism as a separate reality. Today, in light of the emerging Black middle class, we must ask what is the impact of class upon our lives and the lives of other poor Black and Third World women and men.

Another way of addressing the class issue in the church is to recognize the fact that although our race/sex analyses may force us to realize that Blacks and women should share in the leadership of the church, the style of leadership and basic structures of the church virtually insure the continuation of a privileged class.

Contemporary Black women, in taking seriously the Christ mandate to be among the least, must insist that we address all three aspects of Black women's reality in our analyses. The challenge here for contemporary Black women is to begin to construct a serious analysis that addresses the structural nature of poverty. Black women must recognize that racism, sexism, and classism each have lives of their own, and that no one form of oppression is eliminated with the destruction of any other. Though they are interrelated, they must all be addressed.

The third and final challenge for Black women is to do constructive Christology. This Christology must be a liberating one, for both the Black women's community and the larger Black community. A Christology that negates Black male humanity is still destructive to the Black community. We must, therefore, take seriously only the usable aspect of the past.

To be sure, as Black women receive these challenges, their very embodiment represents a challenge to White women. This embodiment (of racism, sexism, and classism) says to White women that a holistic analysis is a minimal requirement for holistic theology. The task of Black women, then, is constructive.

As we organize in this constructive task, we are also challenged to adopt the critical stance of Sojourner with respect to the feminist analysis as reflected in her comment:

> I know that it feel a kind o' hissin' and ticklin' like to see a colored
> woman get up and tell you about things, and woman's rights. We

have all been thrown down so low that nobody thought we' ever get up again, but we have been long enough trodden now; we will come up again and now I am here . . .

. . . I wanted to tell you a mite about Woman's Rights, and so I came out and said so. I am sittin' among you to watch; and every once in a while I will come out and tell you what time of night it is.[26]

26. Ibid., 96–98.

# PART FOUR

# Sexuality

# 13

# Human Sexuality—The Rest of the Story

LAST SPRING I RECEIVED an email from an MDiv student at a seminary in the Midwest. This student was in a class on contemporary theology and had just read an article that I had written fifteen years ago on womanist theology and sexuality, specifically on the role or place of Black lesbians in womanist theological discourse. The seminarian wanted to write a paper on my work—I was surprised. I realized how much I have changed while theological discourse on Black lesbian lives seems to have stayed much the same. What is different? I am not a part of the formal academic world. I do not currently work in a church. I am not as optimistic as I was then about the power of Christianity and Christian people to transform the world through love and justice. I have explored and participated in religious traditions outside of Christianity. What is still the same? I am still an Episcopal priest. I maintain my belief in the potential for hope-filled action rooted in a broad range of faith and spiritual practices. I am still an African American lesbian of faith who is willing to talk about God, community, justice and love, though I talk about them and experience these things in a different way.

There was a poignancy to the request from that seminarian. So many years after writing this article there still is not much theological discussion by out lesbians of color. There has been some voice and visibility of lesbians of color and our allies, but it is clear that it is still difficult and dangerous to speak and write in religious academia and especially in the church as openly lesbian, gay, or bisexual theologians or religious professionals. Transgendered and intersexed people of faith are not even considered. So I am curious, which way *is* indeed forward for the Black theologies? For Womanist theologies? For the church? Can there be movement in the academy in relation to questions concerning human sexuality?

As an Episcopal priest I am a part of a worldwide Anglican Communion that has in recent years struggled deeply, almost to the point of schism, over the issue of homosexuality, including ordaining lesbians and gay men to all orders of clergy (the deaconate, priesthood, and most recently the episcopacy) and the volatile issue of same-sex marriage. As an organizer in faith communities and in African American communities in support of same-sex marriage I have experienced firsthand the rejection, hatred, and even the internalized oppression in some Black faith communities around the acceptance of lesbians and gay men. On the other side are the profound gestures of love, support, and acceptance that are also evident in individual acts and in some Black communities. In both my secular work and faith community work, a major sticking point in struggles around homosexuality is the Bible, how it is read and how it is understood as a source of authority. Other sticking points include varying degrees of understanding and acceptance of the social construction of gender, varying perspectives on psychological and sexual development, and a largely unexamined overt acceptance of a narrow and limited model of family life. All of this has a profound impact on the shape and pace of discussion and action to develop healthy, liberating, and transformative perspectives on human sexuality.

Perhaps the greatest obstacle to moving the discussion on human sexuality is conflating "human sexuality" with "homosexuality." Human sexuality includes sexual health and reproduction, relationship issues including family violence, divorce, polygamy, and sexual abuse. Human sexuality also includes human trafficking, rape as a tactic of war, and sex work/prostitution, just to name a few issues. Closely related to issues of human sexuality are issues of gender justice, including women's rights and transgender issues. If our discussions of human sexuality are limited to homosexuality alone we risk missing an opportunity to deepen and expand our political and theological thinking to include critical issues that impact people of African descent around the world.

I am not suggesting that there is not a great deal more work to be done in terms of activism and reflection in Black theologies and womanist theologies to challenge the injustices of heterosexism and homophobia. Indeed our reflection and action on homosexuality and the lives of GLBTQ people[1] needs to be expanded beyond questions of church participation and sanction to look at real life issues that GLBTQ people face including issues of anti-gay violence and human rights abuses; discrimination in housing, employment, and health care; and critical issues of survival and nurture for GLBTQ youth. Too often GLBTQ people are portrayed as a problem to be solved rather than people, part of creation, who deserve safety, dignity, respect, and liberation from oppressive power, whether sacred or secular. Reflecting on civil and human rights for GLBTQ people and liberating theologies that support these rights within a broader context of human sexuality will enable us to have a moral base for activism in the service of *all* aspects of healthy sexuality, respect and justice for *all* Black people.

## POWER

It is critical that we not lose sight of the role of power in these religious and theological struggles around sexuality. In our culture sex and power go together. When we talk about sex we are not simply engaged in a discussion about morality or even what is correct in terms of biblical interpretation. These struggles have everything to do with who has the power to define who is "in" or "out" in terms of secular or religious group acceptability. These struggles have to do with the power to determine who is or is not worthy of safety and respect, who does or does not have the right to be self-determining/self-defining. It has to do with the power to lead institutions, to control reproduction, to define the norms for family structure. The power struggles that underlie the contentious religious debates over human sexuality are struggles over who gets to speak for God.

In the Anglican Communion the power struggles connected to the intense debates about human sexuality (read: homosexuality) are also evident in the long-standing and on-going conflict around women's ordination. These debates are also deeply entwined with the relatively recent power struggles between church authorities in the Global South (which, with the exception of the South African Church, have tended to be more conservative on issues of human sexuality and women's ordination), and those of the North, which have tended to make more liberal

---

1. Gay, lesbian, bisexual, transgendered, queer people.

decisions on these issues. The strong subtext to this struggle is who will have the authority to define the boundaries of the church, interpret its doctrine and teaching, and define its future. In short, who is in charge?

Related to this struggle are the actions of those who benefit or think that they benefit from hetero-patriarchal structures, and who fiercely protect and maintain those structures. The rigid boundaries of gender identity and sexuality are maintained in order to sustain power and control in a hetero-patriarchal system. This is one reason that bisexuality and transgender expression are perhaps even more deeply feared, silenced and made invisible.

## HUMAN SEXUALITY: STORIES AS BASIS FOR THEOLOGIES AND ACTION

Theological reflection for me has its origins in stories of real individuals and communities. The issues of human sexuality addressed in this paper have all arisen in Black communities that I have been a part of as an organizer or clergy person. These stories are not uncommon. Indeed they are all too common. I am sure that many of you have heard stories like these. Many of you could tell similar stories. They offer some, but certainly not all, of the issues that a more comprehensive theological reflection on human sexuality needs to address. It is in the telling, hearing, reflecting, and acting on the depth and breadth of human sexuality that Black theological reflection can grow in its ability to respond to the complex realities of human sexuality today. It is a way to inspire theological movement while at the same time a way to address present and continuing issues of human sexuality that urgently need to be responded to.

## SEXUAL ABUSE/INCEST

Maya was a young Black girl in a parish that I served. At thirteen years old, she was living with extended family and attending her local public school. With the help of another clergyperson Maya had worked her way to the promise of a scholarship to attend a private boarding school in New England. By all appearances, she led the life of most of the kids in her neighborhood. There were the manifold struggles that poverty or near poverty bring. Yet Maya continued to grow and learn and even excel in some ways. The cracks in Maya's world began to show when one of her uncles accidentally killed another while restraining him as he thrashed around in a drug-induced rage. Family violence and the ravages of drug use shone through the cracks. A few weeks later when the horror of that accident began to shift, we learned that Maya was pregnant. Months later she gave birth to a baby girl and became a middle-school-aged mother. At the news of her pregnancy, the clergyperson who had been helping Maya to get into the private school quickly withdrew her support. However, her family and the community of the church continued to support Maya and her baby daughter. She was not rejected or in any way blamed for getting pregnant at such a young age as are other girls in different communities. This response by family and church community holds clues for how we might think theologically and politically about teen pregnancy and parenting. At the same time, the father of Maya's baby was never identified. There was never any in-depth inquiry into how this thirteen-year-old child became pregnant to begin with. There were rumors about an adult male who lived in the same building as Maya and her family. There were other rumors about an uncle.

Dr. Joycelyn Elders, former Surgeon General of the United States during the Clinton Administration, has written, "sexual abuse is a major public health problem, which is made more complex by the attitudes of our society in addressing issues involving sex."[2] These attitudes are most certainly impacted by our religious attitudes about sexuality, including those that are held in place by silence, shame, and fear. What do Black theologies/womanist theologies have to say to a child like Maya? What do they have to say about incest and child sexual abuse? How do we incorporate the realities of teen pregnancy and teen parenting into our liberating religious reflection on human sexuality? What does womanist theology/Black theologies have to say in support of family structures that fall outside of an idealized norm of mother/father and 2.5 kids?

## DOMESTIC VIOLENCE

Layla was a fifteen-year-old faithful acolyte in another church that I served. Layla was being raised by her grandmother in the projects that shadowed the parish. She had participated in the life of St. Rita's ever since she was a young child. She attended Sunday school. She helped out in the soup kitchen and sang in the choir. She found her way to the

---

2. Joycelyn Elders, quoted in Robin D. Stone, *No Secrets, No Lies: How Black Families Can Heal from Sexual Abuse* (New York: Broadway, 2004) xiii.

church largely on her own. No other adult family member attended the church. In many ways the church was an extension of her family. It was a place that accepted her and valued and invited her participation.

One day Layla showed up at the church just before a service; her face was swollen and bruised. Her hair and clothing were disheveled. It turned out that her twenty-one-year-old boyfriend who had just been released from prison had beaten her earlier that morning. Some of the women in the church quickly gathered her up, smoothed her hair, patted her back, and in hushed tones meant to sooth, told her "to get used to it, that's just the way men are."

Relationship violence is all too common in American society, in-cluding Black communities. It touches married couples, people who are dating, adults, elders, and a growing number of teens. Women and men are targets of relationship violence, though women are targeted at greater rates. It impacts straight, gay, bisexual, and transgendered members of our communities. Relationship violence injures and kills thousands of women each year. It seems that almost every day the media reports a man who killed or seriously injured a girlfriend, wife, or ex-wife, some-times also children and other relatives and sometimes himself. And yet somehow it remains one of the deep secrets of many communities, including faith communities. Silence is kept because we fear exposing less than perfect marriages, partnerships, and families. I also think it is kept because we still lack courage in naming and confronting patriarchal oppression in too many of our communities and institutions, including the church.

## HIV/AIDS

I buried Georgette nine months after I met her. She had brittle hair, an ashen face, and she weighed less that one hundred pounds. At age thirty she appeared to be twice her age. She was tough. She was a vocal advo-cate for herself insisting on attention and service to the point of being annoying to most of the professional staff in the facility where she lived. Georgette's path to the residential center for people with AIDS where I served as chaplain was defined by prostitution and drug use.

At her funeral I wanted to remember her not as a sugar-coated ide-alized figure, but as someone who was deeply flawed and yet had tried to make change in her own life. Her young son was at the funeral. He had been able to see her only a few times in the last years of her life. I wanted his final memories of his mother, who had most certainly had a difficult life, to include the story of his mother's choice to be baptized only a few months earlier and of his mother's love and concern for her son. My pastoral concern was in assuring family and friends of God's love even in the most difficult circumstances.

Just as I was about to conclude the service, which was being held in a local funeral home, a man who had been sitting in the back row cradling his huge leather Bible leapt to his feet, marched toward the casket containing Georgette's body, slammed the Bible down on the lid of the casket, and launched into a diatribe about Georgette's sinfulness and the fact that she was certainly burning in Hell at that very moment. According to this man, who was a distant cousin (and a self-identified minister of the Gospel) AIDS was God's judgment on this woman. She had gotten what she deserved.

According to The Balm in Gilead, Inc., a faith-based organization whose stated mission is "to stop the spread of HIV/AIDS throughout the African Diaspora," tells us the real story:

- "While only 12 percent of the total American population, African Americans make up 37 percent of total American AIDS cases."

- "Black children in the U.S. represent almost two-thirds (62 percent) of all reported pediatric AIDS cases."

- "Black senior citizens represent more than 50 percent of HIV cases among persons over age 55."

- "HIV/AIDS infection rates in the Caribbean are among the highest in the world second only to Sub-Saharan Africa."

- "More than 1.4 million Nigerian children have been orphaned by AIDS."

- "The leading cause of HIV infection among African Americans is heterosexual contact, followed by injection use."[3]

Clearly it is essential that we address HIV/AIDS and its impact on Black communities around the world if we want to engage human sexuality through a librating theological lens.

3. All statistics are taken from the "Balm of Gilead" website: www.balmgilead.org.

## ANTI-GAY VIOLENCE

In the early morning hours of May 11, 2003, Sakia Gunn, a fifteen-year-old African American lesbian was waiting for a bus with four friends in Newark, New Jersey. They had just returned from a night out in Manhattan's Greenwich Village. As they were waiting, a car with two men pulled up. The men began flirting with the girls who quickly identified themselves as lesbians and said that they were not interested. The men became enraged by their rejection. An argument erupted. One of the men got out of the car and began to choke one of the girls. Sakia Gunn came to her aid. In the struggle, the man stabbed Sakia in the chest. She died a few hours later in the hospital. The man who stabbed her turned himself in to the police.

Over 2,500 students attended Sakia's funeral. The principle of Sakia's high school was quoted as saying, "If someone chooses to live a certain lifestyle, they must pay a certain price." He refused to honor student's request for a moment of silence in Sakia's honor because she was a lesbian.

This murder highlights how lethal homophobia and heterosexism can be. It is literally a matter of life and death. We lose sight of this in too many of our debates about human sexuality/homosexuality. We tend to focus on issue like ordination and marriage, not on violence and death. No one should face the death penalty because of his or her sexual expression or gender identity. There are places in this world where imprisonment and even death are the penalty for homosexuality. We need to keep this reality clear in our minds when we approach questions of human sexuality and most specifically homosexuality.

## CONCLUSION/MOVING FORWARD

All of the issues raised by these stories of individuals and communities point out the complexity of what it means to do theology that is truly liberating, healing, and empowering—theologies that include the lives and experiences of all Black people. We must be willing to embrace and stand with survivors of violence, with GLBTQ people, and people with HIV/AIDS when we say that we want to move forward with regard to human sexuality in our theologies and in our actions in community. We cannot afford to delay or hide behind a limited view of one aspect of human sexual experience, namely, homosexuality, in an attempt, consciously or unconsciously, to avoid engagement with a wider range of issues that many of us will find frightening, disconcerting, and even painful. These stories also raise the question: Who needs liberation from us? It is only with this type of complex engagement, self-examination and solidarity that we can move toward sexual health, sexual justice, and well-being for all Black people.

If we are willing to cast our theological thinking and faithful action about homosexuality/GLBTQ issues within a larger framework of human sexuality we will open new possibilities and avenues for reflection, discussion, and activism for justice for GLBTQ people in African American communities to emanate from religious sources. For example, if we are willing to recognize and affirm diverse family structures, and indeed the success of diverse family structures as survival strategies in Black communities, then we might find a way to recognize and affirm lesbian and gay families, including same-sex marriage. We might even decide to judge a relationship by its quality (love and care) rather than its form (heterosexual), an essential step to stopping domestic violence. If we are willing to try on the idea of fluidity in gender identity, then we might find ourselves able to acknowledge and accept the blessing of people of transgender expression in our congregations and communities. In this way we can deny the gay-bashers God's permission or endorsement of their crimes.

Clearly a holistic, comprehensive engagement with human sexuality opens up possibilities for empowerment, healing and justice for us all. These stories do not necessarily point to any new concept; theology from the underside is our history and heritage. These stories do point to the underside of our own communities, and the importance of continuing to embrace God's preferential option for the most vulnerable. They challenge us to act upon our theology: how do we live out our belief that human beings—all human beings—are the image of God and therefore sacred? How do we express in words and actions the value of mutuality in relationship, and an ethic of care and protection for those considered to be the least of the children of the earth?

In addition to this wholistic approach to addressing human sexuality in our theological, congregational, and community lives I want to suggest three tasks as we work in our various faith contexts to move in directions that will result in greater liberation, empowerment and healing for all Black people.

First, we need to expand out theological, religious, and spiritual conversations to include religious perspectives other than Christianity. Black Christian theologians have an opportunity to engage theological, social and political ideas in conversation with Black people who practice Islam, Buddhism, Orisa traditions (including Lukumi, Santeria, Vodu), Judaism, and Ethical Humanism just to name a few traditions. How might this type of conversation help us to expand our understanding of divinity, humanity, and the role of sexuality in religion and spirituality?

Second, we must open our own theological roads by allowing fluidity with respect to identity and categories. It is important not to slip into essentialism. This is especially critical in discussions about human sexuality, gender, and race. What does it mean to be a "woman?" What does it mean to be a "man?" How do these questions complicate for us the way we articulate Black liberation theologies or Womanist theologies? How do they enable us to think about and act beyond boundaries set by institutions and structures of power, as well as those that are self-imposed? And, how do we act and write and speak in solidarity with those on the margins?

Finally, I wish we would develop cooperative models for shaping theologies and activist faith communities. Collaborations and discussions that bring together scholarship, activism, and experience from congregations, communities and the academy are a critical step in developing cooperative models for theological reflection and faithful action. With our differences and our commonalities, it is my hope that we find shared paths on our various journeys that will lead to constructive, powerful, liberating theologies and strategies for action for all Black people. This will entail being conscious of our power as well as our marginality. It means allowing for permeability in identity boundaries and categories that we use to define ourselves. I wonder what a Black liberation, Womanist, African diasporic model of shared thinking and action would look like? It might be celebratory and self-aware; it might honor and enjoy our bodies; it might reflect and support the whole community; it might be flexible and fluid, self-critical and self-determining. It might be the way forward.

# 14

## Black Churches, the Bible, and the Battle
## over Homosexuality

### HORACE L. GRIFFIN

W HEN BLACK FILM DIRECTOR Spike Lee popularized a common
Black cultural understanding of sex as "doing the nasty," few
African Americans may have grasped the negative implications of shame
and filth that come with such a reference, even when the reference is
made in a humorous manner. And while most African Americans could
hardly be considered sexually repressed (the display of sex in Black hip-
hop music and music videos and a disproportionate number of teen
pregnancies would disprove such a claim), historical circumstances that
demonize Black sexuality and create sex-negative Black religion are
largely responsible for the lack of progressive sexual ideology and theology among African Americans. After centuries of white racism depicting Black sexuality as animalistic and perverse, many African American
religious leaders and others have internalized a negative appraisal of
sexuality in general and Black sexuality in particular. They have been
engaged in a perpetual reaction to this depiction by adopting dualistic
notions of sexuality and promoting conservative sexual mores in order
to gain respectability from the mainstream.

And while conservative gender and sexual views are not easily
missed in Black churches, no part of human sexual expression creates
more discomfort and rage in African American heterosexuals, and others for that matter, than same sex sexual expression and relationships.
The Black church's teaching that homosexuality is immoral has created a
crisis for gay Christians in Black churches. It is a teaching that I charac-

terize as oppressive and duplicitous. Homophobic preaching creates psychological and theological problems, both for lesbians and gays in Black churches, and their heterosexual friends, family, and fellow congregants. And while I, as a gay son of the Black Church, join with other openly gay African Americans in celebrating the rich worship experience and numerous ways Black churches have helped Black people, I deplore the ways that Black church leaders and others denigrate gays.

The strong opposition to civil rights marriage legislation of African American gay relationships and that of other gays is the most recent evidence of this fact. And while homophobia can be found in all communities, for the purposes of this paper, I will focus on Black church homophobia as problematic and antithetical to the Gospel of Jesus and the Black liberation theology tradition. I offer other approaches to understanding scripture and homosexuality through a pastoral theology of Black liberation, providing reconciliation for gays and heterosexuals in families and Black faith communities.

Understanding and appreciating homosexuality as a legitimate sexual expression continues to be a challenge for African Americans. Even amid the significant number of gays, lesbians and bisexuals in Black families and communities; the ever growing number of openly lesbian and gay African Americans like the Black icon, Angela Davis; and the awareness of prominent and revered African American lesbian and gay Christians in history such as George Washington Carver, James Cleveland and Barbara Jordan, many Black heterosexuals display a stubborn resistance to viewing homosexuality as anything but a white aberration, often dismissing its relevance to Black people. Even when there are attempts to present African Americans as more accepting, the evidence of this struggle is apparent as in the following example.

In *One More River to Cross: Being Black and Gay in America*, Keith Boykin cites that only "29 percent of blacks surveyed said that homosexuals should remain in the closet, while 65 percent disagreed." Many Blacks continue to argue that they "do not object to homosexuality [but] object to *open* expressions of it."[1] Such a position is contradictory. To say that a gay person is accepted as long as she/he does not demonstrate the very thing that makes her/him gay is no acceptance at all. This attitude is strikingly similar to that of white racists who feigned acceptance of

---

1. Kevin Boykin, *One More River to Cross: Black and Gay in America* (New York: Anchor, 1996) 188.

Blacks as long as Blacks stayed in their place and exhibited behaviors that did not reflect Black cultural expressions. The expectation that gays be both invisible and out of the closet, reflects the shame, discomfort and embarrassment that African Americans feel about same sex affection. Given that no heterosexual is saying that heterosexuals should not display open expressions of their heterosexuality, this reaction is more than cultural modesty about sexual relationships. Rather, this kind of silencing is a means of domination and control over gays and, like all silencing, works toward the death of a people. In the current climate, there are two areas that continue to be used to keep African Americans homophobic or opposed to loving same sex sexual expression. The first is theological (using the Bible to oppose homosexuality as in same sex marriage) and the second is cultural (arguing that homosexual desire or acceptance is not Black).

Many Black church leaders and others align themselves with the heterosexual supremacist President, George W. Bush, in a vitriolic campaign against civil rights marriage legislation of gay relationships. And while it is true that some who oppose gay marriage may not consider other legal discriminations and attacks on gays as justified, their marriage opposition nonetheless points to their perspective that gays and heterosexuals should not be treated equally.

## SAME SEX MARRIAGE

The recent marriage debate has divided African Americans largely into two camps: marriage traditionalists and marriage advocates.[2] Black Christians stand as some of the most ardent defenders of marriage as a special right for heterosexual couples, both civilly and religiously. Their position has won them many friends from conservative white Protestant Christians who ordinarily are not interested in hearing from African Americans or Black clergy on important issues of the Black majority, including Affirmative Action programs, better public schools for Black children, Black poverty and the racism of our police and penal system.

In February 2005, ministers who worked on the reelection of George W. Bush urged conservative Black ministers in California to join them in a campaign against gay marriage entitled, "Black Contract

2. Marvin M. Ellison, *Same-Sex Marriage: A Christian Ethical Analysis* (Cleveland: Pilgrim, 2004) 1.

with America on Moral Values." A summit held at the 27,000 member Crenshaw Christian Center in Los Angeles, hosted by renowned televangelist, Fred Price, included the showing of a video, designed to present all gays as white sex fiends using Martin Luther King's name. Price commented, "the marriage issue has moved [me] to act." The event exacerbated the homophobia of the Black pastors present (as if this group were not homophobic enough). Seventy Black pastors "nodded affirmatively" as they pledged allegiance to this campaign. Frank L. Stewart, an African American bishop, argued, "black people have to change their whole paradigm of thinking. This is a philosophical war going on." With such tactics that resurrect the language and actions of former segregationists and Klan members, it is not surprising that Black lesbian activist Jasmyne Cannick would say, "I feel like I am at a KKK meeting." She questioned how Black leaders who have experienced discrimination could challenge the rights and struggles of others, including gay blacks."[3]

Across the country, Black church leaders can be heard defending marriage from the Bible, pointing out that the Bible only sanctions marriage between a man and woman in a similar manner as many ante-bellum white ministers pointed out that the Bible sanctioned slavery. Like past efforts to keep marriage as an institution only for free white people or members of the same race, the Bible has become a defense mechanism in preventing marriage from being extended to another group of citizens. The irony this time is that African American heterosexuals are leading the charge of denying marriage to another oppressed group.

On March 22, 2004, in a historic stand against marriage equality, "the Reverend Clarence James and 29 other [African American] pastors . . . signed a declaration outlining their beliefs on marriage . . . The declaration [stated] that marriage is not a civil right, and marriage between a man and a woman is important because it's necessary for the upbringing of children."[4] Reverend James stated "when the homosexual compares himself to the black community, he doesn't know what suffering is."[5] While James' statement reflects a common Black response, there are problems with this statement. First of all, James makes an untrue

3. "Black Clergy Wooed for Values Fight"; online: www.latimes.com/news/local/la-me-pastors2feb02.

4. "Black Clergymen Come Out Against Gay Marriage," *Atlanta Journal Constitution*, March 23, 2004.

5. Ibid.

statement about gay people. In his word choice of "the homosexual," he identifies gays as white and the same. This is noted in his contrast of "the homosexual" with "the Black community." He conveniently ignores the millions of African American gays in order to keep "gay rights" as solely a part of privileged wealthy white men, a group that is perceived as spared discrimination.

Furthermore, the sentence in this document, "to equate a lifestyle choice to racism demeans the work of the entire civil rights movement," makes false claims about both homosexuality and the Civil Rights Movement. Homosexuality is no more a "lifestyle choice" than heterosexuality and the Civil Rights Movement is an effort to ensure all Americans equal rights under the Constitution. Some of the most committed leaders of the Civil Rights Movement of the 1950s and 60s were also lesbians and gays such as Bayard Rustin (King advisor and organizer of the March on Washington, 1963), James Baldwin, Audre Lourde, and the Reverend Malcolm Boyd, a white gay Episcopal clergyman.

The present injustice against lesbians and gays has everything to do with the Civil Rights Movement. To reduce the movement to racism is a gross misunderstanding. Martin Luther King Jr. understood that while the movement committed itself to transforming evil racist structures into systems of equality, his work with the poor people's campaign is consistent with his belief that "a threat to justice anywhere is a threat to justice everywhere." In other words, if a society can justify discrimination toward gays, similar reasons can be used to justify discrimination against skin color, gender, religion, or any other categorization of human beings.

Perhaps King knew the limits of using the argument of choice to deny civil rights and marriage. For those who continue to argue that gays can be discriminated against because they chose their homosexuality, they should remember that in the days of Nazi Germany, a group was discriminated against because of their religious choice. The argument that Judaism is a religious choice and one can simply choose another religion to avoid persecution highlights the injustice of discriminating against a group simply because a segment of the population has made a choice that another group does not like. With such an approach, there would be an unending attack on groups that make choices disliked by others. The ugly history of denying marriage to individuals who chose

someone of another race is too recent in our history for us not to have
learned a lesson.

Rev. James's claim that gays do not know what suffering is lacks
credibility. Since gays experience pain from lies about themselves, losing
their jobs within and outside of the U.S. military, housing discrimination, being ridiculed, ignored, and disowned by their family members,
denied their children, and experience physical assault and even death
because they are gay, it is simply not true that gays do not understand
suffering. If James cannot understand *this* as suffering, then he, not gays,
does not know the meaning of suffering.

On December 11, 2004, Black heterosexual ministers led another
anti-gay march in Atlanta. Considering King's position against any discrimination, the March beginning at the Martin Luther King Jr. Center
for Nonviolent Social Change was especially problematic. Led by Bishops
T. D. Jakes and Eddie Long, thousands of demonstrators turned out to
oppose marriage equality between gay and heterosexual couples. Earl
Hutchinson of *Black News* wrote that the sight of the daughter of Martin
Luther King Jr., the Reverend Bernice King, "standing at the gravesite
of her father with thousands of demonstrators to denounce gay marriage was painful and insulting." Hutchinson feels "given [King's] relentless and uncompromising battles against discrimination during his life,
it defies belief that he would back an anti-gay campaign." Even though
Bernice King is an outspoken evangelical, many who know her would
find it surprising that she has marched, written letters, and petitions de-
nouncing gay marriage.[6]

Stating that it will "never allow the sanctioning of same sex marriage by its clergy nor recognize the legitimacy of such unions," in its
recent proclamation, the Church of God in Christ, led by the Presiding
Bishop, Gilbert E. Patterson, expresses pride in exclusive heterosexual
marriage.

The other six historically Black denominations hold similar positions; no Black denomination supports marriage equality for gay couples
and heterosexual couples. The Church of God in Christ proclamation
identifies all lesbian and gay unions as sinful. This proclamation, however, does not address other biblical marriage models that most Black
Christians would also view as immoral, for example traditional polygynous marriages as in the case of Abraham and Solomon. And while po-

6. Earl Hutchinson, *Hutchinson Report Newsletter*, December 13, 2004.

lygynous marriages are not found in the New Testament, they are never condemned by God as sinful or inappropriate. Let me be clear, I am not an advocate for polygynous marriage, but rather I point out that it is not true that Black Christians are opposed to gay marriage simply because they are not found in the Bible. In an attempt to end discussion, the Church of God in Christ, uses the Bible as a last defense of exclusive heterosexual marriage and resistance to lesbian and gay marriage, much like most Black denominations continue to resist women's equality and ordination. Marriage advocates would say that a responsible theological response to marriage is more than just citing certain scripture that presents one marriage model as a way to exclude others, especially since these same Christians do not adhere to a number of biblical passages.

Many ignore biblical mandates, for example, of stoning disobedient sons (Deuteronomy 21:21), granting divorce only in cases of sexual unfaithfulness (Matthew 19:9), giving up wealth (Matthew 19:21), and greeting everyone with a kiss (2 Corinthians 13:12). Interestingly, Paul's biblical injunction on kissing appears more times than his writing on homosexual activity. I am not suggesting that Christians observe strict and abusive passages, as in the case of stoning children, but rather that Black Christians should also recognize the irrelevance of using the above passages on homosexual activity when addressing lesbian and gay relationships that model Christian values of love, support, nurture, care and compassion.

Like the double standard of condemning the sexual activity of gay relationships while heterosexuals engaging in the same sexual activity escape such ridicule, there is also a double standard between the two groups regarding the passage to "be fruitful and multiply." Despite the fact that heterosexuals engage in the same kinds of sexual behavior as gays, with heterosexuals also engaging in genital intercourse, the Church of God in Christ Marriage Proclamation centers the opposition to same sex relationships on biblical grounds of procreation, "be fruitful and multiply." It reads "marriage between male and female provide the structure for conceiving and raising children. Compliance with this command of God is a physical and biological impossibility in same-sex union." This statement ignores the fact that it is also impossible for many married heterosexual couples (elderly and infertile) to fulfill this command. In this respect, what can occur in a committed non-procreative heterosexual relationship that cannot also occur in a committed homosexual relationship?

One can readily assess that the reason why Black church heterosexual Christians deny African American lesbian and gay Christian couples marriage is their problem with sexual expression between two women and between two men. When presented with the fact that procreation cannot occur between all heterosexual couples, Black Christians often shift the argument of procreation to one that is "for the upbringing of children." This position disrespects the many single parent/mostly single mother headed families and those without the biological father and mother that provide nurture, love, care and the successful upbringing of Black children. This does not mean that many fathers and mothers do not provide wonderful home environments for the upbringing of children, but rather it calls for the recognition of other nurturing parental configurations without making male-female headed household superior and ignoring the unhealthy and abusive male-female headed structures.

With the current abundance of Black children within our society and 90% of children of darker color in adoption homes, procreation is an unnecessary concern.[7] What is needed from African American church leaders is encouragement from responsible adults, be they heterosexual, lesbian, or gay, to take care of needy Black children, instead of disparaging comments about non-procreative lesbian and gay couples. Rather than a threat to Black families and communities, African American gays are often financially and emotionally devoted to their families and communities. And in the cases of lesbian and gay headed households, studies show that children are as equally well-adjusted as those coming out of heterosexual headed households.

When there are so many problems in Black families and communities, especially heterosexual male absence or violence in homes, gangs, alcohol and drug abuse, large prison populations, teenage pregnancies, high rates of AIDS and other sexually transmitted diseases, it is curious why Black pastors continue opposing lesbians and gays for desiring to honor their committed relationships in a positive way through marriage. Perhaps, such a focus here is a result of frustration shared by these pastors from unsuccessful efforts in resolving the above ills in Black families and communities. Anti-marriage equality is a diversion from such fail-

7. Dan Woog, "Adopting a Family," *The Advocate* issue 750/751, January 20, 1998, 70.

ures and conveniently scapegoats African American lesbians and gays as causing major problems in Black families and communities rather than many heterosexuals.

This heterosexual supremacist approach to marriage is also upheld by African American Howard Divinity School professor Dr. Cheryl Saunders. Saunders finds that gay relationships "severely undermine the heterosexual family."[8] To state that gays "severely undermine the heterosexual family" suggests that the heterosexual family and heterosexuality are not as strong as marriage traditionalists argue but rather weak units that crumble under a more powerful and attractive lesbian or gay configuration.

Such a claim does not speak favorably or convincingly to the stability and quality of heterosexuality. The "severely undermine" language used by Saunders, creates hysteria for heterosexuals, that gays are to be feared, and threaten the moral fabric of society. This rhetoric has created a frenzied African American heterosexual population, influencing church leaders in their present stand against gay marriages and dismissal of homosexuality as African or Black.

When I was a professor at the historically Black Fisk University, I was under constant siege by students decrying homosexuality as a perverse European sexual practice, unknown to Africans until Europeans imposed it on them.[9] Interestingly, these same students spent an enormous amount of energy "proving" that Europeans stole everything from Africa. Everything that is, except homosexuality. With the prevalence of homosexuality throughout the world in both the human and animal world and people's dishonesty about their same sex sexual desire, I found the students' resistance to African homosexuality having more to do with their discomfort about homosexuality rather than a great untruth about African people.

---

8. Cheryl Saunders, "The Black Church and Homosexuality." This paper was presented on February 12, 1998, at a conference sponsored by the Carpenter Program in Religion, Gender and Sexuality and the Kelly Miller Smith Institute of Vanderbilt Divinity School. The quote is taken from *The Tennessean*, February 13, 1998, 2b.

9. Marc Eprecht, "Good God Almighty; What's This! Homosexual Crime in Early Colonial Zimbabwe," in *Boy-Wives and Female Husbands: Studies in African Homosexualities*, ed. Stephen O. Murray and Will Roscoe (New York: St. Martin's, 1998) 198–99; and Ron Simmons, "Some Thoughts on the Challenges Facing Black Gay Intellectuals," in *Brother to Brother: Collected Writings by Black Gay Men*, ed. Essex Hemphill (Boston: Alyson, 1991) 213.

Why are many Africans and African Americans resistant to a ho-mosexual presence in Africa even when there is considerable evidence otherwise? In a world that continues to view African peoples as less developed, less moral and perhaps less human, and given the stigma of homosexuality as an immoral expression, it becomes clear that the myth about homosexuality satisfies a cultural need. The assertion that homo-sexuality is a perverse sexual practice of Europeans imposed on Africans is a reflection of the human tendency to attribute stigmatized behavior to a despised group. Thus, the view—homosexuality is an outside aber-ration imposed on sacred African people.

How could whites be responsible for sexual feelings in Black Africans or Black people? Are Blacks also granting that whites even have power over their sexual desires? Anthropologist Marc Eprecht had a similar question when he examined the hundreds of homosexual cases in Zimbabwe and surrounding African countries involving only a few whites. "Were this a white man's disease, how to explain that nearly 90 % of all cases of homosexual crime involved African men [having sex with] other African men or boys."[10]

Although Africans and African Americans are right to criticize European colonialism, the accusation that colonialism imposed homo-sexuality is simply untrue. Since homosexuality is a part of human sexu-ality, identified throughout time in various forms on all continents by anthropologists and sociologists, it becomes a racist claim to state that Africans do not express themselves with same sex love like the rest of the world. In their brilliant work, *Boy Wives and Female Husbands: Studies of African Homosexualities,* anthropologists Stephen Murray and Will Roscoe refute the claim that homosexuality is not African in the follow-ing statement: "although contact between Africans and non-Africans has sometimes influenced both groups' sexual patterns, there is no evidence that one group ever 'introduced' homosexuality to another."[11]

Despite the presence of homosexual expression in European coun-tries, most of Europe, prior to and during the African slave trade, strongly rejected same-sex sexual practice. European Christians were generally sex negative and anti-homosexual. Hence, European Christian mis-sionaries, slave traders, and colonialists who went into African countries were more prone to condemn homosexual practice rather than condone

10. Eprecht, "Good God Almighty," 206.

11. Murray and Roscoe, eds., *Boy-Wives and Female Husbands,* 267.

or encourage it. Under colonial rule in the former Rhodesia, "African men's own testimony also shows that they generally expected and often feared the stern disapproval of whites and sought, for that reason, to keep their homosexual practices secret."[12]

The cultural teaching that homosexuality is a white perversion, provides the convenience of disowning homosexual reality in Black people. The courageous gay Black South African, Simon Nikoli, stated that his mother, perceiving his homosexuality as a bad thing, told him, "I knew that I should not have sent you to that white school."[13] This common response prevents Black Africans from reassessing homosexual expression and its relevance to those within their families, communities and themselves. This homophobia promotes harsh responses toward fellow gay and lesbian Africans or those who engage in sexual relationships with the same sex, and places many Africans as victimizers like the Europeans who colonized them.

In the spring of 2001, two women in Somalia were sentenced to death for "unnatural behavior." Also, "In Uganda, church leaders of the Uganda House of Bishops called on the government not to register a gay and lesbian group called Integrity Uganda. The church group reportedly described the gay organization as unbiblical and inhuman." Since no one is being violated, harmed, or killed by two people who share a loving sexual relationship, the hostile reaction by Africans and African Americans is confusing. It is precisely these hostile reactions and violent laws that prevent Africans from acknowledging homosexual practice, thus contributing to the false notion that there are no African homosexuals.

Sociologist David Greenberg notes in *The Construction of Homosexuality* that Africans recorded very little about African culture period. It is important to keep in mind that given the cultural taboos against speaking about sex, it would be virtually impossible for homosexual practices to find record.[14] The absence of records, however, should not be interpreted as the absence of homosexual practice. People can and do express themselves sexually, in a variety of ways, without ever writing or talking about such expressions.

Despite the fact that African people did not leave their own records of homosexual practice, African same-sex sexual expression did not

12. Eprecht, "Good God Almighty," 218.

13. Murray and Roscoe, eds., *Boy-Wives and Female Husbands*, 45.

14. Greenberg, *The Construction of Homosexuality*, 19.

go totally undocumented. Murray and Roscoe identify many African homosexual practices and the moral condemnations of early European missionaries: "from late sixteenth-century Portuguese reports of 'unnatural damnation' in Angola, . . . John Burchardt's 1882 report of 'detestable vices' in Nubia, to the 1893 report of copulation contre nature in . . . Senegal and the 1906 report of . . . Herrero men forsaking the natural use of a woman."[15]

Like in all cultures, there are cases of physical affection that have nothing to do with sex, there are many that have to do with sex. Twentieth century anthropologist Kurt Falk documents that for Africans in West Africa and Angola "speaking about homosexual sex is considered disgusting . . . nevertheless, homoeroticism, gender variance (and exchanging sex for material goods) are not phenomena alien to Africa, just as silence does not mean absence.[16] He further states "because to the natives having sex is as normal as eating and drinking and, by all means, tobacco-smoking . . . Because they view homosexual intercourse with unbiased eyes, they have known and practiced it from time immemorial.[17]

It is common for the same behavior described as sexual between a man and a woman to be denied as sexual if it involves two people of the same sex. African researchers are also beginning to tell the truth about same sex sexual expression, regardless of whether or not it is identified as gay or homosexual. Researchers find that in case after case, Africans have not been honest about their homosexual expression. Nii Ajen's (Falk's) research shows that "even the man you may have just done everything with sexually will say no if you ask him if he is gay. And if you should ask that same man if there is homosexuality in Africa, a likely response will be 'no, there is nothing like that in Africa.'"[18]

In Lesotho, boarding school girls form "same-sex couples composed of a slightly more "dominant" partner, called a "Mummy" and a slightly more "passive" partner called a "Baby" . . . The girls do not describe these relationships as sexual, although they include kissing, body rubbing, possessiveness and monogamy, the exchange of gifts and promises, and

15. Murray and Roscoe, eds., *Boy-Wives and Female Husbands*, 11.

16. Ibid., 132, 168.

17. Kurt Falk, "Homosexuality among the Natives of Southwest Africa," in *Boy-Wives and Female Husbands*.

18. Ibid., 131.

sometime genital contact."[19] Some Basothu women in Southern Africa also resist the idea that their interaction with each other could be construed as sexual in spite of the eroticism, intimacy, and "kissing each other on the mouth with great tenderness, exploring each other's mouth with tongues . . . for periods of time in excess of sixty seconds . . . [and] the longest kisses take place out of view of men and children."[20] This present context of dishonesty about same-sex sexual desire and practice has implications for an often touted absent homosexual past in Africa.

This denial is disappointing as well as using the Bible as an oppressive tool in the way white racists used it for the support of slavery and segregation. History informs us that during slavery Christian missionaries converted slaves into a rigid Christianity. Since the majority of African American slaves became Christian through the evangelical efforts of Methodists and Baptists during plantation missions, they also adopted their conservative Christian traditions and strict adherence to the Bible. This biblical indoctrination by conservative white Protestants laid a foundation for African Americans' understanding of scripture in strict literal and legalistic ways. Conservative white Protestants generally taught Blacks that it was the Bible itself that insisted they were to be slaves to whites. Slavery survived for such a long time because most white Christians maintained a faithful adherence to the Bible that sanctioned slavery as moral. Unlike the majority of white Christians, most African American Christians did not find the slavery passages compelling. African American biblical scholar, Vincent Wimbush notes, "from the beginning of their engagement with [the Bible] African Americans interpreted the Bible differently from those who introduced them to it, ironically and audaciously seeing in it—the most powerful of the ideological weapons used to legitimize their enslavement and disenfranchisement—a mirroring of themselves and their experiences, seeing in it the privileging of all those who like themselves are the humiliated, the outcasts and powerless."[21]

As Black Christians embraced biblical stories of Jesus' love and God's liberating power, it became more and more difficult to reconcile

19. K. Limakatso Kendall, *Basali! Stories By and About Women in Lesotho* (Kwazulu Natal, South Africa: University of Kwalzulu Natal Press, 1995) 231.

20. Ibid., 231–32.

21. Vincent L. Wimbush, ed., *African Americans and the Bible: Sacred Texts and Social Textures* (New York: Continuum, 2000) 17.

a God that delivered Israelites from oppressive Pharaohs with a God who kept them enslaved. In this approach to scripture, Blacks, like other groups, demonstrate a practice of selectively choosing scripture. In this "selection bias" there is more attending to information that confirms what is already believed and offers validation while viewing other biblical injunctions as irrelevant to their present status. Thus, the Bible can, and historically has been used by the oppressor and the oppressed for their own liberation and benefit. It is much too simplistic to refer to the Bible in binary ways as an oppressive book or a liberationist document. As noted by African American biblical scholar Dr. Renita Weems, the Bible has less to do with either oppression or liberation. Christians read the Bible and assign meaning to create oppression or liberation in their lives and the lives of other human beings.

Nancy Ambrose, the slave grandmother of African American theologian Howard Thurman, expressed this dilemma in the following case: "during the days of slavery, . . . master's minister would occasionally hold services for the slaves. Always the white minister used as his text something from Paul. Slaves be obedient to your masters as unto Christ. Then he would go on to show that if we were good and happy slaves, God would bless us. I promised my maker that if I ever learned to read and if freedom ever came, I would not read that part of the Bible."[22]

This example points to the limitations of scripture and the different hermeneutical lenses that a Christian culture brings to a passage. As Wimbush's analysis and Ambrose's Christian experience affirm, Black people's experience of God's grace and Christ's presence in their lives made them full and equal children of God. For Ambrose, Paul's biblical writing failed to convince her that it was God's intention for her to be subordinate to white masters. Her faith and relationship with God told her that she was a child of God and should be treated the same as whites who claimed God's favor, regardless of what was stated in the Bible. The above example shows that African American Christians demonstrate that you can be faithful Christians without accepting all scripture as authoritative. The rejection of Scriptures supporting slavery is the clearest example. This approach is valuable and appropriate when examining passages that have been traditionally used against gays and their relationships.

22. Howard Thurman, *Jesus and the Disinherited* (New York: Abingdon-Cokesbury, 1949) 30–31.

The first reality about homosexual practice in the Bible is that the biblical writers were not as preoccupied with the issue of homosexuality as present-day church leaders. There are no more than six or seven passages that address homosexual activity: Genesis 19:1–29 (Judges 19); Leviticus 18:22; 20:13; Romans 1:18–32; 1 Corinthians 6:9-11; and 1 Timothy 1:8–11.[23] Moreover the biblical passages cited do not speak to early Christians' negative perspectives on homosexuality. Since the writers only refer to homosexual activity (a practice that was assumed to be a deviation from a natural heterosexual construction), there is no reference, or condemnation for that matter, of two people of the same sex cohabitating in a loving, committed, and long-term sexual relationship.

Many point out with good reason that it is anachronistic to use the Bible to address the homosexual reality of the twenty-first century unknown to ancient and first-century biblical writers. New Testament scholar Robin Scroggs offers the following brilliant summary: "The basic model in today's Christian [gay] community is so different from the model attacked by the New Testament that the criterion of reasonable similarity of context is not met. The conclusion I have to draw seems inevitable: *"Biblical judgments against homosexuality are not relevant to today's debate.* They should no longer be used in denominational discussions about homosexuality, should in no way be a weapon to justify refusal of ordination, *not because the Bible is not authoritative*, but simply because it does not address the issues involved."[24]

A pastoral care approach that honors Black liberation for gays in Black churches and families must teach that the Bible does not offer itself as an adequate source for responding to the issue of homosexuality anymore than it sanctions organizing a free society or providing women and men with equal authority in the home and church. It is not a radical request to expect people not to apply the above homosexual activity passages to gay people. African American Christians, like other Christians, treat so literally the references to homosexual practice in the Bible, while

23. Although this passage has traditionally been used to refer to homosexual activity, the words "defile themselves with mankind" are quite ambiguous and are in no way clear that this has to do with two men having sex with each other. Scholars Patricia Jung and Ralph Smith note that the Greek word *arsenokoitai* used in this passage is usually, but not exclusively, translated as "sodomites."

24. Robin Scroggs, *The New Testament and Homosexuality: Contextual Background for Contemporary Debate* (Philadelphia: Fortress, 1983) 127.

at the same time they interpret biblical texts on almost every other topic with considerable flexibility and non-literalness.

Unlike the critical "hermeneutic of suspicion" approach of an African American majority on this culture's response to slavery and segregation, African Americans, by and large, have followed the teachings of the white majority culture. Few raise this logic: since whites were wrong on their view of slavery, perhaps the white majority is also wrong on its view that homosexuality is immoral. Or if the majority Christian culture today recognizes that earlier Christians should not have adhered to certain biblical passages on slavery and supported the subsequent racial oppression, how does the same Christian culture justify the present adherence to a few biblical passages that depict same sex sexual expression as immoral?

Finally, Jesus' silence on homosexuality in all four gospels ought to give African American Christians the greatest pause that homosexuality is the great sin as defined by a majority of Black and white churches.[25] A reasonable response is that if homosexuality were a great sin or a sin at all, Jesus would certainly have addressed this terrible way of life, as he did other sins, at some point during his ministry. The fact that the Black church has been able to assert the dominant position that "the Bible opposes homosexuality and is definitive for what the church should think and do about it" supports Wimbush's point that it is the culture's interpretation rather than a biblical emphasis.

According to its progenitor, James Cone, Black Liberation Theology "must take seriously the reality of black people—their life suffering and humiliation . . . When black people affirm their freedom in God, they know that they cannot obey laws of oppression. [And in light of] the Biblical emphasis on the freedom of [humans], one cannot allow another to define his [or her] existence."[26] If liberation is at the heart of the historical Black church as Cone and others claim and if it is to be consistent with Jesus' gospel mandate to "liberate the oppressed" (see Luke 4:18 and 19), then African American heterosexuals *must* work to end legal discrimination and church teachings and practices that are demeaning

25. This statement should not read that predominantly Asian and Latino churches do not have similar views. However, the level of emotion, attack and politicization of this issue tends not to be as high as is true in Black and white congregations, especially in the conservative Protestant denominations.

26. James H. Cone, *Black Theology and Black Power* (New York: Seabury, 1969) 117, 137–38.

and oppressive to African American gays and contribute to their suffering and death.

As an African American heterosexual Black theologian, Dwight Hopkins, has argued that any teaching or practice that does not support the full equality of lesbians and gays is inconsistent with Christian Black liberation theology. In light of this, there is no reason why Black heterosexual church leaders cannot move toward a true Black liberation theology that affirms all loving sexual relationships as reflecting God's purpose in creation. And in her groundbreaking *Sexuality and the Black Church*, Womanist theologian, Kelly Brown Douglas, asserts that "to choose Jesus as the center of one's life and faith is to choose one whose very being . . . in the world compel[s] an appreciation for the sanctity of human sexuality. Thus, to render sexuality as a taboo issue is, in effect, to preclude the possibility of knowing God's intimate presence and activity in human history."[27]

As documented in Gary David Comstock's *A Whosoever Church* and Larry Kent Graham's *Discovering Images of God: Narratives of Care Among Lesbians and Gays*, narratives of gays' Christian witness as saints washed in the blood of Jesus and living righteous lives provide evidence that gays are children of God. These narratives reflect God's image of compassion, love, and peace, and have the potential for moving all people from viewing homosexuality as immoral and taboo to celebrating same sex love as good, wholesome, and fulfilling. When we take it upon ourselves to resist the bondage of homophobia and heterosexual supremacy, it is then, and only then, that we will be able to celebrate that we are a liberated people of God.

27. Kelly Brown Douglas, *Sexuality and the Black Church* (Maryknoll, NY: Orbis, 1999) 142–43.

## 15

# Spirit in the Dark

## *Sexuality and Spirituality in the Black Church*

DENNIS W. WILEY

When i (*sic*) listen to Aretha, i know that there is a holy spirit because nothing else could make me feel so alive. As far as secular music goes, vintage Aretha is about the closest i come to "getting happy." Listening to her wail, it's as if i'm not here anymore, but transported to another space and time, where i experience heal-ing, connection, and a sense of peace. Her music has often been the antidote to my sorrow, protecting and strengthening me to keep pressing on.

I believe that the Spirit dwells in many places. I know that it lives in Aretha because my soul has gone there and been renewed.[1]

## ARETHA LIVE AT FILLMORE WEST

IN SAN FRANCISCO, CALIFORNIA, February 5–7, 1971, Aretha Franklin, the undisputed "Queen of Soul," recorded an electrifying album titled, "Aretha Live at Fillmore West."[2] Rebounding from a failed marriage and attempting to reach a wider, more diverse audience, Aretha gave a performance for the ages in Haight-Ashbury—West Coast hippie head-

1. Margo V. Perkins, "The Church of Aretha," in *My Soul Is a Witness: African-American Women's Spirituality* (Boston: Beacon, 1995) 129–30.

2. Aretha Franklin, *Aretha Live at Fillmore West*, originally issued as Atlantic #7205, May 19, 1971.

quarters. Although the entire recording is an ever-ascending joy ride, the absolute climax of the occasion occurred on the final night when, toward the end of the concert, she sang the title song from an earlier album she had recorded in the studio just the previous year. The name of that song, composed by Aretha, was "Spirit in the Dark."

What is so special about that song, that performance, and that night is how Aretha, so naturally and seamlessly, wove together the falsely-separated aspects of life (especially, African American life) into a richly beautiful tapestry of spiritual harmony and ecstasy. Through her artistic genius, the superficial lines of division between the sacred and the secular, the soul and the body, the church and the world, religion and life, and spirituality and sexuality were all erased. And in erasing those lines, she brought together not only people of African descent, but also people across racial, ethnic, class, gender, age, cultural, religious, and even sexual orientation boundaries. In other words, as per the title of the song, she literally ushered into that place and into that moment in time the "spirit in the dark."

If we were to exegete the "text" of that moment, we would discover profound insights about human sexuality and the Black religious experience (especially as manifested in and through the Black Church). Since the musical "pericope" under consideration is the performance of "Spirit in the Dark," we are aided in our understanding of the significance of this selection by briefly reviewing the selections that immediately precede and succeed it on the recording.[3]

## DR. FEELGOOD

The preceding song, jointly composed by Aretha and her volatile ex-husband/former manager, Ted White, is titled, "Dr. Feelgood." Aretha introduces it by asking the audience, "Does anybody feel like hearing

3. The liner notes inform us that, of the ten tracks included on this album, tracks 1–7 were recorded on Friday, February 5, and tracks 8–10 were recorded on Sunday, February 7. Therefore, whereas tracks 8 and 9 ("Spirit in the Dark" and the extended version of the same) and track 10 ("Reach Out and Touch [Somebody's Hand]") were recorded on Sunday night, track 7 ("Dr. Feelgood") was recorded on Friday night. This essay assumes that the order of selections was the same each night and that, therefore, on Sunday evening, the track 7 selection immediately preceded the track 8 selection. Even if this was not the case, however, it would have little impact on this essay since our specific point of reference is the *virtual* "live" performance, as presented on the album, rather than the *actual* "live" performance that occurred on Sunday evening.

the blues?" The people promptly respond with a rousing, "Yeah!" Aretha says, "Alright." And after playing a brief musical prelude by masterfully and provocatively tickling the keys of her electric piano, she begins, slowly but deliberately, belting out a song that basically proclaims: "I don't mind having company sometimes, but I don't care *who* you are— whether you're my mother, my brother, my father, or my sister—I don't want *anybody* sitting around smiling, chit chatting, making small talk, and in the way when me and my man want to make love. Period."

Toward the end of the song, so as to emphasize that there is only one kind of physician who can fix what is wrong with her, she declares (with the audience enthusiastically joining in to help):

> Don't send me no doctor
>    Filling me up with all of those pills
> I got me a man named 'Dr. Feelgood'
>    And, oh yeah, that man takes care of all my pains and my ills.
> . . .
> And after one visit to Dr. Feelgood
> You'd understand why Feelgood is his name.

Finally, after a plethora of erotically suggestive moans, groans, wails, oohs, and aahs, Aretha concludes the song with the following vocal and emotional crescendo:

> Oh, yeah, oh, good God Almighty, the man sure makes me feel real
>    Goooooooooooooooooooooooooooooooooooooooood!!!!!![4]

Even though Aretha is not graphically explicit here, as many younger and more contemporary rock, rhythm and blues, and hip hop artists are inclined to be, she leaves no doubt concerning what she is talking about. She is talking about (1) the need for absolute privacy when she is having sex with her man; and, (2) the fact that, for her, a la Marvin Gaye, sex brings not only *pleasure*, but *healing* as well.[5]

---

4. Internet source of lyrics: www.sing365.com.

5. This is a reference to Marvin Gaye's hit single titled "Sexual Healing," which was released by Columbia Records in October 1982 (Columbia #03302, October 1982). The song was featured on an album by Gaye titled *Midnight Love* that was released at the same time (Columbia #38197, October 1982). For a comprehensive analysis of Gaye's struggle with the relation between sexuality and spirituality, see Michael Eric Dyson, *Mercy, Mercy Me: The Art, Loves & Demons of Marvin Gaye* (New York: Basic Civitas, 2004).

Interestingly enough, however, there is another dynamic also at work here. A parallel, more subtle message is found not in the words of the song, but in the evolving development of the sound, style, and innuendo of the music. Stylistically, it began as blues, but it is ending up as gospel. Emotionally, it began at the Fillmore West, but it is ending up in church. Artistically, it began as a song, but it is ending up as a sermon. And, erotically, it began concerning a *sexual* union between a woman and her man, but it is ending up involving a *spiritual* communion between a woman and her God.

In other words, by the conclusion of the song, it seems as if Dr. Feelgood has been transformed from a human being who can provide sexual thrills into a Divine Being who can provide all Aretha's wants and needs. That explains why she so easily slides into a style and mood of singing that is literally indistinguishable from that which occurs in many Black churches. The ad libbing, the improvisation, the repetition, the call-and-response, and the heightened anticipation, as one level of ecstasy surpasses the former, are all reminiscent of the expressive praise, unspeakable joy, and spiritual possession that characterize innumerable Black worship experiences.

It is vitally important to understand, at this point, that Aretha is not playing church or being sacrilegious. Even a cursory reading of her life, her upbringing, her experiences, and her music reveals that she is not pretending or simply putting on a show. Instead, she has been catapulted, beyond her control, into a realm in which her spirituality and her sexuality cannot be neatly compartmentalized. The only thing that matters to her now is the honest expression of a genuine love-encounter with God, whether that encounter is experienced through the powerful gift of sex or through the positive energy and affirming responsiveness of her audience (or, should we say, her "congregation"?) at the Fillmore West. Either way, for her it is all about love. And the love she feels, the spiritual vitality she experiences, and the authentic affirmation she receives in this priceless moment is what allows Aretha to momentarily "turn it down a notch" and segue so smoothly into the real highlight of this album— "Spirit in the Dark." But before turning to "Spirit in the Dark," let us first utilize "Dr. Feelgood" as a background for exploring heterosexuality— one aspect of the question of sexual orientation that so vexes the Black Church and the broader society in which we live.

## HETEROSEXUALITY: ARETHA AND "DR. FEELGOOD"

Of course, in the song "Dr. Feelgood," Aretha is talking about a hetero-sexual love relationship between a woman and a man. On the surface, it appears to be a positive relationship, although there is no way we can tell for sure. Ike and Tina Turner's relationship also seemed positive—on the outside. Aretha's infatuation with Feelgood appears so total that it may border on the fanatical and obsessive. If this is the case, the question becomes, "Does she simply *love* Feelgood, or does she *idolize* him?" If she loves him, that is fine, as long as he loves her in return. But if she *idolizes* him, we have a problem . . . or, I guess we should say, *Aretha* has a problem. Pastoral care experts would call this problem "*relationship* addiction."

But, then, we really don't know what kind of relationship Aretha and Feelgood have, do we? Is he her husband, her lover, her part-time lover, or simply someone she calls when she's horny and someone who calls her whenever he wants to make a "booty call"?[6] It could be that there is no substantive relationship at all between Aretha and Feelgood, other than a mutual agreement to satisfy each other's sexual needs and desires on an as-needed basis. If this is the case, then it may well be that sex itself has become an idol for Aretha. Pastoral care experts would call this "*sexual* addiction." I call it "*sexolatry*"—i.e., the idolization or romanticization of sex to the extent that we celebrate its pleasure at the expense of disregarding its pain. In her relationship with Feelgood, has Aretha somewhere crossed over from enjoying the beauty of sexuality to experiencing the tragedy of sexolatry? If so, the question is, "Where is that line and how do we know when we have crossed it?"

Another way of viewing this same situation, however, is to under-stand that, even if Aretha is not married to Feelgood, and even if they

---

6. According to the *freedictionary.com*, "A *booty call* is a telephone call, other com-munication or visitation made with the sole intent of achieving sex with the person being contacted. Such a call is usually made later in the evening and often after consum-ing alcohol." Even though this term is used above with reference to the man calling the woman, "Traditionally this phenomenon, especially the term *booty call*, is associated with a woman calling aman, when both parties are already in a sexual relationship. The term itself is more likely to be used by the person answering the call or others in his/her company than the person making the call. It is often derisive, but not always. For example, "Did John take off?" "Yeah, he had to answer a booty call." A 1997 comedy film starring Jamie Foxx, Tommy Davidson, Vivica Fox, and Tamala Jones was titled "Booty Call." It was directed by Jeff Pollack and released by Columbia Pictures.

have no long-term commitment to each other, could it be that she is neither the victim of relationship addiction nor sexolatry? Could it be that
she is simply, as one of her song titles suggest, a "natural woman" who has
not yet found "Mr. Right," and yet experiences the same natural sexual
drives and urges that most normal human beings experience? Could
it even be that she is a Christian woman—maybe divorced, widowed,
middle-aged, biological clock is either running down or has already run
down—or an even younger woman, attractive, unattached, available, and
alone, who simply wants to satisfy her sexual yearnings behind closed
doors because she has always been discreet, respectful, and private in
matters concerning her personal life?

And if she engages in this consensual, sexual activity on Saturday
night, is she consumed with guilt and remorse on Sunday morning? Can
she still go to church, sing in the choir, usher on the usher board, or even
minister in the pulpit without feeling like the worst sinner and biggest
hypocrite who ever walked the earth? Is it her fault that she has found
Dr. Feelgood, but cannot find Mr. Goodman—a man who has a job, is
not incarcerated, is not a player, is not gay, and is not a man who will
make love to her one moment and beat her to a pulp the next?

Sure, Feelgood is not the best man in the world. Sure, he is not ready
to make a commitment, and probably never will be. Sure, he is trifling,
lazy, under-educated, and unemployed. But he makes her *feel* so good.
And she doesn't call on his services every night, or even every week for
that matter. In fact, she tries to be good, she tries to hold out, and every
time he leaves her place to go home in the wee, wee hours of the morning, she says to herself, "Alright. That's the last time. I'm not going there
anymore." But, sure enough, after she's prayed and fasted and held out as
long as she can, before she knows it those natural urges swell up inside
of her once again, she cannot hold out any longer, and old, reliable Dr.
Feelgood is at her service one more time. What's a woman to do? And I
haven't even told you Feelgood's side of the story yet.

I have shared this imaginary tale of Aretha and Dr. Feelgood simply to point out some practical issues regarding human sexuality that
the Black Church needs to grapple with in an open and straightforward
manner. When it comes to the issue of managing one's sexual needs and
wants, the church is not very helpful, especially when it comes to single
adults. Paul wrestled with this issue in his first letter to the Corinthians
and the best advice he could offer was (1) he wished everyone could be

celibate like him, but he conceded that celibacy was a "gift" and different people have different gifts;[7] and, (2) if single folk cannot control their sexual urges, he advised them to get married, "For it is better to marry than to burn [with passion, that is]."[8]

In my opinion, this is not only *bad* theology—it is *impractical* theology for the twenty-first-century Black Church. In the first place, as Paul acknowledges, everyone does not possess the gift of celibacy. The sex scandal among priests in the Catholic Church, for example, provides compelling evidence that when people who do not have the *gift* of celibacy make the *vow* of celibacy, a whole lot of innocent people—including children—get hurt.

Secondly, it is extremely poor advice to tell a woman or a man, in this day and time, that the lack of sexual self-control is a sufficient reason to get married. This advice (a) ignores the plethora of dysfunctional marriages in which two people end up bringing each other, and their children, nothing but heartache, misery, and pain because they never should have gotten married in the first place; and, (b) overlooks the fact that for Black women, there is, for a variety of reasons, a serious shortage of eligible and available heterosexual Black men.

My wife, a pastoral psychotherapist who has counseled and conducted workshops for numerous Black Christian women, revealed that whereas men tend to reach their sexual prime in their twenties, women tend to reach theirs in their thirties. With a particular burden for some of these women who desire to marry, but have not found anyone to marry, she makes the following incisive observation concerning the question of sex outside of marriage:

> It is never dealt with forthrightly in the Church universal. We never say, "It's alright to do it." We do say, "It's *not* alright to do it." But we don't help people deal with the struggle of being in their sexual prime and having no committed relationship. How do they express their sensuality and sexuality? What's allowed?[9]

Whereas Paul lived in the first century, in which Jesus' imminent return was expected, we live in a completely different situation. In fact, according to my wife, we live in a time in which, in the mental health

7. 1 Corinthians 7:7 (NRSV).

8. 1 Corinthians 7:9 (KJV and NRSV).

9. From a telephone conversation with Dr. Christine Y. Wiley on Monday, October 31, 2005.

community, "eyebrows are raised if a person has reached a certain age and has not had sex."[10]

Thus, it seems to me, the church must do more than give unwise and impractical counsel to people—men *and* women—who are struggling to live holy lives in the midst of complex circumstances. Am I advocating sex outside of marriage? No, I am not, because I realize that that advice also carries with it the potential for a lot of serious and complicated problems. What I am saying, however, is that the Black Church should stop always trying to take the easy way out by giving people black and white answers to gray questions. Otherwise, the church simply sets itself up for harmful and hypocritical sexual behavior that extends all the way from the pew to the pulpit.

The fact of the matter is that we, in the church, have become remarkably astute at preaching one thing and practicing another. That is because there is often a gap between our *spoken* theology—what we *say* —and our *lived* theology—what we *do*. We do God, ourselves, and the people under our care a grave disservice when we perpetuate this inconsistency by continuing to propagate antiquated and unrealistic moral advice instead of earnestly seeking to hear anew what God is saying to us for such a time as this. In the meantime, while being castigated by our pious pronouncements, our children witness our inconsistent and hypocritical conduct. No wonder so many of them have turned their backs on the church.

While sex outside of marriage is a major issue for Christian heterosexuals, there are many other issues that the church should also address to help persons deal with the reality of their sexuality in healthy and wholesome ways. For instance, what about masturbation? Is it a sin or is it, also, a gift from God that can relieve some of the tension, stress, and horniness surrounding sexual loneliness? What about oral sex, even within marriage—is it acceptable or unacceptable? Among our adolescents, should we only advocate abstinence or should we also distribute condoms? What about abortion—is it right or is it wrong? And, of course, how should sexually active human beings protect themselves from HIV/ AIDS and other sexually transmitted diseases? These are only a few of the questions involving human sexuality that the church must confront carefully, deliberately, and in a non-sensational, non-reactionary manner

10. Ibid.

if it would provide wise, responsible, and compassionate sexual guidance to the people under its care.

## SOFT ON SIN?

One of the charges leveled against churches that attempt to be progressive in their understanding and handling of complex sexual issues is that they are "soft on sin." If nothing else, this charge raises the question, "Where should the Black Church draw the line between sexual freedom and sexual restraint?' If there are no standards, no guidelines, no clear-cut rules and regulations pertaining to appropriate Christian sexual conduct, does not the church send a message that "anything goes"?

Some of us may have grown up in a church where, if a young, teenage girl became pregnant, she was publicly humiliated by being paraded before the congregation, reprimanded for her misconduct, compelled to confess and ask for forgiveness, and then forced to withdraw from active participation in the choir, the ushers, and all highly visible church leadership positions until after the child was born. Please note that, in most cases, no process of accountability was required for the father of the child, but only for the mother. Furthermore, when the child was born, often the request to have the baby "blessed" in a public baby blessing ceremony was denied because the child was born out of wedlock and, therefore, considered "illegitimate."

While I would assume that most churches have moved away from the public humiliation spectacles, those of us who are pastors do face some difficult and delicate decisions pertaining to the care and protection of *every* member of the congregation. I will briefly share two challenging situations I have had to confront. One has to do with an unwed, young adult who became pregnant, started showing quite visibly, and sang on the front row of the choir. My pastoral dilemma was whether or not to ask her to temporarily step down from the choir until after the baby was born, not for the purpose of humiliating her, but for the purpose of not sending the wrong message to the youth and children of our congregation who looked up to her as a role model. Would her continued presence on the choir signal to them that our church condones premarital sex and pregnancy? Fortunately, after sitting down and discussing my dilemma with the young woman, she graciously agreed to take a temporary leave of absence from the choir.

Another instance, with a less favorable outcome, involved a baby blessing ceremony. Now, let me briefly explain that, in the Baptist Church, a baby blessing ceremony is primarily symbolic. It is not believed to bestow any special protection or benefit upon the baby. Its primary purpose is to challenge the parents and God-parents (who are chosen by the parents) to commit themselves to raise the child "in the nurture and admonition of the Lord." With this in mind, consider the following situation.

A young man, who had been a member of our church when he was a teenager, eventually stopped coming, got into trouble, and was incarcerated. In fact, I testified in court on his behalf. Several years later, after being released from prison, he came back to the church and rededicated himself to the Lord. Shortly thereafter, he informed me that he and his fiancé, with whom he was living, would like to have their newborn baby blessed in a Sunday morning worship service. They were planning to be married in about six months. After much prayer, agony, and deliberation, I explained the meaning of the blessing ceremony to him and recommended that either he wait until after the wedding to have the baby blessed or that I would be glad to include the baby blessing ceremony as an integral part of the marriage ceremony. In the meantime, I believe I also offered to have private prayer with him, his fiancé, and the baby. He reluctantly said he understood, and I have not seen him, his fiancé, or the baby since. Did I make the right decision? Could I have handled it better? For even those of us who consider ourselves "progressive" ministers, questions like these haunt us every day of our lives.

## SPIRIT IN THE DARK

Whereas the studio version of the song begins, "I'm gettin' the spirit in the dark," Aretha begins this live performance by asking, "Are *you* gettin' the spirit"? The implication is that Aretha has already received the spirit and her only concern now is that it touch and, indeed, *move* as many other people as possible. The song itself, however, is somewhat of an enigma. Unlike "Dr. Feelgood," it is not clear what kind of spirit Aretha is really talking about here. On the one hand, she talks about people "movin'" and "groovin'" and "dancin'," reminiscent of a high school house party in which the parents are not home, the music is turned way up, and the lights are turned way down. On the other hand, a good portion of the lyrics are borrowed from an old nursery rhyme about Little

Sally Walker who sits (and then rides) in a saucer, wipes her weeping eyes, and then shakes it to the east, shakes it to the west, and, ultimately, turns to the one that she loves the best. Many of us can remember little African American girls singing and dancing to this rhyme in schoolyard playgrounds at recess, shaking their little hips from side to side with an innocent, though defiant, sense of spirit and pride. But is this what Aretha is talking about?

Perhaps Mark Bego, author of a biography of Aretha, best summarizes the mystery surrounding the meaning of "Spirit in the Dark":

> Is the "spirit" spiritual, or is it physical? When a reporter from *Ebony* magazine asked Aretha what the song meant, she answered evasively, "Well, it's true that I have to really *feel* a song before I'll deal with it, and just about every song I do is based either on an experience I've had or an experience that someone I know has gone through. Spirit in the Dark? . . . Hmmmmm . . . that's one I'd rather not talk about. It's very, very personal and I don't want to get into it right now." It makes one wonder exactly what—or who—inspired the revival-meeting-type rejoicing that the song celebrates.
>
> The song starts out slow, like a grinding seduction, and then the pace begins to pick up as Aretha urges everyone who feels "the spirit" to get up and "move" and "groove." There are four different places in the song where the pace accelerates, and Aretha's delivery becomes more and more frenzied. By the end of the song, the tambourines are shaking, the Sweet Inspirations are quaking, and Aretha is joyfully testifying about the virtues of putting your hands on your hips and getting "The Spirit in the Dark." This song is either about an uplifting religious revelation, or an incredible sexual experience.[11]

By the end of this song, the church feeling is, perhaps, even more intense than it is at the end of "Dr. Feelgood." At any rate, it is more energetic and upbeat as the song is written to escalate into a high tempo, hand-clapping, foot-stomping, Pentecostal rhythm that seems intentionally designed to bring the house down.

But what makes this song so unique, so special, and so germane to our discussion of human sexuality and spirituality is not the rhythm, the music, the lyrics, or even the fact that it is sung by Aretha Franklin,

---

11. Mark Bego, *Aretha Franklin, The Queen of Soul* (New York: De Capo, 2001) 132–33.

the Queen of Soul. What makes it so pertinent here is that on the *Live at Fillmore West* album, Aretha, after singing a 5-1/2 minute version of the song, is joined onstage by Ray Charles who, at Aretha's request, spontaneously moves "with the spirit a little."

Remember, now, Ray Charles, as gifted and creative as he was, was never known for being a highly religious man. In fact, when he first began playing his music in nightclubs and bars, some church folk vehemently protested because they did not think it right that he should apply secular lyrics to gospel-sounding music. What Ray Charles eventually did earn a reputation for was the antithesis of what most people would characterize as spirituality—i.e., womanizing, carousing, and drugging.

Nonetheless, despite this rather tainted profile, Ray Charles has always been a highly revered and esteemed icon among a large segment of the African American community. Why do we so readily excuse his frailties while we so quickly condemn the weaknesses of others? Is it because he became blind at an early age? Is it because his younger brother suffered a tragic drowning death while Ray stood by paralyzed by shock, confusion, and disbelief? Is it because Ray had so many problems, difficulties, and challenges in his life? Or is it because his musical genius was so awesome that, despite his shortcomings, we knew that talent like that had to have come from God?

I do not know. But what I do know is that when Aretha walked back onstage at the Fillmore West, with Ray clinging tightly to her arm, and proclaimed, "I discovered Ray Charles!" the crowd went crazy. Never mind that Ray did not know the words to the song. Never mind that he and Aretha had never practiced or performed it together before. Never mind that the whole affair was completely unrehearsed, totally spontaneous, and absolutely unpredictable. The fact of the matter is that nothing could have more effectively testified to the power of the *spirit* to move, even *in the dark*, than what happened in San Francisco on that Sunday night.

Not only did Ray Charles sing, but Aretha also turned the electric piano over to him to play at one point. And as he became more and more comfortable within the security of his own improvisational dexterity, Aretha could be heard in the background exclaiming, "It's funky up in here!" It became clear, as the magic moment continued to build, that Ray's primary reference point for the spirit was what he knew best—music, women, and maybe even booze. At one point, when he couldn't recall the words, he made up some words: "Just like a movie star, talkin' to Ray Charles." At another point, he demanded:

> Can you feel it?
> Can you feel it?
> When you hear Aretha sing, y'all, oh, Lawd,
>> Can you feel the spirit?
>> When my woman wake me up in the mornin',
>> She give me the spirit.
>> Oh, when I'm on my last go 'round,
>> I need a little spirit,
>> It's good for my soul, oh, yes it is,
>> Every now and then, oh, Lawd,
>> I git me a little spirit.

Finally, as Ray neared the close of his brilliant impromptu performance, he said,

> I'm goin' home, y'all,
>> 'Cause I feel the spirit,
> I've got to find me a woman tonight,
>> 'Cause I feel the spirit,
> It's gettin' next to me now, oh, Lawd.

The key point here is that, despite all of this ambiguity surrounding the spirit and exactly what the spirit in the dark truly represented at Fillmore West, the spirit moved like a charm on that dark night in San Francisco. It made no difference that Aretha and Ray may have been talking about two or more different things when they talked about the spirit. The fact of the matter is that the Spirit brought it all together and made it all work. And despite Ray's tendency toward the profane and the risqué, guess what an emotionally overwhelmed and spiritually blessed Aretha Franklin called him as he walked off stage after his stellar performance: "Ray Charles! The Right Reverend Ray. The Right Reverend Ray. The Reverend Righteous Ray. . . . Ray Charles. What can you say about Ray Charles, except he's the Right Reverend, ain't he? He's the sho' 'nuf Right Reverend!"

What could Aretha possibly be thinking by christening Ray "The Right Reverend"? After all, Aretha is the daughter of a preacher who, before his untimely death, was one of the most highly acclaimed "Reverends" in the city of Detroit. Aretha grew up in the church and began singing solos in the choir at age 12. Aretha used to travel around

with her father on evangelistic campaigns and revivals. Surely, she understood what a "Right Reverend" was. Why, then, would she bestow such
a hallowed honor upon someone like Ray Charles, who was not only a
notorious womanizer, but one who had even been indicted, convicted,
sentenced, incarcerated for drug use?

Without our excusing any shortcomings that Ray may have had, it
appears that Aretha understood that the Spirit, like God, is no respecter
of persons. She may have also remembered the passage from the book of
Romans that says, "All have sinned and fall short of the glory of God."[12]
She may have realized that she herself was far from perfect. And, last
but not least, she may have comprehended that if we believe that *our*
spirituality is the only *legitimate* spirituality, then we will be inclined to
believe that our race is the only legitimate race, our gender is the only
legitimate gender, our class is the only legitimate class, and our sexual
orientation is the only legitimate sexual orientation. The "spirit in the
dark" reminds us, then, that the spirit can, indeed, shine a light of hope
and harmony even in the midst of that which the world has deemed
hopeless, dissonant, dark, evil, dirty, and of absolutely no account. With
this in mind, let us briefly consider homosexuality.

## HOMOSEXUALITY: WHO MADE ALICE AND STEVE?

If I were to ask you the question, "Who made Alice and Steve?" you
would probably look at me as if I had lost my mind. In the first place,
you would doubtless want to know, "Who in the world are Alice and
Steve?" Secondly, if you were a God-fearing person, and I continued
to harass you by asking you this same question over and over again,
you might—just to appease me, shut me up, and get me to leave you
alone—desperately respond, "*God* made Alice and Steve!" Finally, you
would probably reach the height of frustration and confusion if, after
your answer, I walked away with a satisfied look on my face saying, "See,
I *knew* you were not homophobic."

I share this hypothetical situation with you to make a point. So often,
those whose hearts are burning with the passion of intolerance, whose
eyes are flaming with the fire of hatred, and whose lips are spewing out
the rhetoric of homophobia arrogantly proclaim, "God made Adam and
Eve—not Adam and Steve!" My response to this tired, time-worn cliché

12. Romans 3:23 (NRSV).

has become, "Alright, but *who* made Steve? *Somebody* had to make Steve, and if *God* didn't make Steve, *who made Steve?*" Because the reality is that Steve the homosexual does exist, and somebody had to place him here on this earth.

Although I think my response is a pretty good one, I recently realized that it is probably a sexist response to a sexist statement. After all, the statement automatically kicks Eve to the curb. We never hear these same homophobic voices proclaim, "God made Adam and Eve—not *Alice* and Eve." In other words, why are they just focusing on our gay brothers and ignoring our lesbian sisters? Hence, in the interest of equal time, I contend that if God made Adam and Eve, I want to know who made Alice and Steve.

To paraphrase a famous question by Howard Thurman, "Why is it that Christianity and, more specifically, the Black Church seem impotent when it comes to dealing with the question of sexual orientation? Has the church, indeed, betrayed the religion of Jesus, or is there a defect inherent in the Christian religion that prevents a more effective, loving, and humanitarian response?"[13] We have wrestled with this question in my own congregation and are still seeking the answers. While our process has not been an easy one, we have had some victories and some setbacks.

Openly gay and lesbian couples are joining our congregation as the word spreads among the homosexual community that we are a welcoming and affirming congregation. One gay couple has even joined with three young children that they have adopted. Furthermore, I have witnessed considerable spiritual growth concerning this issue among the heterosexual members of our church. Although we have lost some who did not agree with our inclusive posture, those who have remained have made tremendous progress as they have earnestly and honestly struggled with the issue of heterosexism. For instance, in a men's retreat, facilitated a few years ago by Dr. Randall Bailey, and in a men's workshop, conducted last month by Dr. Alton Pollard III, heterosexual and homosexual men came together to discuss our relationship with each other and with God.

13. Howard Thurman, *Jesus and the Disinherited* (Richmond, IN: Friends United Press, 1969) 7–8. In the paraphrase I have substituted "sexual orientation" for "race, religion and national origin."

As you can probably imagine, a pastor is faced with daunting challenges when shepherding a congregation through the transformation of a predominantly heterosexual congregation into one that is openly welcoming and affirming toward persons of other sexual orientations. I will briefly mention two. One challenge is how to make the church a safe place for homosexuals while, at the same time, keeping it a safe place for heterosexuals. I have discovered that, on the one hand, when homosexuals find a church that genuinely welcomes them, many of them go out, spread the word, and bring others back with them. On the other hand, just the opposite tends to happen with many of the heterosexuals. Perhaps because of their uneasiness with—and maybe even embarrassment by—the perception that we are becoming a "gay" church, they cease spreading the word, rarely if ever invite anyone to church, and may even become less active themselves. I can sense this tendency, perhaps most keenly, with regard to our ministry to men. With many predominantly heterosexual congregations already struggling to get more men involved in the church, this task becomes an even greater challenge when heterosexual men are uncomfortable with being in the presence of homosexual men and vice versa.

Another challenge has to do with expecting homosexuals to abide by the same standards of sexual morality that are expected of heterosexuals, so as not to communicate a double standard. The following example may help to explain what I mean. In our church, as perhaps in most churches, we discourage heterosexual couples from living together outside the institution of marriage. We believe that if they are serious enough to live together, they ought to be serious enough to make a Christian commitment to each other. And, of course, for heterosexual couples, marriage is the ultimate Christian commitment.

For gay and lesbian couples the situation is quite different. While they may be living together, it is more difficult to determine the level of commitment they have made to each other because marriage is prohibited in most jurisdictions. This is why I, personally, am in favor of gay marriage. I think we put homosexuals in a "catch-22" situation when, on the one hand, we frown on their supposed promiscuity and, on the other hand, forbid them to consummate their relationship in the form of the most sacred commitment this society legally recognizes—marriage.

## AMAZING GRACE

A little less than a year after the Fillmore West engagement, Aretha recorded another historic live album entitled, *Amazing Grace*. This time, it was a gospel album instead of a secular album, it was recorded in Los Angeles instead of San Francisco, and she collaborated with James Cleveland instead of Ray Charles. On the final night of the two-night recording session at the New Temple Missionary Baptist Church, Cleveland invited Aretha's father, the Reverend C. L. Franklin, to come forward to give remarks. Toward the end of his comments, he shared the following incisive story:

> I went in the cleaners one day in Detroit to pick up some clothes, and Aretha had appeared on a recent television show. And [the lady at the cleaners] told me, "I saw your daughter, Aretha, last night." I said, "Yes, how did you like it?" She said, "It was alright, but I'll be glad when she comes back to the church." I said, "Listen, baby, let me tell you something. If you want to know the truth, she has never left the church." I said, "All you have to do is have something [within], and the ability to hear, and the ability to feel, and you will know that Aretha is still a gospel singer." And the way she sings in this church, she sings anywhere she sings.
>
> She took me with her to Switzerland and France and Italy this past summer and we were over there about five or six weeks. And I was thinking about, reminiscing over, recapitulating . . . how the crowds responded in the same way. The Italians, as well as the French and others—many of them could not speak English . . . not conversationally, but they remembered the English words of Aretha's songs. They had . . . memorized them. And they would say, eventually during the program, "Arree-thra! Arree-thra! Spirit in the Dark!"[14]

What Rev. Franklin is saying here is that there is something about the Spirit that transcends the superficial barriers that divide human beings from each other. His claim that Aretha "has never left the church" is critical when considering the relationship between the sacred and the secular, the church and the world, and spirituality and sexuality. It is tantamount to his saying that the church has never left her. She carries the church with her, in her heart, wherever she goes, whether it is the Temple Missionary Baptist Church of Los Angeles or the Fillmore West in San

14. Aretha Franklin, *Amazing Grace: The Complete Recordings*, Rhino Entertainment Co., 1999 (originally issued by Atlantic Recording Corp., 1972.

Francisco. And if she carries the church with her, this means that she also carries the Spirit with her ... even in the dark.

## REACH OUT AND TOUCH (SOMEBODY'S HAND)

The final track on *Aretha Live at Fillmore West* is the song originally recorded by Diana Ross titled, "Reach Out and Touch (Somebody's Hand)." It may not be a "spiritual" song in the strictly religious sense of the term, but it is spiritual in the sense that it promotes physical contact and bodily connection among human beings based, not on categories of sameness, but on the simple desire to "make this world a better place, if you can." Aretha's journey from sexuality ("Dr. Feelgood") to spirituality ("Reach Out and Touch [Somebody's Hand]") has demonstrated that these two seemingly opposite concepts do not have to remain separate and apart, but can indeed coexist in peaceful, positive, and productive harmony ("Spirit in the Dark").

# 16

## Black Church Homophobia

### *What to Do about It?*

KELLY BROWN DOUGLAS

T HE ISSUE OF SEXUALITY, especially non-hetero expressions of sexuality, is a complex matter within the Black church community. Even
with all of their diversity, Black church people are regarded as strikingly
similar in their attitudes toward non-heterosexual sexualities. They are
viewed as not simply homophobic but more homophobic than other
populations of society. Recent polls suggest that while various constituencies of American society are becoming more supportive of gay and
lesbian rights, African Americans are not.[1] In fact, the African American
community appears to be trending in the opposite direction. There
is probably no issue that better highlights Black church views toward
non-hetero sexuality than that of same-sex marriages. A recent Pew
study indicated that the Black church community was more opposed to
these marriages than other communities. The study cited 64 percent of
African Americans opposing same-sex marriages, a percentage that had
held steady for several years, while the overall population had become

---

1. A 2004 Pew Forum-University poll indicated that while support for gay and les-
bian rights had grown in American society from 35 percent to 45 percent since 1992,
this was not the case within the African American community. A plurality of African
Americans opposed gay and lesbian rights, whereas four years prior 56 percent of
African Americans favored those same rights. Consult the *Pew Forum on Religion and
Public Life* website: pewforum.org/gay-marriage.

less opposed to these marriages (from 41 percent in 1996 to 30 percent in 2003).[2]

The Black church community's obstinate stance in regard to issues surrounding gay and lesbian rights is most striking when one considers both the historical Black struggle for social equality and the Black church's prominent role within that struggle. It appears inconsistent, if not hypocritical, for the Black church to be in the forefront of racial justice concerns, yet resistant if not repressive when it comes to the rights of non-heterosexual persons. How are we to account for this close-mindedness when it comes to non-hetero expressions of sexuality? Is it possible to move the Black church community toward a more equitable view? If so, how? These are the questions that I will attempt to address in this essay. Given the recent attention given to the debate on same-sex marriages, I will address these questions in relation to this particular concern. For, to be sure, Black church people's responses toward same-sex marriages reflect the complicated nature of their attitudes toward homosexuality in general. As stated earlier, the Black church community's views toward non-hetero sexualities is not a simple matter. They are rather a result of a complex interaction of socio-political, historical, and theological realities. In order, therefore, to understand the heterosexism/homophobia of the Black church community as well as to move this community toward more reliably just views, this complex socio-political/historical/ theological interaction must be apprehended. Again, I will attempt to do this through an exploration of the same-sex marriage debate. Before doing so, however, two things must be recognized.

The first thing that must be appreciated is the Black church's heterogeneous character. The Black church community is not a monolithic reality. This church is a disparate collective of churches that reflect the diversity of the Black community itself. These churches are diversified by origin, denomination, doctrine, worshiping culture, spiritual ethos,

2. This study is cited by *Religious Tolerance.org: Longitudinal U.S. Public Opinion Polls Same-Sex Marriage and Civil Unions*; online: religioustolerance.org/hom_poll5 .htm. It should be noted that various polls are constantly conducted with varying results. Some suggest that the gap in opinion between the overall population and that of African Americans is closing. For instance, a study taken later in November 2003 revealed that opposition to same-sex marriage within the general population had grown to 59 percent even as the African American population remained steady at 60 percent. The Pew Research Center for the People and the Press, "Religious Beliefs Underpin Opposition to Homosexuality"; online: people-press.org/reports/display7 .php3?PageID=765.

class, size and other less obvious factors. They may be within white denominational structures or independent of them. They can reflect congregational, connectional or episcopal polities. They can be urban, suburban, or rural. They range in size and structure from storefronts to mega-churches. Yet, as disparate as Black churches are, they share a common history and play a unique role in Black life, both of which attest to their collective identity as the Black church. In short, Black churches emerged as a fundamental part of Black peoples active resistance to dehumanizing white racist oppression, even as they have played a central role in Black peoples struggle for life and freedom.

Moreover, while this essay focuses on the prevalent and pervasive homophobic sentiment of the Black church, it recognizes that there are various Black churches with more liberating and progressive views toward sexual expression and even same-sex marriages. One such prominent Black church is Covenant Baptist Church in Washington, D.C., with co-pastors Christine Wiley and Dennis Wiley. This church not only welcomes gay and lesbian persons, but its pastors also perform same-sex blessings.[3]

Second, before proceeding in this discussion I must also clarify the vantage point from which I speak. I am a Black female Episcopal priest who also claims my voice as a womanist theologian. Thus, I represent that aspect of the Black church community that is a part of a white denominational system. As a Black Episcopalian, however, my story of faith is inextricably linked to the story of Absalom Jones, a former slave, co-founder of the Free African Society and co-initiator of the independent Black church movement (along with African Methodist Episcopal founder Richard Allen), and the first Black Episcopal priest. Jones signifies the persistent Black presence within the Episcopal church that constantly advocates for racial justice within the denomination and whose primary identification is with the wider Black community in the struggle against white racism.

Furthermore, even though the denominational system of which I am a part might be considered more progressive in its views toward non-heterosexuals as it allows for the blessing of same-sex unions, ordains self-identified non-heterosexual persons, and recently consecrated

---

3. This church was featured on a PBS documentary (July 16, 2004) titled *Black Churches and Gay Marriage*. Again, Covenant was highlighted as a church where gay and lesbian persons are welcomed and pastors perform same-sex marriage blessings.

a gay Bishop (though this latter act has in fact divided the world-wide Anglican communion), the Black Episcopal community with which I identify tends to mirror the prevailing attitudes of the wider Black church community.[4] While there are Black Episcopal voices that are supportive of gay and lesbian rights within the church, there are also significant Black voices that are not. Interestingly, the most strident opposition to the recent consecration of a gay bishop has been from the African continent, suggesting perhaps a consistency of passion throughout the African diaspora when it comes to non-heterosexual sexualities.[5] For instance, during a recent address to a national gathering of Black Episcopal clergy, those who were most strident in responding to my lecture on sexuality were several clergymen from the African continent. They were quite clear that homoeroticism was something that the African continent could simply not tolerate. Even more telling, perhaps, were the responses from the African American clergy: they were conspicuously silent as if refusing to engage such a topic.[6] Nonetheless, it is from out of and to the wider Black faith community, of which Black Episcopalians are a part, that I speak.

Denominational affiliation notwithstanding, my womanist identity further compels me to speak about matters of sexual injustice. As a womanist theologian I am committed to the survival and wholeness of entire people, male and female.[7] I am, therefore, obliged to speak to any form of injustice whether it is present within the Black community or in the wider society. More specifically, womanist scholars are compelled

4. In November 2003, Gene Robinson, an openly gay priest, was consecrated as the ninth Episcopal Diocesan Bishop of New Hampshire.

5. It should be noted that at the Third International Conference on Afro-Anglicanism held in Toronto, Canada, July 20–27, 2005, an accord was agreed upon that addressed, among other issues, the issue of human sexuality. In regard to sexuality the accord states: "We have wrestled with deep sincerity with the complex issues of human sexuality . . . The vast differences of approach have been evident in our dialogue. Nevertheless, we have not departed from the sacred truths of our common humanity. We have all been created in God's image. God's compassion and love are extended to all whom God has created . . . We yearn together for the day when the human body will become the symbol, and source, and sacrament of unity among us and no longer a cause of division or an instrument of strife."

6. I am referring to the Seventh Triennial Black Clergy Conference and the First Convocation for the Recently Ordained, sponsored by The Episcopal Church Office of Black Ministries. The conference was held in Atlanta, Georgia, October 23–26, 2005.

7. Consult Alice Walker's four-part definition in *In Search of Our Mothers' Gardens: Womanist Prose* (San Diego: Harcourt Brace Jovanovich, 1983) xi–xii.

by our very womanist identity to interrogate homophobic attitudes and heterosexist systems and structures as they exist within the Black church community in an effort to debunk and dismantle them.[8] These very attitudes and systems have certainly infringed upon the lives of many Black women and men. They have most notably contributed to the Black church community's slow response to the HIV/AIDS crisis which now ravages the Black community.[9] Thus, if for no other reason, the womanist commitment to survival and wholeness compels a discerning theological response to issues of sexuality. Womanist theologians, therefore, cannot ignore that aspect of the womanist definition which states that a womanist loves other women sexually and/or non-sexually.[10] It is the inherent task of those of us who claim our voice as womanist theologians to work toward creating a Church and community where non-heterosexual persons are able to love themselves and those whom they chose to love without social, political or ecclessiastical penalty so that they along with all other Black men and women may enjoy life and wholeness. It is out of my commitment as a womanist theologian that I address the homopobia/heterosexism of the Black church community. Let us now examine the complex nature of homopobia/heterosexism within the Black church community as it has been most recently manifest in the debate surrounding same-sex marriages.

## THE BLACK CHURCH AND SAME-SEX MARRIAGES

The Black church community and its leadership has not been silent on the issue of same-sex marriages. In April 2004, The Church of God in Christ, a predominately Black denomination of 5.5 million members, issued a proclamation that stated marriage should be reserved for heterosexual couples. This proclamation specifically asserted that marriage as ordained by God is meant for procreation, that homosexuality is sinful and a direct violation of the law of God, and that regardless of whether or not same-sex unions gain social acceptance or legal legitimacy, the Church of God in Christ will stand resolutely firm and never allow the

8. Womanist theologian Katie G. Cannon used the term "debunk" in reference to the womanist task to deconstruct the methods and notions of white patriarchal ethical and theological systems.

9. Consult my discussion of this in *Sexuality and the Black Church: A Womanist Perspective* (Maryknoll, NY: Orbis, 1999).

10. Walker, *In Search of Our Mothers' Gardens*, xi.

sanctioning of same-sex marriages.[11] Several months later the African Methodist Episcopal Church expressed similar sentiments. In July 2004, delegates to the AME convention unanimously voted (and reportedly without debate) to forbid its clergy from performing same-sex marriages or civil union ceremonies. This vote by a denomination which claims about 2.5 million members was the first vote of its kind by a predominately Black denomination.[12]

Black pastors have also been very vocal within their local communities in rallying support against same-sex marriages. For instance, in February 2004, three major associations of Black clergy within the Boston, Massachusetts area joined together to issue a statement against non-heterosexual marriage. The Black Ministerial Alliance, the Boston Ten Point Coalition, and the Cambridge Black Pastors Conference, all primarily made up of clergy from historically Black denominations, stated that they believed "marriage to be a unique covenant established between a man and woman" and supported "the call for a Constitutional Amendment to define marriage as a covenant between a man and a woman."[13] In that same year, Reverend William Owens, a 65-year-old Black pastor in Memphis Tennessee, established the Coalition of African-American Pastors. This nationwide coalition has joined with several white pro-family groups in the fight against same-sex marriages. All across the country Black clergy have come to the forefront to defend heterosexual marriage and to vehemently oppose same-sex marriages even to the point of aligning with groups not typically in the forefront of racial justice concerns.

What is it that has stirred the passions of the Black church community when it comes to this issue? What has provoked so many Black pastors to speak out against same-sex marriage, especially since the Black church community has typically remained silent on issues of this nature? Even though it has long been understood that the Black church community generally considers homosexuality to be sinful, this community has never before issued official proclamations or public statements on the

11. "Marriage: A Proclamation to the Church of God in Christ Worldwide," reprinted by *The Human Rights Campaign*.

12. Consult *Human Rights Campaign* news release on African American Episcopal Church.

13. "Black Clergy Statement on Marriage," February 6, 2004; online: www.boston .com/news/local/massachusetts/articles/2004/02/07/black_clergy_statement.

topic. What, therefore, has prompted such a public display of emotion and opinion in regard to this particular topic? Given the general lack of priority granted to these type of sexual concerns within the Black church community, why has the idea of same-sex marriage pricked the social/ theological consciousness of this community?

The issue of same-sex marriage came into national prominence in 1996 when President William Clinton signed into law the *Defense of Marriage Act* (DOMA) in response to the controversy that had occurred in Hawaii when voters passed a law prohibiting same sex marriage. DOMA defined marriage as a legal union between one man and one woman and most importantly granted states the right to make their own decision concerning the legality of same-sex unions. Still, this topic did not seem to capture the general publics imagination until seven years later when in November 2003 the Massachusetts Supreme Judicial Court determined that its state's ban against same-sex marriage was unconstitutional. This Massachusetts decision was the catalyst for cities across the country, most notably San Francisco, to begin issuing marriage licenses to gay and lesbian couples. With this, the battle was on between supporters and non-supporters of gay and lesbian couples right to state, if not church, sanctioned marriage.

The nationwide debate which quickly ensued over same-sex marriages formed a perfect storm in relation to the Black church community. This debate struck several chords within the Black political, historical and theological psyche that brought to the surface long and deeply held sentiments concerning homosexuality in general and the fight for gay and lesbian equality in particular. Donna Brazile, Black female political operative and 2000 campaign manager for Al Gore, described it as the mother of all wedge issues for the Black community.[14] Let's now look to see why this is the case. What are some of the specific factors that created a perfect storm compelling the Black church community to respond and thus to expose the complicated reality of Black church homophobia/ heterosexism?

### An Issue of Civil Rights

Much of the public discourse surrounding the fight for same-sex marriage has framed same-sex marriage as a struggle for civil rights. One

14. Brazile quoted by Candi Cushman, "Pastors Provoked," *Citizens Magazine Feature*; online: www.family.org/cforum/citizenmag/features/a0033970.cfm.

of the central claims made by the gay, lesbian, bisexual, and transgendered community is that their fight for social equality is a civil rights
issue. They clarified this point through their participation in the fortieth
Anniversary celebration of the March on Washington. Even though
they were invited by the planning committee of the event, many Black
church leaders (especially those who had previously participated in the
1960s Civil Rights movement led by Martin Luther King, Jr.) were in-
censed when the National Gay and Lesbian Task Force bought several
busloads of mostly white people to the Lincoln Memorial to join the
celebration. One Black minister said, "[Gay and lesbian persons] know
nothing about what we went through . . . How can they even compare
that? They've hijacked the civil rights movement."[15] The Reverend Jesse
Jackson surprised many when he criticized gay-marriage advocates
for equating their battle with Black people's historical struggle for civil
rights. Speaking at Harvard Law School he said, "The comparison with
slavery is a stretch . . . gays were never called three-fifths humans in the
Constitution."[16]

Black church leaders' vehement resistance to viewing the gay and
lesbian struggle for social equality and same-sex marriage as a civil rights
issue is about more than homophobia, as some have suggested. It is also
more than a chauvinistic response to Black people's marginalized status
in America. Rather, it speaks to a profound awareness of the racialized
character of oppression in American society. The fact remains that social
and economic privilege and penalty is characteristically predicated upon
skin color. As many have pointed out, the lack of economic resources,
lack of job and educational opportunities, disproportionate numbers of
Black people especially men in prison, and even inadequate funding for
HIV prevention and AIDS treatment in certain communities is a matter of race. In essence, the color-line remains a pressing problem within
contemporary society.[17] Therefore, many Black leaders resent the equation of the gay and lesbian movement with the civil rights movement
not solely because of their feelings about homosexuality, but because to
do such a thing obscures the complex and persistent actuality of Black
oppression. It in effect glosses over the reality that racial oppression is a

15. Ibid.

16. Ibid.

17. In his discussion on racism in America in *Souls of Black Folks*, W. E. B. Du Bois
argued that the problem of the twentieth century was the problem of the "color-line."

part of the fabric of American society in a way that perhaps the oppression of gays and lesbians is not. The Reverend Irene Monroe, an openly lesbian African American theologian and columnist, further points out that Black people's reluctance to affirm the movement for Lesbian, Gay, Bisexual, Transgendered, Queer people's (LGBTQ) rights as a civil rights struggle is because it seems that civil rights gains have come faster for queer people than Black people. She explains, From the Stonewall Riots of 1969 to May 17, 2004, the LGBTQ movement has made some tremendous gains into mainstream society, a reality that has not been afforded to African Americans.[18] Others have observed that the gay and lesbian movement itself, reflecting the racialized character of America, is not free from racial discrimination. As one Black gay man pointed out, even as the Human Rights Campaign was pushing to equate gay civil rights with Black civil rights, this mostly white gay organization had no visible Black leadership or tangible support from Black leaders.[19] Irene Monroe acknowledges the fact that racism is as rampant in the white queer community as it is in the larger society.[20] She further argues that because the LGBTQ movement persistently [dons] a white face, it marginalizes the people of color who are a part of the movement, and makes Black claims that the LGBTQ movement is pimping the civil rights movement appear legitimate.

Given the apparent whiteness of the gay and lesbian movement, it is taken as a sign of white privilege and arrogance when white gay and lesbian organizations glibly usurp the language of and piggy-back on the Black civil rights movement, especially when they themselves are not more pro-active in eliminating racial discrimination, even within their own organizations. One gay Black man perhaps put it best when he said, "While the anger of Black heteros is sometimes expressed in ways that are in fact homophobic, the truth of the matter is that Black folks are tired of seeing other people hijack their [stuff] for their own gains, and getting nothing in return. Black non-heteros share this anger of having

18. Irene Monroe, "No Marriage between Black Ministers and Queer Community," *The Witness Magazine*; online: thewitness.org/agw/monroe060204.html.

19. Kenyon Farrow, "Is Gay Marriage Anti-Black???" *ChickenBones: A Journal*; online: www.nathanielturner.com/isgaymarriageantiblack.htm.

20. Monroe, "No Marriage between Black Ministers and Queer Community."

our blackness and Black political rhetoric and struggle stolen for other peoples gains."[21]

Though it should be noted that notable Black ministers and/or civil rights advocates such as Congressman John Lewis and Reverend Al Sharpton recognize the gay and lesbian struggle as a matter of civil rights, there is no constituency within the Black community that would perhaps be most outraged by the equation of Gay and Lesbian rights with the Civil Rights movement than the Black church community. As mentioned earlier, much of Black church history and identity is tied to the Black people's struggle for rights. The Black church has been the in- stitutional center of Black people's struggle for freedom, from slavery to the present. Moreover, the 1960s Civil Rights Movement emerged out of the Black church community and was sustained by Black churches. For many Black church people, the civil rights battle was not simply a social- justice matter. It was most significantly a matter of faith. Martin Luther King, Jr., Baptist minister and leader of the Civil Rights Movement, made plain the connection between Black faith and the Black struggle for civil rights. In his first speech during the Montgomery bus boycott, the begin- ning of the 1960s Civil Rights Movement, he stressed the inextricable link between being a Christian and being involved in the battle against racial injustice. He said: "we are not wrong in what we are doing . . . If we are wrong God Almighty is wrong. If we are wrong Jesus of Nazareth was merely a utopian dreamer who never came down to earth."[22]

Moreover, many Black church leaders have made personal sacrifices to the civil rights struggle at the same time that many Black lives were lost. Whether or not they are valid, it is no doubt for these reasons and more that Black ministers have felt compelled to passionately respond when the fight for same-sex marriage is framed as a civil rights issue. Essentially, regardless of whether it is actually a matter of civil rights and homophobia/ heterosexism notwithstanding, to equate the struggle for gay and lesbian rights as a civil rights issue appears to many within the Black church community as sign of disrespect and disregard for Black peoples historical struggle against white racist oppression in America

21. Farrow, "Is Gay Marriage Anti-Black???"

22. Martin Luther King Jr., "Address to the Initial Mass Meeting of the Montgomery Improvement Association," Holt Street Baptist Church, December 5, 1955, King Center Archives.

and most importantly an attempt to usurp and/or marginalize Black people within the very movement for which Black lives were lost.

The fight for same-sex marriage and gay and lesbian rights is considered an affront to Black people's history for yet another reason. Support of homoerotic lifestyles, in the minds of many, only serves to reinforce the destructive consequences of white racist oppression upon the Black community and family. In general the issue of homosexuality becomes an issue about the Black community's historical oppression and survival particularly as that oppression has impacted the Black family. Again, no issue made this more clear for many in the Black church than that of same-sex marriage.

### An Issue of Oppression

There is no Black leader who has been more vocal in proclaiming same-sex marriage as a threat to the Black family than long-time civil rights activist Reverend Walter Fauntroy. In testimony given before Congress voicing support of the Federal Marriage Amendment (an amendment to designate marriage as only between a man and a woman), Fauntroy argued that the legalization of same-sex marriage would have a detrimental impact on society and most especially on Black families. He stated, "For most black Americans who know our history, we do not want any further confusion about what a marriage and family happen to be." He went on to say, "We have not yet recovered from the cruelties of slavery which was based on the destruction of the family."[23] Various Black church people have expressed similar sentiments regarding the impact of same-sex marriages upon the Black family. One Black pastor said, "The black community has witnessed firsthand the havoc wreaked by the destruction of the family unit first through slavery and then through welfare . . . so black people are poised to lead a rebellion against the further destruction gay marriage would cause." While, as many Black leaders have pointed out, to cast gay marriage as a particularly significant threat to Black families is misguided given the actual social/political threats to the Black family (i.e. lack of employment, educational, housing and healthcare opportunities), what this argument does aptly point to is the

23. Cited by Phuong Ly and Hamil R. Harris, "Blacks Gays in Struggle of Values: Same-Sex Marriage Issue Challenges Religious, Political Ties"; online: www.washingtonpost.com/ac2/wp-dyn/A58627-2004Mar14.

reality of Black oppression that has shaped Black people's attitudes toward sexual issues, especially those issues involving same-sex sexuality.

White racist oppression of Black people, as manifest in the slavocracy, did not respect the Black family. Typically, Black people were not permitted to marry. For various reasons, marriage was not considered a viable option for the Black enslaved. As chattel they had no rights as human beings, of which marriage was one. In addition, the slavocracy viewed marriage as a threat to the slavocracy's re-productivity. It was thought to interfere with the enslaveds' ability to be good breeders. Most significantly, the very notion of enslaved marriages ran counter to the white supremacist ideology that undergirded the slavocracy. This racist ideology projected Black women and men as hypersexualized beasts controlled by lust (i.e., the sexual urgings of their genitalia). Black men and women were characterized as immoral beings driven by abnormal sexual proclivities. They were, therefore, deemed suited for breeding, but not for intimate loving relationships. If, however, enslaved men and women were permitted to marry, such permission did not imply that their marriages would be respected. The exigencies of the slavocracy as well as the racially sexualized ideology that undergirded it, prevailed over the marriage commitment. Thus, the master retained the right, and usually exercised it, to use the husband and wife as breeders, or to sell them away from one another. Any children that were issued forth from the marriage were also likely to be sold away from their parents. In short, Black marriages and hence families were not respected within the slavocracy. They were simply not privileges granted to a people viewed as hyper-sexualized beastly chattel.

Restrictions upon Black marriage rights did not end with the slavocracy. Black men and women were still not permitted to freely choose the person with whom they would make a family. Long after slavery Black/White marriage unions were prohibited. It would not be until June 12, 1967, with the *Loving v. Virginia* Supreme Court decision, that legal restrictions on interracial marriages were completely lifted. Prior to this decision sixteen states maintained laws which forbid Blacks from marrying whites. The lifting of miscegenation laws again did not suggests respect for the Black family. As has been pointed out on numerous occasions, Black families have been consistently under siege by the interacting and interlocking social/political economic systems of white racism.

Black people's persistent history of racially sexualized oppression with its concomitant attacks upon the family, has shaped their responses to social issues and especially sexual matters. Essentially, in an effort to offset white racist hyper-sexualization of them (that is, that they were overly sexualized beasts), Black people have adopted perhaps unwittingly a *hyper-proper sexuality* in a effort to mitigate if not sever the link made between blackness and abnormal sexuality. This hyper-proper sexuality is characterized by a strident determination to engage sexuality in a proper manner and to present the Black community as an exemplar of proper sexuality. What it means to be proper is shaped by what is deemed acceptable in society and thereby defined by social-cultural narratives of power. Proper sexuality is thus discerned according to heterosexist, patriarchal notions of proper sexuality. The point being, within a society defined by white patriarchal heterosexist standards of acceptability, non-heterosexuality is viewed as improper. Thus, the Black church community's responses to issues of sexuality, such as homosexuality or gay and lesbian rights, are significantly shaped by a heterosexist sensibility.

Furthermore, the history of white racist attack upon the Black family has also compelled the Black community to become hyper-vigilant in protecting the well-being of the Black family. This vigilance is also influenced by white heterosexual patriarchal norms; family therefore is defined accordingly. Consequently, despite the fact that it has historically developed effective family models (i.e. extended family units) and despite the socio-economic pressures that prevent it from being so in the main, the Black community has consistently struggled to conform to white patriarchal standards of family; thus maintaining a male-centered nuclear family unit.[24] Ironically, the end result is that Black people's history of oppression has compelled the Black community to adopt standards of sexuality and notions of family that are consistent with the

24. One should note, for instance, the 1965 Moynihan Report that opens by stating that the "deterioration of the Negro family," was the "fundamental source of the weakness of the Negro community." The report further argues that the Negro family is at the heart of the "tangle of pathology" that perpetuates poverty and antisocial behavior within the Black community. The report identifies the centrality of the Black mother as opposed to the father within the Black family, erroneously identified as a "Black matriarchy," as the root cause of the Negro family's deterioration. It cannot be emphasized enough, however, that this report was just one example of the way in which the Black family was attacked for not conforming to white patriarchal standards at the same time that it provided a scapegoat for the white racist system and structures that actually contributed to the poverty and social problems within the Black community.

very ideologies that have served to oppress them, that is, white patriarchal standards. Hence, the Black church community as a whole has
adopted sexual values that are non-accepting of homoerotic sexuality
and most certainly non-accepting of same sex marriages. Both are seen
as an affront to proper Black family structures as well as to Black sexual
propriety.

At the same, it has not been just Black people's history of sexualized
oppression that has shaped their sense of proper sexuality and thus their
responses to homo-erotic sexuality. Most importantly Black people's
views on family and sexual values have been shaped by their faith. Black
people's history of oppression and faith have come together in such a
way to create an almost impregnable position on same-sex marriage.
Theologian Imani-Shelia Newsome-Camara explains, Marriage was traditionally undervalued in slave communities, not by slaves, but by owners, so the Black religious institutions sought to give African-Americans
legitimacy as human beings, and that history has been woven together
with the theology that God created man and woman for marriage.[25] Let
us now examine the faith that informs Black church views on same-sex
marriages.

## An Issue of Faith

Reverend Fauntroy again makes the issue plain when he says that his
church teaches him that same-sex marriage is an abomination. His view
is echoed by numerous Black ministers as they assert that the Bible
condemns not simply same-sex marriage, but also homosexuality. The
bottom line according to many Black church people, is that the Bible says
homosexuality is wrong. In fact, whether they are churchgoers or not,
Black people often argue that the Bible makes clear that homosexuality
is a sin.[26] As a Black clergyman said to me at the Episcopal Black clergy
conference mentioned earlier, the Bible has not changed and it makes
clear to me that homosexuality is damningly wrong. Even if the biblical

25. Quoted by Michael Paulson, "Black Clergy Stirs Gay Marriage Backers," *The
Boston Globe*; online: www.boston.com/news/local/articles/2004.02/10/black_clergy
_rejection_stirs_gay.

26. Consult the November 18, 2003, Pew Study, "Republicans Unified, Democrats
Split on Gay Marriage: Religious Beliefs Underpin Opposition to Homosexuality."
According to this study, three-quarters (74 percent) of Black Protestants considering
homosexuality sinful. The only group with a higher percentage of persons considering
homosexuality sinful was white evangelicals (88 percent).

texts customarily referred to as proof against homosexual practices (i.e. Genesis 19:1–9; Leviticus 18:22; 20:13; Romans 1:26–27) have been misconstrued or distorted, by invoking biblical authority a sacred canopy is placed over oppressive views toward gay and lesbian persons. This canopy renders homophobia and heterosexism within the Black church community practically intractable and certainly renders same-sex marriage an intolerably sinful deed.

As central as the Bible is to the Black faith tradition there is another key element of Black faith that also informs Black peoples responses to homoerotism: that which I refer to as a *platonized theology* and what Black novelist James Baldwin has aptly described as Protestant Puritanism. Platonized theology shapes an influential strand of the Christian tradition. This theology notably places the body in an antagonistic relationship with the soul. The soul is divinized while the body is demonized. The soul is revered as the key to salvation. The body is condemned as a source of sin. The locus of bodily sin is human passion, that is, sexual pleasure/lust. This sacred disdain for the sexual body pervades the Christian theological tradition, particularly as it has given way to a definite sexual ethic. Specifically, platonized Christianity advocates a dualistic sexual ethic. That is, it suggests only two ways in which to engage sexual activity, one tolerable, not inherently sinful and the other intolerable, sinful. Procreative use is tolerably good; non-procreative use is intolerably evil. Characteristic of platonized Christianity, a third possibility is not permitted. A platonized sexual ethic does not allow for sexual activity to be an expression of an intimate, that is, loving relationship. For all intents and purposes, platonized Christianity severs intimate sexuality from loving relationality. The implications of platonized Christianity are obvious.

First, platonized Christianity makes clear that the site for procreative sexuality is marriage, even as marriage is viewed as the privileged context for procreative sexuality. Second, platonized Christianity provides theological shelter for the denigration of certain human beings. For inasmuch as certain people are sexualized, (as is characteristic of any marginalized people) then those people can be deemed sinful by nature since to sexualize them is to suggest that they are unavoidably given to lustful sexual behavior.

Platonized Christianity became an influential part of the Black faith tradition during the eighteenth-century religious revivals. During these revivals a significant population of Black men and women were converted to Evangelical Protestant thought, the principle conduit of platonized Christianity in America. Black church people most affected by this evangelical, that is platonized tradition, tend to affirm the assertions of the apostle Paul that one should make no provision for flesh, but if one must engage in sexual behavior, it is better to marry than to burn (1 Corinthians 7:9). At the same time, reflecting this platonized tradition, Black church people tend to view homoerotic sexuality as lustful, sinful behavior. Since it is not viewed as procreative, it is not considered a proper form of sexual expression and thus is not seen as deserving the shelter of marriage. In this respect, Black church peoples concept of a hyper-proper sexuality is driven not simply by white patriarchal heterosexist norms, but most significantly by a platonized Christian theology, though the two narratives coincide when it comes to homosexuality and same-sex marriages.

It is also interesting to note that these narratives also coincide when it comes to women. Both define women's sexuality in terms of their capacity to procreate, thus in relation to men. Such a view ostensibly denies Black women the possibility of non-procreative and hence non-male centered sexual expression. Such recognition once again compels a womanist response. For just as white patriarchal heterosexist social narratives and platonized theology disavow the propriety of non-heterosexual expressions of sexuality, they also work together to uphold the center of patriarchal power: a heterosexual male-centered family where women's primary role is to procreate or at least to support the male-centered family. There was no greater example of this insidious interplay between patriarchal and heterosexist narratives than a sermon given by a prominent Black pastor in Washington, DC. From his Sunday pulpit, he vulgarly attacked homosexual persons, particularly lesbians. He argued that Black lesbianism is a result of strong Black women who believe that they can survive without a man (specifically Black women who earn more than their husbands).[27] The implications were clear, inasmuch as Black women defined themselves independently of Black men they were

27. This refers to a sermon delivered by Reverend Willie Wilson on July 3, 2005, at the Union Temple Baptist Church in Washington, DC. In this sermon Reverend Wilson made vitriolic comments toward gay and lesbian persons and vulgar innuendos about homoerotic intimacy.

in danger of becoming lesbians and they were certainly a threat to the Black family; hence independent Black women needed to be subdued.

More to the point, however, Black church people's vehement responses to same-sex marriage as well as homosexuality reflects a *theo-historical dynamic* that is grounded in a platonized theology and propelled by a history of racial sexualized oppression. James Baldwin puts it best when he says: "It is very important to remember what it means to be born in a Protestant Puritan country, with all the taboos placed on the flesh, and have at the same time in this country such a vivid example of a decent pagan imagination and the sexual liberty with which white people invest Negroes and then penalize them for . . . Its a guilt about the flesh. In this country the Negro pays for that guilt which white people have about flesh."[28] And indeed Black people do pay for that guilt, at least in their views toward sexuality. With this understanding we can now answer what it is that has compelled the Black church community to respond with such passion regarding same-sex marriages.

The issue of same-sex marriages is considered a direct affront to Black peoples sense of struggle, experience of oppression and faith tradition. As such this issue exposes the social, historical and most importantly theological factors that coalesce to provide a perfect storm for bringing to the surface prevailing Black attitudes toward non-heterosexuality. While homophobia and heterosexism may be the result of this storm of issues, it is a homophobia and heterosexism born from the struggle of being Black in a society hostile to Black humanity. Nevertheless, both are still a problem because they limit the life options of non-heterosexual women and men and perhaps even more sinfully support violence against them. So, while we may appreciate the complexity of Black homophobia and heterosexism, it still must be addressed and hence eradicated. Left to answer is how to move the Black church in the direction of becoming a more equitable and just community in regard to matters of non-heterosexuality.

Before I continue further, I must offer a caveat. What I will now briefly put forward reflects only my preliminary thoughts as I move toward a fuller understanding of the issue of same-sex marriage and what it might mean in regard to the Black church community. Thus, that which follows are at this point for me theological signposts that compel further theological reflection.

28. James Baldwin, interviewed by Studs Terkel, 8–9.

The first signpost is found in Black people's own historical experience with contested marriages. To reiterate, the Black enslaved were routinely denied the privilege to marry. Marriage was considered a right granted to human beings capable of loving relationships. Because Black people were considered less than human, that is beastly chattel, they were thought incapable of such loving relationality. Consequently, they typically were not granted the right to marry. Yet, despite the hardships and brutality associated with doing so, enslaved men and women routinely risked both life and freedom in order to marry the one they loved. The question is why? What was it that was so significant about the marriage union that compelled enslaved men and women to pursue it despite the oppressive conditions that mitigated against it? The answer is perhaps found in the words of Black novelist William Wells Brown. In his nineteenth-century novel *Clotel*, Brown says this of the enslaved determination to be married:

> Although marriage . . . is a matter which the slaveholders do not think is of any importance . . . it would be doing that degraded class an injustice, not to acknowledge that many of them regard marriage as a sacred obligation and show a willingness to obey the commands of God on this subject. Marriage is, indeed, the first and most important institution of human existence . . . It is the most intimate covenant of heart formed among mankind; and for many persons the only relation in which they feel the true sentiments of humanity.[29]

Two things immediately stand out in Browns observations regarding the enslaveds views of marriage. First, Black people's tenacity to be married despite the obstacles imposed by the rule of slavery, witnessed not primarily to their need to conform to white cultural/social conventions, but rather to their desire to affirm before God and community the sanctity of their intimate relationships. At stake was not so much the propriety of their marriages, as the sacredness of their loving relationships. Such an emphasis on the sacredness of relationships was perhaps informed by an African theological heritage that stressed the theological significance of maintaining loving harmonious relationship with one another as a reflection if not in response to the harmonious relationship that God maintains with all of creation. To be sure, the enslaved determination to be married suggests the theological foundation for discerning

29. William Wells Brown, *Clotel* (New York: Arno, 1969) 57.

the Church's response to same-sexed marriages, that foundation being the sanctity of *loving relationality*.

Any appreciation for what it means for human beings to be created in the image of God and thereby to reflect that image must begin with the imperative to engage in loving relationality with one another. The Genesis Creation narrative puts it thus, So God created humankind in [Gods image, in the image of God [God] created them male and female [God] created them (Genesis 1:27). What is made clear in this creation account is that human beings are not meant to live in solitary existence, but to live relationally. In this regard, the emphasis is not on the biological creation of male and female but on the existential creation of human relationship. Essentially, made clear in the creation of male and female is that the fullness of one's humanity is to be found in loving relationship. And so it is perhaps that what the Church must fundamentally affirm is what many enslaved men and women apparently understood, the sacredness of loving relationality. The theological imperative of human creation is not for men and women to categorically conform to social/ historical contrivances of marriage, but for them to adhere to what it means to be *imago Dei*. Given this, the Church has an absolute obligation to nurture and to provide a space for loving relationality, regardless of its sexual identity.

The second thing that stands out in Brown's observation concerning enslaved responses to marriage is his emphasis on their humanity. Clearly, marriage for the enslaved was a marker of their very humanity. As Brown puts it, it is . . . the only relation in which they feel the true sentiments of their humanity. The implication for the Black church community is clear. If Black church people are to take seriously the meaning of their own history of struggle for their humanity, particularly as that struggle was informed by their faith, then they must realize the justness of non-heterosexual women's and men's struggle for full affirmation of their humanity. Most importantly, as Black church people witness to a God who enters into *compassionate solidarity* with the Black oppressed in the struggle for their humanity, they must also recognize that this God is no respecter of persons when it comes to the oppressed. That is, just as God has revealed Gods self on the side of Black people as they strive toward freedom and justice so is God on the side of non-heterosexuals as they do the same. Rev. Kelvin Calloway, pastor of the Second A.M.E. Church in Los Angeles, perhaps best describes the mandate for the Black church when he said, "Oppression is oppression is oppression ... Just because we're not the ones who are being oppressed now, do we not stand with those oppressed now? This is the biblical mandate. That's what Jesus is all about."

In this regard, Black people's demand that those in the gay and lesbian struggle for justice respect their history of struggle, i.e. the significance of the civil rights movement, does not mitigate the need for the Black church community to recognize the parallels between white cultural contempt for them and heterosexist contempt for non-heterosexual persons. Just as white racist culture has historically refused to admit the humanity of Black women and men, and thus has variously denied that Black people are created in the image of God; so too does heterosexist culture repudiate the humanity of non-heterosexual men and women and thereby implicitly disavows that they, as non-heterosexuals, are created in the image of God. Indeed, the Black church often mimics white cultural contempt for their humanity as it virtually asserts the non-humanity of gay and lesbian persons by proclaiming that God did not create human beings to be gay and lesbian, thus regarding non-heterosexuality as a sin. Once again, Black church people must recognize the similarity between white racism and heterosexism, even as heterosexism is perpetuated within the Black community itself. It is in this way that even though Black people may be unable to acknowledge the gay and lesbian struggle as a civil rights issue, they must admit it as a human rights issue. As such, the Black church community is obliged by its own faith affirmations to affirm the divine worth and sacred rights accorded to all human beings, i.e. life, dignity and the freedom to live out their full potential as divinely created beings. And most significantly, again in accordance with Black people's own history of struggle, these sacred rights include the privilege to marry and have it recognized by the church and state.

Finally, the Black church is compelled to recognize that platonic Christianity spawns and sanctions structures of oppression. Inasmuch as it maintains a sacred dualism that demonizes the body and deems non-procreative sexuality as evil, it provides the theological framework for dehumanizing ideologies that routinely sexualize their victims. Black people must reclaim their own faith heritage that maintains the sanctity of the body and thereby recognizes that true salvation is not simply about what happens to the soul, but also what happens to the body. In

other words, there is a significant Black faith tradition that has historically recognized that soul salvation means nothing less than bodily freedom. This is what pulsates through the sung testimony of the enslaved
found in the spirituals. As we know, the spirituals maintained in their
hidden/coded language the connection between heavenly salvation and
earthly freedom. That is, enslaved men and women testified in song to
the urgency to save their souls while simultaneously singing about the
urgent need to free their bodies. The point of the matter is, the spirituals
point to a faith tradition that did not readily admit soul/body splits but
maintained the inextricably connection between the two. Such a tradition suggests a response to a platonized (i.e. Protestant puritan) tradition
that is characterized by body/soul splits. To be sure, it is only in reclaim-
ing its own non-platonized religious heritage that I believe that the Black
church will become more consistent and equitable in responses to matters of sexuality.

The problem of homophobia/heterosexism and most particularly
same-sex marriages within the Black church community is a complicated one. Yet, regardless of the complexity of the matter, it is one that the
Black church must address. It is, to be sure, time for the Black church to
truly live into its justice-affirming social, political, historical, and theological tradition and thus to eradicate any manifestation of the sin of
homophobia/heterosexism from its very midst.

# PART FIVE

# The Future of Black and Womanist Theologies and the Church

# 17

# Black Theology/Womanist Theology in Dialogue

JEREMIAH A. WRIGHT JR.

I APPROACH THIS TASK of entering the personal dialogue between Womanist theologians and Black theologians and entering the intellectual conversation between Womanist theology and Black theology with great fear and trembling. Let me lay before you the issues that cause my fear and trembling in order for you to understand the perspective I bring and some of the proposals I make for the future of the dialogue, the future of the academy and the future of the church.

The first issue that complicates this task for me is the complex issue of location. I write as a person who was born in the Black church, raised in the parsonage, nurtured by Black preachers, and taught by a wide variety of vastly different professors (Black and white)!

On the white side of the ledger, my professors run the gamut between Mircea Eliade (the premier historian of religions), Martin Marty (the nation's leading church historian forty years ago), Jonathan Z. Smith (the University of Chicago's resident scholar in the field of Jewish studies thirty years ago), Gösta Ahlström (the professor of Hebrew Bible with a concentration in the history of religions and a PhD from Uppsala, Sweden), and Fazlur Rahman (the University of Chicago's brilliant Islamist in the 1970s).

Mircea Eliade was a practicing Catholic who went to Mass every morning. Martin Marty was a lifelong Lutheran who understood personally and painfully the rift between Missouri Synod Lutherans and the Evangelical Lutheran Church of America. Jonathan Z. Smith never talked about the synagogue as one who worshipped there. Gösta Ahlström was so turned off by the chauvinism, the patriarchal perspective, the misogyny, the sacred justification for stealing another people's land and the genocidal hatred found in the Hebrew texts that he did not know what to believe in the mid-1970s. And Fazhur Rahman was a committed member of the Sunni community, the *ahlul kitab* (the people of the Book), and a lifelong student and scholar of Sufism who guided my studies of the Tijaniyya (a nineteenth-century Sufi sect) as they swept into West Africa converting or killing the Bambara, the Fube, and the Tukolour. These are the non-African professors who shaped my perspective and contribute to my "location," the place from which I approach today's task with fear and trembling.

On the Black side of the ledger of my professors, the diversity (and the dichotomies at times) are even greater. There is Dr. Samuel DeWitt Proctor on one end of the spectrum who was a professor, a preacher, and a pastor, a man with one foot in the academy and one foot in the local congregation—a model I grew up seeing and a modality most of my professors at the University of Chicago Divinity School told me was impossible. On the other end of the spectrum there was Dr. Charles Long, the absolutely awesome professor in the history of religions who did not belong to a church, believe in the church, or go to a church unless he was invited to speak at that church or he had to attend a family function at church like a baby baptism, a wedding, or a funeral. In between Dr. Proctor and Dr. Long there was Dr. E. D. McCreary, my ethics and humanities professor who taught both at the undergraduate level at Virginia Union University and at the School of Theology at Virginia Union University while pastoring the Mt. Carmel Baptist Church in the Church Hill community of Richmond, Virginia (Church Hill was hardcore ghetto in the 1960s!). There was John Lovell, the country's leading authority on the Spirituals, the sacred songs produced by a people of faith who knew God long before chattel slavery and the coming of the European conquerors and colonizers to their shores. There was Sterling Brown, a Harvard graduate and a product of the Harlem Renaissance, a personal friend of Langston Hughes, Lorraine Hansberry, and Zora Neale Hurston. Sterling was ambivalent about the church because of what he had seen and what he had experienced.

The seeds of racism and raw hatred sown by white Christians yielded a harvest of "strange fruit" that left a bad taste in millions of Black mouths (including Sterling Brown's). And the crops of that crap calling itself "Christianity" were weeds that choked out the possibility of belief for many a son and daughter of African descent.

There was Sterling Brown's colleague, Arthur P. Davis, who along with Brown and Ulysses Lee published *The Negro Caravan* (an anthology of Black writings) in the 1940s.[1] And then there was Dr. Stanley Alsop, the Dean of the Jamaican campus of the University of the West Indies whose work in linguistics opened up a whole new world for me— an African-centered world peopled by professors like Dr. Cheikh Anta Diop, whose mind-boggling insights would never again let me be your average, garden-variety "colored preacher" cut off from the Continent or the cultures that make us who we are as African Americans.

The first issue that complicates today's task for me is the complex issue of location. I write as a person who was born in the Black Protestant church; and in deference to and out of respect for my co-presenter this afternoon, I need to say that my best friend in childhood was a Roman Catholic, while my father's only surviving brother was a layreader at the St. Thomas African Episcopal Church in Philadelphia. St. Thomas was the Anglican Church started for Africans in the late 1700s. My perspective of Black Protestantism was shaped by an exposure to Black Catholics, Black Anglicans, and seminary-trained Black Baptist preachers.

I write as a person who was born in the Black church, raised in a Black parsonage, nurtured by Black preachers, and taught by a wide variety of vastly different professors—Black and white. My collegial relationships across the years, moreover, make the issue of location even more complex for me.

I am a colleague of Carlos Moore, Molefi Asante, Cornel West, Na'Im Akbar, Asa Hilliard,[2] and Iva Carruthers. I have been in constant communication and dialogue across the years with Gayraud Wilmore, Jackie Grant, and Randy Bailey (Randy and I were students together at the University of Chicago Divinity School). My work with Anderson Thompson and John Kinney, Elkin Sithole and Janice Hale, Kariamu Welsh Asante, and Ivan Van Sertina have made the journey even more interesting. I am a friend and student of Clarice Martin, Kelly Brown Douglas, Linda Thomas, Dwight Hopkins, James Cone, Jerome Ross,

---

1. Sterling Allen Brown, Arthur P. Davis, and Ulysses Lee, editors, *The Negro Caravan: Writings by American Negroes* (New York: Beaufort, 1969).

2. Asa Hilliard, *The Maroon within Us: Selected Essays on African American Community Socialization* (Baltimore: Black Classic Press, 1995).

Obery Hendricks, Renita Weems, and Henry and Ella Mitchell. Dennis Wiley is my cousin (my blood cousin!) and I am Julia Speller's Pastor. Each of these persons adds to my understanding of the Black church, Black theology, and Womanist theology. The first issue that complicates today's task for me is the complex issue of location.

The second issue that makes me tackle today's task with fear with trembling is the issue of vocation. By vocation I am a pastor *and* I teach seminary! Now remember! I grew up seeing that model. Before I got to Virginia Union University as a student (in January of 1959) I had been steeped in the culture of Virginia Union University. My mother's brother, Dr. John B. Henderson, was a graduate of Virginia Union University and the Oberlin School of Theology. He was also Dr. Samuel DeWitt Proctor's pastor in Norfolk, Virginia!

My mother's second oldest brother was Dr. Thomas Howard Henderson. Dr. Thomas Henderson was the Dean at Virginia Union under Samuel DeWitt Proctor. He and Sam Proctor became close friends. (He was also the first non-minister to be the President of Virginia Union University.) Dr. Samuel DeWitt Proctor was always in our home and in our Pulpit as I was growing up. He was a pastor and a professor. Dr. John Malcus Ellison was both a pastor and a professor. Dr. Alex Bledsoe James was a pastor and a professor. Dr. E. D. McCreary, whom I referenced earlier, was also a pastor and a professor. I grew up seeing the model of men who loved the Lord and men who loved learning. In the 1940s, 50s, and 60s when I was in school, there were no women pastors or women professors in the world I knew.

My mother was a minister, but she was born in an era when it was not permissible to call her a "minister." So, my mother never went to seminary. She had four earned degrees, but seminary was unheard of for sisters in the 1930s and 1940s. My mother stayed a "Women's Day Speaker" until the day she died.

Now when the truth is told, my mother could preach circles around most males that I had heard, but she was still called publicly just a "speaker." My mother loved learning, however, and she loved the Lord. So I grew up seeing the model of men and women who loved the Lord and who loved learning—but the women were not considered "legitimate preachers" in my world.

I had not met Ella Mitchell when I went away to college. Yvonne Delk was still an undergraduate student at Norfolk State Teachers

College when I went away to Virginia Union University. Bishop Vashti McKenzie and Dr. Ann Lightner-Fuller (like Dr. Jackie Grant) were still in elementary school when I went away to college.

As a result, the only women preachers I knew of were the storefront pastors in Philadelphia who had not been to seminary. My understanding of ministry, however, forged in the frames of the Black church that was born in the barn of Beth-racism out behind the Big House of segregation. My understanding of ministry was that authentic Black ministers with integrity were those ministers who had graduated from college and finished three years of seminary.

Just as there was no line of separation between the sacred and secular in African culture—sacred and profane, yes! but not the sacred and so-called "secular," the secular was an alien European concept to Africans—there was also no line of separation between the spiritual and the intellectual in the African-American culture in which I was nurtured.

I grew up seeing the model of pastor and professor, and by vocation, by divine calling, that is who I am! I am a pastor of a church, and I am a seminary professor.

And just a sidebar here if you don't mind. I had that model reaffirmed for me (the model of pastor and professor) after having been beat up and beat down by Black seminary professors who did not know my world, Black seminary professors who were mad at the Black church, and Black seminary professors who gave up on the Black church because of the endless politics, the eternal "poo-nanny" chasing, the poor academic preparation (or the lack thereof), the deep anti-intellectual strain that strangles the Black church, and a large amount of Black parishioners who don't want to be taught *how* to think, but who want to be told *what* to think!

Those disgruntled, disenchanted, and disgusted professors saw the concept of a person being a Black pastor *and* a Black professor as an oxymoronic manifestation of paranoia, schizophrenia, or deep denial. They beat me up and they beat me down. I was battle-scarred and battle weary, but as a member of the board of directors of the Black Theology Project, I was providentially positioned in 1984 to be at the "Jornada Theologia" (the theological consultation) sponsored by the Cuban Counsel of Churches in Havana, Cuba.

We traveled one day during the conference out to the seminary in Matanzas, and during a paper presented there by a professor of comparative religions, the professor said, "We do not allow anyone to teach in our seminary who is not the pastor of or active in a local church." To do so, he explained, would be to have a bunch of intellectual theories (or philosophical fantasies) totally unrelated to existential reality. He argued that professors who were not members of congregations would be teaching theory that was totally unrelated to congregational facts. What that would be doing, he argued, was having professors who were preparing persons for the pastorate who themselves were cut off from the church. That would produce propagators of philosophical fantasy that was in no way connected to existential reality!

That Cuban professor articulated for me both the position I had held since my exposure to the life, world, and culture of a Black seminary in the 1950s and the reality I had lived since entering the Divinity School at the University of Chicago in 1969. That Cuban professor was "killing me softly with his song" because he was describing my vocation, describing what God had called me to, and talking about where it was I worked. He was not only "on my street" (in the language of the Black church), he also had my address and he was sitting in my living room!

By vocation I am a pastor, and I am a professor; and that gives me a perspective when approaching this dialogue that not only gives me pause. It also makes me enter this conversation (as I said at the outset) with fear and trembling.

Having said that by way of prolegomenon, let me offer just one person's response to the question of "How long?"—a response offered from the perspective of a pastor and a professor. How long will the dialogue and the discussion, the disagreement and the distrust go on between Black theologians and Womanist theologians? How long will there be a gap between the Academy and the pew when it comes to the issues addressed by Black theology and Black theologians and the issues considered crucial by the average Black parishioner across the broad-based denominational spectrum which makes up the Black church?

On the intellectual side from where I sit, rapprochement has already taken place; where we are on the verge of a meeting of the minds that will be made manifest by a moving together theologically with a common agenda that is determined to set all of God's people free. We have come an awfully long way from the days of the pioneers in Womanist theology who had to give the Black theologians a "wake-up call." Running parallel to the paradigm established by the Civil Rights Movement and the Black church, the Black Theology Movement purported to say a word on behalf of all of the oppressed in general (in 1969 and the early years of Black theology) and the Black oppressed in particular.

The same problem that plagued the Civil Rights Movement and the Black church, however, was being perpetuated in the Black Theology Movement and our Womanist sisters quickly, radically, and sometimes irritatingly brought that to our attention! The Civil Rights Movement spoke on behalf of Black people in America, but it spoke only with a male voice. It spoke only with a male perspective, and its view and treatment of Black women in America (and in the world) ran a strange, contorted, and sometimes confused gamut.

Male chauvinists never considered the possibility of a Black female perspective or any remote chance of a Black female being "out front" in a leadership position. Sexists and misogynists (Black men!) preached a Gospel of liberation in the 1960s, but they practiced a religion of domination, subjugation, and exploitation when it came to Black women.

We had our "symbolic" icons like the First Lady in the local Black church. We had Rosa Parks, whom we put on a pedestal but we never let her speak as a leader from the podium! We had Black women whom we lifted up as important figures in our litanies of leaders in the fight against segregation. We talked about (or mentioned in litany-form) Harriet Tubman, Sojourner Truth, Jarena Lee, Ida B. Wells, and Fannie Lou Hamer in our speeches and sermons as we rehearsed the line-up of our rich historic legacy. But we perpetuated the model of keeping Black women "in their place" when it came to leadership positions in the Civil Rights Movement and keeping them publicly silenced not only in the church but also in the Movement.

The cadre of Black clergy who come to mind when recalling the Civil Rights Movement and its leadership includes Martin Luther King Jr., Ralph David Abernathy, Fred Shuttlesworth, Walter Fauntroy, Wyatt Tee Walker, William Augustus Jones, Andrew Young, Samuel Billy Kyles, and even the young whippersnapper who was still in seminary, Jesse Louis Jackson. That cadre of Black leadership in the Southern Christian Leadership Conference, the leadership of SNCC, the leadership of CORE, and the leaders lifted up as spokespersons were all male! The only voices being heard were male. The only perspective being voiced was the male perspective.

As I look back at that era, I also think about the Urban League and the NAACP, which were also male-dominated. They were not liberation-oriented, however! Those two groups (back during the Movement) had assimilation, desegregation, and mis-defined "integration" as their agendas. They did not have liberation as their agendas. Even as I think of those groups, however, I can't recall more than one or two females who were ever the presidents of SCLC, SNCC, CORE, the Urban League or the NAACP. If a woman were elected president, the TV cameras and the media focus were always on the men!

Following the model of the historic Black church in America, the Civil Rights groups used women as things but *mis*used women by keeping them down in the ranks and silencing their voices in terms of leadership. Women who might have had thoughts of their own, concerns of their own and issues which needed addressing from a female perspective were never "out front." The men just never considered that a possibility!

As I said a moment ago, Black sexists and misogynists preached a Gospel of liberation in the 1960s but they practiced a religion of domination, segregation and exploitation when it came to Black women—both in the church and in the Civil Rights Movement (both of which were led by Black male leaders of the Black church).

Sexism was not the only gorilla sitting in the living room, however. Heterosexism and heterosexist attitudes rendered same-gender loving people (like Bayard Rustin) invisible! Same-gender loving people were invaluable in terms of their contributions but they were invisible in terms of their recognition.

The same problem that plagued the Civil Rights Movement forty years ago was being played out in a "remix" in the Black Theology Movement. Womanist theologians, however, quickly brought that inconsistency to the world's attention as they addressed the male-dominated perspective of the Black theologians in the 1970s. Over the past twenty-five years, however, since the pioneers in Womanist theology gave the Black theologians their wake-up call, from where I sit, it seems as if we have come an awfully long way. Rapprochement has already taken place or we are on the verge of a meeting of the minds that will be made manifest by men and women scholars moving together theologically with a common agenda that is determined to set all of God's people free.

James Cone and Jacqueline Grant are working on the same agenda. Linda Thomas and Dwight Hopkins are working on the same agenda. Dennis Wiley and Kelly Brown Douglas are working on the same agenda. Alison Gise Johnson and Jerome Ross are working on the same agenda. Iva Carruthers and John Kinney are working on the same agenda. Obery Hendricks as a New Testament scholar and Renita Weems-Espinosa as an Old Testament scholar are working on the same agenda. Black scholars in religion are moving together theologically with a common agenda that is determined to set all of God's people free; and that is exhilarating! That is what I see on the intellectual side of the equation.

On the congregational side of the equation, however, the vision is not as exhilarating. In fact, it is somewhere between frustrating and debilitating! Black theology as articulated initially by James Cone and as developed over the past thirty-five years by a "great cloud of witnesses" is untouched by the average Black pastor in the year 2005. In fact, Black theology is untouched by the *majority* of Black pastors in the year 2005!

The reasons for that reality are "legion" like the man in Mark 5; but I would like to lift up two of those reasons. 1) The majority of Black pastors in the African-American church are not seminary graduates. Those pastors, as a result, have not been exposed to James Cone (except on the Tavis Smiley–Tom Joyner TV show). They have not read the works of Gayraud Wilmore, Deotis Roberts, Kelly Brown Douglas, Homer Ashby, Jacqueline Grant, Theresa Frye Brown, Dwight Hopkins, Randy Bailey, or Jerome Ross. 2) The issues being wrestled with at the seminary level, therefore, are non-issues for the majority of local Black church pastors. As a result, Black theology is on the verge of a breakthrough thirty-five years into its systematized development. Black theology is now in dialogue with African theologians, African philosophy, and the rich legacy of African epistemology (as is evidenced in Dwight Hopkins's latest book on *Being Human*.)[3]

While Black theology is on the verge of a breakthrough today, in touch with its roots and in lock step with its sisters who bring the Womanist perspective to the table as an equal partner with equal force (and not as a stepchild with the "minority"), and while Black theology is on the verge of a breakthrough thirty-five years into its systematized

3. Dwight N. Hopkins, *Being Human: Race, Culture, and Religion* (Minneapolis: Fortress, 2005).

development in dialogue with African thought, in touch with its African roots and in step with its African sisters, that is not the case with the Black church!

There is so much that is exciting and exhilarating on today's scene when it comes to Black theology. Dwight Hopkins is uncovering connections with the Dalits, Africans on the Continent, and Africans in the North American Diaspora. Hopkins is bringing that perspective to the table, and while he is doing that, Carlos Moore is opening up a whole new dimension in understanding the depth of thought behind Cheikh Anta Diop's Two Cradle Theory. Diop was arguing for the feminization of civilization in his Two Cradle Theory! Diop argues that what changed humans from being hunters, gathers, killers, and conquerors into civilized humans with sedentary homes and families was the influence of women—the feminization of civilization! The influence of women on African theology and African world-view (Moore argues) was Cheikh Anta Diop's biggest contribution. These exciting developments are now being placed on the theological agenda of Black theology; but while Black theology is on the verge of a breakthrough, the Black church in North America is on the verge of a breakdown! I say that for the following reasons.

Members of the Black church are flocking to "religious" leaders who are totally out of touch with the liberation agenda and who are wholeheartedly preaching greed as the "new level" of spirituality to which they have "transitioned." Creflo Dollar apparently never heard of the Dalits. T. D. Jakes never read one sentence by Cheikh Anta Diop and probably has never heard of Carlos Moore. Jakes said at Rosa Parks's funeral that he had never even met her!

Black parishioners are interested in "Negro Fests" where Darfur, Sudan, Angola, the Congo, and Colombia never get mentioned. Black parishioners are interested in large gatherings of praise where they can gather for an entire week of getting their praise on and getting their shop on, speaking in tongues, and spending their dollars.

What is going on in the Black church with 50,000 believers gathering to get high spiritually is comparable to 80,000 Blacks gathering to hear Nelly or 50 Cents with his empty head! Between Nelly and Negro preachers, between Dollar and 50 Cents, however, the Black church in North America is on the verge of a breakdown. She is severing all ties with the church that produced a Gabriel Prosser, a Denmark Vesey, a Nat Turner, and a *Kairos Document*.

As a result, Black theologians are talking to themselves while trying to shape the thinking of those entering the pastorate; and only a remnant is listening as they talk! The average seminarian, incidentally, wants to be like Jakes and not like Jesus!

On the congregational side of the equation, the view is not so exhilarating. We have taken a quick look at Black theology. Now let us look at the world of Womanist theology as it pertains to the local church. Womanist theology is not even on the radar screen of most Black pastors. This is particularly true in the historic Black churches. In the majority of the churches in the largest Black Baptist denomination (The National Black Church Incorporated) and the National Baptist Church Unincorporated (and all of their subset splinter groups of Baptist) if there is any *one* thing that most of the churches and pastors can agree on it is that there should be no women in ministry! Most of those churches still do not allow women to stand in the pulpit when they speak; and the Baptists are not alone!

Dr. Cheryl Townsend Gilkes as a scholar of and Dr. Robert Franklin as a son of the Church of God in Christ both attest to the fact that women can organize a COGIC congregation. Women can start a COGIC congregation and women can supply the pulpit of a COGIC congregation until "a real pastor" is called—meaning a male Pastor is in place; but no women are allowed to pastor a COGIC congregation. (The happy exception to this sexist rule is the diocese of Bishop McKinney in Southern California down in the San Diego region). A woman can organize the church, start the church, and supply the church but she cannot pastor that church! Now you can shout all over your sanctuary with the saints in praise. You can cry and weep tears of joy and tears of relief with Judy McCallister being your Psalmist; but you can bet your last sanctified dollar that Judy will never be your Pastor in a COGIC congregation.

In the AME church, the delegates elected their first female Bishop in the 113 years in the year 2000. (Now they have three female Bishops after 118 years of existence.) The AME Zion Church and the CME church are still playing catch-up, but they are not really trying to keep up when it comes to women being Bishops in those denominations!

Womanist theology can't even hope to get a hearing in a place that is still struggling with the notion of allowing women to be ministers or having women in positions of power. After all, Paul said, "he permits no woman to be *over* a man!"

Womanist theology, as I just said, is not even on the radar screen of most Black pastors and most Black parishes. This is painfully true in the historic Black church, and this is especially true if there is any talk of same sex inclusion; and Womanist theology keeps raising that issue (along with the disowned, disparaged, and disrespected sons of the Black church who labor in the field of Black theology).

Same sex relationships may be as normal as breathing for womanist theologians, but Womanist theologians, please remember, are on the intellectual side of the equation. On the congregational side of the equation, same-sex relations are not only not normal (or *ab*normal); they are considered an "abomination to the Lord." So Womanist theology that raises the issue (or any womanist theologian who raises the issues) becomes anathema to "Aunt Jane and Uncle Robert." The average Black parishioner in the Black church in America is clear on what "the Bible says"—especially the King James Bible and not one of those new-fangled translations of the Bible!

Jacqueline Grant can raise the crucial question: Is the Black church hazardous to the health of Black women (her spiritual health and her psychological health both of which are under attack in the average Black church) and Kelly Brown Douglas can address that same question and others in her powerful book *What's Faith Got to Do With It*;[4] but as long as Kelly mentions the unmentionable abominations she mentions in her book *Sexuality and the Black Church*, Black parishioners (male and female) will continue to be divided and in denial![5]

As a Pastor, I have seen this painful reality in the congregations where I have served. When it comes to the acceptance and embracing of Womanist theology, I have seen Black parishioners first of all behave as addicts in denial. Here is what I mean. A *recovering* addict acknowledges that there is a problem. They own the fact that they have a problem. That is the first step on the long and treacherous road to recovery. They have to "name the demon." If they cannot *name* the demon as Jesus did in Mark 5, then they cannot *tame* the demon in their own lives! That is the perspective of a *recovering* addict or an addict in recovery.

4. Douglas, *What's Faith Got to Do With It: Black Bodies/Christian Souls* (Maryknoll, NY: Orbis, 2005).

5. Douglas, *Sexuality and the Black Church: Womanist Perspective* (Maryknoll, NY: Orbis, 1999).

An addict in denial, however, does not even acknowledge that there is a problem; and I see and hear many female parishioners every week who still say and will go to their graves saying, "Father God!" They sprinkle their prayers in almost every other sentence with the sexist spice of "Father God." They are spiritual addicts in denial. They see nothing wrong with that term, and if you will let me be honest, I need to say to you that I hear that term not just from senior citizens and from serious and sincere parishioners. I also hear that term from young male and female preachers in the year 2005. I also hear it from some women in seminary and I hear it from some who have finished seminary!

Just as addiction is a chemical problem, sexist language is in the spiritual DNA of these believers! They cannot help it and they will attack you if you call them on it! In addition, moreover, I also see, hear, and serve believers who are anti-woman preachers! If being against women preachers is the mindset, you can completely forget about the notion of entertaining Womanist Theology as a possible hermeneutic for approaching the Word of God.

As a pastor, I repeat, when it becomes an acceptance of and an embracing of Womanist theology, that notion is not even on the radar screen of most Black believers. I have also seen parishioners who are devotees to the cult of "The King" and devotees occasionally to the cult of "The Queen" or "The Diva!" If the King or the Queen, the pastor, does not endorse Womanist theology, the people of the cult are most liable never to even have heard that term.

The third reason I say this about Womanist theology, however, is the fact that I have seen, heard, and served (and I have been a clergy colleague of) believers who are suspicious of anything or anyone perceived of as "pushing the homosexual agenda." That is how womanist theologians are perceived, and that is how most Black theologians are perceived—especially Black theologians who are in the United Church of Christ! Please don't forget the historic July 4, 2005, of the General Synod of the United Church of Christ.

So the question of "how long?" is still on the table. The question of how long will the dialogue and the discussion, the disagreement and the distrust go on between Black theologians and Womanist theologians is still being asked. More specifically, however, the question of how long will there be a gap between the academy and pew when it comes to the issues addressed by Black theologians and Womanist theologians and the issues considered crucial by the average Black parishioners across the broad-based denominational spectrum which makes up the Black church is still with us? As a result, how long translates for me into how *do*? How do you change perceptions and perspectives of preachers, pastors, and parishioners without losing your mind?

Let me offer three quick responses to that question in the interest of time and then we can dialogue. 1. You change perspectives and perceptions one person at a time. 2. You won't ever change the perspectives and the perceptions of some preachers, pastors and parishioners. But then, 3. You learn how to live with your differences without getting a divorce!

The example of Anthony Campolo offers the best paradigm in this area for me. Pastor Campolo and his wife disagree over the issue of homosexuality. They both believe that homosexuals are made in the image of God, that they are loved by God, that Jesus Christ was sent by God to save homosexuals and to save heterosexuals. They both believe that there should never be any discrimination against a homosexual when it comes to employment, civil law, and civil rights; but they disagree as to whether or not the church should bless homosexual unions. Tony and his wife are not divorcing over the homosexual issue, however! That paradigm of learning how to live with difference without getting a divorce is what some of us are working on us in the Samuel DeWitt Proctor Pastor's Conference right now. We are calling it "Constructing a Theology of Disagreement." This is where you learn how to disagree with another colleague in ministry without getting a divorce!

We need each other to be fully human. The Zulu articulate that reality with their firm belief in *unmtu gumntu, gbantu*! An individual can only be an individual by virtue of being in relationship in community with other individuals. With all of our differences I believe we are still— all of us!—the children of God.

# 18

# Communion Ecclesiology and Black Liberation Theology

## Jamie T. Phelps, OP

THE INTERNATIONAL BISHOPS' SYNOD of 1985 identified *communio* or *koinonia* as the fundamental idea of the Second Vatican Council. This judgment has promoted a notable emphasis on ecclesial communion in subsequent papal and other magisterial documents. In most instances, this has led to increased emphasis on the internal relationship between the local churches and its members and has led also to stress on communion as the goal for ecumenical and inter-religious dialogue.[1] While these discussions are important to a fuller understanding of the mission of the Church, this new emphasis on the Church as communion also provides a term by which to argue its mission to foster the recognition and manifestation of the essential unity of the whole human family.

Here I argue that the central theme of the unity of the human community is the teleological focus of both Black liberation theology and communion ecclesiology. The synodal and papal documents on social justice promulgated following Vatican II were an elaboration of the churches' self-understanding of communion that linked the intraecclesial communion of the Christian churches with the extraecclesial communion of the human community. This unity of the human community is also an explicit central value of African traditional religions and the African American religious tradition.

---

1. Synod of Bishops, "The Final Report," *Origins* 15 (December 19, 1985) 444–50.

The historical development of the Black Church and Black organizations and conferences within predominantly white churches has been motivated by the desire of Black people to maintain their human dignity and their sense of human equality in the context of a dominant social and ecclesial context previously denied to them. Protestant and Catholic churches compromised Christianity by conforming to the social institutions that embodied a white supremacist ideology and the social patterns of slavery, segregation, and Black servitude. Ecclesial institutions themselves adopted the white supremacist ideology that allowed its members to own slaves, and restricted the participation of its Black members. The emergence of a formal Black liberation theology, within the context of the Civil Rights Movement, provided a theological interpretation of Black people's quest for liberation. It identified and critiqued the structures and patterns of relationships that continued to marginalize, devalue, exploit, and otherwise perpetuate the oppression and dehumanization of Black people in the United States as antithetical to the gospel of Jesus Christ. This theology focused on racism as the root ideology that legitimized the oppression of Black people. In a similar vein, Latin American liberation theology provided a theological interpretation for the class oppression experienced by the poor and marginalized people within Latin America. Both theologies reread the tradition to identify a previously de-emphasized image of the historical Jesus. Jesus is and was the Liberator and God of the oppressed. Many U.S. Catholic social-justice activists, including theologians, engaged Latin American liberation theology and took up the war against poverty and oppression in Latin America. But many of these same activists, blinded by bias, ignored Black liberation theology and the racial oppression identified as a root cause of poverty and oppression within the U.S.

Black liberation theology has called the churches to become a model of the pattern of relationship that it seeks to establish in the world. It challenges all churches to refute the dehumanization of Blacks and all oppressed peoples within their communities as they assist the oppressed in the struggle to obtain full freedom and equality in society. This challenge of Black liberation theology makes clear that the final goal of liberation theology is identical with the ultimate goal of communion. At the 1985 synod the bishops focused on intraecclesial communion, ecumenical communion, and the social challenges facing society. These foci suggest that commitment to justice, peace, and freedom of men and women, and to a new civilization of love, is a fundamental perspective for the Church as communion. Commitment to communion is integrally related to commitment to liberation. Human freedom or liberation is a precondition of ethical living since persons cannot form an authentic visible community unless they are free.

The new emphasis on communion ecclesiology and Pope John Paul II's call for repentance and conversion provides a new opportunity for the Church in North America to become a living sign of the unity of the human community. Toward this end, the Church in the U.S. must speak the truth of its sinful past, ask and give forgiveness, and commit itself to creating a visible worldwide ecclesial and human communion of reconciling love and solidarity. In this human communion the full humanity, dignity, and equality of Blacks and others who had been historically oppressed peoples will be recognized. In ecclesial communion peoples of all cultures and classes will be recognized as full human beings empowered by the Holy Spirit to be active and primary agents of the Church's mission.

## ECCLESIAL COMMUNION AND HUMAN COMMUNION

The human dimension of the Church as communion implicit in the documents of Vatican II was further elaborated in the social justice documents issued by the popes and various bishops' conferences from 1965 to 1975. The goal of communion was the promotion of a worldwide communion within the Church, between the particular churches, between the churches and other religious faiths, and ultimately within the whole human family. Vatican II's Dogmatic Constitution on the Church, *Lumen gentium*, argued that God's plan of salvation includes all those who seek to know God, live a good life, and persevere in charity. The document explicitly identified Catholics, other Christians, members of other religious faiths such as Jews and Muslims, as well as those who seek the unknown God, those who do not know the gospel or the Church of Christ, and those who have no explicit knowledge of God. The Church is to preach the gospel "to the ends of the earth."[2]

The bishops at the council understood that God's universal salvific will implies that no living person is beyond God's will for salvation.

2. *Lumen gentium* no. 1. See also nos. 14–17. I cite from *Vatican Council II: The Conciliar and Post Conciliar Documents*, ed. Austin Flannery, inclusive language ed. (New York: Costello, 1996).

Consequently, no living person is beyond the call to live in communion with others. God's plan has made Christ the source of salvation, for the whole world. This communion gathers every good found in the hearts, minds, rites, and customs of peoples, purifies and perfects them to glorify God and to ensure the happiness of humanity.[3] Clearly, *Lumen gentium* suggests that a central aspect of the Church's mission is to transform the whole world from a situation of disunity based on race, class, nationality, religion, gender, or age to one of unity or communion.

The papal and episcopal documents following Vatican II made more explicit the ultimate goal of the social justice mission of the Church as the realization of human or world communion. Pope Paul VI's encyclical *Populorum progressio* (1967) noted that the social question "tied all human beings together." Catholics must work to address social inequities by "building a human community where men and women can live truly human lives, free from discrimination on account of race, religion or nationality, from servitude to other men or women . . . where liberty is not an idle word . . . where the needy Lazarus can sit down with the rich man at the same banquet table."[4]

*Octogesimo adveniens* (1971), Paul VI's apostolic letter on the 80th anniversary of *Rerum novarum*, decried the egoism and domination that still characterized some human relationships within an urban industrialized world. The need for greater justice and sharing of responsibility among workers was noted. Attention was focused on the division between youth and adults, men and women, and the need to recognize the place and dignity of marginalized groups such as "the handicapped and the maladjusted, the old, and different groups . . . on the fringe of society."[5] *Octagesimo adveniens* noted in particular the sufferings of victims legally discriminated against because of "their race, origin, color, culture, sex or religion."[6]

The document of the 1971 Synod of Bishops, *Justice in the World*, strongly underscored that social justice directed both toward the

---

3. Ibid., no. 17.

4. Pope Paul VI, "Populorum progressio" no. 47, in *Proclaiming Justice and Peace: Papal Documents from Rerum Novarum through Centisimus Annus*, ed. Michael Walsh and Brian Davies, rev. ed. (Mystic, CT: Twenty-Third, 1991) 234. See no. 63 for the pope's extended comment on racism.

5. "Octagesimo adveniens," nos. 14–17, in *Proclaiming Justice and Peace*, 252–53.

6. Ibid., no. 16.

transformation of the world and relationships within the Church were "a constitutive dimension of preaching the gospel."[7] Acknowledging the continuance of the ancient division between "nations, empires, races, classes" it warned about the intensification of such division due to the development of new technological means of destruction. Economic growth had contributed to the increase of "marginal persons" bereft of food, housing, education, political power, and responsible moral agency.[8] All of these conditions of injustice require Christians to discover new paths toward justice in the world. Like Jesus, our actions and teachings must unite in an indivisible way, the relationship of men and women to God and to one another. Like Jesus, Christians must be willing to give their total lives for the salvation and liberation of men and women by defending the dignity and fundamental rights of the human person.[9] Men and women must be able to exercise their freedom of expression and thought both within Church and society.[10]

Finally, Paul VI's summary of the 1974 Synod of Bishops, *Evangelii nuntiandi* (1975), echoed the previous documents in identifying social transformation as an essential aspect of evangelization. Through the power of the gospel the Church evangelizes "by upsetting [hu]mankind's criteria of judgement, determining values, points of interests, lines of thought, sources of inspiration and models of life which are in contrast with the word of God and the plan of salvation."[11] Most notably *Evangelii nuntiandi* emphasized the "profound link between evangelization, and human advancement—development and liberation—in the anthropological order . . . which touches the very concrete situations of injustice."[12]

This short and incomplete survey of the Catholic Church's teachings on social justice indicates a strong ecclesial tradition that understands its mission as proclaiming the gospel through the twin actions of preaching and embodying Jesus's call to liberation and communion. The social sins of racism, sexism, classism, homophobia, ethnocentrism,

7. "Justice in the World," nos. 6, 7–8, 40–46, in *Proclaiming Justice and Peace*, 270–71, 277–78.

8. Ibid. nos. 9, 10.

9. 9 Ibid. nos. 31, 37, 39.

10. Ibid., no. 44.

11. "Evangelli nuntiandi," no. 19, in *Proclaiming Justice and Peace*, 292–93.

12. Ibid., no. 31.

imperialism, etc., limit the freedom of, some and divide the whole human community. These patterns of oppression contradict the gospel that proclaims the essential unity of all human beings who are made in the image and likeness of God and are called to unity by Jesus's proclamation of the reign of God.

Liberating the Church and society from the interpersonal and socially unjust structures and patterns of relationship that oppress and divide the human community is an essential aspect of evangelization. Those who call themselves disciples of Christ have by their baptism begun a journey of faith that is a gradual process of being liberated from sin and all that oppresses. By the power of the Spirit acting in and through us we are enabled to cease participation in oppressive patterns of relationship and to enter into full communion with God, one another, and all creation.[13]

## BLACK AND WOMANIST LIBERATION THEOLOGIES

The social justice mission of the Catholic Church elaborated in its document are in harmony with the social justice mission as articulated by Black and Womanist liberation theologies. The distinguishing focus of Black and Womanist theologies is the insistence that this mission needs to include the particular experience of Black people. These theologies also focus on the realities that divide the human community but place emphasis on those root dynamics at the heart of Black alienation and oppression within society, namely the social sins of racism, sexism, and classism. Both the social justice mission at the heart of the Church and the social justice mission at the heart of Black and Womanist theologies is ultimately directed toward liberation, the overcoming of the oppression of human division, and communion, the visible realization of full human communion.

## TRADITIONAL AFRICAN AND AFRICAN AMERICAN
## RELIGIOUS VALUE OF COMMUNITY

The emphasis on communion, the communion of churches and peoples rooted in the presence of the Holy Spirit, has been a source of hope for those of us who recognize in this emphasis a continuity between tradi-

---

13. Ibid. That liberation from sin and all that oppresses (social systems) is an integral part of evangelization is noted in no. 9 and carefully nuanced in nos. 29–36.

tional African and African American religious values that are the foundations of Black theology. The term of this continuity is a central value
that characterizes African and African American religious tradition
namely belonging to a community. John Mbiti, the African philosopher,
has noted:

> [T]raditional religions are not primarily for the individual, but for
> the community of which he is part. Chapters of African religion
> are written everywhere in the life: of the community, and in the
> traditional society, there are no irreligious people. To be human
> is to belong to the whole community, and to do so involves par-
> ticipating in the beliefs, ceremonies, rituals and festivals of that
> community. A person cannot detach themselves from the religion
> of his group for to do so is to be severed from one's roots, one's
> foundation, one's context of security, one's kinships and the entire
> group of those who make a person aware of their own existence
> . . . To be without religion amounts to a self-excommunication
> from the entire life of the society, and African peoples do not
> know how to exist without religion.[14]

The African thirst for "community" was not destroyed but strengthened
through the ordeal of the Middle Passage. Our African ancestors longed
for the intimacy and comfort of the family, kin; and clan. To meet this
need, they forged an extended family as well as a new culture from the
diverse African cultures, that were fused during slavery. Peter Paris
reminds us that when African American slaves and their descendents
referred to themselves using the terms African, Negro, and Colored, they
were reconstituting themselves into a new tribal unity or community.
Through this community they sought to preserve their dignity and self-
respect, even though the same terms were used by the dominant culture
to denigrate, divide, and oppress Africans. They therefore adhered to
"the primary goal of African moral life [which was] the preservation
and enhancement of the community." When the "slave appropriated the
formal features of their slave holders' Christianity, with respect to ritual
practices, language and symbols, they invested each of them with new

---

14. John S. Mbiti, *African Religions and Philosophy*, 2nd rev. ed. (Portsmouth, NH:
Heinemann, 1990; orig. ed. 1969) 3. For a more extended discussion of African and
Black American continuity in values, see also Jamie T. Phelps, "Black Spirituality," in
*Taking Down Our Harps: Black Catholic in the United States*, ed. Diana L. Hayes and
Cyprian Davis (Maryknoll, N.Y.: Orbis, 1998) 179–98.

meanings . . . [Community remained] the paramount moral and religious value among African peoples."[15]

The concept "Black community" became the metaphor for the community understood as an extended family that was not restricted to blood-relatives but embraced neighbors and friends. The use of family appellations such as brother, sister, uncle, aunt, and cousin to refer to playmates, family friends, and neighbors, common in African communities, persisted among succeeding generations of African Americans.[16]

## KING AND THURMAN

The writings of two of the most prolific activist theologians and spiritual leaders born and initially nurtured in the Black community during the twentieth century were Howard Thurman and Martin Luther King, Jr. Their writings emphasize the continued centrality of community in the African American religious ethical tradition and the integral relationship of love, justice, and community within that tradition. Katie Cannon has correctly observed that "for both Thurman and King everything moves toward community."[17] Although each offered distinct interpretations and application of the concepts of *imago Dei*, love, and justice, both argued that love and justice are to be ordered toward community. Both insisted that all men and women, including Black men and women, were made in the image and likeness of God who is the source and means of the inter-relatedness of all human beings. Luther Smith has summarized the essence of Thurman's theological ethics as follows:

> Thurman's greatest legacy may be his vision of inclusive community: a community based on reconciliation, which recognizes and celebrates the underlying unity of life and the inter dependence of all life forms. Justice and a sense of innate equality are ruling principles for community, and love-ethic established and maintains the community's creative character. Person identity is affirmed while unity is sought with one's fellows. Thurman's inclusive community harbors all races, classes, faith claims and ethnic groups, for in the eyes of God, every human being is His beloved child. Difference among people are not ignored or

---

15. Peter Paris, *The Spirituality of African Peoples: The Search for a Common Moral Discourse* (Minneapolis: Fortress, 1995) 63, 64, 72.

16. Ibid., 89.

17. Katie G. Cannon, *Black Womanist Ethics* (Atlanta: Scholars, 1988) 168.

depreciated, though their importance does not overshadow the bond of kinship between individuals. And because of this bond, difference can he appreciated rather than feared, for the variety of truth perspective they bring to understanding. In cultural pluralism persons come to know the many faces of God, and what God is doing in diverse ways. Hopefully, this will give individuals a proper sense of self and neighbor such that one does not fall into destructive righteousness, inclusive community confirms what Thurman understands as God's will for human relationships.[18]

As Cannon also observed, Thurman held that "mystical experience, love and community relatedness are part of the same continuum. Inclusive community is nonspatial. It is qualitative."[19]

Martin Luther King, Jr.'s leadership in the Civil Rights Movement, although public, was never essentially political; rather, it was a theological and ethical movement grounded in a notion of community quite similar to that of Thurman. King's dream of the future for America and the world was expressed in his concept of "the beloved community," his metaphor for the achievement of a qualitatively inclusive community. King's creative activism involved three basic strategic principles "assessing the character and logistics of the situation; naming the primary evil to be dramatized; and identifying the meaning of non-cooperation with evil."[20] King was outlining strategic principles for the achievement of political and civil rights, but the purpose of that achievement was ultimately the establishment of an inclusive human community rooted in the Judeo-Christian love ethic. King once noted: "It is true that as we struggle for freedom in America, we will have to boycott at times. But we must remember . . . that a boycott is not an end in itself . . . the end is reconciliation, the end is redemption, the end is the creation of the beloved community."[21]

The writings of both Thurman and King are precursors of the liberation theology that would emerge in the late 1960s. Their speech, writings, and actions demonstrate the integral relatedness of liberation and communion. Both initially struggled for the liberation of oppressed Black people within the U.S. Both eventually expanded their concerns to

18. Luther Smith, as quoted in Cannon, *Black Womanist Ethics*, 169.

19. Ibid.

20. Ibid., 173.

21. Martin Luther King Jr., as quoted in Cannon, *Black Womanist Ethics*, 173.

include all oppressed people and their oppressors as their analysis and vision took on global dimensions.

## CHURCH DISUNITY: THE RACIAL DIVIDE

The Black struggle for liberation and community within Church and society has an interrelated history. Both the Protestant and Roman Catholic churches in the U.S. compromised their authentic Christian identity by imitating within their own structures the same racial division characteristic of the surrounding society. Black members were subjected to the same segregation, marginalization, and devaluation within the Church as they were accorded in society. The churches uncritically adopted the prevailing racist ideology and relegated the Christian principle of the unity of humankind exclusively to the spiritual realm. Historically, white supremacist ideology and an uncritical ethnocentrism led to the relegation of Blacks to the back pews of white churches.[22] The separation of the Protestant churches on the basis of racial discrimination or the relegation of Blacks, both rich and poor, to the invisible margins within Roman Catholic and other "predominantly white" congregations or denominations was and is common.

African Americans responded creatively and constructively to their oppressive marginalization. Excluded from community within slave-holding congregations or denominations, separate Black Protestant denominations began to be established in 1750.[23] The first Black Protestant denominations arose out of the desire of Blacks to overcome the structural oppression of the white "Christian" churches whose social and religious practices denied the full humanity of its Black members and thus their identity as person made in the image of God.[24] In separate churches, Black Protestants were able to nurture and sustain their God-given identity, dignity, and culture as well as to experience community as a spiritual and visible reality. The use of the adjective "African" suggests that these separate Black Protestant churches sought to adhere to the cultural value

22. Ibid., 78.

23. Melva Wilson Costen, *African American Christian Worship* (Nashville: Abingdon, 1993) 78; for a listing of separate Black Protestant congregations and denominations founded between the years 1758 and 1908, see 83–86.

24. See Carol V. R. George, *Segregated Sabbaths: Richard Allen and the Emergence of Independent Black Churches, 1760–1840* (New York: Oxford University, 1973).

of community within their new churches in a manner that characterize their African ancestors and the authentic Christian tradition.

Black Catholics, in their attempts to hold fast to the Christian tradition of class and racial inclusion (Galatians 3:28), initially resisted the formation of separate parishes. They chose to establish "colored Catholic" organizations and fraternities. These groups focused on three activities simultaneously. First, they provided the spiritual nurture and affirmation of their full humanity and dignity denied to them in mixed congregations. Secondly, they combated the mistreatment of Blacks within Church and society. Finally, they struggled for inclusion by active participation within the mission and ministries of the Church as religious women, ordained men, and active laity.[25] During the first three-quarters of the nineteenth-century Black women were not accepted into congregations of religious women. Black men were not admitted to seminaries in the U.S., and Black laypersons had to struggle to have their voices heard. The establishment of separate religious congregations for Black woman in 1829 and 1842 was the official beginning of Blacks engaging in the mission of the Church within the U.S. Catholic Church.[26] The first "Black priests" in the Catholic Church in the U.S. were three sons born to Michael Morris Healey and his slave mistress. The eldest, James Augustine Healey, was ordained in 1854. Because of their mixed ancestry, many did not recognize the Healey priests as Blacks. Augustus Tolton, the first recognized Black priest was born in 1854 and ordained in 1886.[27] The emergence of vocal laity is documented by the record of

25. See *Three Catholic Afro-American Congresses* [reprint] (New York: Arno, 1978; orig. ed. 1893). These nineteenth-century lay congresses sought to combat the impact of racial prejudice on Blacks within the Church. In addition they provided a space where Blacks could act as agents of their own mission and evangelization in collaboration with white priests, religious women and men, and others engaged in Catholic ministry among Blacks. See also Jamie T. Phelps, "John R. Slattery's Missionary Strategies," *U.S. Catholic Historian* 7 (Spring 1988) 202–5. Black Catholics often argued against separate churches since these accommodated racial prejudice rather than combating it. Slattery argued for separate churches for Blacks.

26. Cyprian Davis, *The History of Black Catholics* (New York: Crossroad, 1990) 98–115. The first congregation of women religious was a failed attempt started in Kentucky in 1824. Five years later in 1829 four women took vows as the first members of the Oblate Sisters of Providence founded by a French refugee priest from Haiti and four Haitian women. The Sisters of the Holy Family were founded in New Orleans in 1842.

27. Cyprian Davis's work just cited is the most succinct record of this history. For an excellent account of the ordeal of admitting Black men to priesthood in the U.S., see

the Black Catholic Congresses initiated by Daniel Rudd in 1888.[28] Prior and during the emergence of Black ordained, religious, and lay leadership, white bishops, priests, and sisters and several congregations of men and women religious committed themselves to ministry among Black Americans.[29]

Most of the attention of the Catholic Church during the nineteenth and early-twentieth century focused on issues facing immigrant Catholics. The majority of church leadership and members remained neutral or silent about the social and moral evil of slavery as well as the subsequent segregation, subjugation, lynching, and other forms of social violence that victimized Black people in America. Catholics considered these practices as social rather than moral issues. Hence the actions were not judged as a proper concern of official church decision-making bodies.[30] While there were notable exceptions, all too many ethnic European

---

Stephen J. Ochs, *Desegregating the Altar: The Josephites and the Struggle for Black Priests, 1871–1960* (Baton Rouge: Louisiana State University, 1990).

28. See *Three Catholic Afro-American Congresses*; and Davis, *History of Black Catholics*, 163–94.

29. Davis, *History of Black Catholics*, 28–56. While the history of this ministry has not been fully documented the presence of Black Catholics in the U.S. dates back to 1536 and the population of Black Catholics in the Spanish, French, and English colonies was notable. Many of these Catholics were slaves. In a letter written by Bishop John Carroll in 1785, he noted that of the 16,000 Catholics in Maryland about 3,000 of them were Negro slaves from Africa. See Jamie T. Phelps, "The Mission Ecclesiology of John R. Slattery: A Study of an African American Mission of the Catholic Church in the Nineteenth Century" (PhD. dissertation, Catholic University of America, 1989) 368. The first parish committed to the mission of the Catholic Church to Blacks was St. Francis Xavier, founded by the Jesuits in Baltimore.

30. Catholic bishops during the nineteenth century were divided over the question of slavery and the inclusion of slaves in the ministry of the Church. Some supported slavery and others condemned it. Some Catholics made provision for ministry to the slaves while others were preoccupied with the demands of the immigrant population. At the Second Plenary Council of Baltimore in 1866 the question of the emancipated slaves was delayed until after the official closing so that the record of the discussion is not contained in the official *Acta et decreta*. The *Josephine Newsletter* for November, December, and January containing the English translation of the post-council discussion and the original Latin text are located in the Archdiocese of Baltimore Archives: AAB9A-D4 and AAB 39A-D4. For a detailed and nuanced summary of this issues, see Jamie T. Phelps, "Caught between Thunder and Lightning: An Historical and Theological Critique of the Episcopal Response to Slavery," in *Many Rains Ago: A Historical and Theological Reflection on the Role of the Episcopate in the Evangelization of African American Catholics*, ed. Secretariat for Black Catholics, National Council of Catholic Bishops (Washington: United States Catholic Conference, 1990) 21–34.

Catholics conformed to the ethos that perceived negroes and Blacks to be inferior and marginalized.[31]

John Richard Slattery (1851–1926), the second superior of the Josephites, was one of the nineteenth-century missionaries working in ministry among Blacks within the U.S. Catholic Church. He struggled to found a seminary open to Black seminarians. During the Third Plenary Council of Baltimore (1884) he submitted a proposal advocating the creation of separate churches for "Negroes" because interracial congregations tended to neglect Blacks. Slattery wrote:

> It is admitted generally that if the Negroes who have been baptized Catholics are to be kept in the Faith, and if the non-Catholic [Negroes] are ever to be brought into the Church, it must be under God's blessings, by priests. [These priests must be willing to devote themselves exclusively to the colored people of their parish with the same care which they bestow on the White members of their congregations. Yet now . . . the colored people of their flock gradually diminish in number, while their attendance usually grows in number when chapels are set apart for their exclusive use.[32]

Oppressive patterns of segregation, marginalization, Black servitude, and racism rooted in a white supremacist ideology tear at the very heart of the central meaning of Jesus's universal call to salvation. They violate the essential meaning of the concept of communion and distort the meaning of Jesus's mission and that of the Church. The resistance to accept Black men and women in the seminaries and religious congregations denied the call of Black people to act as subjects, that is as evangelizers and mediators of peace and justice in the Church and society. The call of Black men and women to discipleship and participation in the liberating mission of Jesus and the Church was and is often muted and strained by racist resistance to the presence of Blacks within all strata of the Church and society. The past and present exclusion of Black men and women from ministerial roles within the Church is a denial of their equality and full humanity. While today there are many, though not enough, Black

31. Ibid.

32. Josephite Archives (henceforth JFA), 3-H-13: JFA: Copybook 3 (henceforth CB-3). This citation is from Slattery's original proposal that describes a system of "large centers whence missionaries might radiate to a distance of, say 200 miles." For details of the early efforts of evangelization of Blacks in the U.S. Catholic Church, see Jamie T. Phelps, "The Mission Ecclesiology of John R. Slattery," 273.

Catholic priests, religious women and men, deacons and an increasing number of Black Catholic lay ecclesial ministers, the assumption of Black intellectual or moral inferiority still clouds their full acceptance and integration within the Catholic ministerial community. Often they are marginalized within the broader Catholic community and denied legitimate inclusion as full participants in the ministerial and hierarchical priesthood and the common priesthood of the faithful.[33] Marginalization and denial militates against an effective increase of Black Catholics engaged in full time church ministry and Black Catholic evangelization. The universal aspect of Jesus's proclamation and saving actions as well as the nature of the Church as a universal sacrament of salvation are abrogated. That the Church is a locus of revelatory communion of the human community with one another and all creation with God was and is often suppressed or ignored in discussions of the Catholic Church's presence in the Black community.[34]

The tragic history of racism within the Catholic parishes of the urban North during the 1940s, 1950s, and 1960s is documented by John T. McGreevey's research. A misguided ethnocentrism became the springboard for the overt racist rejection of Blacks and other non-white people within Northern Catholic parishes. The efforts of white Catholic leaders like John LaFarge and Daniel Cantwell of the Catholic Interracial Councils to struggle against racism within the Church were overshadowed by daily encounters in local parishes.[35] In the case of the Archdiocese of Chicago, misled by their pastor's affirmation and insis-

---

33. *Lumen gentium*, no. 10.

34. Economic rather than theological considerations seem to be more prominent in such discussions.

35. John T. McGreevey, *Parish Boundaries: The Catholic Encounter with Race in the Twentieth-Century Urban North* (Chicago: University of Chicago, 1996). This excellent history chronicles the perspective of white Catholics. It does not however reflect the involvement of Black Catholics as subjects in the struggle against racism nor does it discuss the Black Catholic organizations who struggled against racial segregation and racism. For this perspective see Cyprian Davis, *The History of Black Catholics in the United States*, and *Black and Catholic: The Challenge and Gift of Black Folk*, ed. Jamie T. Phelps (Milwaukee: Marquette University, 1997). For additional information on the Church and reflection see, Jamie T. Phelps, "Racism and the Church: An Inquiry into the Contradictions between Experience, Doctrine and Theological Inquiry," in *Black Faith and Public Talk: Critical Essays on James H. Cone's Black Theology and Black Power*, ed. Dwight N. Hopkins (Maryknoll, NY: Orbis, 1999) 53–76. For reflection on environmental racism see, Bryan Massingale, "The Case for Catholic Support," in *Taking Down our Harps*, 147–62.

tence that segregation was not wrong, many parishioners of European ethnic heritage resisted the admission of African American Catholics to their parishes and schools.[36] The movement of one single family into an ethnic Catholic neighborhood or parish was often cause for protest. In one such crowd one Catholic man was heard to say, "I don't want those jigs sitting in the same pew with me!" while a seventeen-year-old quickly responded that "those niggers don't join the Church anyhow."[37] The phenomenon of the "changing parishes" and migration of European ethnic Catholics to the suburbs seemed to have been fueled both by a complex mixture of ethnocentrism, the desire for economic prosperity, and racism. Still, courageously, some ethnic European Catholic clergy and religious condemned the "middle class materialism" that attempted to "justify segregation by saying that it produces peace and harmony by keeping separate people who would otherwise be in conflict."[38] During the social transformation, which occurred during the Civil Rights Movement, many ethnic European Catholics were blinded by their fear and their desire for security and economic stability. Many turned deaf ears to the cries for justice from their Black Catholic and Protestant brothers and sisters and to the Catholic social teachings that condemned segregation and racism. Too many Catholic men and women failed to respond to the vision of an inclusive community and the call to be in right relationship with one's neighbor that was central to Jesus's proclamation of the Good News illustrated through the Parable of the Good Samaritan. They took flight to the suburbs abandoning the possibility of truly integrated churches and neighborhoods. Blacks were not seen as neighbors nor as brothers and sisters created by a common God and made in the divine image. Blacks were perceived as enemies who were to be feared and despised rather than loved.

## BREAKING THE SILENCE:
## BLACK THEOLOGY OF LIBERATION

Until 1958, most U.S. Catholic bishops were silent and appeared indifferent to racism.[39] Even when some bishops took public stances against

36. For data on select Chicago parishes during the 1940s, see McGreevey, *Parish Boundaries*, 89–93.

37. Ibid., 97.

38. Ibid.

39. See *Many Rains Ago*, passim.

racist behavior,[40] the majority of Catholic theologians and lay people persisted in their silence. Martin Luther King, Jr., as theologian and pastor, was the first prophetic voice that effectively challenged the Christian churches and the U.S. to confront their complicity with racial injustice. King galvanized the prophetic spirit. Black Christian clergy and laity and attentive and committed white and Black members of predominately white churches, including Catholics, began to protest the racism that divided both Church and society. King welcomed all who were prepared to march and protest as a necessary prelude to the realization of his vision of the world as the beloved community.

Inspired by the Civil Rights Movement, James Cone attempted to confront the silent complicity of Christian theologians and the churches in the continued perpetuation of racism. His initial work called for a profound paradigm shift in theology as well as within ecclesial structures and social patterns of relationship. Such a shift required an examination of the limits of the prevailing interpretations of Christology and ecclesiology that had legitimized ecclesial and social "American Apartheid."[41]

The formal articulation of liberation theology emerged almost simultaneously on the North and South American continents in the writings of James Cone, *Black Theology and Black Power* (1969), and shortly thereafter in his *A Black Theology of Liberation* (1970), as well as in the volume of Gustavo Gutierrez, *A Theology of Liberation* (1971).[42]

40. Fortunately this silence was broken by the U.S. Catholic Bishops in their issuance of a series of letters beginning in 1958 addressing racism. In 1979 the U.S. Catholic Bishops issued a pastoral letter *Brothers and Sisters to Us* (Washington, DC: United States Catholic Conference, 1979). The pastoral was encouraged by the Black Catholic community; its actual writing and development was shepherded by Bishop Joseph Francis, SVD. Later the Vatican's Pontifical Commission Iustitia et Pax issued *The Church and Racism: Toward a More Fraternal Society* (Washington, DC: United States Catholic Conference, 1988).

41. Douglas S. Massey and Nancy A. Denton, *American Apartheid: Segregation and the Making of the Underclass* (Cambridge: Harvard University Press, 1993). This text provides a historical and sociological examination of how the Black ghetto was created by whites during the first half of the twentieth century in order to isolate the growing urban Black population. This systemic segregation continues today to perpetuate Black economic poverty.

42. Unfortunately many Catholic theological texts and essays ignore this reality and make no mention of Black liberation theology, exploring Latin American liberation theology exclusively. Collections or summaries of modern theology and theologians published by Catholic publishers sometimes omit the category of Black liberation theology as well as the names of James Cone and other Black and Womanist Protestant theologians.

Interestingly, both these expressions of liberation theology began by challenging the interpretations about Jesus and the Church in the prevailing theologies of the period. Thus, each theologian took up his own "quest for the historical Jesus." Cone and Gutierrez began to reread the Bible and theological traditions from the perspective of the oppressed. Cone gave emphasis to the plight of oppressed Blacks in the U.S., Gutierrez focused on the oppressed indigenous peoples in Latin America. Both discovered a Jesus who did not condone slavery or the devaluation and dehumanization of human beings. Both discovered a Jesus who was God of the oppressed, a Liberator.

In their search for the full meaning of the Bible and Christ for those whose existence is characterized by oppression, both Cone and Gutierrez touched and embraced the profound mystery of Jesus's sojourn on earth. Both identified Jesus as the heart of Christian life and the gospel. For Cone, Jesus Christ is the essence of the Gospel.[43] For Gutierrez, Jesus Christ is the center of God's salvific design.[44] For Cone, "Jesus is the Oppressed One whose task is that of liberating humanity from inhumanity. Through him the oppressed are set free, to be what they are."[45] For Gutierrez, "[t]he work of Christ . . . a new creation . . . is presented simultaneously as a liberation from sin and from all its consequences; despoliation, injustice and hatred."[46] Both acknowledged Jesus's option for the poor. "He was" declared Cone, "for the poor and against the rich, for the weak and against the strong."[47] Gutierrez wrote: "Jesus accompanied this criticism with a head-on opposition to the rich and powerful and a radical option for the poor."[48]

---

43. James H. Cone, *A Black Theology of Liberation*, 2nd ed. (Maryknoll, NY: Orbis, 1986; orig. ed. 1970) 119–23.

44. Gustavo Gutierrez, *A Theology of Liberation*, trans. Sister Caridad Inda and John Eagleson (Maryknoll, NY: Orbis, 1988; orig. English ed., 1973) 151.

45. Cone, *A Black Theology of Liberation*, 117.

46. Gutierrez, *A Theology of Liberation*, 158.

47. Cone, *A Black Theology of Liberation*, 120.

48. Gutierrez, *A Theology of Liberation*, 228. Cone and Gutierrez differ in their attitudes toward the rich. While both see the rich as the object of Jesus criticism, Gutierrez sees the condemnation of the actions of the rich not as being against them but rather as an invitation to conversion. I agree with Gutierrez's approach since this is consistent with the concepts of Jesus as a universal Savior who calls rich and poor alike to salvation and liberation.

Both theologians see contemporary liberation movements as a central aspect of the mission and meaning of Jesus Christ. According to Cone: "The life, death and resurrection of Jesus reveal that he is the man for others, disclosing to them what is necessary for their liberation from oppression. If this is true, then Christ must be Black with Black people so they can know that their liberation is His liberation."[49] Similarly, Gutierrez insists: "All the dynamism of the cosmos and of human history [is] the movement towards creation of a more just and fraternal world. The overcoming of social inequalities among men, the efforts so urgently needed on our continent, to liberate man from all that depersonalizes him, physical and moral misery, ignorance and hunger, as well as the awareness of human dignity . . . all these originate and are transformed and reach their perfection in the saving work of Christ."[50]

Both Cone and Gutierrez see the death and Resurrection of Jesus Christ as the central mystery of Christian life, a mystery that calls for the profound and salvific transformation of the oppressed from their stated of dehumanized oppression to a new creature as human beings. Cone writes: "His death is the revelation of the freedom of God, taking upon himself the totality of human oppression; his resurrection is the disclosure that God is not defeated by oppression but is transforms it into the possibility of freedom."[51] Gutierrez affirms that "the center of God's salvific design is Jesus Christ who by his death and resurrection transforms the universe and makes it possible for man to reach fulfillment as a human being. . . . The redemptive action of Christ, the foundation of all that exists, is also conceived as recreation."[52]

Although the Christological perspective of both these theological pioneers is analogous, their work was received differently in the U.S. Catholic theological community. In the earliest reviews of their work only two Catholic critics engaged their texts. The reviewer in the *Journal of Religious Thought* addressed Cone's second book, *A Black Theology of Liberation* and identified Cone's approach as extreme. The reviewer

49. Cone, *A Black Theology of Liberation*, 120.

50. Gutierrez, *A Theology of Liberation*, 178.

51. Cone, *A Black Theology of Liberation*, 118.

52. Gutierrez, *A Theology of Liberation*, 151 and 158. As I reread these texts almost thirty years later, the continuity and distinctions in the work of these two theologians is more apparent to me. Both insist that Christian salvation is intimately connected with our historical liberation. Cone's work is anthropocentric whereas Gutierrez's work is creation centered.

correctly asserted, however, the necessity of an authentic Black theology to be rooted in the indigenous art and thought forms found in the Black community but failed to acknowledge Cone's social location as an authenticating source for his views. Using loaded rhetorical phrases such as "the simplistic nature of his analysis," the reviewer seems to challenge his intelligence and his authenticity. Indeed, the reviewer comes perilously close to personal attack in concluding: "such a 'Black theology' . . . [becomes possible only when a Negro intelligentsia has arisen [and has] become alienated from the living context of the Black community."[53] On the other hand, the reviewer of Gutierrez's *Theology of Liberation* in the Jesuit weekly *America* applauded his attempt "to explore the relation between the redemptive work of Christ, of the Church, and movements for liberation of men from oppressive and dehumanizing conditions."[54]

## CATHOLICS' SILENCE: THE BLACK EXPERIENCE AND BLACK LIBERATION THEOLOGY

Cone has challenged Catholics who are concerned about justice regarding their indifference and silence on racism and their lack of knowledge about Black history and culture. He has been equally critical about their lack of interest in Black theology.[55] The majority of ethnic European American Catholic theologians men and women have failed to engage the Black liberation theology that emerged over thirty years ago in the U.S. Even many of the theology departments and seminaries that teach other forms of liberation theology, such as Latin American, Feminist, Latino/Latina, African omit U.S. Black theology of liberation from their curricula and syllabi. Cone noted many years ago that this omission of the Black experience suggests that "the black experience is not and has never been regarded as essential to the life and work of the church."[56] The silence of most Catholic theologians on the issue of racism and the

---

53. Rosemary Ruether, "Review of *A Black Theology of Liberation* by James Cone," *Journal of Religious Thought* 28 (Spring-Summer, 1971) 75–77.

54. Joseph A. Komonchak, "Review of *A Theology of Liberation: History and Politics of Salvation*, by Gustavo Gutierrez," *America* 128 (March 31, 1973) 291.

55. James H. Cone, "A Theological Challenge to the American Catholic Church," in *Speaking the Truth: Ecumenism, Liberation and Black Theology* (Grand Rapids: Eerdmans, 1986) 50–60; and "White Theology Revisited," in *Risks of Faith: The Emergence of Black Theology of Liberation, 1968–1998* (Boston: Beacon, 1999) 130–37.

56. Cone, *Speaking the Truth*, 57.

U.S. Black theology of liberation, in contrast to the number of Catholic theologians who engage and teach the theology of Gutierrez and other liberation theologians in Latin America speaks volumes.[57]

The papal letters that I cited earlier in this article as well as several individual and collective letters by U.S. Catholic Bishops from 1958 onwards clearly identify racism as a social and moral evil or sin.[58] Bryan Massingale looks closely at the publications of the U.S. Catholic bishops in the light of Cone's writings. But how does one explain the collective and loud silence of American Catholic theologians? The annual proceedings of the Catholic Theological Society of America from 1946 to 1972 produced only two references to race as a moral issue. Even the "Notes on Moral Theology" published from 1940 to 1993 in Theological Studies produced similarly meager results. This silence is astonishing in a country in which the "Negro problem" dominated the first-quarter of the twentieth century, a country in which racism and its negative impact on Black life and freedom was so dramatically challenged during the Civil Rights Movement in the third-quarter of that same century. Until the recent emergence of Black Catholic and Protestant theologians and ethicists, as well as other liberation theologians, with a few exceptions, the theological academy has failed to acknowledge or discuss and develop a moral argument against racism as a moral issue and social sin.[59]

57. One must balance this dismal portrait with the seeds of hope seen in the steady and relatively large number of Catholic theologians who participate in the annual session of the Black Theology Group of the Catholic Theological Society of America. Some have attended these sessions faithfully for years and each year one sees new faces of colleagues taking seriously the need to engage the theological thought arising from the perspective of the Black experience. The special issue of *Theological Studies*, in which this essay first appeared, honoring the work of James Cone is the fruit of Euro-American Catholic theologians engaging their Black Catholic colleagues at a session of the Black Catholic Theological Symposium at Marquette University held recently.

58. Note the U.S. Catholic Bishops' 1979 letter *Brothers and Sisters to Us* and the Pontifical Commission Iustitia et Pax, *The Church and Racism: Toward a More Fraternal Society*, cited above in n. 40. See also, Jamie T. Phelps, "Racism and the Church: An Inquiry into the Contradictions between Experience, Doctrine and Theological Theory," in *Black Faith and Public Talk*, ed. Dwight N. Hopkins (Maryknoll, NY: Orbis, 1999) 53–76.

59. Bryan Massingale, "The African American Experience and U.S. Catholic Ethics: Strangers and Aliens No Longer," in *Black and Catholic: The Challenge and Gift of Black Folk*, ed. Jamie T. Phelps (Milwaukee, Wisconsin: Marquette University Press, 1998) 81–86. Notable exceptions among moral theologians include Gerald Kelly, John La Farge, Joseph Leonard, Daniel Maguire, Barbara Hilkert Anderson, Paul Wadell, Bryan Massingale, and Anne Patrick. In more recent conferences of the AAR, the Catholic

Why has Cone's work and the subsequent work of Black and Womanist theologies of liberation been ignored by most Catholic theological scholars? Why are so many systematic, biblical, and moral theologians mute about the contradiction between our theological traditions and the racism that is embedded in our national psyche and institutional patterns? Why do liberal, contextual, and global theologians often overlook the racism that permeates the U.S. and world reality? Are we suffering from a hardness of heart that blinds us and makes us deaf to the implications of the way and teachings of Jesus within, our own local and global context? "You shall indeed hear but not understand, you shall indeed look but never see. Gross is the heart of this people, they will hardly hear with their ears, they have closed their eyes, lest they see with their eyes and hear with their ears, and understand with their heart and be converted and I heal them" (Matthew 13:14–15). Massingale suggests that the white tendency to treat Blacks as objects of white study, analysis, and charity rather than subjects capable of independent action or creative initiative has inhibited the recognition of Black agency and the possibility of engagement of Blacks in Catholic moral discourse.[60]

Paul Wadell submits three reasons for this "pattern of omission and neglect" of racism as sin.[61] First, he locates a problem with the prevailing methodological assumptions of Roman Catholic moral theology that equate Christian ethics with human ethics. In its effort to demonstrate that Christian ethics and human ethics are basically the same, too often Christian ethics is collapsed into an abstract and unhistorical understanding of humanity so that our concrete and particular beliefs have little or no impact on moral thinking. Once Christian ethics has been made so abstract and unhistorical, Roman Catholic moral theology loses all sight of the concrete and particular."[62] Second, Wadell argues that American Catholic ethics and moral theology have failed to engage African Americans about their experience of racism, they have rendered

---

Theological Society, and other Catholic theological societies, questions regarding the silence of the theological communities on race relations and on racism have surfaced and a positive engagement of the issue seems promising. The U.S. Catholic Bishops' pastoral on racism, *Brothers and Sisters to Us*, already cited, clearly states: "Racism is not merely one sin among many, it is a radical evil that divides the human family and denies the new creation of a redeemed world" (10).

60. Ibid. 84.

61. Paul Wadell, "Response to Bryan Massingale," in *Black and Catholic*, 102–6.

62. Ibid., 102–3.

themselves incapable of generating an ethics of justice that moves beyond "enlightened self-interest." As such, American Catholic ethics fail to recognize the "limitations, bias and self-deception that creeps into so much of what ethicists take for granted."[63] Third, American Catholic ethics and moral theology neglect the Black experience because it is marked by "too much fantasy and not enough reverence and repentance." Wadell uses the definition fantasy provided by Iris Murdoch. Accordingly, fantasy is "a distortion of moral vision based on a chronic misreading of the world and other people precisely because to see them truthfully would challenge us to conversion."[64] Persistence in ethical fantasy prohibits one's vision and actions from being truthful.

Drawing on the work of Bernard Lonergan, M. Shawn Copeland develops the concept of bias that is related to the concept of fantasy used in Wadell's analysis. She argues that the notion of "intellectual bias" provides a rational explanation of the silence and lack of solidarity for liberation on the part of many theologians from the dominant culture in the U.S.

> [In]difference, ignorance, egotism and selfishness are the obstacles to solidarity. We must push pass our own personal indifference, ignorance, egoism and the selfishness of our society. These obstacles to solidarity can be understood comprehensively as failures in authentic religious, intellectual, and moral living they can be expressed compactly as bias. By bias, I do not mean unswerving commitment to personal preference in the face of contrary and contradictory evidence; nor do I refer to personal temperament. Rather, by bias I mean the . . . less conscious decision to refuse corrective insights or understandings, to persist in error. Bias, then is the arrogant choke to be incorrect. Thus anti-Semitism racism, sexism, homophobia, class exploitation, and cultural imperialism, are explicit concrete forms of individual and group bias . . . Moreover, [these instances of bias] are forms of consciousness that, at once sustain the hegemony of the patriarchal, white supremacist ordering of the society in which we live, and undermine our efforts, to critique the consciousness, to participate in the person and social transformation and thus move authentically beyond mere rhetoric about solidarity.[65]

---

63. Ibid., 104.

64. Ibid.

65. M. Shawn Copeland, "Toward a Critical Christian Feminist Theology of Solidarity," in *Women & Theology*, ed. Mary Ann Hinsdale and Phyllis H. Kaminksi, Annual Publication of the College Theology Society 40 (Maryknoll, NY: Orbis, 1994) 3–38.

Copeland's analysis implies at least that silence about a particular issue or question in fact represents an active, intentional choice and statement about an issue.

Berel Lang's intriguing book-length essay, *Heidegger's Silence*, thematizes bias as silence or omission in the presence of evil and oppression. Lang's thesis is that Heidegger's view of the Jewish Question, his denial or silence—is reflectively articulated thought and the view emerges as reflective and thought, notwithstanding the fact that it sometimes expresses itself in the same forms that otherwise suggest mere prejudice or the influence of social or cultural tradition."[66] Heidegger's silence before and after the Holocaust, Jacques Derrida writes, "leaves us the commandment to think what he did not think." Heidegger's silence suggests that "it was by thinking, not its absence, that Heidegger chose silence."[67] Heidegger's own words, "Man speaks by being silent," condemns him and supports Lang's thesis.[68]

The arguments of Massingale, Wadell, Copeland, and Lang lead me to conclude that the silence of U.S. Catholic theologians about racism is parallel to the silence of leading German theologians and intellectuals during the Nazi atrocities and prosecution of the so-called "final solution" against Jewish people. The theologians' failure to engage the experience and thought of Black people in America is, in my judgment, parallel to the failure of German theologians and philosophers to engage the experience and thought of the Jewish people.

66. Berel Lang, *Heidegger's Silence* (Ithaca, NY: Cornell University, 1996) 6. This intriguing essay articulates one of the many perspectives by which philosophers have sought to explain Heidegger's silence during the Holocaust. In some way's Lang's arguments provide a lens through which to interpret the silence of Catholic theologians and other intellectuals on the question race and racism as parallel to Heidegger's silence on "The Jewish Question" and the Holocaust. Gunnar Myrdal's classic, *An American Dilemma* (New York: Harper & Brothers, 1944), is an extensive analysis of the white denial of "a Negro Problem" as a conscious choice of masking the thoughts about Negroes that occupied their minds. See "Explaining the Problem Away," 1:30–31.

67. Lang, *Heidegger's Silence*, 29.

68. Here Lang is quoting Heidegger's "What is Called Thinking," 13. Heidegger's silence about the Jews and the Holocaust has been often discussed. See "And into Silence," in *Heidegger and the Political: Dystopias* (New York: Routledge, 1998) 146–62.

## BLACK LIBERATION THEOLOGY AND COMMUNION

Examining the meaning and mission of the Church from the perspective of Black liberation theology can both strengthen and challenge the theological understanding of "communion." Black liberation ecclesiology, according to Cone, insists that "the Church is that people called into being by the power and love of God to share in his revolutionary activity for the liberation of man ... The Church ... consists of people who have been seized by the Holy Spirit and who have the determination to live as if all depends on God. It has no will of its own, only God's will; it has no duty of its own, only God's duty. Its existence is grounded in God."[69] Therefore, the Church of Christ is not bounded by standards of race, class, or occupation.

The Black liberation ecclesiology of James Cone has emphasized that the Church as the Body of Christ must exhibit five characteristics: it must suffer with the suffering;[70] it must proclaim the kerygma of liberation to Blacks—and other oppressed peoples and nations—as the liberating message of God's reign, confronting the world with the reality of Christian freedom:[71] it must join in the struggle for liberation against the political, economic and social systems that contradict the Good News of Jesus liberating activity;[72] it must be in its own community what it preaches and what it seeks to accomplish in the world, it must be a visible manifestation that the gospel is a reality;[73] and it must challenge both Black and white churches to refute the dehumanization of Blacks and all oppressed peoples in their own communities as they struggle with them to obtain full freedom and equality in the society.[74]

As his conversations with womanists, feminists, and other liberation theologians from other cultural contexts such as Africa, Latin America, and Asia multiplied, so Cone's understanding of the liberating mission of the Church expanded. His understanding began to embrace not only the Black victims of racial oppression, but also the victims of gender,

69. Cone, *Black Theology and Black Power*, 63, 65.

70. Ibid., 66. For a fuller development of Cone's theology of suffering see his "Divine Liberation and Black Suffering," in *God of the Oppressed*, 163–93.

71. Cone, *Black Theology and Black Power*, 67; and Cone, *A Black Theology of Liberation*, 131.

72. Cone, *Black Theology and Black Power*, 67.

73. Ibid., 70–77; see also Cone, *A Black Theology of Liberation*, 131–32.

74. *Black Theology and Black Power*, 110; *A Black Theology of Liberation* 132–35.

cultural, and class oppression within both the Black and white Protestant and Catholic congregations.[75] Cone had always understood that the Church must be on the side of the poor, because Jesus was for the poor;[76] but his understanding of the poor in his later thought has embraced not only the Black poor in the U.S. but the poor all over the world. His Black, Asian, and Hispanic women students and their friends and associates at Union Theological Seminary were among the first articulators of womanist, mujerista, and Asian women's liberation theologies in the U.S. As he deepened their social and theological analysis of racial oppression, they made him more cognizant of the oppression of the distinct nature of the oppression of Black, Hispanic, and Asian in Church and society.[77]

Cone's most recent essays on Black theology and the Black Church continue to challenge the Black churches to embrace both the demand of being agents of liberation and the creation of a new heaven and a new earth. The broadening of the horizons of Black liberation theology and the realization that the whole world is caught up in one dynamic struggle between estranged members of one culturally diverse human family, has led to understanding the relationship between the diverse forms of liberation theology within and beyond the U.S. This helps us to understand that we are seeking liberation from oppressive divisions in the human community and *liberation for* a new or beloved community that embraces all into one communion under God.

75. James Cone, *My Soul Looks Back* (Nashville: Abingdon, 1982) 93–94, 99–108. Cone recognized the continuity and discontinuity of the theologies of liberation in Africa and Latin America. While all theologies of liberation focus on the dehumanization, marginalization, and oppression of the poor, African liberation theology outside of South Africa, focused primarily on cultural oppression or imperialism while the later focused on class oppression (ibid., 108–13). These different foci have implications for the mission of the Church. In the former, there is a dramatic focus on inculturation of the local churches; in the latter, there is a struggle to have the Church identify with the struggle and liberation of the economically poor masses.

76. Cone, *A Black Theology of Liberation*, 120.

77. Among Cone's students who have published are: Jacquelyn Grant, *White Women's Christ and Black Women's Jesus* (Atlanta: Scholars, 1989); Kelly Delaine Brown, *The Black Christ* (Maryknoll, N.Y.: Orbis, 1994); Chung Hyun Kyung, *Struggle to be Sun Again: Introducing Asian Women's Theology* (Maryknoll, N.Y.: Orbis, 1990). Through the years many other women theologians participated in the student circle of women theological students at Union Theological Seminary. Among those who have published are Katie Cannon, Delores Williams, Ada Maria Isasi Diaz, and JoAnn Terrell. These women—and many others—were directly or indirectly influenced by Cone and influenced his thought through the years.

## THE CALL TO REPENTANCE AND CONVERSION

In his 1998 apostolic letter, *Tertio Millennio Adveniente*, Pope John Paul II declared that the year 2000 was to be a Jubilee Year during which Catholics were called to embrace the joy of repentance and conversion, a joy based upon the forgiveness of sins.[78] Foremost in the Pope's mind was disunity within the Christian Church, intolerance, the use of violence in the service of truth and religious indifference.[79] Because those sins "have been detrimental to the unity willed by God for his People" are among those that require a greater commitment to repentance and conversion, the Church has been invited to become "more fully conscious of the sinfulness of her children recalling all those times in history when they departed from the spirit of Christ and his Gospel and instead of offering to the world the witness of life inspired by the values of faith, they indulged in ways of thinking and acting which were truly forms of counter-witness and scandal."[80]

In his post-synodal apostolic exhortation, *Ecclesia in America*, summarizing the Synod of America held in late 1997, John Paul II had also stressed this call for repentance and conversion.[81] He urged Catholics on the American continents to engage in a new evangelization. He emphasized that conversion is possible only if it is rooted in one's encounter with Jesus in the New Testament, in the liturgy, and in the "real and concrete situation" of the complex reality of America.[82] Only by being reconciled with God can we be "prime agents" of "true reconciliation with and among [our] brothers and sisters."[83] The Catholic Church, which "embraces men and women of every nation, race, people and tongue (Revelation 7:9) is called to be 'in a world marked by ideological, ethnic, economic and cultural division,' and 'living sign of the unity of the hu-

---

78. John Paul II, "*Tertio millennio adveniente*," *Origins* 24 (Nov. 24, 1994) 401–16, at no. 32. More recently the International Theological Commission addressed various issues raised by the pope's call to repentance, "Memory and Reconciliation: The Church and the Faults of the Past," *Origins* 29 (Mar. 16, 2000) 525–44.

79. *Terti millennio adveniente*, nos. 34–36.

80. Ibid., no. 33.

81. John Paul II, "*Ecclesia in America* (The Church in America)," *Origins* 28 (Feb. 4, 1999) 565–92, at no. 3. The theme of the American Synod was "Encounter with the Living Christ: The Way to Conversion, Communion and Solidarity in America."

82. Ibid., nos. 12–13.

83. Ibid., no. 32.

man family."[84] The Church in America is being called to a communion within and beyond the American continents.

Commitment to communion is integrally connected to a commitment to Black and other forms of liberation. A social historical appropriation of communion ecclesiology in the context of the Americas in general and the U.S. in particular will require a radical conversion by which we acknowledge the sinful nature of the systems of oppression within our ecclesial institutions and society that divide the human community.

Acknowledgment of our complicity in the social sins that divide us is only the beginning of our conversion. Secondly, we must seek the forgiveness of those whom we have victimized by our past injustices. Finally, both parties must work together toward human solidarity rooted in our spiritual communion. Concretely this reconciliation will be manifested in the development of more inclusive patterns of relationship. These patterns will allow the full participation in decision making, ministerial and social actions of Church and society according to their capacity by those who previously were excluded, devalued or marginalized by the overt and covert boundaries of racism, classism, sexism, homophobia, cultural imperialism, and all other systems of oppression.

The call to communion resonates with our deepest desire for liberation from the oppression of dehumanizing patterns of relationships of racism, sexism, and classism manifest by our continued marginalization, devaluation as responsible and active participants of the church mission of ecclesial and social transformation. This call to communion resonates with our deepest desire for inclusion within community of humankind as respected and capable human agents of God's mission. Most marginalized and oppressed peoples passionately desire to be in union with one another and all of humankind and creation. Yet true community is only possible if it is founded in the radical truth of our personal and collective history of joy and sorrow.

Posing the question of what it means for a local church to live in "Pentecost communion," Richard Marzheuser suggests that a local church or parish must "welcome all Catholics . . . regardless of their nation, people, tribe or language . . . In the triumph of Pentecost 'there is no longer Greek and Jew, circumcised and uncircumcised, barbarian,

---

84. Ibid.

Scythian, slave, and free, but Christ is all in all' (Colossians 3:11)."[85] In view of the history of oppression within the U.S. and the world, I most heartily agree with Marzheuser's interpretation regarding the ideal of Pentecost communion. But I also insist that such a reality is possible only if we engage in the process of conversion here outlined.

## BROADENING OUR THEOLOGICAL HORIZONS

Conversion within the context of the theological community has specific implications. The social justice tradition of the Catholic churches impels Catholic and Protestant theologians in the U.S. to break their silence about the marginalization, devaluation, and systemic oppression of Blacks and other groups with the ecclesial, social, academic, economic, and political institutions of this nation. Catholic and Protestant theologians must begin to engage the new theological voices that have emerged in the last half of the twentieth century. A global approach to theology requires that one critically engage the new African/African American, Latino/a, Hispanic American, Asian/Asian American, and Indigenous/ Native American, European/European American theological perspectives both male and female that have emerged in the U.S. and around the world.[86] These voices must continue to mature and deepen as they engage people and theologians whose cultural, class, and religious traditions differ from their own. Such a theological dialogue will reveal areas of continuity and discontinuity. New questions will be raised and new understandings of God, Christ, and Church will emerge. Both liberation theologies and communion ecclesiologies compel us to engage in a rigorous and expansive dialogue with scholars from diverse cultural contexts within this nation and around the world as we search the images and metaphors for God and God's mission that embody the truth and justice of those who desire to live in communion with God.

Theologians are called to use their resources for the empowerment of the poor, the weak, and the marginalized. Black theologians and

85. Richard Marzheuser, "The Holy Spirit and the Church: A Truly Catholic Communio," *New Theology Review* 11 (Aug. 1998) 63–64.

86. Admittedly this is a daunting task, but in a global society such as ours to omit any theological voice might lead to a too narrow interpretation of God's rich and complex revelation and self-expression and a too narrow understanding of the Church's mission in today's society. The task requires a shift from an individualist narrow approach to theological scholarship to the formation of intentional broader, interdisciplinary and multicultural community of men and women scholars.

Black Christians, Catholic and Protestant, must move beyond a mere reaction to white racism in America and begin to extend their vision of a new human and cosmological community for the whole inhabited world. Christians must be concerned about the quality of human life not only in the urban centers and the small rural towns of America, but also that of their brothers and sisters in Africa, Asia, and Latin America. Oppressed people live on the margins of their societies and are the victims of systemic oppression and violence both within and beyond the U.S. Humanity is one, and, as Martin Luther King Jr. observed many years ago, no one is liberated until all are liberated. While maintaining a commitment to those who are oppressed locally, theologians must also broaden their horizon to those who are oppressed globally. They must recognize that oppressed peoples within the U.S. and those beyond the U.S. exist in a culture of death, one that was created by the dominant culture and characterized by the poverty of unemployment and unending debt, political and economic corruption, racial and cultural discrimination, inadequate or irrelevant education, personal devaluation, and marginalization.[87] Refusal to hear the voices of poor Black people and other marginalized people throughout the world condemns many to live by an alternate violent economy of a global drug community.[88] Those who practice theology from the perspective of the poor and marginalized must continue to create liberating communities with all whom they encounter so as to discover and embody the power of Spirit that enables patterns of complicit silence about social sin to be broken.

Black theology of liberation must continue the rich legacy and creative vision of human liberation and include in it the distinctive contributions of the Black experience that our ancestors have passed on. Black people have been struggling for more than 430 years. We must identify the wisdom that our experience has taught us would be useful in the creation of a new historical future for all oppressed people. Black theologians must seek what others can teach us from their historical experience in the struggle for justice as we participate in the liberation of the world from its patterns of oppression.[89] America and the world must be liberated from the image of a Church and society that continues to be a nightmare for the masses of Black and oppressed people. America

87. See "*Ecclesia in America*," nos. 59–64.

88. Ibid., no. 61.

89. Cone, "Black Theology and the Black Church," in *Risks of Faith*, 45–47.

and the world must embrace that communion imaged by the metaphor of the beloved community envisioned by Black liberation theology and communion ecclesiology.[90]

Cone's early experience made him initially less optimistic than King about the possibility of U.S. Christians and other citizens transcending the boundaries of racism and the other systems of oppression that mitigate against the full historical embodiment or visible manifestation of communion in our ecclesial, national, or world communities. Still he holds fast to the image of King's beloved community and urges the Black churches to engage in the ongoing conversion and transformation that will signal the full realization of this vision of communion in its broadest and most inclusive manifestation in our world. Cone insists with Malcolm X that the distinct contribution of the Black experience and scholarship including Black theology must become primary agents of both liberation and communion. With King he asserts: "We are created for each other and not against each other. We must, therefore, break down the barriers that separate people from one another. As we seek the beloved community of humankind."[91] Cone's vision is faithful to that of the Church understood as communion. Fidelity to that vision will lead church theologians to broaden their horizons to embrace the whole human community through intraecclesial, ecumenical, and interreligious dialogue. Such a broadening of horizons will enable the theological community to provide the theological interpretations that enable the community to grasp more fully the truth about ourselves and God's self-revelation to us. Such a broadening will lead to commitment to the

90. See Cone, *Martin & Malcolm & America: A Dream or a Nightmare* (Maryknoll, NY: Orbis, 1991) 111, 127. Malcolm X called our attention to the fact that for most Blacks in the U.S., life was not characterized by Martin Luther King Jr.'s dream of a community that would judge people by the content of their character rather than the color of their skin. Malcolm argued separation to make it possible to nurture Black self-love as the road to Black authenticity and full humanity. King recognized that one cause for the nightmare was the consequence of our having broken community. "Through our sin, through our evil and through our wickedness, we have broken communities." Cone wisely concludes that both Malcolm and King are right. Malcolm was right in encouraging Blacks to embrace liberation, that is, their own human dignity and freedom as Black people to avoid participation in Black genocide. King encouraged liberated Black people to stand against racism and poverty while seeking the beloved community. Later Black, Womanist, and other liberation theologians would add sexism, class exploitation, imperialism, and homophobism to the list of those demonic "isms" from which we must be liberated to embrace one another in love.

91. Ibid., 318.

realization of a just Church and society in which brothers and sisters dwell together in the communion of love.

## CONCLUSION

Black liberation theology and communion ecclesiology are not opposing theologies. One presupposes the other. No one can enter into full communion with an individual, group, nation, or world if one's relationship to the other is marked by indifference or oppression. Communion is predicated on the assumption that such a union is freely embraced and that both partners are freely saying a "yes." Human freedom is a precondition for the ethical action of living in right relationship with one another and with God. As Christians celebrate the start of the third millennium, they have an opportunity to acknowledge their past individual and social sins, to ask forgiveness of one another, and to commit themselves to the living in communion as the people of God that Jesus envisioned at the end of his earthly sojourn.

One can become one with others only if one can speak the truth of one's sinful past, asking and granting forgiveness, and reaching out to one another in a spirit of reconciling love and solidarity. Oneness cannot be built on lies, denial, or the pretense of reconciliation. Oneness or unity in diversity is the pattern of communion manifest in the Triune God. This oneness can serve as a model of ecclesial and human communion. Rooted in that communion born of the Spirit, this oneness will be manifest concretely as diverse individuals and cultural groups are allowed to use freely their gifts and talents. As more people exercise their human freedom and responsibility to participate in service motivated by the love of God and focused on justice within ecclesial and social communities, authentic communion will deepen. Only when Christians speak and live in truth can they become a Church and a nation whose patters of relationship become a sacrament of radical unity in diversity. To get to the truth one must break silent complicity with the social evil that has marred the past and continues to mar the present reality. What must be confronted are the white supremacist, gender, and class ideologies that lead to the current patterns of interpersonal, social, and ecclesial relationships that contradict God's call to communion.

Today many are questioning the relevance and necessity of liberation theology or pronounce its death with the emergence of contextual and global theology.[92] I suggest that liberation theology will cease to be necessary when and only when all men and women are free of sin and all that oppresses. Then and only then will it be possible for us to experience the fullness of communion that was the basic ecclesial paradigm of the Second Vatican Council. Then and only then will our world truly image the unity in diversity that characterizes the nature of the Triune God. Only then will we be embraced into the ones for which Jesus prayed in fulfillment of his mission to lead all creation back to the fullness of communion with God, with one another, and with all creation.

92. Congregation for the Doctrine of the Faith, *Instruction on Certain Aspects of the Theology of Liberation* (Boston: St. Paul, 1984). This document did not totally condemn liberation theologies but spoke rather against "certain aspects," most notably a too exclusive use of Marxist analysis, and an understanding of liberation emptied of its theological and spiritual dimensions and restricted to class analysis borrowed from Marxism (see Parts 6-10). Much of the document seems to affirm, as the introduction suggests, that "The Gospel of Jesus Christ is a message of freedom and a force for liberation ... from the radical slavery of sin and the many different kinds of slavery in the cultural, economic, social and political spheres, ... derive[d] ultimately from sin ... that of preventing people from living in a manner befitting their dignity" (5). See the development of this major theme as it relates liberation to the Bible and earlier teachings of popes and bishops, including evangelization and social justice (Parts 1-5, 11).

# 19

## Called to Be the Salt of the Earth

### Black and Womanist Theologies—Which Way Forward?

IVA E. CARRUTHERS

THIS QUESTION *How Long Oh Lord? The Future of Black Theology— Womanist Theology Dialogue in Church and Academy* is one with which I am hardly a stranger. It is a routine question associated with why we do what we think we are doing. But in preparing this essay, I was drawn to reread Carolyn Rodger's poem, "It Is Deep." Rodgers's poetry, written in the late 1960s, reflects a personal understanding of the tensions between church and academy, religion and liberation. The tension between her aspirations for the Black power movement and her abandonment of the Negro religion and church of her mother was a foretaste of a posture for womanist theology. In "It is Deep," Rodgers talks about that personal tension. In the end, she concludes:

> My mother, religious-negro, proud of
> Having waded through a storm, is very obviously,
> A sturdy Black bridge that I
> Crossed over, on.[1]

It is this metaphor of a bridge that positions the perspective of this essay. A bridge allows people to traverse from one point to another, often over an otherwise impassable barrier such as water; a bridge connects generations of experiences and possibilities; a bridge can be an intersecting

---

1. Carolyn Rodgers, "It Is Deep," in *Songs of a Black Bird* (Chicago: Third World Press, 1973).

point of reconciliation, healing, compromise, and vulnerability. A bridge can be that vantage point from which you envision new possibilities, discover new realities and meet new people to transform the world.

## A VIEW FROM THE BRIDGE

A view from the bridge tells me that we are on the precipice of a regrouping in new ways, with new authority, and with new partners to transform the world. A view from the bridge tells me that we are wrestling with difficult questions close up, but answers are unfolding that will guide our feet as we remain willing to look in the mirror and yet remain the salt of the earth for the people of God. According to Luke 14:34–35, "Salt is good; but if salt has lost its taste, how can its saltiness be restored? It is fit neither for the soil nor for the manure pile; they throw it away. Let anyone with ears to hear listen!"

Three questions help to inform my response to the question raised above. The first question is Benezet Bujo's question on the trajectory of academic discourse: "What are we to say of an African theology that never gets beyond the lecture halls of universities and congresses, mostly outside of Africa? No one could take seriously a theology which preached the necessity of inculturation, but simply ignored the surrounding social misery."[2] The second question is Jacquelyn Grant's critique of the position of Black women in the institutionalized church: "Is the Black church detrimental for Black women's physical and psychological health?" "How do we reconcile all of these unhealthy activities in the church with the other side of the church's story—that story we like to tell and tell over and over again?"[3] The third question is Gayraud Wilmore's condemnation of our proclamations: "[How can it be that] the burning issues of the 21st century—preventive war, terrorism, gay rights, human sexuality, family structures and values, the hip-hop culture, prison construction and reform, abortion, stem-cell research, genocide and ethnic cleansing, Afrocentrism and the explosion of African Christianity, globalism, HIV/AIDS and the desperate needs of the Two-Thirds World—are scarcely

---

2. Benezet Bujo, *African Theology in Its Social Context* (Maryknoll, NY: Orbis, 1992) 70.

3. Jacquelyn Grant, "Freeing the Captives: The Imperative of Womanist Theology," in *Blow the Trumpet in Zion: Global Visions and Action for the 21st Century Black Church*, ed. Iva E. Carruthers et al. (Minneapolis: Fortress, 2005) 86, 90.

touched by our Sunday sermons, conference addresses, church governing bodies, or literature?"[4]

With these overarching questions, I want to look internally at the
corporate "we" and the contemporary landscape, and externally at the
corporate "them" and the contemporary landscape, and personally and
collectively at us at this very moment. An introspective critique suggests
that Black theology and womanist theology are challenged by three realities: the culture of amnesia, the crisis of leadership, and the compromise
of mission. The perpetuation of each of these realities will surely destroy
a people. But likewise, the identification of each of these realities as a tar-
get for transformation can shape our battle plan to empower and move
forward a more matured and strategic agenda for Black and womanist
theologies.

## THE CULTURE OF AMNESIA

The culture of amnesia is the complete embodiment of collective forget-
fulness. It is to a people what Alzheimers is to an individual. It is totally
incapacitating and wipes out the synapses of memory that reminds a
people from where and how far they have come. It destroys human will
and the desire to be fully human as God created us to be. The culture of
amnesia is characterized by a people of God who have forgotten to tell
their story of faith and victory to their children, in this case multiple
generations. A consequence is a major dissonance of appreciation and
understanding of the prophetic word and courageous action that came
from those who appropriated their faith to energize the continuous
struggle for liberation, empowerment, and institutional development.
We now have generations of persons in the pulpit and pew, churched
and unchurched, who are clueless about how they got where they are,
why they are where they are, and what they ought to be doing.

An individual who has no sense of historical grounding as a member of a family and community or a generation that has no sense of its
history as a link to a people's journey, becomes the cancer within that
devours. Black theology and the Black power movement emerged as a
part of the continuum and legacy of African struggle and self-expression
for liberation, liberation in mind, body, and spirit. Then and now, the

4. "The Black Church in the Age of False Prophets: An Interview with Gayraud
Wilmore," in ibid., 167–68.

question of the rootedness of Black Theology in Western or African epistemological approaches to theological reflection cannot be ignored.

Over the past forty years, we have come some distance towards
the road back to self-understanding. However, the culture of amnesia
certainly propels this inquiry and reflection into the Southern Cradle as
a crucible of epistemological direction.[5] The justification for this is revealed in the wisdom of our people who in Ghana, West Africa, with the
imagery of the Sankofa bird, whose beak touches its tail as a reminder
that in the circle of life, we must always look back to move forward.
This same circular view of time and space is expressed in Kenya, East
Africa by the concept of Zamani—moving backwards into spiritual understanding and, ultimately, through death, experiencing perfect peace
and reconciliation with God. This backwards view of time and space is
circular, not linear, where a people's faith in the future sustains them in
the present, thus the richness of the African concept of Imani or faith.
For both the individual and community of faith, the Sasa, potential and
dynamic present time, is being secured by the foundation of the past and
being bonded with all other created and yet to be created things.

This epistemological understanding of faith and departure from
Western linear time and space was with the slaves in the brush arbors
and on the Underground Railroad, and the 80-year-old grandmother
who just stood on a ladder all night and prayed to her Jesus as the waters
surrounded her in Katrina. For generations, this way of knowing, feeling,
and using time and space for a divine purpose has been embodied in the
African American faith which claims the not yet in the already and vows
that because we are, I am, or that I may not get there with you, but we
will get there.

Cecil Cone's epistemological critique that there was more to Black
theology than political liberation is worth repeating: "When the slaves
were introduced to Christianity, they brought with them their African
"pre-understanding." Thus it may be said that Africans were not converted to Christianity but that they converted Christianity to themselves
. . . Thus Black Theology is called to be loyal to its African elements if it
wishes to be faithful to the Black religious experience. The Black religious experience has in common with its African roots the concept of

---

5. Consult Marimba Ani, *Yurugu: An African Centered Critique of European Cultural Thought* (Trenton, NJ: Africa World Press, 1994); and Cheikh Anta Diop, *The Cultural Unity of Black Africa* (Chicago: Third World Press, 1990).

the divine as all-encompassing."[6] Indeed, Black theology is a connector to the transcendental God awareness and belief that Africans had before, during and after the slave trade—a God awareness and belief that is manifest in Spirit and Spirits. To say, "we are an African people and we will be free," is to claim one's identity and commitment to struggle not as a mere political activity, but to struggle out or a sense of divine righteousness.

This divine righteousness is linked to African ontological concepts of Ntu and Nommo that affirm the ever-present universal force and its manifestations and the word that wakes up the spirit and becomes flesh. Typically, this Ntu/Nommo dynamic fuses the sacred and secular. It is communal and it has both male and female expression. Worthy of more explication in another context, the Ntu/Nommo dynamic is relevant here in that it points us to the African faith tradition that affirms prayer and power from the collective that crosses time and space, links the ancestors with the yet to be born, and indwells in the spirit of those engaged in active resistance to captivity. The Ntu/Nommo indwelled in Tubman, Vesey, Turner, Truth, and Boukman, all servant leaders who fought with a sense of divine righteousness and belief in a just God. The Ntu/Nommo is the unprecedented spirit that overwhelmed Howard Thurman on his first sail to Africa. As he reflects: "I look out on the full moon and the ghosts of my forefathers rise and fall with the undulating waves . . . In the deep, heavy darkness of the foul-smelling hole of the ship, . . . they held their breath against the agony . . . What tools of the spirit were in their hands with which to cut a path through the wilderness of their despair?"[7] This same Spirit, that was in the beginning and still lives among us, commands that we remember and tell the story. We are commanded to establish the rocks of remembrance that we shall never forget and share their meaning with our children's children.

I shall never forget the time I went in search of finding the remnants of a slave cemetery on Hilton Head Island (South Carolina) where hotel development occurred years ago despite vigorous protest by the Black community. I asked a Black gardener of this now commercial area to direct me to the site and with a startled look, he said, "I am so glad

6. Cecil Wayne Cone, *The Identity Crisis in Black Theology* (Nashville: AMEC, 2003) 42.

7. Howard Thurman, *With Head and Heart: The Autobiography of Howard Thurman* (New York: Harcourt Brace Jovanovich, 1979) 193.

someone cares. You are one of the few who have ever asked." He then walked me to the small fenced in area. In another area of that county, where Harriet Tubman served as nurse and the enslaved first heard the reading of the Emancipation Proclamation, I wanted to revisit an historical marker that I had witnessed the dedication of several years before. I asked a well-educated pastor for the location of the marker that was dedicated to commemorate one of the last slave ships landing in the U.S., and he told me I had to be mistaken because he had not heard of any such place.

From the bridge between academy and church, we must ask: what happens when the memory of a people lies dormant in the silence of the marginalized? What happens when the memory of a people is negated by the ignorance of its privileged? A recent conversation with a young, intelligent, energetic female pastor, seminary graduate, ordained for eight years and serving in one of the largest prophetic and activist Black churches in a fairly large city reveals what happens. My one-on-one conversation with her was at a recent Women in Ministry conference, where she was trying to process references to Black theology and a specific mention of a she-God. (I did not know her.) She shared that these references were intriguing, yet jolting to her understanding of ministry and personal identity. Because these ideas seemed to pull her away from a more universal view of God and salvation by Christ, she was not sure how they were relevant to her. On the other hand, she saw the Hurricane Katrina realities raise questions of gross inequities to which the church needed to respond, but not as a witness for Black or womanist theology. Her view was that Black and womanist theologies tended not to yield a spirit of cooperation among the people of God, whoever they are, and that lack of cooperation is the sin. In eight years of ordained ministry, the first time she witnessed or heard of the Black church cooperating across denominational barriers, though minimal, has been in response to Hurricane Katrina.

This pastor graduated from Dallas Theological Seminary, but she had no real knowledge of the role of the church in the Civil Rights Movement, had never heard of the Negro Convention Movement, and did not view the liberating acts of a Tubman, Truth, Vesey, and Turner as particular acts of faith and appropriations of Christian theology. She was honest, open to conversation, and receptive to an educational moment. Now, whatever this conversation says about her, it says much more about us. We have not taught our children their history. This young pastor is the consequence of a culture of amnesia. Unless and until we take on this culture of amnesia as we move forward, we are becoming a people who are victims of "mentacide." The antidote is for us to dig deeper into the Southern Cradle of epistemology and ontology and *unearth* our African spirituality in the expression of our African American faith.

We can unapologetically research, teach, preach and celebrate the revelations of our African religious continuity through the prism of Black and womanist theologies, studied and experiential. With over 450 scripture language projects all over Africa, new synapses are made continuously. For example, in Cameron, "truth of God" and the "word of God" are not static but dynamic and mean "the lived-word" as articulated by Black theology. In the Irreg language of Tanzania, Yahweh is a feminine God—a possibility articulated by womanist theology. These examples of what can be unearthed for the academy and the church in the crucible of the Southern Cradle affirm Wilmore's self admonishment that "Womanist theology is not a branch of Black theology, nor is it a substitute for Black theology. Womanist theology *is* Black theology."[8] They affirm Grant's declaration that today, this Christ, found in the experiences of Black women, is a Black woman."[9] They affirm that a Pan African view of theology is the way forward for Black and womanist theologies.

Indeed, the antidote for the culture of amnesia and mentacide is for the word to be lived in the collective and individual memories of our people, and that will not happen by wishing it to happen. Our Black churches must become sites of study, oral history engagement, "edutainment," and sacred rituals of commemoration of the stony road we trod with a faith that has us still here. The words of Papa Dllas guide this very moment: "Don't cry for me now, daughter. I want you to promise me one thing. I want you to promise me that you gonna tell all the children my story."[10]

8. Gayraud S. Wilmore, *Pragramatic Spirituality: The Christian Faith through an Africentric Lens* (New York: New York University Press, 2004) 70.

9. Jacquelyn Grant, *White Women's Christ and Black Women's Jesus: Feminist Christology and Womanist Response* (Atlanta: Scholars, 1989) 220.

10. Papa Dallas, "Remember Me," *Voices of Our Ancestors*, U.S. Library of Congress.

## CRISIS OF LEADERSHIP

The next observation I want to discuss is our crisis of leadership, which threatens the very future of the race. As we examine this crisis in leadership, the first step is to understand leaders are chosen and made. Divine leaders can be preordained in the womb, but even they need a nurturing womb to answer the call. Our challenge is to thus successfully cast a net for leaders who are willing to take off the veil of privilege and protection of "made in the USA." Our challenge is to create and sustain leaders who will risk the lack of affirmation and even ostracism that comes with being opposed to the gatekeepers of the status quo, be we in the academy, the judicatory, the denomination, the schoolhouse, the courthouse, the jailhouse, or the hospital corridor. Wherever the vocation of ministry leads us, the challenge remains the same.

Today's view from the bridge sadly reveals that many who came through the academy under some tutelage of Black and womanist theologies have walked back into the church, men desirous of being deified and sister divas choosing to wear markings of a royal crest over a crown for righteous struggle. To those served by the church, it appears that womanist theology is being morphed into divadom and Black theology is being measured by how much money cometh and how close you can get to Pharaoh.

To be sure, Black and womanist theologies compel a special call to leadership in ministry for the academy and the church. That call is grounded in the role of a prophet. With a faith in God and unwavering commitment to the vision, a few named biblical prophets and many unnamed women overpowered and outnumbered the majority. As Christians today, our commitment to prophetic witness ought to be measured by our willingness to witness for Jesus Justice, despite its lack of popularity.

To be sure, the wilderness experience for a prophetic leader is a norm. Biblical prophets stood their ground against powerful rulers and fearful, uninformed silent people as well as sanctified Pharisees and Sadducees. The lamentation of "How Long, Oh Lord" is a constant refrain. Because of this reality, so few in the academy or church want to stay the course. Speaking truth to power will get you killed. With revisionist history, it is sometimes easy to forget the pains and disappointments of a prophet. Prophets are safely embraced and celebrated when they are dead and unable to walk among the people. Ahistorical, comfortable myths suggest that the prophet was well received in his/her time. Romanticization of a totally unified Black church, Black community or Black leadership during any period in time is just that—romanticized revisionist history.

In fact, most prophets are persecuted and find themselves repeatedly up against betrayal, backstabbing and berating. This has been no difference for the prophetic leaders of the academy and Black church than it was for those of biblical tradition. A prophet over here may yield many Judases over there, setting traps for intellectual and spiritual confusion. Always lurking to distract and destroy prophets are traitors, naysayers, the uninformed and misinformed, and the educated fools.

A view from the bridge reminds us that Tubman's husband and brothers were her greatest fear. So she, upon saying goodbye to her mother Christmas day, stole away when they least expected her to. Gabriel Prosser's revolt of over 9000 slaves was betrayed by two informants. Note that, in terms of the civil rights movement it was two women (an unsung sheroe, a high school student and niece of Rev. Vernon Johns and the matriarch of the movement, the late Rosa Parks) who gave life to the movement. And it was a divided National Baptist Convention under the leadership of Rev. J. H. Jackson that charted the course options for Rev. Dr. Martin Luther King, Rev. Dr. Gardner Taylor, and the Civil Rights Movement. And we cannot forget that Black men pulled the trigger on Malcolm X.

The way forward is to recognize that the tensions between academy and church, taught word vs. preached word, prophetic word vs. safe word, soul's salvation vs. people's liberation, are not new tensions. These tensions fuel a saga of crisis in leadership.

> The minister needs the best possible training, because he [or she] is the real leader among his [or her] people . . . It is beyond the power of any being in heaven or on earth to teach what he [or she] does not know. A call to preach is no guarantee of one's fitness to preach . . . [it] simply guarantees the possibilities. A longing and burning desire without knowledge is of very little advantage; it may be a positive disadvantage both to the man [or woman] and to those who are made to listen.[11]

This statement, relevant in 1902, is what Katie Cannon calls the funk-making manure of the past. "Much of our religion smells from that ma-

11. Professor A. W. Pergues, DD, of Shaw University made this statement in 1902 at the Negro Young People's Christian and Educational Congress.

nure of the past. So we ought to be on our knees in repentance to God for carrying that sack of manure too long into the present. We need to repent for not taking a stand against jacklegs right here in our midst who are rehearsing that old funkmaking in preparation for perpetuating that same good-for-nothing religion in the pews in today's black church."[12] Those committed to Black theology must lead the charge to reevaluate the relationships among the academy, community, and church, the criteria for licensing and affirming ministry, and the standards by which success is measured in the academy and the pulpit.

A view from the bridge argues that womanist theology also must not get comfortable with switching seats with men and counting its impact by just being present. To the contrary, womanist theology must remain true to its foundation: the tradition of the "race women" of faith. In the tradition of Esther, women like Mary McLeod Bethune, Ida Wells Barnett, Rosa Parks, and Dorothy Height found no dissonance between being Black, female, activist, a person of Christian faith, and being with the people.

The way forward in resolving this crisis in leadership is to examine for whom we are working and our destination. Leadership for the kingdom is evidenced by what we do for God—our actions and deeds—not merely by what we say. In the end, God is more concerned with our acts of Godliness than the genitalia He/She created. Serving God through the Jesus model of leadership directs our steps at this juncture. Jesus was a revolutionary and fearless leader, leaving the temple to go to the streets; eating, touching, and healing the least of these. He said come as you are and defied the priestly protocols and state powers. He was inclusive and welcoming, and he came with an attitude of servant leadership, humbly and humanly. If Black and womanist theologies are to produce leaders that model Jesus, a correction course in the academy and church is in order. The way forward is to identify prophets willing to stand on the edge and engage in more research on our authentic (not glamorized) past and our contemporary communities, to serve in the unpopular places where God meets people every day and in the communities where the presence of God even appears not to be present.

12. Katie Geneva Cannon, *Teaching Preaching: Isaac Rufus Clark and Black Sacred Rhetoric* (New York: Continuum, 2002) 177.

## COMPROMISE OF MISSION

We confront a culture of amnesia and a crisis of leadership. What is also clear from the bridge is that we are witnessing a compromise of mission. The silence of the academy and church in the wake of Hurricanes Katrina, Rita, and Wilma, are deafening. But by God's grace and mercy, we are also being granted a kairos moment of revival.

The challenge for us in the academy and church is to reclaim and proclaim with even greater fervor Black and womanist theologies because it is right and the Gospel will not be silenced. We should do so despite all the obstacles.

At this historical point in time, the compromise of mission puts the academy and the church at risk to become mere extensions of the state. A view from the bridge sees the compromise of mission engendered by a lure of African American scholars and scholarship, church, and church ministries away from its tradition of fighting for human and social justice and prophetic witness at a time when such analysis and witness is needed more than ever. What it means to be Christian and Black in this twenty first century age of technology ought to be self-evident, given all that we see and know about national and global human and social injustice. But to the contrary, self-absorbed, sanctimonious and personal "Churchianity" has replaced selfless, godly, and compassionate Christianity in the name of Jesus, "the giver of prosperity." This shift within our rich faith tradition to prosperity religion is more than mission drift or a move away from the center. It represents a fundamental compromise of mission, warranting a strategic organized plan of action. Our immunological system is being successfully attacked by slick televangelists and political operatives in a manner designed to co-opt or destroy.

Race is still the most complex and defining predictor for life outcomes for most Black Americans, despite an increase in middle-income African American families and a few very wealthy African Americans. Race connectors are even more apparent in a global context, making a mockery of real triage approaches for humanitarian aid. In fact, the genocide of 800,000 and the refugee crisis in Rwanda are not as compelling as genocide of 200,000 and the refugee crisis in Bosnia. $3 billion + of aid to Israel, a country of less than 7 million, is not as strategic as an African aid package of $760 million for fifty-four countries and 800 million people. This kind of differential aid and its attendant outcomes, correlated with race, only sharpens the double-edged sword in the heart of African Americans relative to what it means to be the oppressed in one situation and the potential oppressor in another.

Because race is also no longer fashionable as a construct of analysis, it gets marginalized and diffused by real and imagined patterns of classism, ethnic diversity, and sexism. The delusion, through a few personalities and theological propaganda, of equal access to prosperity and rights to Jabez' increased territory prop up this myth that race does not really matter and class is the issue. Class is definitely an issue, a wedge issue that serves the interest of the status quo. From the perspective of being Christian and Black, race matters even more. For despite gender and sexual orientation, as one becomes more privileged, as they say in Brazil "to buy one's way around the meaning of race," one must also look in the mirror and ask: how can I not become the evil against which I have fought?"

So whatever we do, we must understand that the gospel will not be silenced and we must be clear what it means to be the salt of the earth. In the sacred texts, salt connotes sacrifice, discipleship, and courage to bring unity and peace to the kingdom. Salt is also used to preserve manure. So it follows that in our midst there will be many false prophets who deceive many more. There will be many teachers of the law with flowing robes in the academy and pulpit, seeking accolades and important seats of honor. They will personify the culture of amnesia, the crisis of leadership, and the compromise of mission.

The rocks are crying out from hamlet to hamlet. Our people and institutions are dying. We knew this was so before Hurricane Katrina and we know it is still so. Think about the plight of Morris Brown, an African Methodist Episcopal (AME) college established in 1885. What kind of neglect, academic and church, under the watch of a generation more educated, more prosperous, more worldly, and more privileged than any generation before it and certainly more so than the generation that built it, could allow such deep financial problems to happen?

Black and womanist theologies going forward cannot have a static view of the academy or the church; to the contrary, we need more dynamic and incisive strategies for proclamation and affirmation, requiring a ministry of presence among the people (Luke 4:18). We must fetter out, build capacity, mentor, transplant, and ultimately connect those in the academy and churches who share the values and commitment for making Black and womanist theologies lived theologies in the lives of the least of these, in the U.S. and throughout the world. This will not be a popular run. The cost is too great for those unwilling to stay fit. This will not be a network televised run. The risk is too great for those who benefit by our inability to connect. But it can be a successful run, because our sacred work is God's vision in the first place. And where God has given vision, God has also given provision. The move forward for Black and womanist theologies requires intentional and strategic propagation of ourselves to forthrightly stand in the breach amongst the crying rocks?

## ETHIC OF ENTITLEMENT

To effectively chart our course forward, we have to thoroughly assess the battlefield. James H. Cone's words ring loudly: "Do not underestimate evil's power to confuse and corrupt the mind and the spirit. We are struggling not just against flesh and blood, not just against an individual instance of oppression, but against structural evil."[13] A brief penetration of the external environment tells us that we confront an ethic of entitlement –twenty first century style, being masked as a culture of enlightenment.

The eighteenth-century European American Enlightenment, from the obverse side of African humanity, is historically and contemporaneously more appropriately characterized as European American Entitlement. From slave plantation brush arbors to the Negro Convention Movement to the Civil Rights Movement, from house Negro to White House Negro, the Black church in the U.S. has wrestled theologically with a dynamic construct, *a race-class absorption matrix*, embedded in a European American ethic of entitlement. The operative question of this race-class absorption matrix framed the parameters around the extent to which African Americans both can and want to be acculturated and assimilated in the dominant American democracy as full participatory citizens with rights and privileges appertaining to.

The historical context in which W. E. B. DuBois could proclaim the "question of the 20th century would be the question of the color line" was one in which there was a clear color hierarchy, a creed of equal rights and a principle of common good, advantaged by a sense (though always

13. James H. Cone, "Loving God with Our Heart, Soul, and Mind," in *Blow the Trumpet*, 62.

illusional) of numeric superiority. The past few decades, however, have revealed a major shift in the landscape upon which the ethic of entitlement and its attendant institutional expressions and economic order find expression. We have moved from a color hierarchy to a genomic technocracy, a creed of equal rights to a system of meritocracy, and a principle of common good to an imperative of cultural good. It is against this shift in the landscape of the European American ethic that today African Christians, liberation, Black theology, and womanist theology must cast their lot, despite how unpopular it might be.

We are reminded that it is in hallow institutions like the University of Chicago and various think tanks where some of the strongest intellectual and influential pillars of this ethic of entitlement have been carved and propagated. Edward Shils, Professor Emeritus at the University of Chicago, provides a framework for understanding the flow of scholarship, communication, and ideas informing. His analysis on opposing loci of authority, "center" and "periphery," suggests the potential role of "isolated cliques of scholars" to either sustain or pull toward the periphery the core values and beliefs which govern society.[14] We are one such clique, competing with a dynamic environment grounded in an ethic of entitlement. His work also informs a church on its way to being peripheral to the needs of a people.

In terms of global geopolitics, predicting the ultimate marriage of communism and capitalism, Escott Reid, former director of the World Bank (while at the University of Chicago's Adlai Stevenson Institute), crafted a policy based on the gulf "between the rich northern whites and colored southern poor."[15] In terms of the potential to effect American hegemony as a system of democracy, Harvard professor B. F. Skinner's redaction of behavioralism to sociobiology left his final words about the obsolescence of democracy and the overriding imperative to move to a genetic meritocracy: "If man has emerged as a master species, . . . why not look forward to a master subspecies or race? . . . Why not a master culture? . . . A culture survives if those who carry it survive, and this depends in part upon certain genetic susceptibilities to reinforcement."[16]

14. Edward Shils, *Center and Periphery: Essays in Macrosociology* (Chicago: University of Chicago Press, 1975).

15. Escott Reid, *Strengthening the World Bank* (Chicago: Adlai Stevenson Institute, 1973) 30.

16. B. F. Skinner, *Beyond Freedom and Dignity* (New York: Vintage, 1972) 133–34.

In terms of laws of survival at any cost, Ben Wattenberg's argument in the "Birth Dearth—What Happens When People in Free Countries Don't Have Enough Babies?" is a demographic imperative for sustaining western values at any cost by asking: "Will our values continue to dominate in a world where our populations shrinks: Shrinks to 9 percent? 5 percent? Shrinks even lower . . . Our economic and military power go down . . . This view should not be seen as simply Western chauvinism."[17] And no doubt, Milton Friedman's fundamental argument is at the core of the Walmartization of the global economy. According to Friedman, Professor Emeritus at the University of Chicago, "few trends could so thoroughly undermine the very foundations of our free society as the acceptance by corporate officials of a social responsibility other than to make as much money for their stockholders as possible."[18]

We have been invited into citadels of global academic hegemony (i.e., like the University of Chicago and other elite institutions) from whose bowels have come pillars of the ethic of entitlement. But, by our very presence and activity, we bring authentic theological meaning to Black and womanist theologies. And there are some white people who will not be silenced either. The same Bill Moyers that propelled the media icon, "Black man as endangered species," has twenty years later experienced the vitriolics of the media. With disdain for the increased compromise of the media he cautioned: "We are moving toward an oligarchic society where a relatively small handful of the rich decide, with their money, who will run, who will win, and how they will govern. The defenders of the present system will fight hard to hold on to their privilege, and they write the rules. Nothing less than our democracy is at stake."[19]

Other progressive white scholars and activists include Jennifer Ladd, strong believer in God, but committed to no particular religious institution, and co-founder of Class Action, Inc. She humbly introduces herself as a person who inherited wealth and, at the same time, works to educate the public about the negative impacts of class, race, and money. Similarly Susan Thistlewaite and James W. Perkinson are theologians who dare to call for a dismantling of white theology. Perkinson, in par-

---

17. Ben J. Wattenberg, *The Birth of Dearth* (New York: Pharos, 1987) 7, 48, 98.

18. Milton Friedman, *Capitalism and Freedom* (Chicago: University of Chicago Press, 1962) 133.

19. Si Kahjn and Elizabeth Mennich, *The Fox in thte Henhouse: How Privatization Threatens Democracy* (San Francisco: Berrett-Koehler, 2005), from the frontispiece.

ticular, writes: "White theology . . . must learn to confess and analyze the historical reality of whiteness as a social structure of oppression for people of color . . . its destiny is finally that of disappearing in the on-going struggle against the organization of whiteness as oppression."[20]

In terms of dismantling the Western, Northern Cradle epistemo-logical approaches, we are talking about Black and womanist theologies causing a seismic shift in the organization of the world ethic. That does not happen by happenstance and lone ranger scholarship. It happens by well-organized networks of scholarship, resource development, and mission driven local church growth. If you have ever been exposed to the inside of a think tank, as I have, you will witness what can be ac-complished by a small group of persons who know who they are, with whom they share an agenda, where they are headed, and what the mis-sion is, short and long-term. Our work demands not only the retrofitting and strengthening of the bridge, in the context of this landscape shift, but also the revitalizing and innovating of new alliances among Black, womanist, African, liberation, feminist, and other prophetic theologies.

Together, we must engage in dismantling the axis of privilege and evil—an ethic of entitlement that is driven by an ethic of private profit over public good. Theologian, preacher, and parishioner can ill afford to do business as usual. Passive critique; transcendental, trite sermons; and sanctuary-only worship must be transformed to model the ministry of Jesus, who read the scroll in the temple but then went out to the hurting and oppressed to change their condition. Jesus' interpretative prism for action must penetrate the vocation of the theologian, the hermeneutic of the preacher, and the understanding of the worshiper, regardless of race, class or gender.

The vocation of the theologian demands courageous, plural, and interdisciplinary study that informs the word of God in an era of Black and white bibliolatry. It must connect ethics to the other sciences. The hermeneutic of the preacher requires connecting the Word to people where they are in these times. The understanding of the parishioner must be made manifest by faithful service to the least of these. We have

---

20. James W. Perkinson, "A White Theology of Solidarity in the Making, Beyond Essence, Between Categories, Before Responsibilities," unpublished paper. See also his *White Theology: Outing Supremacy in Modernity* (New York: Palgrave Macmillan, 2004).

not done it in the face of the HIV/AIDS pandemic, but perhaps we can in the face of Hurricane Katrina.

## THE PROPHETIC CALL OF KATRINA

In a chronological sense we may have turned the corner into a new century, but the record and reality reveal a people of God struggling against going backwards into captivity. African Americans, and by extension the African American church, confront a reality that parallels a people characterized by external oppression in a Pharonic or Babylonian culture committed to their demise. It likewise affirms a people of God on the water's edge confronting an internal culture of amnesia, a crisis in ` leadership, and a compromise of mission.

The torrid waters and winds from Africa in the wake of hurricanes Katrina and Rita have slapped the Black church with revelatory and prophetic meaning that cuts to the questions, "How Long, Oh Lord? And if not now, then when?" James H. Cone's brilliant and prophetic words were a preface to Hurricane Katrina:

> Connecting racism with the degradation of the earth is a much-needed work in . . . black liberation theology and the black churches.
> . . . For the first time in history, humankind has the knowledge and power to destroy all life—either with a nuclear bang or a gradual poisoning of the land, air, and sea . . .
> [T]he poor bear an unequal burden for technological development while the rich reap most of the benefits. This makes racism and poverty ecological issues.[21]

The ongoing revelations about Hurricane Katrina bring back vivid reflections of what must have been the crisis and relief effort after the Emancipation Proclamation and the actualizing of the Freedmen's Bureau. Two months after Katrina, there were rural communities which still had not seen a Federal Emergency Management Agency (FEMA) or Red Cross relief resource. And evacuees had been sent to places of complete isolation and alienation. There was also the privatization of human suffering with corporate controlled trailer camps in isolated areas in dirt fields, and a prison population which included people charged with misdemeanors. This population went without food for five days and

21. James H. Cone, *Risks of Faith: The Emergence of a Black Theology of Liberation, 1968–1998* (Boston: Beacon, 1999) 139, 142, 141.

many more were dispersed throughout the nation representing, a double bounty in the prison for profit market. There were several thousand children disconnected or missing from parents and body bags piled high deep in New Orleans morgues with family members still trying to claim their loved ones. And it is unlikely their loved one will ever be properly identified. There were also possible events of euthanasia; and cities, churches, and organizations were caught in the federal government shell game of "you pay up front and we may reimburse you."

How Long, Oh Lord? And if not Now, when?

FEMA and Red Cross subcontractors of the Southern Baptist Convention and Pat Robertson's Operation Blessing precluded Black church relief and ministry, from hot meals to professional counseling services. This is the same Pat Robertson who called for the assassination of the President of Venezuela. President Bush first said the government was doing a good job, but it has now been proven that his flight over the levees were fixed, and conversations with the troops were staged media events. And for the "good job" former director Brown did at FEMA, he was rewarded with an appointment to oversee an $85 million New Orleans reconstruction contract. Let us not overlook the farce of bi-partisan Congressional hearings, as well as suspension of affirmative action and wage protections in the reconstruction effort (though that was eventually reversed due to the need for damage control in the White House).

But there is more at the water's edge proving that everybody your color is not of your kind. Leading the charge for the ethic of entitlement are people of color: a former Secretary of State (Colin Powell) who has been beat down into silence; a Black woman Secretary of State, (Condoleezza Rice) saying the revelations surrounding Katrina have nothing to do with race; a Black male Secretary of Housing and Urban Development (Alphonso Jackson) saying ultimately the competition for housing reconstruction in terms of low income vs. high income housing will be resolved by "the free enterprise market"; and a Black preacher (T. D. Jakes) representing a Judas council, standing and holding fort with the powers that be. In the wake of their proclamations, a former Secretary of Education, William Bennett, spews a Herod-like message for the world to see, suggesting the abortion of Black children as one solution for problems in America.

The African proverb reminds us that silence makes a mighty noise. Where is our righteous indignation? "For people who were blind but now they see," we have an obligation to make sure that righteous people understand these are not aberrations, but evidences of a callous heartless system built upon a culture and ethic of entitlement and global profiteering and piracy.

And as we ask the questions "How Long, Oh Lord? And if not now, when?" some have already gone back in the water, resurrecting the fundamental question of our African identity. While thousands marched on Washington for the Million More March, a few well-connected persons are arguing a position for the full de-Africanization of Black America, calling for the de-utilization of the word "African American" and the re-identification of African Americans as Black Americans.

And so, answers to the questions "How Long, Oh Lord? And if not now, when?" will ultimately be driven by what strategies, beyond a march, for transformation of the academy, church, and community, to create, globalize, and sustain a position for Black, womanist, liberation, and African theologies, grounded in the principles of Jesus Justice.

Jerome C. Ross reminds us that all the sacred biblical texts were written under one of six forms of oppression.[22] The biblical story is a story of tensions between the oppressed and the oppressor, the liberated and the captive. And yet we often identify with, teach, and preach the God of the Oppressor. Dwight N. Hopkins implores us to acknowledge that the sacred texts are also the stories of our lives in both the hell of captivity and the full love of our humanity.[23] It is in the intersection of these sacred texts in the lives of people that the hermeneutical lens from Black and womanist theologies in dialogue will bind the academy and church. We must be not only a voice to the people but also a partner on the journey towards Jesus justice, where God of the oppressed and the disinherited meets the people at their point of need and hope in a future.

Let me conclude with a final observation. The answer to the question, "How Long, Oh Lord?" may be "Never." But we will stay on the

22. Jerome Clayton Ross, "The Cultural Affinity between the Ancient Yahwists and the African Americans: A Hermeneutic for Homiletics," in *Born to Preach: Essays in Honor of the Ministry of Henry & Ella Mitchell*, ed. Samuel K. Roberts (Valley Forge, PA: Judson, 2000) 22–39.

23. Dwight N. Hopkins, *Being Human: Race, Culture, and Religion* (Minneapolis: Fortress, 2005).

battlefield, for the struggle continues and the bridge upon which we stand oversees the awesome power of tributaries three layers deep: the academy, church, and community with the God of the Oppressed, a Liberating Christ, and a Liberated People. We should be empowered to keep on keeping on, for if not us then who?

With authority we must continue to move forward towards what I call a Pan African theopraxis. This direction will surely connect our discourse with African theologies that enrich our understanding and knowledge of God, Christianity, and our people. For centuries, the Lemba people of Southern Africa have claimed their descent from the Lost Tribe of Judah to the ridicule of Western religious scholars. The recent genetic testing by labs in the U.S., Britain, and Israel proved they have a higher genetic marker for the Levite priestly class than those priests in Israel today.

The answer to the question "How Long, Oh Lord?" may be "Never." But with righteous indignation we must continue to offer the complaint of Habakkuk with the courage of Esther.

> How long, O LORD, must I call for help,
>     but you do not listen?
> Or cry out to you, "Violence!"
>     but you do not save?
> Why do you make me look at injustice?
>     Why do you tolerate wrong?
> Destruction and violence are before me;
>     there is strife, and conflict abounds,
> therefore the law is paralyzed
>     and justice never prevails.
> The wicked hem in the righteous,
>     so that justice is perverted. (Habakkuk 1:2–4 NIV)

> And the LORD answered,
> Write the vision, and make it plain. (Habakkuk 2:2, KJV)

> And the woman declared:
> . . . and if I perish, I perish. (Esther 4:16)

The bridge is where we meet. On the bridge is where the intersection of Black and womanist theologies will produce a Talmud born out of the remembrance of the Maafa[24] and a declaration that we are an African

---

24. St. Paul Community Baptist Church (Brooklyn, New York, Johnny Rae Young-blood, senior pastor) produces an annual, Hollywood-like musical and theatrical

people and we will be free. The bridge is where we meet and reclaim our children through the telling of our story, from the glorious age of Africa to Katrina, so they will pick up the refrain and declare never again. The bridge is where we must confront the pain and silence around sexuality and Black bodies, sexual abuse, exploitation, and homophobia. On the bridge we have met and conversed on liberation, and survival and quality of life; we have spoken of patriarchy in the family and Black male as endangered species; we have reflected upon Jesus the Man and Christ as a Woman. We have gotten naked in our human sexuality, and in our nakedness we find mission and purpose.

Those in the academy must see the academy as the mission field and transform the academy, but they also must see the mission field as the academy and be with the people. Those in the church must lead and be led by a sense of Jesus Justice for the least of these, not only because it is the most practical thing to do (and it is), but most importantly it is the right thing to do and an imperative of a Christian walk. This ought to be a moment of revelation and revival where we ask ourselves: Guess who's coming to dinner? The answer: The poor and dispossessed of Katrina, and from around the world (i.e., like the lessons of the Parable of the Great Feast in Luke 14:15–24).

So we are called to continue to be the salt of the earth, not for the manure pile like some, but for the Kingdom of God. How Long, Oh Lord? Maybe Never. The God we serve does not expect us to finish the work. *But,* He/She does expect us to stay the course.

---

production called the "Maafa." The production also travels to major cities nationally. Some titles on the Maafa are: Erriel D. Roberson, *The Maafa and Beyond* (Columbia, MD: Kujichagulia, 1995); S. E. Anderson, *Black Holocaust for Beginners* (New York: Writers & Readers Publishing, 1995); Marimba Ani, *Let the Circle Be Unbroken: The Implications of African Spirituality in the Diaspora* (Lawrenceville, NJ: Red Sea, 1994); Raymond A. Wimbush, ed., *Should America Pay: Slavery and the Raging Debate on Reparations* (New York: Amistad, 2003); James Forman, "The Black Manifesto," in *Black Theology: A Documentary History, 1966–1979,* ed. Gayraud S. Wilmore and James H. Cone (Maryknoll, NY: Orbis, 1979) 80–89; Arnold Schuchter, *Reparations: The Black Manifesto and Its Challenge to White America* (Philadelphia: Lippincott, 1970); and Richard America, *Paying the Social Debt: What White America Owes Black America* (Reston, VA: Reston Institute Press, 2001).

# 20

## Strange Fruit

### *The Cross and the Lynching Tree*

JAMES H. CONE

---

They put him to death by hanging him on a tree. (Acts 10:39)

The South is crucifying Christ again
By all the laws of ancient rote and rule;
The ribald cries of 'Save Yourself' and 'Fool'
Din in his ears, the thorns grope for his brain,
And where they bite, swift springing rivers stain
His gaudy, purple robe of ridicule
With sullen red; and acid wine to cool
His thirst is thrust at him, with lurking pain.
Christ's awful wrong is that he's dark of hue,
The sin for which no blamelessness atones;
But lest the sameness of the cross should tire
They kill him now with famished tongues of fire,
And while he burns, good men, and women, too
Shout, battling for his black and brittle bones.[1]

Southern trees bear a strange fruit,
Blood on the leaves and blood at the root,
Black body swinging in the southern breeze,
Strange fruit hanging from the poplar trees.[2]

1. Cited in Anne P. Rice, *Witnessing Lynching: American Writers Respond* (New Brunswick, NJ: Rutgers University Press, 2003) 221–22.

2. "Strange Fruit" was written by Abel Meeropol and became Billie Holiday's

PETER'S POWERFUL DESCRIPTION OF Jesus's death as a "hanging on a tree"; Countee Cullen's 1922 gripping poem, "Christ Recrucified"; and Billie Holiday's haunting song, "Strange Fruit," are poignant reminders that the cross and the lynching tree, separated by nearly 2000 years, are not usually thought of as being symbolically connected, except by Black poets, novelists, and other reality-seeing artists. Lynching was such an unspeakable crime that Blacks and whites seldom talk about it, especially not in mixed racial settings. The lynching of Black Americans is an atrocity that white Americas would rather forget, but they cannot. The memory of disfigured Black bodies "swinging in the southern breeze" is so painful to African Americans that they also try to keep these horrors buried deep down in their consciousness: but like a dormant volcano, they erupt uncontrollably, causing profound ontological agony and pain. But like the atrocities of the Middle Passage, chattel slavery, and Jim Crow segregation, Blacks and whites and other Americans who want to understand the true meaning of the American experience need to remember lynching. To forget this unspeakable crime leaves people with a fraudulent perspective of this society and of one's understanding of the meaning of the Christian gospel for this nation.[3]

In contrast to the lynching tree, the cross is one of the most visible symbols of America's Christian origin. America is a "nation of believers," a "beacon on the hill," called to be "a righteous empire," "the people of God" like Israel in the Hebrew Bible. Many Christians believe that Jesus died on the cross to redeem humankind from sin. He took our place and suffered on the cross for us so that we will not burn forever in hell. Jesus was our substitute, the Son of God, who gave "his life a ransom for many" (Mark 10:45). We are "now justified by [God's] grace as a gift, through the redemption that is in Christ Jesus, whom God put forward as a sacrifice of atonement by his blood, effective through faith" (Romans 3:23–24). Without Jesus's death on the cross we would not be accept-

---

signature song. For a history of "Strange Fruit," see David Margolick, *Strange Fruit: Billie Holiday, Café Society, and an Early Cry for Civil Rights* (Philadelphia: Running Press, 2000).

3. On lynching, see Philip Dray, *At the Hands of Persons Unknown: The Lynching of Black America* (New York: Modern Library, 2003); W. Fitzhugh Brundage, *Lynching in the New South: Georgia and Virginia, 1880–1930* (Urbana: University of Illinois Press, 1993); W. Fitzhugh Brundage, ed., *Under the Sentence of Death: Lynching in the South* (Chapel Hill: University of North Carolina Press, 1997).

able before God. The cross, therefore, is the great symbol of salvation for Christians.

Unfortunately, during the course of 2000 years of Christian history, this orthodox understanding of the cross has become a fixed doctrine that many believe *must* be accepted as the definition of what it means to be a Christian. It has become a form of "cheap grace," as Dietrich Bonhoeffer put it, an easy way to salvation, completely without cost. The cross has been transformed into a harmless, non-offensive religious object that Christians wear around their necks as a sacred fashion piece and place on church steeples and altars to decorate their sanctuaries with a symbol of holiness. The classic Christian view of the cross claims to know too much about *how* salvation is accomplished and thus removes the element of mystery in our understanding of salvation. The cross, therefore, needs to be rescued, that is, liberated from the superficial pieties of Christians because their transformed cross blinds them from seeing the true meaning of the one who was crucified on Calvary's hill. Unless the cross and the lynching tree are seen together, there can be no genuine understanding of Christian identity in America and no healing of the racial divide in churches and seminaries as well as in the society as a whole.

I know the cross and the lynching tree are not comfortable subjects to talk about together. Who wants to think about lynched Black bodies when doing a theological reflection on Dietrich Bonhoeffer's question, "Who is Jesus Christ for us today?" This is exactly what I contend the gospel requires Christians to do, especially preachers and theologians. I claim that no American Christian—white, Black, or any other color—can appreciate the full theological meaning of the American Christ without identifying his image with a "recrucified" Black body hanging from a lynching tree.

I begin this reflection in the only place I feel confident to speak as a theologian: the Black religious experience. I was born into this reality and have wrestled with its paradoxes and incongruities since childhood. If I have anything to say to the Christian community in America and around the world, it will happen as I stand as a theologian on the reality that sustains and empowers Black people to resist the forces that seem designed to destroy every ounce of dignity in their souls and bodies.

The Black church community was my place of resistance, the place where I took my stand to declare theological war on white supremacy.

That was why I entered the ministry, went to seminary, and, to my surprise and that of many others, earned a PhD degree in systematic theology. I wanted to get as much of the intellectual resources as I could because white theologians were well armed with a weighty theological tradition and would fight back fiercely when challenged. Though my seminary education prepared me to do theology, introducing me to the great thinkers in the Western theological tradition, I knew that I would never be able to engage the intellectual giants like Barth, Tillich, Niebuhr, and Bonhoeffer on the territory of their white Euro-American theology. I had to engage the Christian gospel and white theology's interpretation of it on my territory: the Black religious experience and the struggle for justice that emerged out of it.

While whites may have produced the most influential theologians in the Christian tradition, the Black church community has produced some of the greatest preachers of the gospel of Jesus the modern world has ever known. From the nineteenth century untutored evangelists like Black Harry, Jarena Lee, and John Jasper to twentieth-century learned orators like Howard Thurman, Martin Luther King Jr., Prathia Hall Wynn, and Gardiner C. Taylor, Black preachers have been word-warriors for the Lord. They make the gospel plain and real to ordinary people, so that the Bible becomes a liberating message coming directly from God. I marvel at the exegetical and homiletical skills of the Black preacher—his/her ability to speak the truth to power with the wisdom of a sage and the passion and courage of a prophet. The Black preacher is a "genius of the spontaneous word" and a master of biblical truths and stories about God's work of salvation. Black preachers took a white gospel designed to enslave them and transformed it into a Black liberating gospel of Jesus.

I first heard Black preachers in rural Arkansas at Methodist, Baptist, and Sanctified churches. Each denominational minister had his/her own distinctive preaching style. While the way they preached was different, the subject of their message often focused on the suffering Jesus and the salvation accomplished in his death on the cross. I noticed how the passion and energy of the preacher increased whenever he talked about the cross, and the congregation responded with outbursts of "Amens" and "Hallelujahs" that equaled the intensity of the sermon oration. People shouted, clapped their hands, and stomped their feet, as if a powerful, living reality of God's Spirit had transformed them from nobodies in white society to somebodies in the Black church. Nothing, absolutely nothing, dominates Black church worship like talk about Calvary and the one who died on the cross for the sins of the world. Most Black sermons take their climax on Calvary and the people often wait patiently for the preacher to take them there. When preachers think they may be losing their audience, they retell the story of Jesus's crucifixion, emphasizing how he died so we might live eternally. Paradoxically, the cross can resurrect dead sermons and enable ill-prepared preachers to enliven a bored congregation.

One word of caution is in order here, lest we get too carried away. Because Black preaching in particular and Black worship generally creates a great deal of emotionalism, there is always the danger that unscrupulous, self-seeking preachers will corrupt the gospel of the cross for personal financial gain. The Black church, therefore, needs to find ways to bring charismatic preachers under the control of critical theological reason and the prophetic judgment of God. The Black church needs seminary-trained, prophetic theologians, who are as committed to their intellectual vocation as pastors are to their call to preach. The preacher proclaims the gospel and the theologian explains it so the preacher will not get too carried away with his/her eschatological rhetoric. The preacher inspires people to make a commitment to the gospel and the theologian analyzes the preached word and subjects it to the justice and mercy of the God revealed in Jesus Christ. To be a profound preacher, therefore, one must be a critical theological thinker. As preacher, one proclaims God's love for the poor, and as theologian one reflects on the meaning of divine love for the poor when their poverty seems to deny that claim.

How can one believe that God loves Black people in a world defined by four hundred years of white supremacy? These contradictions and incongruities challenge theologians and preachers to a deeper understanding of the knowledge of God. Some preachers, as Paul said, have "the zeal of God but not according to knowledge." Theology probes the mysteries of God, what the German scholar Rudolph Otto called the "*Mysterium Tremendum*" and what the Black preacher called, quoting the Bible, "the truth that passes all understanding." The theologian teaches preachers about the ontological and existential significance of divine mysteries of the cross so that they can proclaim the true gospel and not a counterfeit version of it.

For a minister to become a prophetic preacher like Martin Luther King Jr., he/she has to become a committed theologian, a pastor who reads and thinks as well as prays. But a minister must be more than a preacher-theologian. It is not enough to just teach and preach the gospel. It is necessary also to *live* the gospel that one preaches and teaches. Martin Luther King Jr. was an *activist* preacher-theologian. He deeply believed that the truth of the gospel could only be taught and preached in a world that is being actively transformed.

What is this gospel that must be taught, preached, and lived in the world? There are so many ministers who claim to speak for God. Many white evangelical ministers frequently say they have a direct word from God, as if God speaks to them as one talks to a human being. President George W. Bush spoke about his "heavenly Father" as if God commanded his declaration of the war in Afghanistan and Iraq. I have even heard Black preachers speak with the same certainty, especially when they express their opposition to women in the ministry, abortion, same-sex marriage, and other controversial issues.

The true word of God, however, is not something we possess, as if God were an object under our control. We don't possess the gospel; it possesses us and transforms our lives. The gospel is not derived from this world because it is not a human word, not a pious feeling or a sophisticated idea that comes from intellectuals in seminaries, no matter how smart they may be. Faith, and not the intellect, is the primary way to gain knowledge of the gospel.

The gospel is God's message of liberation in an unredeemed and tortured world. On the one hand, the gospel is a transcendent reality that lifts our spirits to a world far removed from the hurts and pains of this one. On the other, it is an immanent reality, that is, a powerful liberating presence among the poor right *now*, "building them up where we are torn down and propping them up on every leaning side." The gospel is in the world but not of the world. That is what makes God's word *paradoxical* or as the old untutored Black preacher used to say "inscrutable." It is here and not here, revealed and hidden at the same time.

The Word of God is also *offensive*. It is not a word that we want to hear, even though we say we do. God's Word is not a popular word, not a successful word, and not an entertaining word. The gospel is the suffering word of the cross, a lynched word hanging from a tree. The gospel is a tortured word, a Black word in the world of white supremacy.

The gospel and the cross cannot be separated. The cross stands at the center of the gospel. Take the cross away and the gospel is no longer the gospel of the God of Jesus. I know that such a theological claim would be fiercely rejected by many womanist and feminist theologians.[4] When one considers how corrupt and misguided Christian preachers and theologians have used the cross of Jesus to oppress marginal people, especially women and children, urging them to accept passively their suffering in the home, church, and the society, who can blame womanists and feminists for saying, "no more crosses for me." But we must remember that every good theological insight or ethical deed is always corrupted by sin, that is, our self-interest and thus theologians and preachers should always speak with humility and self-criticism and never with dogmatism. As theologians our responsibility is to show how self-glorification corrupts the Christian ministry and theological reflection. Before God we are all guilty. As Paul confessed, "I do not understand my own actions. For I do not do what I want, but I do the very thing I hate . . . I can will what is right but I cannot do it. For if I do not do the good I want, but the evil I do not want is what I do. Now if I do what I do not want, it is no longer I that do it, but sin that dwells in me" (Romans 7:15, 18–20). That is a powerful self-critique that Paul derived from the cross. All Christians need to internalize this cross-critique daily. We, therefore, should not turn away from the cross because people use it for evil. The cross is the most empowering symbol of God's loving solidarity with the "least of these," the unwanted in society who suffer daily from great injustices. We must face this cross as the terrible tragedy it was and discover in it, through faith and repentance, the liberating joy of eternal salvation.

The cross is not good news to the powerful or for anyone whose understanding of the world is defined by established religion. That was why Jesus's disciples slept through his agony in the Garden and ran away from his crucifixion. One disciple betrayed him and another denied him because the crucified Messiah was not the one they expected. "We had hope that he was the one to redeem Israel" (Luke 24:21). We today don't want any part of Jesus's cross either, not the old rugged

---

4. See especially Delores S. Williams, *Sisters in the Wilderness: The Challenge of Womanist God-Talk* (Maryknoll, NY: Orbis, 1993); Joanne C. Brown and Carole R. Bohn, eds, *Christianity, Patriarchy and Abuse: A Feminist Critique* (New York: Pilgrim, 1989).

cross on Calvary's hill. The cross is a "stumbling block" to the religious and the pious, and "foolishness" to the wise, the secular scholars in the universities. But God's foolishness is wiser than human wisdom, and God's weakness is stronger than human strength" (1 Corinthians 1:25). For "God chose what is foolish in the world to shame the wise; God chose what is weak in the world to shame the strong; God chose what is low and despised in the world, things that are not, to reduce to nothing the things that are, so that no one might boast in the presence of the Lord" (1 Corinthians 1:27).

Today as yesterday, the cross reveals God's loving solidarity with the "unspeakable suffering of those who are tortured," and "put to death by human cruelty . . . In the person and fate of the one man Jesus of Nazareth this saving solidarity of God with [the oppressed] is given its historical and physical form." "The Word became flesh and lived among us" (John 1:14). "In Jesus' cross God took up the existence of a slave and died the slave's death on the tree of martyrdom" (Philippians 2:8).[5]

Great preachers preach the cross as the heart of the Christian message. The Apostle Paul preached the cross and transformed a little Jewish sect into a faith for the world. Martin Luther preached the cross and started the Protestant Reformation. Karl Barth preached the cross and created a Copernican revolution in European theology. Martin Luther King Jr. preached the cross and transformed the social and political life in America.

One has to have a powerful religious imagination to see redemption in the cross, to discover life in death and hope in tragedy. "Christianity," Reinhold Niebuhr wrote, "is a faith which takes us through tragedy to beyond tragedy, by way of the cross to victory in the cross."[6] What kind of salvation is that? To understand what the cross means in America, we need to take a good long look at the lynching tree in this nation's history—"the bulging eyes and twisted mouth," that "strange fruit" that Billy Holiday sang about, "blood on the leaves and blood at the root." The lynched Black victim experienced the same fate as the crucified Christ.

The cross and the lynching tree interpret each other. Both were public spectacles, which were usually reserved for hardened criminals, rebellious slaves, and rebels against the Roman state and falsely accused

5. Martin Hengel, *Crucifixion*, trans. John Bowden (Philadelphia: Fortress, 1977) 88.

6. Reinhold Niebuhr, *Christianity and Power Politics* (New York: Scribners, 1940) 213.

Blacks who were often called "monsters in human form" for their audacity to challenge white supremacy in America. Any genuine theology and any genuine preaching must be measured against the test of the scandal of the cross and the lynching tree. "Jesus did not die a gentle death like Socrates, with his cup of hemlock . . . Rather, he died like a [lynched Black victim] or a common [Black] criminal in torment, on the tree of shame."[7] The crowd's shout "Crucify him!" (Mark 15:14) anticipated the white mob's shout "Lynch him!" Jesus's agonizing final cry from the cross, "My God, my God, why have you forsaken me?" (Mark15:34) was similar to the Georgia-lynched victim Sam Hose's awful scream, as he drew his last breath, "*Oh, my God! Oh, Jesus.*"[8] In each case, it was a cruel, agonizing, and contemptible death.

The cross and the lynching tree need each other: the lynching tree can liberate the cross from the false pieties of well-meaning Christians. The crucifixion was a first-century lynching. The cross can redeem the lynching tree and thereby bestow upon lynched Black bodies an eschatological meaning for their ultimate existence. The cross can also redeem white lynchers and their descendants too, but not without profound cost, not without the revelation of the wrath and justice of God, which executes divine judgment, with the demand for repentance and reparation, as a presupposition of divine mercy. Most whites want mercy and forgiveness but not justice and reparations; they want reconciliation without liberation, the resurrection without the cross.

As preachers and theologians, we must demonstrate the truth of our proclamation and theological reflection in the face of the cross and the lynched Black victims in America's past and present. When we encounter the crucified Christ today, he is the humiliated Black Christ, a lynched Black body. Christ is Black not because Black theology said it. Christ is *made* Black through God's loving solidarity with lynched Black bodies and divine judgment against the demonic forces of white supremacy. Like a Black naked body swinging on a lynching tree, the cross of Christ was "an utterly offensive affair," "obscene in the original sense of the word," "subjecting the victim to the utmost indignity."[9]

7. Hengel, *Crucifixion*, 90.

8. Cited in Leon F. Litwack, *Trouble in Mind: Black Southerners in the Age of Jim Crow* (New York: Knopf, 1998) 281.

9. Ibid., 40.

A crucified Jesus and lynched Black bodies were not pretty objects to look at. That was why Christians transformed the cross into a sacred fashion symbol and seldom show images of lynching. But the trauma of lynching lives on in the blood and bones of Black people. We cannot forget the terror no matter how hard we try. We can go to churches and celebrate our religious heritage but the tragic memory of the Black holocaust in America's history is still waiting to find theological meaning. When Black people sing, "Were you there when they crucified my Lord," they often think of Black lives lost to the lynching tree. "Oh! Sometimes it causes me to tremble, tremble, tremble." "Were you there when they nailed him to the tree?" "Were you there when they pierced him in the side?" "Were you there when the blood came twinkling down?" "Were you there when he bowed his head and died?" The "Were you there?" was a rhetorical question. Black people were there! Through the experience of being lynched by white mobs, Blacks transcended their time and place and found themselves existentially and symbolically at the foot of Jesus's cross, experiencing his fate. If Blacks could identify with Jesus suffering on his cross, Jesus also could *not only* identify with hanging and burning Black bodies on the lynching tree but also redeem Black suffering and make beautiful what white supremacy made ugly. "Black is beautiful, baby!"—a popular phrase in the Black community in the 1960s—has for more theological truth than most people know.

In a penetrating essay, Reinhold Niebuhr wrote about "the terrible beauty of the cross." "Only a tragic and a suffering love can be an adequate symbol of what we believe to be at the heart of reality itself." The cross prevents God's love from sinking into sentimentality and romanticism. "Life is too brutal and the cosmic facts are too indifferent to our moral ventures to make faith in any but a suffering God tenable."[10]

The gospel of Jesus is not a beautiful, Hollywood story. It is an ugly story, the story of God snatching victory out of defeat, finding life in death, transforming burning Black bodies into transcendent windows for seeing the love and beauty of God.

Mark D. Jordan writes: "What makes the ugliness of Jesus' crucified body important is not that it was the greatest physical ugliness, but that we are asked to see through it to the unspeakable beauty of God. The crucifixion inverts our ordinary bodily aesthetic by claiming that

10. Reinhold Niebuhr, "The Terrible Beauty of the Cross," *The Christian Century*, March 21, 1929, 386–88.

the radiant source of all beauty was disclosed to us in a scourged, crucified dead body . . . Paradoxical assertions about Jesus' beauty on the cross invite us to learn that bodies can be beautiful in ways we hadn't expected—or were perhaps afraid to think."[11] God's loving solidarity can transform ugliness into beauty. Take a look at the atrocity photos of lynched Black bodies in the book *Without Sanctuary*,[12] and through the powerful imagination of faith, discover the tragic beauty of them, the "terrible beauty" of the lynching tree.

The church's most vexing problem today is how to define itself by the gospel of Jesus's cross revealed through lynched Black bodies in American history. Where is the gospel of Jesus's cross revealed today? Where are Black bodies being lynched today? The lynching of Black America is taking place in the criminal justice system where nearly one-third of Black men between the ages of 18 and 28 are in prisons, in jails, on parole, or waiting for their day in court. One-half of the two million people in prisons are Black. That is one million Black people behind bars—more than in colleges. Through private prisons, whites have turned the brutality of their racist legal system into a profit-making venture for dying white towns and cities throughout America. One can lynch a person without a rope or tree.

The civil rights movement did not end lynching. Whenever society treats a people as if they have no rights or dignity or worth, as the government did to Blacks during the Katrina storm, they are being lynched covertly. Whenever people are denied jobs, health care, housing, and the basic necessities of life, they are being lynched. There are a lot of ways to lynch a people. Whenever a people cry out to be recognized as human beings and the society ignores them, they are being lynched.

When I heard and read about the physical and mental abuse at the Abu Ghraib prison in Iraq, I thought about lynching. The evil Roman empire that killed Jesus at Calvary was similar to the American empire that lynched Blacks in the U.S. and also created the atrocities in Iraq. Many white Americans seemed surprised and even shocked that such abuse could come from the U.S. military. But most Blacks were neither

11. Mark D. Jordan, *Telling Truths in Church: Scandal, Flesh, and Christian Speech* (Boston: Beacon, 2003).

12. James Allen, *Without Sanctuary: Lynching Photography in America* (Santa Fe, NM: Twin Palms, 2003).

surprised nor shocked. We have been the object of white America's abuse for nearly four hundred years.

People who have never been lynched by another group usually find it difficult to understand why Blacks want whites to remember lynching atrocities. Why bring that up? Is it not best forgotten? Absolutely not! The lynching tree is a metaphor of America's crucifixion of Black people. It is the window that best reveals the theological meaning of the cross in this land. In this sense, Black people are Christ-figures, not because we want to be but because we had no choice about being lynched, just as Jesus had no choice in his journey to Calvary. Jesus did not want to die on the cross and Blacks did not want swing from the lynching tree. But the evil forces of the Roman State and white supremacy in America willed it. Yet, God took the evil of the cross and the lynching tree upon the divine self and transformed both into the triumphant beauty of the divine. If America has the courage to confront the great sin and ongoing legacy of white supremacy, with repentance and reparation, there is hope "beyond tragedy."

# PART SIX

# New Voices in the Black Church

# 21

# Too Young to Be Black

## *The Intergenerational Compatibility of Black Theology*

BRANDEE JASMINE MIMITZRAIEM

### BENT, LIKE ELBOWS: AN INTRODUCTION[1]

My first experiences with Black theologies came in a Contemporary Theology course where we discussed James H. Cone's *God of the Oppressed* and Jacquelyn Grant's *White Women's Christ and Black Women's Jesus.*[2] Though I understood the significance of both works to the discipline, society, and class, I experienced a fundamental disconnect from the texts. My comments and critiques caused concern among my fellow classmates. The white students could not understand my lack of cohesion with Black thinkers, and the Black students questioned my blackness. In an effort to mediate the discussion, another Black woman—who was significantly older than me—declared, "Brandee, of course you don't agree. You're not old enough to be Black. Wait until you're my age—or at least thirty-five. Then you'll see what it means to be an African American." The truth in her statement is not that there is some magical age a person must reach

---

1. OutKast, "ATLiens." *ATLiens*, Verse 1: "I heard it's not where you're from but where you pay rent / Then I heard it's not what you make but how much you spent / you've got me bent / like elbows amongst other things but I'm not worried / cause when I stepped into the party like a mouse you scurried."

2. James H. Cone, *God of the Oppressed* (San Francisco: Harper & Row, 1975; rev. ed. 1997); Jacquelyn Grant, *White Women's Christ and Black Women's Jesus*, American Academy of Religion Academy Series 64 (Atlanta: Scholars, 1989).

before they *become* Black. Rather, its value is in its implications. My disconnection from the text was a result of experiential incompatibility. Cone's and Grant's experiences in the 1940s, 1950s, 1960s, and 1970s did not resonate with my experiences decades later. I felt abandoned by the Black theological discourse.

This incident of ideological abandonment led me to question the ability of Black theology to be relevant to generations who know only of its foundational context through history books. The inherent experiential element of Black theology and its focus on the context in which it was formed make it difficult for those who did not experience that context to locate themselves in the discipline. Further, I question if it is possible for theologians in my generation to participate in Black theological discourse. That is, are theologians who are not yet thirty-five able to do Black theology from their context and experiences? This paper is the result of wrestling with these questions. I do not expect to find the ultimate answer. Through an examination of Black theology and a careful consideration of its purpose and method, I hope to find a way to construct Black theologies of liberation from the culture and lived experiences of the emerging generation.

I use the term "Black theology" when speaking generally of the theological discipline done by Black people. This is not to say that I understand the male-dominated strand to be primary or that I consider the female-dominated theology to be a component of that strand. Black theology denotes, simply, those theologies as done by Black people—female and male. To indicate the male-dominated strand of Black theology I use the term "Black liberation theology." Likewise, when speaking of the female-dominated strand I employ the common term "womanist theology." These theological systems, though similar, are distinct and treated as such. However, it is not the purpose of this paper to discuss the commonalities and differences between the discourses of Black theology. This work assumes the differences as evident in the theological norms, sources, themes and foci of each discourse.

In *Risks of Faith*, James H. Cone discusses his interaction with college students in the late seventies. The article, "Black Theology and the Black College Student" condemns the college students at a lecture for their inability to critically engage Black theology. Insisting on an intergenerational approach to intellectual discourse, Cone assesses the ability of Black theology to do the same. He writes, "It is an interesting and sad contradiction that many nationalists of the sixties and seventies had little or no place for their elders in the struggle. The struggle was almost exclusively youth-oriented . . ."[3] The students are evidence that the struggle of the sixties and seventies was not just youth-oriented but focused solely on those who were youths in those decades. Then, not only did the struggle not interact with its history, it made no room for its future. Gayraud Wilmore asks, "How many of our children can speak intelligently about Black theology?"[4] Children's lack of historical knowledge is far too often viewed as a problem within their generation. It is clear, however, that children can only know what they are taught. Then, if future generations of theologians are to speak of and do Black theology intelligently, the current generation must clear the way. Black theologians must begin to teach, write and understand Black theology as an intergenerational discipline.

Intergenerational efforts begin by taking seriously the voices and experiences of other generations. Notably, Black theology's historical critique and evaluation is strong. But the theological understanding of history is outside the focus of this paper. Instead, I examine the ability to critically consider the future. To this end, when I speak of Black theologians I specifically speak of those theologians currently teaching and writing. I assume this group of Black theologians to be over thirty and, therefore, juxtapose them with the generation of emerging theologians under thirty. Because 2005 celebrates the twenty-fifth anniversary of the emergence of hip-hop in Black culture, I will look directly at the experiences and culture of those people twenty-five and under. This generation has been labeled "Generation Y" by the media and "The Hip-hop Generation" in other circles. Labels run the risk of misrepresenting the labeled. These labels are no different. Bakari Kitwana identifies the hip-hop generation as being born between the years 1965–1984.[5] Generation Y, as defined by the marketing industry, encompasses the birth years of 1981–1994. The over lap in these definitions is significant. There is obvious difference in the lived experiences of a person born in 1967 and a

3. Cone, *Risks of Faith: The Emergence of a Black Theology of Liberation* (Boston: Beacon, 1999) 123.

4. Gayraud S. Wilmore, "Black Theology at the Turn of the Century," in *Black Faith and Public Talk: Critical Essays on James H. Cone's Black Theology and Black Power*, edited by Dwight N. Hopkins (Maryknoll, NY: Orbis, 1999) 240 [232–45].

5. Bakari Kitwana, *The Hip Hop Generation: Young Blacks and the Crisis in African American Culture* (New York: Basic Civitas, 2002) xii.

person born in 1982. Therefore, this paper focuses on the lives of those Black American born since 1979. For the purpose of this paper, I will refer to them as, simply, "The Generation."

## PART I: CATCH THE BEAT
## —THEOLOGICAL EXAMINATION

In 1969, James H. Cone penned *Black Theology and Black Power* thereby beginning the Black liberation revolution in academic theology.[6] This very provocative work led to the more systematic *A Black Theology of Liberation* (1970).[7] Both volumes, necessarily, focus on theologically understanding racism in America. In the late sixties, racism was a visible entity with which Black people were at war. This war was raged in the public eye. Televisions throughout the nation blared vivid pictures of the blood and water spilt in the tumult. Still, theology remained unchanged by this war. Theology was taught and written without considering its social location. Cone writes, "When I asked my professors about what theology had to do with the Black struggle for racial justice, they seemed surprised and uncomfortable with the question, not knowing what to say and anxious to move on with the subject matter as they understood it. I was often told that theology and the struggle for racial justice were separate subjects, with the latter belonging properly in the discipline of sociology and political science."[8] Theological discomfort and unwillingness to address the lived experiences of Black Americans infuriated Cone. In order to win the war against racism, Black people needed a theological framework that took seriously the reality of being Black in America. Black liberation theology surfaced in response.

Black liberation theology makes primary the experiences of oppressed Black men in North America. Black men, dehumanized by racism, are empowered through the very construction of theology. Black liberation theology was constructed in an academic setting to respond to the call of a community. It cannot be understood apart from its social location. Likewise, it cannot be fully understood without considering its formative influences. Martin Luther King, Jr. and Malcolm X played a

6. Cone, *Black Theology and Black Power* (New York: Seabury, 1969; 20th anniversary edition, 1989).

7. Cone, *A Black Theology of Liberation* (Philadelphia: Lippincott, 1970; 20th anniversary edition, Maryknoll, NY: Orbis, 1990).

8. Cone, *Risks of Faith*, xiv.

large role in Cone's ideological development. Diana Hayes writes, "James Cone . . . speaks of three major catalysts for the development of Black Liberation Theology . . . : the Civil Rights Movement, the Black Power Movement and the influence of Malcolm X on the Black Nationalist Movement, and the reaction to the negative depiction of Black religion as set forth in Joseph Washington's *Black Religion*."[9] So crucial are these movements to Black liberation that Cone writes, "[*A Black Theology of Liberation*] cannot be understood without a keen knowledge of the civil rights and Black power movements of the 1960's . . ."[10] Then, Black liberation theology is a product of and speaks to this era.

Notably, Black liberation theology has grown since 1968. Dwight N. Hopkins posits two separate generations of Black liberation theologians. The first generation includes Cone, Gayraud S. Wilmore, and those who conceived the discourse. The second generation rose in response to the work of the first. The use of the term "second generation" is, however, misleading. Rather than being in another age group, these scholars are the ideological children of the founders. Then, they do not necessarily aid in the intergenerational effort. Their worth to the discourse is, however, unquestionable. Hopkins writes of the second generation, "On the one hand, they have sought to pursue the first generation's pioneering agenda. On the other hand, they also have claimed their own distinct approaches. In a word, the second generation are both heirs to the Black theological founders and ground breakers in their own right."[11] The second generation's agenda included more than racism. They focused on issues such as Afrocentricity, gender, and class issues. The second generation, according to Hopkins, began with scholars such as Cornel West and Jacquelyn Grant, the former accenting class analysis and the latter stressing gender full humanity.

Grant's critique of Black liberation theology's inherent sexism changed the theological discourse at large. She critiqued liberation theologies in general for their lack of consistent focus on liberation. Black liberation theology, specifically, refused to tolerate racism, but participated in sexism. Grant writes, "Ironically, the criticism that libera-

---

9. Diana Hayes, *And Still We Rise: An Introduction to Black Liberation Theology* (New York: Paulist, 1996) 53.

10. Cone, *A Black Theology of Liberation*, xi.

11. Dwight N. Hopkins, *Introducing Black Theology of Liberation* (Maryknoll, NY: Orbis, 1999) 88.

tion theology makes against classical theology has been turned against liberation theology itself . . . Where racism is rejected, sexism has been embraced." Womanist theology picked up on this theme. It refuses to accept the notion that oppression is singularly focused. Instead, it understands oppression as being three-fold—i.e., race, class, and gender. Then, Womanist theology transcends the walls of the academy and encourages the lived-experiences of Black women to become primary in the freedom struggle in the Black community. Black theology's commitment to freedom is evident in two of its themes as delineated by Linda E. Thomas and Dwight N. Hopkins.[12]

### Back, Back, Forth and Forth:[13] Thematic Dialogue

Race, as it is used for determining distribution of oppression, is a prominent theme in Black theology. Womanist theologian Jamie Phelps, in "Racism and the Church: An Inquiry into the Contradictions between Experience, Doctrine, and Theological Theory," discusses race as a social-historical phenomenon. She writes, "Race theory was born as a result of a complex fusion of historical choices, white supremacist ideology, and social, 'scientific,' philosophical, and psychological theories which were used to justify the economic system of slavery in America . . . Race is a socially constructed myth predicated on a false theoretical base . . . "[14]

When this understanding infects social systems, the problem of racism is created. Racism, loosely defined, is the combination of race superiority theories with institutional power. Phelps discusses it as racial injustice and lists seven ways in which it is manifested: (1) Constitutional Injustice, (2) Aboriginal Devaluation, (3) Racial/Ethnic Exclusion from

---

12. Dwight N. Hopkins and Linda E. Thomas, "Womanist Theology and Black Theology: Conversational Envisioning of an Unfinished Dream," in *A Dream Unfinished: Theological Reflections on America from the Margins*, edited by Fernando Segovia and Eleazar S. Fernandez (Maryknoll, NY: Orbis, 2001). For references to the method, aims, and approach of womanist theology, see Stephanie Y. Mitchell, *Introducing Womanist Theology* (Maryknoll, NY: Orbis, 2002) 19; Hayes, *And Still We Rise*, 141; and Teresa Fry Brown, "Avoiding Asphyxiation," in *Embracing the Spirit: Womanist Perspectives on Hope, Salvation and Transformation*, edited by Emilie M. Townes (Maryknoll, NY: Orbis, 1997) 72–94.

13. Aaliyah, "Back and Forth," on *I Care 4 U*. Chorus: "Back, back, forth and forth / Wanna see you go / Back, back, forth and forth."

14. Jamie T. Phelps, in "Racism and the Church: An Inquiry into the Contradictions between Experience, Doctrine, and Theological Theory," in *Black Faith and Public Talk*, 66–67 [53–76].

Full Citizenship, (4) Ethnocentricity, (5) Social Racism, (6) Spontaneous Racism and (7) Anti-Semitism.[15] Womanist theology, in seeking liberation from racism, recognizes these and other manifestations. It understands racism to work as a dehumanizing force in society. People are dehumanized when their moral agency is vanquished. Womanist ethicist Katie Cannon writes, "The vast majority of Black [people] suffer every conceivable form of denigration. Their lives are named, defined and circumscribed by white [people]."[16] Womanist theology works to correct this dehumanization by offering Black women the courage to be, to speak, to see themselves as more than substitutes to humanity.

Black liberation theology, likewise, sees racism as an affront to the personhood of Black men. Yet, Black liberation theology understands race more theoretical than Womanist theology. Drawing literally on the one-drop rule (which states that one drop of Black blood renders a person Black), Cone writes, "Black [people] are those who say they are Black, regardless of skin color."[17] Elsewhere, he declares, "Being Black in America has very little to do with skin color. To be Black means that your heart, your soul, your mind, and your body are where the dispossessed are."[18] Then, blackness is not dependent on racial identification. It is beyond ontology. He further conjectures that it is possible for people without one drop of Blackness to become Black and participate in blackness. He writes, "God's Word of reconciliation means that we can only be justified by becoming Black. Reconciliation makes us all Black."[19] Blackness, for Cone, is synonymous with salvation. His goal is to theologically redeem blackness, opening the doors for the understanding that Black is beautiful, good and worthy. Again, this position cannot be understood outside of Cone's context.

However rigid Cone's context is in determining his theology, it is not dominant. His view of gender, for example, has changed over the last thirty-six years. He came to understand that sexism is as problematic as racism. He admits, "I have not always been supportive of women in

15. Ibid., 62.

16. Katie G. Cannon, *Black Womanist Ethics*, American Academy of Religion Academy Series (Atlanta: Scholars, 1988) 3.

17. Cone, *A Black Theology of Liberation*, 66 and 83; see also Cone, *Black Theology and Black Power*, 8.

18. Cone, *Black Theology and Black Power*, 151.

19. Ibid.

the ministry . . . While I did not publicly oppose gender-consciousness in theology, I just kept silent about it and continued my writing and teaching about Black liberation theology as if gender-inclusive language and Black women's experience made no distinctive contribution to my understanding of liberation and its impact on theology. It was a sexist assumption, just as detrimental to humanity as racism."[20] Black liberation theology, too, made this change. Dwight N. Hopkins, in the second chapter of his constructive theology work *Shoes That Fit Our Fit*, engages Toni Morrison's works to understand constructions of gender in lives of Black women. He employs these fictional tales as cultural sources that display Black women's spirituality. He writes, "In Morrision's [*sic*] novels, poor Black women's spirituality is a manifestation of God's spirit of liberation incarnated in their values and traditions."[21] This valuation of Black women and their lived-experiences in Black liberation theology is far from the norm. Hopkins' willingness to critically consider women's experiences in doing theology is a reflection of the impact of womanist theology on Black theology.

Gender considerations in Black liberation theology include attempting to understand how men are engendered beings. Hopkins insists, "There is a male gender."[22] Black male gender is socially constructed in the dominant society and in the Black community. Hopkins writes:

> In the process of socialization, black men experience a double male gender reality, and both are negative. On one hand, the larger culture of white society defines and portrays black men as subordinate to white men. African American men are socialized as a male gender but as men who are subordinate to the racial supremacy of another male gender. On the other hand, within the African American community, black men are socialized to adopt the normative definition of the male gender that is established and defined by the larger white male culture. As a result, black men strive toward and enjoy male privileges over black women and children within the African American family and community.[23]

20. Cone, *Risks of Faith*, xxv.

21. Hopkins, *Shoes that Fit Our Feet: Sources for a Constructive Black Theology* (Maryknoll, NY: Orbis, 1993) 50.

22. Hopkins, "Theologies in Dialogue." Lecture, October 20, 2004.

23. Hopkins, *Heart and Head: Black Theology—Past, Present, and Future* (New York: St. Martin's, 2002) 94.

This dual socialization leads to problems in the Black community and internal problems in Black men. Black men can choose to accept or discard their constructed gender. The task, then, for Black liberation theologians is to re-conceptualize the male gender—that is, masculinity. Hopkins suggests that this starts by understanding the location of God's love in Black maleness. He writes, "They can begin first by accepting the love of God that is in all black men."[24] Accepting God's love leads to Black male self-love. Self-love, for Hopkins, assists in the liberation movement and is epitomized in Jesus. Further, reconstructing Black male gender depends on understanding God as Black. Hopkins states, "A theological reconstruction of the black male consists . . . of a realization that God is Black for African American males."[25] As in discussions of race in Black liberation theology, a Black God empowers Black men to accept their beings as made in God's image. However, it is first necessary to understand that God both encompasses all genders and is beyond gender. God's love, self-love, Jesus' life and God's blackness begins the process, but Black liberation theologians must be in dialogue with Womanist theologians for the reconstruction to be complete.

As stated earlier, Womanist theologians began Black theology's gender critique. Marcia Riggs's *Plenty Good Room* discusses the role of gender in the Black church. Her analysis works to understand and transform the sexual-gender practices in the Black church. She draws heavily on gender theories. She writes, "The decision to use social construction of gender theory as the framework for this analysis aligns with a quest for a Christian postmodern sexual ethic that . . . suggests that social construction theory offers us in the church a way to hold in tension the desire for relationality and justice that individuals and groups dominated by hegemonic sexual norms seek."[26] Then, understanding gender as socially constructed assists womanist theologians in the search for justice and liberation. Riggs employs the experiences of women in "scenarios" to concretize her points. These scenarios suggest that womanist theology conceptions of gender must be understood through the call for justice in relationships with men. Thomas elaborates, "Gender is an important discussion because violence against girls and women is in epidemic pro-

---

24. Ibid., 96.

25. Ibid., 99.

26. Marcia Y. Riggs, *Plenty Good Room* (Cleveland: Pilgrim, 2003) 25.

portions around the world."[27] Discussions of gender in womanist theology, then, are about survival and the quality of Black women's life.

### All Falls Down:[28] Intergenerational Critique

Is Black theology relevant to the Generation (i.e., Black people born in and after 1979)? That is, are the experiences and reality of the Generation manifested in Black theological considerations? I began this paper with the assumption that Black theology's claim to the primacy of the experience of oppressed Black people necessitated its relevancy to the oppressed Generation. After discussing the formation of and themes in Black theology, we must critically examine this assumption.

Cone writes, "No one can write theology for all times, places, and persons."[29] This statement in his 1986 preface is followed by a delineation of the context and intended audience of *A Black Theology of Liberation*. He claims that the book was written for and to Black people to assist in the struggle for freedom. However, the inclusion of the Generation in his audience of "Black people" is uncertain. The Generation, for instance, does not have the "keen knowledge" of Black theologies formative era that Cone insists is necessary for comprehending his work.[30] The Generation can only understand this era through historical accounts. Then, the Generation is abandoned by this work before it begins. Even if the Generation chose to continue reading past the preface, it would be difficult to join Cone in his passion. In the twentieth-anniversary edition, Cone chose to change the language of *A Black Theology of Liberation* to be less sexist.[31] However, he did not consider the Generation's ability to relate to the language or concepts. Cone writes, for example, "Some readers will object to the absence of the 'universal note' in the foregoing assertions, asking, 'How can you reconcile the lack of universalism regarding human nature with a universal God?' The first reply is to deny that there is a 'universal God' in the normal understanding of the term. As pointed out in the previous chapter, God is Black."[32] To the ear of those formed

27. Linda E. Thomas, "Theologies in Dialogue." Lecture, October 20, 2004.

28. Kanye West, "All Falls Down," on *The College Dropout*.

29. Cone, *A Black Theology of Liberation*, xi.

30. Ibid.

31. I say "less" because, as he admits, merely changing "man" to "people" and "He" to "God" does not change the sexist tones or language in an overtly sexist work.

32. Cone, *A Black Theology of Liberation*, xi.

in an era where the universe ended and began in the Western world and the plea for universalism usually was a call for whiteness, this is readily acceptable. However, to the ear of the Generation, this sounds offensive. First, God's blackness has never been questioned in the Generation's lifetime. God and Jesus as Black is such a part of the Generation's experience it is even in their television shows. An episode of *Aqua Teen Hunger Force*, an adult themed show that airs on the Cartoon Network, entitled "Gee Whiz," places in the mouth of one of the main characters, "Meatwad, Jesus was Black." The response, "I know that, but they said he's up there."[33] Second, the Generation's conception of universal is more global. For the Generation, universal humanity denotes the reality that the whole of humanity is related and emerged from the same source. Likewise, a Universal God is understood by the Generation in the same sense as the Universal Port on computers. It is a God who, though specifically for a certain purpose, is readily available. Cone's point in this assertion is only understandable to the Generation if they abandon their own formative experiences and adopt those of Cone as normative. That this is necessary is contrary to the very enterprise. Black theology assures the Generation of the primacy of the Black experience. But to even engage the discourse, the Generation must reject its experience. Cone's more recent works are no different.

In his 1994 "Demystifying Martin and Malcolm" article, Cone condemns the Generation's embrace of Malcolm X and simultaneously denounces the Generation's experiences. Uncritically accepting the media portrayal of the Generation, he writes, "With no respect for themselves or for anybody else, Black youth are dropping out of school, having babies, joining gangs, selling drugs and killing one another with a frequency that boggles the mind."[34] This statement, first, lacks social critique. He categorically attributes the symptoms of an oppressed and impoverished people to a perceived lack of respect. Second, his statement betrays his own emphasis on liberation. He admits that the strides made in the Civil Rights movement were not far reaching. He is able to assess the situation of "the Black underclass" as a result of this lack of progress. However, he does not make this connection with Black youth. His lack of critical

---

33. *Aqua Teen Hunger Force* is an adult-theme cartoon that features food-themed characters. This episode was about the idea that the face of Jesus (whom they called Gee Whiz, as they explained, to placate the censors) on a billboard.

34. Cone, "Demystifying Martin and Malcolm," in *Risks of Faith*, 97 [96–107].

reflection on the Generation is further evident in his estimation of their "Malcolmania," as he puts it. He writes, "Young Black [people] are making a similar error today. They rap about Malcolm's profound analysis of America's racism without even mentioning how Martin organized a movement to fight against the racism that Malcolm analyzed."[35] Unlike the treatment of Malcolm by Cone's generation, no rapper has ever repudiated King or his work. In fact, in 1988 Big Daddy Kane in "Word to the Mother (Land)" says

> Because the moral of it all is we shall overcome
> The cream will keep rising
> We be sizing/Up, the Asiatic one is enterprising
> Building and building to carry on
> All the way from Malcolm X to Farrakhan
> Martin Luther was a tutor, many were pupils
> Those who fell victim were those without scruples[36]

In his article, Cone advocates for equal acceptance of Malcolm and King. Clearly, Big Daddy Kane does exactly that. Then, Cone's unqualified assertion comes not through interactions with the Generation but through theories based on media portrayal. Still, Cone's failure to critically engage the Generation is less egregious than his colleague's refusal to even acknowledge the Generation's existence.

Karen Baker-Fletcher and Garth Kasimu Baker-Fletcher in their theological dialogue, *My Sister, My Brother: Womanist and XODUS God-Talk*, include a section entitled Generations. In the almost fifty pages that make up this section on generations, not one is devoted to the Generation. Instead, they spend these pages discussing solely the generations that came before them. Karen writes, "To be Womanist is to be generational. Generation has to do with more than the biological activity of child-conception and childbearing. It includes childbearing and moves beyond that to consider care for elders and remembering ancestors."[37] While childbearing necessarily alludes to future generations, her discussion of motherhood focuses not on the needs of the child but on the conception of "mother." Hers is a necessarily historical enterprise. This is not inherently imperfect. However, in a chapter

---

35. Ibid., 100.

36. Big Daddy Kane, "Word to the Mother(Land)," on *Long Live the Kane*.

37. Karen Baker-Fletcher and Garth Kasimu Baker-Fletcher, *My Sister, My Brother: Womanist and Xodus God-talk* (Maryknoll, NY: Orbis, 1997) 173.

called "Unto All Generations" to not acknowledge the existence of a younger generation is deficient. Karen continues to discuss generational activity. She insists that diffusing wisdom intergenerationally has been critical to the Black community. She says, "Carving out space and time for honoring the many generations that make up our communities and remembering the spiritual ground that sustains individuals and communities has often been performed against all odds by African American ancestors."[38] Here, the Womanist theological call to celebrate and include all generations is refreshing. However, her discussion betrays this call. The Generation is conspicuously absent from her discourse. Even in the call to consider future generations, Karen neglects the opportunity to engage the Generation.

In one chapter of each section, Karen and Kasimu have dialogue in print. Their dialogue in "Generations" covers many diverse subjects. They begin by discussing intercultural and interracial relationships and move through discussions of language and embodiment. While crucial to the health of Black theology, the dialogue is remiss. The Generation's culture is mentioned in passing. Karen writes, "In contemporary Black culture, Rappers, who are more often male than female, have great liberty to create new words. While there are women Rappers, few are given respect for their creativity, and it is difficult for women to break into this field ... Rap is a patriarchal and unapologetically sexist industry. We need to consider whether or not there are different and unequal levels of freedom to create new language across gender lines."[39] First, her assertions about the rap industry, however true, do not analytically consider the Generation as she insists is necessary. Rather, they serve to uncritically condemn a major part of the Generation's formative influences. Second, she exploits the culture of the Generation to prove a point foreign to the Generation. While there may be inequality in the ability for women and men to create language, this is not evident in the sexism of the rap industry.

Black theology, then, ideologically abandons the Generation based not on offensive action, but perception. Michael Eric Dyson is one of the few Black intellectuals who evaluate the Generation and its culture honestly. Able to view the discord from both perspectives, Dyson blames the anger of his generation on insincere nostalgia. He writes, "Much of the anger I've seen directed at Black youth, especially from older Black

38. Ibid., 179.
39. Ibid., 222.

[people], is tied to a belief that young Black [people] are very different from any other Black generation. Among esteemed Black intellectuals . . . there is a consensus that something has gone terribly wrong with Black youth. They are disrespectful to their elders. They are obsessed with sex. They are materialistic. They are pathological. They are violent. They are nihilistic. They are ethical depraved. They are lazy. They are menaces to society."[40] These perceptions of the Generation come not through personal interaction, but through media portrayal. The negative media attention has made intergenerational efforts between the Generation and its elders difficult. Dyson writes, "It's hard to open a newspaper or watch television without getting an ugly reminder of the havoc our kids wreak on the streets and the terror they must confront without much sympathy or support."[41] Black theology has bought into the media myths and treats the Generation with anger and indignation. Like a red-headed step-child, the Generation is unwanted, unknown and unclaimed; left to deal with its oppression and fight for its liberation alone.

Black theology as the ideological framework for Black freedom struggles should be both relevant to and receptive of the Generation. This has not happened; perhaps because Black theologians have not been made to see that the experiences of the Generation are valid sources for theology. Perhaps, if Black theologians are able to see the theological benefit of critical reflection with and on the Generation, Black theology will be reconstructed to be more hospitable. The remainder of this work will be devoted to this enterprise.

## PART II: GOD? ARE YOU THERE, GOD?[42] CULTURAL EXAMINATION AND THEOLOGICAL CONSTRUCTION

Delores S. Williams begins her *Sisters in the Wilderness* by explaining her faith journey. She writes, "This can help an audience discern what leads the theologian to the kind of theology she does."[43] She discusses her childhood, the role the Church played in her spiritual development. A theologian's culture, the social context, and the early interactions with

40. Michael Eric Dyson, *Race Rules: Navigating the Color Line* (Reading, PA: Addison-Wesley, 1996) 112.

41. Ibid., 113.

42. OutKast, "God (Interlude)," on *Speakerboxx/The Love Below*.

43. Delores S. Williams, *Sisters in the Wilderness: The Challenge of Womanist God-talk* (Maryknoll, NY: Orbis, 1993) ix.

faith shape theological construction. In no other theological system is this more important than in Black theology. The task of theological construction from the vantage point of the Generation, then, must deal critically with its culture, social context and lived-experience.

To reiterate, the Generation is composed of those Black Americans born in and after 1979. This is the only generation that has never known a world *without* hip-hop music. The ideological formation of the Generation, then, was done in the midst of hip-hop. Further, the Generation's childhood mimics that of the development of Black theology. It came of age in a time of racial uncertainty in this society. The Generation remembers vividly the beating of Rodney King and the violent aftermath of the police officer's trial. The Generation has endured child snatching in epidemic numbers, gang violence, an increase in teenage pregnancies, and state imposed curfews. Kanye West explains,

> We never had nothing handed, took nothing for granted
> Took nothing from no man, man I'm my own man
> But as a shorty I looked up to the dope man
> Only adult man I knew that wasn't broke man
> Flickin Starter coats man, man you don't know man
> We don't care what people say.[44]

His appraisal of the Generation's lifestyle is summed up at the end of the song. He says, "Look at what's handed us."[45] Thus the struggle of the Generation is a result of the history of the Black experience in this nation. In short, the Generation grew up dealing with the implications of the 1960s and 70s liberation movements.

There were positive influences on the Generation's formation as well. The Generation has never known a time without the slogans, "Black is Beautiful" and "The Blacker the berry, the sweeter the juice." The oldest members of the Generation saw Jesse Jackson run for President before they hit puberty; they missed high school classes to attend and watch the Million Man March. The Generation has pride in blackness and has never known a world without that pride. This understanding of blackness was formed by seeing positive, healthy images of blackness on television. In fact, the Cosby Show and Black Entertainment Television (BET) are major cultural icons in the Generation. Television helped transmit the

44. Kanye West, "We Don't Care," on *The College Dropout*, verse 1.
45. Ibid., verse 3.

values and norms found in the culture to the Generation. Like the Black church in Black theology's development, the music of the Generation largely shaped the way it understands God and its faith.

The Generation takes seriously its history. This presents a problem and a solution for Black theology. The lived-realities of Black theologians are the Generations historical sources. However, the revival of Malcolm X as an icon shows the prominent role of history in the Generation's conception. The caution for Black theology is not to make history primary over and against the experiences of the Generation. This short list of the location and culture of the Generation serves as a framework for Black theological construction for the Generation.

Up to this point, we have discussed the way Black theology reflects theologically on issues of oppression. Womanist and Black liberation theological dialogue on race and gender illuminates the function of liberation as the theme and focus of Black theology. However, the task of Black theological construction requires a greater intimacy with the discipline. We cannot do Black theological construction without first understanding its sources and norms. Cone identifies six sources for Black liberation theology: Black experience, Black history, Black culture, revelation, scripture and tradition.[46] *Black experience*, in Black liberation theology, is the experience of the oppressed. This is narrowly defined as those racially oppressed men. Cone writes, "The Black experience is existence in a system of white racism."[47] It is, for him, the struggle for Black men to be understood as fully human. Hopkins expands this understanding. In his restructured sources of Black Liberation theology, he writes, "If Black women make up at least 70 percent of Black churches and over half of the African American community then Black theology must deal with and reflect the intellectual, emotional and body concerns and contributions of Black women."[48] Then, the Black experience is the experiences of all of Black people with oppression—racism, sexism, heterosexism, and classism.

*Black history* as a theological source is especially evident in the products of Womanist theology. Womanist theology uses the historical experiences of Black women as the locus for its discourse. The historical experiences of Black women are given equal authority with the real-lived

46. Cone, *A Black Theology of Liberation*, 23–34.

47. Ibid., 24.

48. Hopkins, *Introducing Black Theology of Liberation*, 45.

experiences of Womanist theologians. Mitchem speaks of this as seeing the lives of Black women as texts for doing theology. She writes, "The texts of lives yield information that mere statistics cannot . . . Viewed as texts, human lives also require interpretation. At the same time, human lives stand in interpretation of their times . . ."[49] Womanist theology, then, uses history to understand Black experience.

*Black culture* is a complex issue. First, it assumes that there is a universal culture in the Black experience. Second, it is often understood to be the arts of Black people—a narrow interpretation of the term. Hopkins understands Black culture to be composed of the "art, literature, music, folktales, Black English and rhythm" of the Black experience.[50] Black theology uses as its source, specifically, the liberation motifs found in these forms. It adopts folktales, the Spirituals and Black athletic participation equally so long as they liberate. Hopkins writes, "A liberating culture is vital for a constructive Black theology."[51]

Cone defines *revelation* as a happening in human history. He writes, "[Revelation] is God's self-revelation to the human race through a historical act of liberation."[52] This is evidenced in the active struggle for liberation. Revelation is understood as God's action as evidenced in human action. Further, revelation is decidedly bound to liberation. Cone says, "Black theology takes the risk of faith and thus makes an unqualified identification of God's revelation with Black liberation."[53] Black theology views God's libratory revelation in *Scripture*. Black theologians find meaning and liberation in several biblical texts. Black liberation theology draws heavily on themes of liberation from the book of Exodus. Womanist theology uses, instead, the framework of a Genesis story. Williams writes, "I began to see that it was possible to identify at least two traditions of African-American biblical appropriation that were useful for the construction of Black theology in North America. One of these traditions of biblical appropriation emphasized liberation of the oppressed and showed God relating to men in the liberation struggles . . . [The second] tradition emphasized female activity and de-emphasized

49. Stephanie Y. Mitchem, *Introducing Womanist Theology* (Maryknoll, NY: Orbis, 2002) 47.

50. Hopkins, *Introducing Black Theology of Liberation*, 45.

51. Ibid.

52. Cone, *A Black Theology of Liberation*, 29.

53. Ibid., 31.

male authority."[54] The stories of female non-Hebrew slaves and Hebrew exodus from Egypt serve as primary evidence of God's concern for the lives of oppressed Black people.

Finally, Black theology emphasizes the importance of *tradition* in the theological construction. Tradition is equitable to the Black church. Hopkins says, "The Black church exists wherever Black Christians come together in their own space and time to worship and live out God's call for freedom for the least in society."[55] The traditions of the Black church are evident in the other sources of Black theology. For instance, the scriptural appropriations Williams discusses are those used by the Black church. Further, Black theology understands the legacy of liberation in the Church. Cone writes, "When we look at the history of the Black Church . . . there are many shortcomings and failures. But there is also the constant theme of liberation and God's will to establish justice in the land."[56] This view of the Church allows Black theology to critique the Church while remaining decidedly within tradition.

Andre 3000's question to God on the 2003 OutKast album *Speaker Boxx/The Love Below*, "God? Are you there God?" frames this discussion. Simply, is the God of Black theology present in the culture and lived experiences of the Generation? If so, what does God say to its oppression and struggle for liberation? These questions necessitate Black theological construction using the Generation as its primary source. Following Black theology's example, this construction takes seriously the revelation of God as evidenced in the encultured experiences of the Generation.

Since slavery, Black people have used their culture as an outlet to express their frustrations with and hopes for their experience as oppressed beings. There is a distinct connection between real-lives and culture. The use of culture as transmission for experiences is "encultured experience." Negro Spirituals are the most widely discussed displays of encultured experience. Wyatt Tee Walker writes, "The Spirituals were created and refined by the slaves themselves as religious and social statements about the context of their lives."[57] Further, as encultured experiences Black theology appreciates the Spirituals as a valid source for theological reflection.

---

54. Williams, *Sisters in the Wilderness*, 2.

55. Hopkins, *Introducing Black Theology of Liberation*, 43.

56. Cone, *Risks of Faith*, 127.

57. Wyatt Tee Walker, *"Somebody's Calling My Name": Black Sacred Music and Social Change* (Valley Forge, PA: Judson, 1979) 40.

Their relevance to the lives of the slaves and descendants of slaves, their ability to convey coded communiqués, and their focus on God allow Black theology to consider and explore the Spirituals as living theology. Cheryl Kirk-Duggan writes, "Spirituals champion the Refiner's Fire, the covenant of Black liberation with divine revelation in which grace heals alienation and brokenness."[58] Further, she discusses the importance of the Spirituals to the foundational influences on Black theology: the Civil Rights and Black Power movements. She writes, "During the Movement, Spirituals helped unify disparate groups as they confronted legalized collective racist evil via moral, nonviolent organized protest and paradoxically exposed the United States' denial of moral and legal rights to persons of color ... The Spirituals embodied African American's sense of self, God, and relationship with God."[59] It is precisely because of this intimate relationship that Black theology is critically concerned with the Spirituals.

Hip-hop and Rhythm and Blues (R&B) are the encultured experiences for the Generation. As encultured experiences, these musical forms play a significant role in the emergence of the Generation as intellectuals. Kitwana writes, "Rap music more than anything else has helped to shape the new Black ... culture."[60] As with the Spirituals, these musical forms critique the societal oppression of the Generation. The encultured experiences of the Generation have included socio-political and economic critique. Public Enemy's "Fight the Powers that Be" encouraged the Generation to wage war against the attack on their personhood. They rhymed,

> As the rhythm designed to bounce
> What counts is that the rhymes
> Designed to fill your mind
> Now that you've realized the pride's arrived
> We got to pump the stuff to make us tough from the heart
> It's a start, a work of art
> To revolutionize, make a change nothin's strange
> People, people we are the same
> No we're not the same
> Cause we don't know the game

58. Cheryl Kirk-Duggan, *Refiner's Fire: A Religious Engagement with Violence* (Minneapolis: Fortress, 2001) 45.

59. Ibid., 46.

60. Kitwana, *The Hip Hop Generation*, 9.

What we need is awareness, we can't get careless
You say what is this?
My beloved lets get down to business
Mental self defensive fitness
(Yo) bum rush the show
You gotta go for what you know
Make everybody see
In order to fight the powers that be![61]

This call for awareness was disseminated to the Generation through its music video. In creating the video for "Fight the Powers that Be," Public Enemy held a public protest rally in the streets of Harlem. Fourteen years later, Jadakiss used those same streets to hold a march for his music video. On his *Kiss of Death*, he asks "Why." Jadakiss spits,

Why would niggaz push pounds and powder
Why did Bush knock down the towers . . .
Why they gotta open your package and read your mail
Why they stop lettin' niggaz get degreez in jail
Why you gotta do eighty-five percent of your time . . .
Why did crack have to hit so hard . . .
Why niggaz can't get no jobs . . .
Why they let the Terminator win the election
Come on, pay attention . . .
Why Halle have to let a white man pop her to get a Oscar
Why Denzel have to be crooked before he took it . . .
Why they ain't give us a cure for AIDS?[62]

Behind Jadakiss's poignant questions, Anthony Hamilton croons, "All that I've been givin' / Is this pain that I've been livin / They got me in the system / Why they gotta do me like that / Try'd to make it my way / But got sent up on the highway / Why, oh why / Why they do me like that?"[63] Not only does he show awareness of the social themes of Black theology, but in "Why" Jadakiss dares asks questions about the major events in the lives of the Generation. His questions show the tendency of the Generation to seek below the given explanations to find the deeper connections.

---

61. Public Enemy, "Fight the Powers that Be," on *Fear of a Black Nation*, verse 2. It is important to note that this is the very same group whose lyrics drew protest and caused Senate hearings.

62. Jadakiss, "Why," on *Kiss of Death*, from verses 1–3.

63. Ibid.

Likewise, the encultured experiences of the Generation include theological reflection. Whether speaking of God or for God, the Generation's music critically engages God's activity in their lives. Then, employing the use of these encultured experiences in Black theological construction is not only appropriate but follows the tradition of Black theology. William Banfield writes, "it is helpful to consider [these] musical expressions as a metaphor for a kind of theological probing. Getting to the music may allow us to get closer to the people who are screaming or celebrating various aspects of life."[64] He sees the possibility of doing theology from the encultured experiences of the Generation.[65] However, it is impossible, in this space, to construct a complete systematic Black theology of the Generation. Instead, this will serve as an introduction to the realized possibility of a theological framework constructed in careful consideration of intergenerational compatibility.

### *Sixteen More Bars to Live:*[66] *Lyrical Examination*

Black theology constructs God through two hermeneutical principles: (1) God's revelatory activity as witnessed in Scripture, and (2) God as participant in the liberation struggle.[67] The doctrine of God in the Generation's Black theological construct upholds these principles. First, the encultured experiences of the Generation insist upon the reality of God and God's interaction with humanity as the solution to oppression.

64. William Banfield, "The Rub: Markets, Morals and the 'Theologizing' of Popular Music," in *Noise and Spirit: The Religious and Spiritual Sensibilities of Rap Music*, ed. Anthony B. Pinn (New York: New York University Press, 20023) 174.

65. However critical this point is, it is important to note that he and the other authors included in Pinn's volume speak of the enculturated experiences of the Generation in abstract. They do not engage them critically nor do they relate them to Black theology. More striking, they include no lyrics in their considerations. Though I have heard there are practical reasons for this, speaking of music as encultured experience without inclusion of the lyrics is like painting a picture of a forest without including the trees. Still, I acknowledge these works take a necessary step closer to intergenerational efforts.

66. Cee-Lo Green, "One for the Road," on *Cee-lo Green and His Perfect Imperfections*, verse 3: "But if I only had sixteen more bars to live / I'd get high and hopefully OD on alternative / I'd give a dim lit dream / a color scheme / and I'd swim for the sun / (so far) / no matter how impossible that may seem / I'd bury my feet in the foundation of a forest / becoming one / with / everything there / I'd be long / I'd be right and wrong / But I'd be rare / Then I would pretend I didn't get misty / already missing / y'all / Then I'd forgive those who rhyme / to kill the time / while mine / cultivates the consciousness and chills the spine / but still sublime."

67. Cone, *A Black Theology of Liberation*, 60.

On their debut album, *Soul Food*, GooDie M.O.B. includes the song "Fighting." "Fighting" discusses the liberation struggle as a battle against United States culture and posits God's identification with the oppressed as the only way to survive this battle. The chorus says simply, "Seems like we're fighting for our spirit and mind / They got us fighting for our spirit and mind / Still fighting for our spirit and mind / Can't stop fighting for our spirit and mind."[68] As the four members of this all-male southern group exchange places at the microphone, each explores the ways they are fighting in their daily lives. Cee-Lo ends the song with spoken word because, as he explains, he did not write a verse. In this poem, Cee-Lo defines, explains the Generation's place and calls for a historical under-standing of God's presence in the liberation struggle. He says,

> As individuals and as a people we are at war
> But the majority of my side got they eyes open wide
> But still don't recognize what we fighting fo'
> I guess that's what I'm writing fo'
> To try to shed some light
> But we been in the darkness for so long
> Don't know right from wrong
> Y'all scared to come near it
> You ignore the voice in your head when you hear it
> The enemy is after yo' spirit
> But you think it's all in yo' mind
> You'll find a lot of the reason we behind
> Is because the system is designed
> To keep our third eyes blind
> But not blind in the sense that our other two eyes can't see
> You just end investing quality time in places you don't even need to be
> We don't even know who we are
> But the answer ain't far
> Matter of fact its right up under our nose
> But the system taught us to keep that book closed
> See the reason why he gotta lie and deceive
> Is so that we won't act accordingly
> To get the blessings we suppose to receive . . .
> We ain't natural born killas
> We are a spiritual people
> God's chosen few
> Think about the slave trade
> When they had boats with thousands of us on board

68. GooDie M.O.B., "Fighting," on *Soul Food*, chorus.

> And we still was praising the Lord
> Know what I'm sayin'
> But now niggaz is ready to die over a coat
> A necklace 'round your throat
> That's bullshit
> Black people ya'll better realize that we losin'
> You better go*damn fight
> And die if you got to for to get yo' spirit and yo' mind back
> And we got to do it together.[69]

GooDie M.O.B's insistence on God as the solution to the liberation struggle is evident even in the construction of their name. Cee-Lo explains, "You take away one "O" and it will let you know / 'God is Every Man of Blackness' / The Lord has spoken thru me and the G-M-O-B!"[70]

The encultured experiences of the Generation posit God's love as primarily for the oppressed. On the album, *Nastradamus*, Nas raps, "God love us hood niggaz (I know) / Cause next to Jesus on the cross was the crook niggaz (I know) / and the killers, God love us good niggaz (I know) / Cause on the streets is the hood niggaz / And I know he feel us / God love us hood niggaz (I know) / Cause he be wit us in the prisons / and he takes time to listen / God love us hood niggaz (I know) / Cause next to Jesus on the cross was the crook niggaz / but he forgive us."[71] For Nas, and much of the Generation, this was a novel concept. The Generation is relentlessly bombarded with messages of its inherent worthlessness. These messages come not only from the media, but from those older parts of the Black community who uncritically accept media portrayal. It was, therefore, necessary for God to reveal this message to Nas. He explains his mystic revelation in the first verse:

> He who ears, let him hear
> And he who has sight, let him see
> He who has life, let him be
> See everything goes through change
> Those who know don't talk
> And those who talk don't know a thing
> Men are born soft and turn tough
> Dead lay a stiffened heart, I've been kissed by God
> I've been hurt, I've been marked for death, almost ripped apart

---

69. Ibid., verse 3.

70. Ibid.

71. Nas, "God Love Us," on *Nastradamus*, chorus.

By the beast but he missed his mark
Alone in the dark my thoughts had sparked up
When I saw my body on the floor, from above I watched it all
Yo, it came to me, the pain in me
Many slain empty skulls where a brain should be
It strangely seemed like it was a dream
But the sirens had never woke me
Only reason I'm here now is cause God chose me
And to me, I'm only just a crook nigga
But God love us hood niggaz.[72]

His revelation comes through his experience of being oppressed, of living in the ghetto. He concludes by simply saying, "Our lives are the worst, on top of that we broke / that's the reason why God love us the most."[73]

Likewise, the Generation understands itself as made in the image of God. For the Generation, this is empowering. Erykah Badu sings, "We were made in God's image / Please call us by our names."[74] This is often misunderstood as an appeal for pantheism. However, Badu's repetitive request in "On and On" reflects the Generation's understanding that the very presence and image of God is the source of its full personhood. Badu, too, understands God to be present in the liberation struggle. In her song, "Otherside of the Game," she discusses the difficulties the Generation has being in relationship in this society. She sings, "Whatcha gonna do when they come for you / Work ain't honest but it pays the bills / Do I really want my baby / Brother tell me what to do / See, I know you got to get your hustle on / So I pray / I understand the game sometimes / but I love you strong / ... / Don't you worry / I know there's confusion/ but that God's gonna see us through / peace after revolution."[75] Here, she critiques the socio-economic situation that forces her partner to connive and scheme in order to survive. Nevertheless, she believes that God is present, calls for revolution, and will bring peace once the revolution is successful.

The revolution, the war, cannot be waged without the incarnational presence of God. Jesus as rebel, Jesus as liberator, Jesus as redeemer is paramount to the success of the Generation's liberation struggle. No

---

72. Ibid., verse 1.

73. Ibid., verse 3.

74. Erykah Badu, "On and On," on *Baduizm*, chorus.

75. Erykah Badu, "Otherside of the Game," on *Baduizm*, chorus, verse 1, and bridge.

where is this clearer than in Kanye West's "Jesus Walks." Laid over a simple beat, this song combines the encultured experiences of Black theology with those of the Generation. The chorus includes a soloists voice singing the words of a Spiritual: "I want Jesus to walk with me." Over this, West places voices of children proudly proclaiming, "Jesus Walks!" Between these declarations, he delivers a simple prayer. He says, "God, show me the way, because the devil's trying to break me down. The only thing I pray is that my feet don't fail me now. And I don't think there's nothing I can do now to right my wrongs. I wanna talk to God but I'm afraid cause we ain't spoke in so long."[76] The beginning of the song, however, holds the most meaning for Black theological construction. Before the music begins, over a simple drum beat West declares, "I need to recruit all the soldiers . . . all of God's soldiers. We at war. We at war with society, racism, terrorism but mostly we at war with ourselves."[77] West, then, delivers two simple verses describing the war the Generation is fighting and the importance of Jesus' footsteps on the battlefield for the Generation's survival. The second verse is the most poignant.

> To the hustlers, killers, murderers, drug dealers even the strippers—
> Jesus walks for them.
> To the victims of welfare, feel we're living in hell here, hell yeah—
> Jesus walks for them.
> Now heary, heary wanna see thee more clearly
> I know he hear me when my feet get weary
> Cause we're the almost nearly extinct
> We rappers are role models—we rap we don't think
> I ain't here to argue about his facial features
> Or here to create atheists into believers
> I'm just tryin to say the way school need teachers
> The way Kathy Lee needed Regis that's the way I need Jesus
> So here go my single, dawg, radio needs this
> They said you can rap about anything except for Jesus
> That means guns, sex, lies, videotape
> But if I talk about God my record won't get played—HUH!?
> Well, if this take away from my spins
> Which will probably take away from my ends
> Then I hope it take away from my sins
> And bring the day that I'm dreamin about
> Next time I'm in the club—everybody screaming out:

76. Kanye West, "Jesus Walks," on *The College Dropout*, chorus.
77. Ibid., introduction.

JESUS WALKS![78]

Not only does the Generation face enumerable difficulties, unmitigated scrutiny by the media and unfair criticism from its elders, but the only tools it has for survival are threatened by those same forces. West's "Jesus Walks" became a quick hit. But it was not the first or the only product of the Generation's encultured experience to speak of God. The sad truth is most of the theological reflections in Generational encultured experience never make it to the radio or music videos as singles. These sources are widely known to the Generation and are completely ignored by its elders. As long as Black theology is only receptive of the image of the Generation as played through the media, it will never be able to truly participate in intergenerational efforts and will remain inaccessible and incomprehensible to the experiences of the Generation.

*Wrong Color, Wrong Sex:*[79] *Womanist Sensibilities in the Generation*

Much of the negative appraisal of the encultured experiences of the Generation focuses on its view and treatment of women. This colors the way Womanist theologians have considered the culture of the Generation. Often, Womanist theologians understand the Generation's encultured experiences as participating in the violent oppression of Black women. For instance, Traci West, in *Wounds of the Spirit*, discusses sex-based cultural assaults against Black women. In her critique of rap music as a cultural assault she writes, "Gangsta' rap music has offered a generation of urban youth and young adults depictions of violence against women . . ."[80] West's goal in this chapter is primarily to point out the sources of violence against women in the culture. While she gives equal attention to sources from various cultures, her critique of the goal of language in rap music discloses an uninformed bias. She writes, "some of the references to 'b-tches' in gangsta' rap illustrate how representations of women as vindictive or conniving help to justify coercive male sexual acts against them."[81] In this, she quotes Snoop Doggy Dogg, an artist

78. Ibid., verse 2.

79. Salt N Pepa, "Negro Wit an Ego," on *Black Magic*, verse 3.

80. Traci C. West, *Wounds of the Spirit: Black Women, Violence, and Resistance Ethics* (New York: New York University Press, 1999) 130.

81. Ibid., 131. Importantly, West acknowledges this is not always true and points to Michael Eric Dyson's *Between God and Gangsta Rap: Bearing Witness to Black Culture* (New York: Oxford University Press, 1996) for further information.

whose use of the word bitch refers, ambiguously to male and female as evident in her quote. Even Michael Dyson consents to this position. He writes, "hip-hop's misogyny is more jolting than the antipathy toward women that came through in some R&B."[82] For a corrective he points to R&B as though the encultured experiences of the Generation can be understood apart from each other. Clearly, the Generation's understandings of women need to be examined.

In the encultured experiences of the Generation, there are two primary sources that speak of women: male artists and female artists. The portrayals of the Generation's misogyny often come from an appraisal of male artists. Many male groups and artists overuse the terms "bitch" and "hoe." In previous generations, these pejoratives spoke only of the female. However, the Generation uses these words to express antipathy towards enemies and weaknesses in both genders. Then, claiming misogyny from the use of these words comes from a lack of critical consideration of the encultured experience of the Generation. Further, male artists such as OutKast and GooDie M.O.B. often use the word "bitch" but advocate for better treatment of women. OutKast's "Jazzy Belle" and GooDie M.O.B.'s "Beautiful Skin" deserve special attention. Notably, these are two songs that were never released as singles. Their impact on the Generation, then, happened outside of the media's eye. In "Jazzy Belle" OutKast raps, "Oh, yes I love her like Egyptian, what a description, her royal highness / so many pluses when I bust this / that there can't be no minus / went from yellin crickets and crows, bitches and hoes to queen things."[83] They continue to discuss the issues they have with women who don't respect themselves. "Havin no mercy for the disrespectful ones/Some be hangin around the crew lookin for funds / Dumb, deaf and fine, they be askin me all about mine / How she doin how she be, I know she's sippin that wine behind my back / They skwaak like vultures / Off and On like Trendz of Cultures baby / Hey, he fakin it like these sculptured nails / But they can go to hell and lay with Lucifer."[84] Big Bo's words display overt disrespect of women who fail to respect themselves. This theme is continued in GooDie M.O.B.'s "Beautiful Skin."

"Beautiful Skin" starts with the words, "This particular song right here / is dedicated to the Black woman / And it doesn't pertain to all

---

82. Dyson, *Between God and Gangsta Rap*, 132.

83. OutKast, "Jazzy Belle," on *ATLiens*, verse 1.

84. Ibid., verse 3.

Black women / because some of y'all disrespect y'allself / because you don't know who you are in the first place / This is out of common respect, for all women period."[85] Over a melodic beat, GooDie M.O.B. pontificates about Black women. They discuss the joys and problems inherent with romantic love in the Generation. Cee-Lo asserts, "our only obligations [are] equality, honesty, independence, intelligence, emotion and devotion."[86] This understanding does not mimic sources outside of the Generation, but shows the Generation's commitment to gender equality. Repeatedly, GooDie M.O.B. sing-songs the words "You're my beginning, my end / You're my sister, lover and friend / God is your light from within / It shines through your beautiful skin / What they say about you ain't true / There's no me if there is no you / I hope that you understand / You've got to respect yourself before I can."[87] This assertion that Black men cannot exist without Black women is powerful in and of itself. When combined with the ways female artists understand themselves, it shows a strong Womanist ethic in the Generation.

In "Negro wit an Ego," Salt N Pepa participate in Womanist theological method. Here, they employ their lived-experience to discuss the ways racism and sexism affect the generation. They rhyme, "All I can talk about is what I know / All I know about is what I witness / What I witness is what I see / Me, way below status quo."[88] They understand their oppression to be caused not just by their race, as the song title implies, but by their gender as well. They relate the normal course of events if they call for emergency help. "When I drop a nine, eleven on my 200-C / the cops are surprise to see / a minority behind the wheel of this car / it must be narcotics / how else could she have got it / a brown-skin female with two problems to correct / wrong color, wrong sex."[89] Though this treatment angers them, they insist on respecting themselves and maintaining their inherent dignity. "I won't settle for that, it's unacceptable / And Salt N Pepa's always very respectable / . . . / I'm proud of who and what I am."[90] The ability to find self-worth in the midst of oppression is at the heart of the Generation's encultured experiences.

85. GooDie M.O.B., "Beautiful Skin," on *Still Standing*, introduction.

86. Ibid., verse 1.

87. Ibid., chorus.

88. Salt N Pepa, "Negro Wit an Ego," verse 1.

89. Ibid., verse 3.

90. Ibid.

### *I Know They Don't Want Me In the Damn Club:*[91] *A Conclusion?*

Black theology's relevance to Baby Boomers and, potentially, Generation X is unquestionable. Those generations, who experienced the degradation of overt institutional racism that permeated this society, readily understand the language and themes of Black theology. However, the Generation knows the formative era of Black theology only through secondhand accounts and history books. James H. Cone writes: "The very existence of Black theology is dependent upon its ability to relate itself to the human situation unique to oppressed persons generally and Black [people] particularly. If Black theology fails to do this adequately, then the Black community will and should destroy it."[92] This work demonstrates Black theologie's failure to be adequately relevant to the Generation as oppressed Black persons. Black theology is not, however, expendable. Its worth and value to the Black community since the 1960s is unprecedented and undeniable. Black theology has a choice; either assume that the Civil Rights and Black Power Movements had no effect whatsoever or acknowledge that the experiences of Black women and men have changed since the 1960s.

This serves as a wake-up call for Black theology to make that choice. As a Black woman born in 1980, the intergenerational compatibility of Black theology is a very personal issue. From constantly being forced to discard and ignore my experience, my culture, my situation when engaging Black theology I experience overwhelming frustration. Further, it is extremely alienating to endure this process in a discipline that proclaims to make primary the experience of people who look like me. As with Womanist reactions to Black liberation theology and feminist theology, I am unable to locate God's liberating work as it relates to my generation anywhere in Black theology. This is, primarily, due to Black theology's lack of critical engagement with and attention to the real-lived and en-cultured experiences of the Generation. If, indeed, God's commitment to liberation is not based on the age of the oppressed, the Generation should inherently be included in Black theology. That it is not is illogical. Black theology needs to become intentional about intergeneration compatibility. Quite simply, Black theology needs to participate in intergen-

---

91. Kanye West, "Never Let Me Down," on *The College Dropout*, verse 2.
92. Cone, *A Black Theology of Liberation*, 36.

erational efforts. That is, Black theology needs to extend its ideological framework to include future generations.

This is not a difficult task. Here, I drew on the Black theological theories and presented a comprehensible Black theology of the Generation. For me, this task required a large amount of historical critique. How much easier it is for Black theologians! Black theologians need only pay critical attention to my generation as emerging adults and scholars. The lyrics examined in this paper represent but a small part of the Generation's encultured experiences. They are the lyrics that have informed me, theologically and as a Black woman in the Generation. The wealth of resources for critical engagement with the Generation is vast. Intergenerational efforts require that Black theologians purposefully enact their experiential methodology and, simply, listen.

From 1979, Black theologians have ignored the Generation. You picked us up to play and put us down so you could think theologically. You hugged and kissed us on the forehead before shoeing us away so that you could engage in your theological banter. You have pretended like we are not real. But we are. And we're here. We are in your classrooms. We buy your books. We attend your lectures. In all of this, we are excitedly expecting to hear a word that is relevant to our real lived-experience. We are consistently disappointed. This paper functions to put Black theologians on notice: the Generation is the future of Black theology. Black theologians must begin to make room for our reality in theological construction. Our experiences need to be reflected in the very essence of Black theology. As a generation of oppressed Black bodies, we should not have to stretch Black theology beyond recognition to derive its meaning for our lives. We struggle for liberation. We seek justice. We are sick and tired of being sick and tired, too. Allow us to perpetuate your legacy. Open the ideological deadbolt on your theological framework that we may enter into dialogue as whole people, bringing all of our experiences with us.

## 22

# Claiming Dinah's Voice

*The Response of a Womanist Ally to the One-Dimensional*
*Advocacy of Black Theology*

D. DARIUS BUTLER

W HAT DOES THE STORY of Dinah in Genesis 34 have in common
with Black women? It is not the story that one would readily use or one that womanist scholars have used historically to speak
about Black women's unique experiences. There does not appear to be
any obvious liberation ethic present in the details for those living under
multi-layers of male-dominance, hoping for a future of equality. Any
critique of the characters or an alternative conclusion would be highly
speculative and would border on eisegesis—God forbid that someone
should read against the "inerrancy" of the biblical writ. All one gets from
the story is violence, silence, and male advocacy. But these are precisely
the reasons why I embark upon this task. As a womanist ally,[1] I shall

1. I am a twenty-four-year-old heterosexual Black male from a Two-Thirds World nation (The Commonwealth of the Bahamas) pursuing a professional degree at Vanderbilt
Divinity School. Raised in poverty by a single-parent mother, I am the last child of five
boys. The voice of mother rings loudly in my consciousness as do the voices of many
other women who contributed to my spiritual formation. Gender hierarchy was present in the Pentecostal church where I was religiously socialized. The only persons who
stood in the pulpit to preach or do anything authoritative were men. Even the church's
secretary (a female) was not extended that courtesy. She made the announcements from
a lectern on the floor. By this time I had women Sunday School teachers, choir directors,
youth group leaders, but had heard of no women preachers.

attempt to provide an in-depth analysis of the multiple issues present in this story—the violence, the silence, and the male advocacy—as they have claimed Dinah's voice and the voices of Black women.

While it is necessary to acknowledge that metaphors, sometimes, do not stand on all four legs, there are sufficient similarities in this biblical account, when juxtaposed to the experiences of Black women, to make the connection. These similarities are used here as explication of the multidimensional reality of oppression Black women face. Although the story, particularly the rape, will be treated metaphorically, I do not trivialize the trauma of rape or any other form of sexual violence perpetrated against women. My work, as a young Black man, does, however, draw from the seriousness of such a reality to speak about the unique experiences of Black women who are, as Kelly Brown Douglas says, "oppressed member[s] of an already oppressed group."[2]

## THE STORY RETOLD

Dinah, daughter of Leah and Jacob, goes out to visit the women of the region. She is seen by Shechem, son of Hamor the Hivite, prince of the region. Shechem takes Dinah forcefully and rapes her. He is "drawn to Dinah" and asks his father to "get [him] this girl to be his wife."[3] Hamor goes to Jacob to negotiate at the same time that Dinah's brothers are coming in from the field. When they hear of what has happened, they are outraged and filled with contempt for Shechem. Hamor's proposal

---

The social arrangements concerning gender become even more pronounced during college. The campus environment of American Baptist College, Nashville, Tennessee, reflected the same culture of its parent-body, the National Baptist Convention U.S.A. Inc. It became obvious through conversation that many male students did not support the legitimacy of their female colleagues, neither of calling or presence. I do admit that my participation in that conversation was complicit with what I thought was expected of me from my male colleagues and I also contributed to making my female colleagues uncomfortable. It was not until my junior year, after hearing a life-altering sermon preached by Forrest E. Harris at the annual session of the convention, that I made a commitment to justice as the vocation of my ministry. This brought me full circle. I am delighted to share that in the fall of 2005 I was able to sponsor a Women's Forum titled, "Claiming Our Voice: A Dialogue about Dinah Genesis 34." That forum served as a wonderful witness for justice and placed the issue of sexism front and center in the ministry of the Black church. From that project came wonderful ideas that support this work.

2. Kelly Brown Douglas, *The Black Christ* (Maryknoll, NY: Orbis, 1994) 92.

3. Genesis 34:4 (NRSV).

of Shechem marrying Dinah and the subsequent intermarriage between the kindred of Jacob and his people is accepted. Jacob's sons answer deceitfully, though, requiring all the men to be circumcised as not to disgrace them. This too is agreed upon and all the men are circumcised. On the third day, when they are still in pain, the sons of Jacob, Simeon and Levi, come upon the city and kill all the males. They take Dinah from Shechem's house, plunder the city, take all the flocks and herds, donkeys, all the wealth, and the people of the land. Jacob does not favor their actions; he speaks harshly to them. But they respond, "Should our sister be treated like a whore?"[4]

### Initial Analysis

On the surface, the story line is simple: Dinah is raped and her brothers get revenge and defend her honor. Having someone to avenge the assault committed against a loved one is the lesson of this story. Isn't it? Perhaps it may have been and it may still be read that way. However, that reading of the story dishonors all involved. It dishonors Shechem and Hamor, for they never did quite right the wrong. It dishonors the survivors of the merciless slayings because they were ruled by those who killed their loved ones. It dishonors Simeon, Levi, and the entire house of Jacob because, in their retaliation, they became just as guilty as Shechem. Sadly, it even dishonors Dinah because it was in her name that these atrocities were "supposedly" committed.

It is upon that very word *supposedly* that this paper turns. It is logical to assume that Dinah's brothers were concerned for her. But were they really? Did they really defend her honor or their own? Who actually benefited from their actions? Certainly it was not Dinah. She was perhaps worse off—emotionally and psychologically—after the retaliation of her brothers than she might have been immediately after the rape. Not only was she a victim of the sexual violence of "male entitlement," but she was also made victim to the insensitive abuse of "male-dominated advocacy," which is just as pernicious.[5]

---

4. Genesis 34:31.
5. Both terms are examined in this work.

## PARALLEL ANALYSIS

Dinah's voice is not heard. PhD candidate Amy Steele, in a sermon on this text, says, "[S]he is silent through the first day, the second day, the third day, and the fourth day. In fact we never hear [a] word from Dinah."[6] Her feelings are not considered, not even in the retelling of the story. One hears from Shechem, "who is entangled by his own sense of himself,"[7] Hamor, the master mediator, Jacob and his sons, who fume with contempt, but not from the victim, Dinah. How is it that the voice of the perpetrator can be claimed while the voice of the victim is suppressed? Why is it that the thoughts and feelings of the advocates/defenders are conveyed, yet Dinah is not afforded the same courtesy? This is where the story of Dinah parallels the experiences of Black women living in America.

Just like Dinah, Black women have been longstanding victims of violence in the most profound sense. Stripped of their virtue and devalued as human beings, they suffered the insane institution of slavery (as did Black men), the immorality of *de facto* segregation, and something else that they never thought would be a problem, but was just as heinous: the sexist attitudes pervading their own African American communities. Not only have they been "raped" by the forceful brutality of the dominant culture—white men and women under the idolatry of white supremacy—but they have also been victims of the insensitivity of Black male advocacy—Black theology—which perpetuated the same exclusion and oppression exacted upon them by the dominant culture. "Everybody in the world was in a position to give [poor Black women] orders," says Dwight N. Hopkins, quoting a passage from Toni Morrison's *The Bluest Eye*.[8] "White women said, 'Do this.' White children said, 'Give me that.' White men said, 'Come here.' Black men said, 'Lay down.' They . . . carried a world on their heads."[9] Suffering under the yokes of racial oppression

---

6. Amy Steele, sermon preached at the Women's Forum, "Claiming Our Voice: Dialogue about Dinah (Genesis 34)," November 18, 2005.

7. Ibid.

8. Toni Morrison, *The Bluest Eye* (New York: Washington Square Press, 1970) 109–10, quoted in Dwight N. Hopkins, *Shoes That Fit Our Feet: Sources for a Constructive Black Theology* (Maryknoll, NY: Orbis, 1993) 52.

9. Ibid.

and gender exploitation, theirs was a reality of "double jeopardy" (being Black and female), says Douglas.[10]

Such oppression was evident even in the 1950s and 1960s civil rights movement. One would not think it to be so, but it was. While women played integral roles in the struggle, they were not recognized for their contributions as were men. The Ella Bakers, Gloria Richardsons, Fannie Lou Hamers, Diane Nashs, Ruby Doris Smiths, and a host of other strong Black women were never celebrated (but their witnesses are claimed in this essay).[11] Jacquelyn Grant assessed this well by saying Black women have always been "invisible" in Black theology.[12] What a shock! They were denied the right to be co-creators of meaning in a theology that would speak of the Black experience in light of God's revelation. As Hopkins surmises in his book, *Introducing Black Theology of Liberation*, Grant's most salient critique is that Black women became both the particular and universal symbol of suffering, for in their experiences were all oppressions combined. She says: "[They] relate to the racial suffering of Black men, the gender discrimination against all women, and the economic exploitation endured by all working-class and poor people. As a result, the tri-dimensional aspect of Black women's oppression not only applies to their particular situation but also covers the experiences of the majority of peoples throughout the globe."[13]

The trauma of rape is bad enough, but to be defended by people who do not care to hear your story is just as bad. This is what Dinah's brothers did to her and what Black theology has done to Black women. While Black theologians came to the defense of the Black community against racism, they did not attend to the other manifestations of oppression—oppression with which they too were complicit. In speaking for this marginalized group they attempted to articulate the full experience of Black people. There was just one thing wrong with that: they could not do that adequately, even though they tried. They purported to

10. Douglas, *The Black Christ*, 89.

11. For further reading on the presence and activity of Black heroines in the Civil Rights Movement, consult Rosetta Ross, *Witnessing and Testifying: Black Women, Religion, and Civil Rights* (Minneapolis: Fortress, 2003).

12. Jacquelyn Grant, "Black Theology and the Black Women," in *Black Theology: A Documentary History, 1966–1979*, ed. James H. Cone and Gayraud S. Wilmore (Maryknoll, NY: Orbis, 1993) 325.

13. Dwight N. Hopkins, *Introducing Black Theology of Liberation* (Maryknoll, NY: Orbis, 1999) 144.

speak *for* Black women without speaking *to* Black women. Thus, Black women's issues were swallowed up into the larger fight: liberation from the hold of racism. Of course one should understand that sacrifices must be made for freedom. Perhaps that is what Black women did: put the issue of sexism on hold while "larger" rights were being demanded. But this logic, if taken seriously, presupposes 1) that the issue of racism, as articulated by Black male theologians, was either the only issue or the most important issue facing Black communities and 2) that the issues of racism and sexism were not and are not interconnected. We know that both presuppositions are wrong.

## CRITIQUE OF THE CHARACTERS

The failure of Dinah's brothers to attend to her story becomes a part of the violence perpetrated against her, just as the failure of Black theologians to acknowledge the interrelation of racism and sexism became a part of the oppression wreaked upon Black communities. It is to this failure that my focus turns. To critique their failure is to critique their methodology, for the two are inextricably linked. Any critique of methodology must first take into account the ideologies that undergird such praxis. In the case of Levi, Simeon, and the house of Jacob, the strong patriarchal character of ancient Southwest Asia is dominant. The story validates what Ramathate T. H. Dolamo, in his critique of Cheryl Exum's feminist interpretation of Hebrew Canon Patriarchy, says of her thesis: "[T]he Bible is an androcentric document arising out of a patriarchal culture. As a result, most of the narratives in the Bible relate men's stories. The stories in which women *do* feature are generally fragmented and told in such a way that they serve only the interests of men and of the patriarchal culture."[14]

Further, the issue of property rights—the personhood of Dinah—as it relates to male entitlement is central. First, it surfaces in Shechem who is emboldened to take Dinah by force. This parallels the dominant culture's perceived "right" to deal with Black people in dehumanizing ways. Second, it surfaces in the house of Jacob as they respond to the rape without care for the victim. This parallels Black theologians' critique of

14. Ramathate T. H. Dolamo, "A Critical Review of Cheryl Exum's *Feminist Interpretation of Hebrew Canon Patriarchy*," in *Global Voices for Gender Justice*, ed. Ramathate T. H. Dolamo, Ana Maria Tededino, and Dwight N. Hopkins (Cleveland: Pilgrim, 2001) 153.

white theology without employing the critical self-test of examining how Black theology itself treats African American women. Third, it surfaces in the actual retelling of the story from the male perspective, which is essentially what Black theology did.

The same issue of patriarchy is prevalent in Black theology. James H. Cone acknowledges that "the distinctive contribution of Black women was not a part of [his] theological consciousness" when he embarked on "the task of developing a Black theology of liberation during the summer of 1968."[15] Cone, like others, "had been socialized into a sexist society," says Douglas.[16] They had come to see the world through lenses that did not take women seriously. She refers to their inability to move beyond their maleness to consider Black women's lives as a "one-dimensional understanding," particularly where Christ was concerned.[17] Her theory exposes the other thoughts that Black theologians have used, mostly unconsciously, to justify the invisibility of Black women in Black theology. The notions of gender hierarchy and the norm of male superiority and female inferiority immediately come to mind. These erroneous ideas have been constructed, by men, from flawed interpretations of the biblical text. Genesis 34 gives some precedence. The ordering of gender roles, as the story is recounted, gives men the *right* to speak for women and portrays them as the only ones capable of discussing important matters, even when those matters involve the specific interests of women. Grant's thought on the invisibility of Black women in Black theology addresses this issue. Essentially, she says the incorrect assumptions that "either Black women have no place in the enterprise, or [that] Black men are capable of speaking for [Black women] . . . arise out of male-dominated culture which restricts women to certain areas of the society."[18] However, such restrictions do not support the ethic of liberation to which Black theology claims to be true. Somehow, while being preoccupied with race relations, Black men adopted the language of white oppressors when talking about the "place of women."[19] How could this have happened? Why did Black theologians marginalize Black women? Why did Black

15. James H. Cone, introduction to "Black Theology and Black Women," in *Black Theology: A Documentary History, 1966–1979,* 279.

16. Douglas, *The Black Christ,* 91.

17. Ibid., 92.

18. Grant, "Black Theology and the Black Women," 325.

19. Ibid., 326.

women allow their voices to be muffled for so long? The most obvious reasons seem to be that Black men were denied manhood and that Black women were self-sacrificing. But to leave it at that would excuse Black men and would say nothing of their responsibility to respond faithfully even to an unfaithful situation.

The dominant ethos of Black theology, in its infancy, appeared to be a preoccupation with the recovery of manhood. This was veiled in the quest for liberation of the entire Black community. Cone admits that Black theologians spoke of the Black experience as if it were exclusively a male experience.[20] Nowhere was this more pronounced than in the Statement by the National Committee of Black Churchmen (June 13, 1969). As they articulated the tenets of Black theology, they quoted Eldrige Cleaver's, "We shall have our manhood," as the summation of their quest.[21] The historical response that the word *manhood* is used generically would hold up except they were explicit when they said they "[did] this as men."[22] Further, it is difficult to validate that claim when the spirit of sexism pervaded that culture. Again, it reflects the far-reaching effects of male privilege.

As for the women, they did not draw attention to their unique experience. Perhaps it was the trauma of the actual experience itself that silenced them. A female student colleague of mine at Vanderbilt Divinity School spoke to this as she recounted the horrific experience of being sexually violated at the hands of someone she knew personally. Her voice was literally gone in the initial stage after the rape. She could not articulate her pain vocally. When she returned home, her mother fussed at her for being late but she could not respond at all. It was not until a few days later that she was able to tell what had happened to her, but then she had to deal with the "credibility factor."[23] This complicates the problem and perhaps discourages many women from coming forward with what has happened to them.

The pain of diminished personhood as suffered by Black women at the hands of the dominant culture was magnified by the brokenness of spirit they suffered at the hands of Black men; thus they recoiled. But one

20. Cone, *Black Theology: A Documentary History, 1966–1979,* 279.

21. "Statement by the National Committee of Black Churchmen, June 13, 1969," in ibid., 39.

22. Ibid.

23. She refers to this with the question: Will they believe me?

thing is certain; they are not to blame for what happened to them—not Dinah, not Black women, not any other person who has been made a victim of violence because of gender.

## CONSTRUCTING ALTERNATIVE WITNESSES

While the deafening silence of this story offers much to critique, surprisingly, it gives more liberty to construct a new model that will "create a narrative for the present and the future."[24] This new model must be the product of Black theologians co-laboring with womanist theologians to use the experiences of Black women as the context for doing theology. As not to privilege men or suggest that this new ideal should begin with them, challenges shall be made to Black women first.

With the Black church as its anchor, womanist theologians must keep the issue of sexism ever on the altar of religious life and public discourse.[25] Never should this problem go unchecked. Black women must muster the courage to name the sin that keeps them bound. Male-dominance should not be dismissed as the norm but must be called what it really is: "demonarchy."[26] Black women must call their oppressors to account. Critical engagement with the biblical text must become a priority for them if the demonic properties of patriarchy are to be exorcised from the ranks of the Black church.

Just as Black women have constructed "survival strategies"[27] to stem the tide of total self-sacrifice, they must continue to "live out a moral wisdom in their real-lived context."[28] Keri Day would call this "making incarnational demonstrations"[29] of their commitment to justice. Hopkins'

---

24. Linda E. Thomas, "Womanist Theology, Epistemology, and a New Anthropological Paradigm," *CrossCurrents* 48 (Winter/Spring 1998–99) 492, quoted in Hopkins, *Introducing Black Theology of Liberation*, 135–36.

25. emilie m. townes, ed., *A Troubling in My Soul: Womanist Perspectives on Evil and Suffering* (Maryknoll, NY: Orbis, 1993) 2, quoted in Hopkins, *Introducing Black Theology of Liberation*, 136.

26. Delores Williams, "The Color of Feminism: Or Speaking the Black Woman's Tongue," *Journal of Religious Thought* 43 (1986) 52, quoted in Stephanie Y. Mitchem, *Introducing Womanist Theology* (Maryknoll, NY: Orbis, 2002) 4.

27. Katie G. Cannon, *Womanism and the Soul of the Black Community* (New York: Continuum, 1995) 25.

28. Cannon, *Black Womanist Ethics*, American Academy of Religion Academy Series 60 (Atlanta: Scholars, 1988) 4.

29. Keri Day shared this in a class discussion on October 3, 2005.

reference to Grant's 1979 article, which says, "Womanists have asserted boldly their presence and their right to think theologically from [their own] perspectives,"[30] best illustrates the point. The right to participate in religious discourse must not be something that is given to Black women from Black theologians. Black women must claim it for themselves, knowing that they are equally capable of articulating Black struggle with the same pathos as their male counterparts. This is the task of womanist theology. In addition, Black women must challenge the biblical authority of a male-dominated clergy, demanding that it moves in a direction more proportionate to the demographics of the overall membership. As Hopkins' assessment of Renita Weem's work, *Just a Sister Away: A Womanist Vision of Women's Relationships in the Bible,* notes, they must "look beneath the obvious in the Bible to discover a place for women . . . in God's new community for humanity."[31]

In *For My People: Black Theology and the Black Church,* James H. Cone sets Black theologians in the right direction when he says, "it is important that [they] learn to listen to women tell their stories of pain and struggle."[32] At the least, Black theologians owe Black women an ear to listen, not mouths that try to tell their stories. Hopefully, this listening would lead to a conversation so that a "full theology" can emerge for the Black community.[33]

More pointedly, Black theologians must renounce the privilege of patriarchy that they have enjoyed and still enjoy, to some extent. They, too, must assess it for what it is worth and denounce it as a hegemonic structure that subjugates and oppresses. With the same "progressive and prophetic pole"[34] that they used to address the issue of racism, it must turn now to employ the self-test regarding sexism, determining whether they too have become corrupt. This is not an easy exercise.

---

30. Hopkins, *Introducing Black Theology of Liberation,* 88.

31. Ibid., 140–41.

32. James H. Cone, ed., *For My People: Black Theology and Black Church* (Maryknoll, NY: Orbis, 1984) 137.

33. Linda E. Thomas, "Womanist Theology, Epistemology, and a New Anthropological Paradigm," in *Living Stones in the Household of God,* ed. Linda E. Thomas (Minneapolis: Fortress, 2004) 38.

34. Cornel West, "The Black Church and Socialist Politics," in *Prophetic Fragments* (Grand Rapids: Eerdmans, 1988) 67, quoted in Kelly Brown Douglas, *The Black Christ* (Maryknoll, NY: Orbis, 1994) 3.

The ethic of giving up one's privilege so that another can be included, as evidenced in the ministry of Jesus, must become a governing principle for male clergy. The students of American Baptist College (Nashville, Tennessee) know this ethic well. In October 2005 during Religious College Day in Columbus, Georgia, the (male) preachers made a conscientious decision not to accept any courtesy that was extended to them and not extended to their female colleagues, who were there in support. The culture of this region does not support female clergy and does not grant them the same ministerial rights as men. Instead of sitting in the front pews at the evening rally service, as is the custom, the male preachers sat on the third and fourth pews with the women. This was an authentic protest by both the male and female students.

In light of the critique that womanist theologians have made regarding the various forms of oppression that plague Black people (i.e., racism, sexism, homophobia, heterosexism, and classism), Black theology must retool if it is to remain on the vanguard for the Black community, calling for justice and liberation. It must follow the lead of Black women and come out from the refuge of the academy to become more practically oriented. It must not attempt to articulate the struggles of the entire community; it must create the space where the grace of God empowers the members of that community to name their own experiences.

Imagine how the story of Dinah could have ended had the men listened to the voice of the victim. Perhaps she would have stayed with Shechem, though that would be hard to imagine. Maybe she did want to be avenged. Whatever it was that she wanted, we will never know because the men did not give her any options. This should no longer be the witness of Black men concerning Black women.

When will our world realize the gifts of God in Black women? When will Black men really cherish, celebrate, and honor the ability of Black women who keep their families and their communities together even through adversities? I do not know if I will see a substantial change in my lifetime, but I am committed to doing my part. I have hope that this issue will not go without an advocate. For my mother, Suzanne Marie Butler, who prays for me, and all the other women who, in my life, embody the love of Christ, I am committed.

# 23

# Black Environmental Liberation Theology

DIANNE D. GLAVE

We, African-American Church leaders, historically committed to justice issues, affirm the unitary nature of life and commit ourselves to the ministry of converging justice and environmental issues that are critical matters of life and death for our Church and for our community."

—"National Black Church Environmental and Economic Justice Summit," 1993

A new generation of Rosa Parks and Martin Luther Kings, Jrs. are meeting in churches to pray and plan and then heading out to work for the health of their communities."

—"African American Denominational Leaders Pledge Their Support to the Struggle Against Environmental Racism," *AME Christian Recorder,* 1998

IN THE UNITED STATES, the government and corporations have long targeted people of color and the poor—including African Americans—by dumping toxins and garbage into marginalized neighborhoods. Some African Americans who are working to remedy these injustices to the African American community have applied a Christian framework to their activism. This model of Christian self-empowerment for environmental justice owes much to Martin Luther King Jr. In 1955, King transformed Rosa Parks's refusal to sit in the back of the bus into a church-based movement igniting the mid-twentieth-century civil rights movement. Throughout his ministry of nonviolent activism, King defined social justice through a biblical lens, agitating for civil rights, condemning the Vietnam War, and, in his final act before he was assassinated, advocating for sanitation workers. His historical and theological legacy has endured and is now a cornerstone of environmental justice. This article introduces a working model for a Black environmental liberation theology (BELT), a strand of Black liberation theology; describes the recent history of environmental justice by the African American church and Christian organizations; and proposes an environmental justice agenda for change based on this theology and history.

Members of the African American church and Christian grassroots organizations launched the environmental justice movement out of a confluence of religious beliefs and civil rights social thought and action. In 1970, James H. Cone articulated and formalized a Black liberation theology or a biblical interpretation of civil rights activism by the African American church through a scholarly lens. Black liberation theology, which decries the oppression of African Americans based on biblical principles—is the foundation of BELT, a nascent theology based on environmental justice history and activism by African American Christians. Like Black liberation theology, BELT is both a theology and an ideology that is actualized by shielding contemporary African Americans exposed to toxins and pollution from landfills, garbage dumps, auto mechanics' shops, and sewage plants.[1]

## THEOLOGY, CIVIL RIGHTS, AND BLACK LIBERATION

How can the language of environmental racism, justice, and liberation theology begin to define BELT? Environmental justice scholars, including Robert Bullard, have documented that some in the public and private sectors have deliberately or passively threatened the lives of Native Americans, African Americans, and Latinos through social, economic, and political policies in the form of environmental racism—the inequitable exposure of people of color to air, water, and noise pollution on a scale sufficient to trigger birth defects, miscarriages, stillbirths, cancer,

1. For the foundations of Black liberation theology, see Cone, *A Black Theology of Liberation* (Philadelphia: Lippincott, 1970); Dwight N. Hopkins, *Introducing Black Liberation of Theology* (Maryknoll, NY: Orbis, 1999) 41. George C. L. Cummings, *Common Journey: Black Theology (USA) and Latin American Liberation Theology* (Maryknoll, NY: Orbis, 1993), suggests that Black liberation theology and Latin American liberation theology emerged discretely and simultaneously in the late 1960s.

and stress-related illnesses documented since the 1980s. Environmental justice seeks to eliminate such racism by demanding the equitable treatment for people of color and the poor through government policy, legislation, regulation, and law enforcement. Environmental justice activists have employed many strategies, including lobbying, legislation, law enforcement, and protest, which were modeled upon civil rights initiatives to counter environmental racism.

The language of theology is a means of combating environmental racism. Black liberation theology is based on scriptures, especially from the New Testament, that hold the promise of environmental equity and justice for African Americans. Galatians 3:28 is one such scripture of equity: "There is neither Jew nor Greek, there is neither slave nor free, there is neither male nor female; for you are all one in Christ Jesus." Psalm 82:3–4 advocates justice for the oppressed: "Defend the poor and fatherless; Do justice to the afflicted and needy. Deliver the poor and needy; Free them from the hand of the wicked." In Luke 10:25–37, Jesus tells the Good Samaritan parable, modeling diversity and social justice. A Jewish man was waylaid and beaten by thieves as he traveled from Jerusalem to Jericho. Two Jewish religious leaders passed without assisting the beaten man. Although Samaritans were excluded from Jewish society, a passing Samaritan stopped to bandage the traveler's wounds, then took him to an inn, cared for him, and left money for his expenses. The parable models caretaking and righting injustice. In this same manner, the modern African American church has sought justice for the African American community who are inequitably exposed to water, air, and noise pollution.[2]

According to Cone in *A Black Theology of Liberation* (1970), Black liberation theology commissioned the African American church to continue to eliminate oppression against African Americans after the civil rights movement. Cone expanded his theological interpretation of Black liberation theology to include environmentalism in his article "Whose Earth Is It Anyway?" in which he argued that mainstream theologians "often include a token black or Indian in anthologies on ecotheology, ecojustice, and ecofeminism . . . But people of color are not treated *seriously*, that is, as if they have something *essential* to contribute to the conversation. Environmental justice concerns of poor people of color hardly

---

2. All biblical quotations in this chapter are from the New King James Version (NKJV).

ever merit serious attention, not to mention organized resistance."[3] At the 1993 National Black Church Environmental and Economic Justice Summit, Reverend Eugene F. Rivers III, the cofounder of the Azusa Christian Community, concurred: "And what we've done in connecting the issue of environmental justice and racism is we've drawn the connection between environmental racism as an expression of white supremacy."[4]

Resistance was not new to African Americans, typical of civil rights activism of the early twentieth century. For example, during the 1917 New York City Silent Protest Parade, approximately ten thousand African Americans marched peacefully with banners against racism. Founded upon this early twentieth-century history, African Americans and their supporters of the 1950s and 1960s organized boycotts, marches, freedom rides, sit-ins, and protests, which shamed the United States government and citizens who harbored racism. As a result of the scrutiny and, more importantly, the dedication of civil rights leaders and volunteers, this activism culminated with the Civil Rights Act of 1964, which legally banned discrimination in public places, and the Voting Rights Act of 1965, which authorized federal employees to register African Americans to vote and suspended discriminatory literacy tests and poll taxes.

Against this backdrop, African American ministers and civil rights activists were catalysts for social change, leading peaceful demonstrations and ultimately influencing a theology much like environmental activists of the African American church and Christian grassroots organizations. Dwight N. Hopkins says that Christian leaders of the civil rights era "religiously told white officials to stick to Christian love and nonviolence . . . preached funerals for nonviolent civil rights workers. And they experienced the pain of having their churches dynamited in the early morning hours."[5] As president of the Southern Christian Leadership Conference (SCLC), a civil rights protest organization led by African American ministers, Martin Luther King helped to define civil rights activism by knitting together social justice and a theology. In his

3. Cone, "Whose Earth Is It Anyway?" in *Risks of Faith: The Emergence of a Black Theology of Liberation, 1968–1998* (Boston: Beacon, 1999) 138–45.

4. "National Black Church Environmental and Economic Justice Summit," National Council of Churches of Christ in the USA, Prophetic Justice Unit, Washington DC, December 1–2, 1993, 51.

5. Hopkins, *Introducing Black Theology of Liberation*, 4.

"Letter from a Birmingham Jail," written to his fellow clergy in 1963, he said: "Just as the prophets of the eighth century B.C. left their villages and carried their 'thus saith the Lord' far beyond the boundaries of their home towns, and just as the Apostle Paul left his village of Tarsus and carried the gospel of Jesus Christ to the far corners of the Greco-Roman world, so am I compelled to carry the gospel of freedom beyond my own home town."[6]

## ENVIRONMENTAL RACISM, ENVIRONMENTAL JUSTICE

Environmental racism by whites has biblical, historical, and contemporary origins. Some Christians have ignored or distorted biblical directives, instead emphasizing the authority granted by God to rule the earth. In the book of Genesis, Adam and Eve named the flora and fauna based on a covenant of stewardship in which God gave humankind control of nature. In return, Adam and Eve cared for the land, plants, and animals. Unfortunately, something went awry in the interpretation of this portion of scripture by some Christians. Lynn White Jr. argues that Christians embraced dominion of nature, ignoring their caretaking responsibilities in this covenant with God: "No new set of basic values has been accepted in our society to displace those of Christianity. Hence we shall continue to have a worsening ecologic crisis until we reject the Christian axiom that nature has no reason for existence save to serve man."[7] Biblical dominion, though subverted, remains the foundation of modern interactions of people with nature in Christian and even secular circles in the United States.[8]

Christian or not, this biblical interpretation of self-entitlement toward nature has seeped into contemporary environmentalism, often rejecting the rights of grassroots activism organized by and for lower-income groups and people of color to ensure a safe environment. Cone wrote: "Blacks and other minorities are often asked why they are not

6. Martin Luther King Jr., "Letter from a Birmingham Jail," April 16, 1963. Online: http://www.stanford.edu/group/King/frequentdocs/birmingham.pdf.

7. Lynn White Jr., "The Historical Roots of Our Ecological Crisis," *Science* (March 10, 1967) 1287.

8. For Western interpretations of biblical dominion, see Mark Stoll, *Protestantism, Capitalism, and Nature in America* (Albuquerque, NM: University of New Mexico Press, 1997) ix, 6–7; Roderick Nash, *Rights of Nature: A History of Environmental Ethics* (Madison: University of Wisconsin Press, 1989) 88.

involved in the mainstream ecological movement. To white theologians and ethicists, I ask, why are you not involved in the dialogue on race?"[9] Mainstream activists, much like the Christians described by White, focus on conserving resources and preserving wildlife, often ignoring the concerns and role of people of color including African Americans. They rely on tokenism to diversify their staff; they are, as Robert Gottlieb has stated, "caught up in the terrain and action that placed their groups apart from the new kinds of environmental politics being influenced by ethnicity, gender, and class factors."[10]

Another aspect of BELT—a strand of Black liberation theology—is the history of environmental justice by the African American church and Christian organizations. Church environmental justice activists, part of the long history of civil rights in the African American community and an underpinning of BELT, struggled to reverse twentieth-century environmental racism. Bullard, in *Unequal Protection: Environmental Justice and Communities of Color* (1994), refers briefly to King's role in the 1968 sanitation workers' strike, in Memphis, Tennessee, which precursored late twentieth- and twenty-first-century environmental justice activism.[11] This strike deserves a closer look. On February 12, 1968, the Memphis sanitation workers went on strike to improve wages, hours, and vacations, with an unhealthy work environment as a subtext. Sanitation workers handling the city's trash were exposed to hospital waste and rotting food, which drew rodents, roaches, and birds, creating a petri dish for rashes and disease. In the words of Leroy Bonner, a sanitation worker: "[One time there were] two maggots right around my navel. I took a bath and they stretched out and they fell off in the tub. And my wife said, 'Lord have mercy, Leroy, wait a minute and let me run that water out' . . . She ran it out and she came in and washed my head and everything, and [she] was pulling them out of my head. You see, that was summertime. I said, 'Well, I can't help it . . . We got to try to make it.'"[12] Bonner's exposure to rotting trash and maggots signified how race and

---

9. Cone, "Whose Earth Is It Anyway?"

10. Gottlieb, *Forcing the Spring: The Transformation of the American Environmental Movement*, rev. ed. (Washington, DC: Island, 2005) 262.

11. Robert D. Bullard, *Unequal Protection: Environmental Justice and Communities of Color* (San Francisco: Sierra Club Books, 1994) 3–4.

12. Leroy Bonner, quoted in Cornell Christion, "The Memphis Sanitation Strike: Blood and Strife Brought Dignity for City Workers," *Commercial Memphis*, February 28, 1993. Online: http://comercialappeal.com.

poverty defined the status and treatment of African Americans in the 1960s. As a poor African American man who had limited choices for employment, his work environment was a hostile place.

African American ministers, local leaders, and church members joined sanitation workers like Bonner who organized a citywide strike and boycott on February 24. A day later, the ministers urged their congregations to support the sanitation boycott and march on behalf of the workers. Throughout March, Memphis mayor Henry Loeb met with the ministers, who continued to lead marches, while their congregations raised money by holding a gospel music marathon. The strike drew national attention when King led a rally on March 18. Later, on April 3, King spoke at the Mason Temple in Memphis, Tennessee, supporting the sanitation workers in his famous speech "I've Been to the Mountaintop," a template for the justice of Black liberation theology and BELT:

> There are thirteen hundred of God's children here suffering, sometimes going hungry, going through dark and dreary nights wondering how this thing is going to come out . . . It's all right to talk about streets flowing with milk and honey, but God has commanded us to be concerned about the slums down here and his children who can't eat three square meals a day. It's all right to talk about the new Jerusalem, but one day God's preacher must talk about the new New York, the new Atlanta, the new Philadelphia, the new Los Angeles, the new Memphis, Tennessee.[13]

King's vision for improving the living conditions of poor African Americans was inherently environmental. He addressed the complexities of wages, safety, and health and gave the plight of sanitation workers context, mindful of the environmental problems in the inner city during the civil rights era. King's speech also evoked something broader—"a moral geography of social and political progress"—and constituted an implicit environmental manifesto decrying and dismantling everything from slavery to segregation set against nature.[14]

After the 1960s, Benjamin F. Chavis Jr., a one-time reverend and the president of the National Association for the Advancement of Colored People (NAACP), advocated for African Americans in a way that was

13. King, "I've Been to the Mountaintop," April 3, 1968. Online: http://www.stanford.edu/group/King/publications/speeches/I've_been_to_the_mountaintop.pdf.

14. Melvin Dixon, *Ride Out the Wilderness: Geography and Identity in Afro-American Literature* (Urbana: University of Illinois Press, 1987) 1.

critical to environmental justice as a national movement. At the 1993 National Black Church Environmental and Economic Summit, he described in biblical language—responsibility, creation, and sin—the foundation of BELT as he described an implicit and explicit culpability of whites and African Americans respectively concerning the environment: "The fact that we [African Americans] are disproportionately dumped on is just consistent with being in America . . . And the demand that God puts on us is that we will face up to the contemporary responsibility that God has given us to not let God's creation be destroyed by sin . . . Environmental injustice is sin before God."[15]

Chavis's previous historical and activist role in Warren County, North Carolina, had been one of the modern catalysts of the national environmental justice movement. In 1978, liquid tank drivers hired by the Ward Transformer Company secretly poured toxic manmade polychlorinated biphenyls (PCBs) along roads across thirteen North Carolina counties. In an attempt to dispose of the tainted soil, the state of North Carolina constructed a landfill in Warren County, which was predominantly African American. In 1984, Christian African American leaders like Chavis joined Warren County citizens to demonstrate against the government's attempt to collect and then dump the soil in the county. Other church leaders, including Reverend Joseph Lowery of the Southern Christian Leadership Conference and Walter Fauntroy, a Progressive National Baptist minister, united with locals to peacefully protest the dumping. The protesters were concerned about the correlation of PCBs with various illnesses including skin disorders, reproductive problems, liver disease, and cancer. African American women mixed prayer and supplication with activism in a rural Baptist church, an underpinning of BELT. As it was later described, these women "got on their knees and prayed to God to give them the strength to lay down in the street in front of those trucks . . . But thank goodness these women said, 'You're not going to dump in my church, you're not going to dump in my community.' And out of that vigilance, out of that resistance, it helped energize a movement that was building in many different places; God helped put it right; it wasn't just the black community."[16] Though these women were arrested, along with other protesters, they succeeded in igniting the national environmental justice movement.

15. "National Black Church Environmental and Economic Justice Summit," 14.
16. Ibid., 15.

The Commission for Racial Justice of the United Church of Christ (UCC) also sought social justice for African Americans—later including other people of color—by picketing with the Student Nonviolent Coordinating Committee during the civil rights era and participating in the 1972 National Black Political Convention in Gary, Indiana. The commission continued its commitment to justice and environmental justice, through their landmark study *Toxic Wastes and Race in the United States: A National Report on the Racial and Socio-Economic Characteristics of Communities with Hazardous Waste Sites* (1987). Chavis said of the UCC's decision to produce this publication: "We believe that the time has come for all church and civil rights organizations to take the issues seriously. We realized that the involvement in this type of research is a departure from our traditional protest methodology. However, if we are to advance our struggle in the future, it will depend largely on the availability of timely and reliable information."[17] This report by a Protestant organization remains a critical source for studying and further developing the environmental justice movement. Later in 1994, the UCC also responded when the Shintech Company planned—but never succeeded—to construct a polyvinyl chloride (PVC) manufacturing plant in Convent, Louisiana.

The activism of local grassroots organizations against environmental racism defines BELT. In 1977, the Reichold Chemical Company located in Columbia, Mississippi, was accused of exposing two hundred cattle to dioxins and exploding Agent Orange, a defoliant herbicide and dioxin. In addition, the company allegedly poured chemicals downstream into Jingling Creek, past a recreational facility and high school frequented by African Americans. Four floods also exposed toxins that Reichold had buried off-site at what is now a Superfund site. In 1992, the Jesus People Against Pollution (JPAP) established a grassroots environmental justice organization, responding to years of toxic dumping by Reichold. JPAP exposed Reichold's disregard for the community and the resulting health problems and increased mortality among African Americans.

During the 1990s, Helping Other People Emerge (HOPE), established by Reverend Buck Jones in East St. Louis, drew upon environmental activism and Christian faith, to battle local problems. Residents

17. Commission for Racial Justice, United Church of Christ, *Toxic Wastes and Race in the United States* (1987) x; online: http://www.ucc.org/about-us/archives/pdfs/toxwrace87.pdf.

approached HOPE because they were being shaken out of bed at 3 a.m., having their windows and dishes broken, and finding the foundations of their homes cracked. This damage was caused by a company that was shredding cars, including contaminated vehicles, and their gasoline tanks, creating explosions. According to Jones, "We marched, we prayed, we threatened to file a lawsuit, we blocked the entranceway to the plant, and we won. They (the shredder company) hired residents to check and inspect the cars; in addition, they also gave a cash settlement." He organized projects reducing lead poisoning among children, cleaning up of Dead Creek, and a rallying against Onyx Environmental Services, which planned to incinerate neutralized nerve gas for the United States Army at the expense of local African Americans.[18] Before Jones's death, he organized toxic tours of East St. Louis, exposing toxic hotspots and the role of the government and corporations in environmental racism in East St. Louis.[19]

Jones based his final initiatives upon the efforts of the National Council of Churches (NCC), which consolidated grassroots into a national effort in December 1993. Leaders of the major African American churches, including the African Methodist Episcopal, African Methodist Episcopal Zion, National Baptist Convention, USA, national Baptist Convention of America, Progressive National Baptist Convention, and the Church of God in Christ met for two days at the National Black Church Environmental and Economic Justice Summit in Washington DC. The attendees emphasized quality of life and health in the African American community, focusing on pollution and dumping rather than the mainstream interests of eliminating global ozone depletion and protecting endangered species. Reverend Franklyn Richardson, the general secretary of the National Baptist Convention, USA, presented the NCC report, containing six specific demands, to Vice President Al Gore. These demands included a presidential executive order on environmental justice and regulation of corporations, the identification of a church representative for the Sustainable Communities Task Force of the President's council on Sustainable Development, and the involvement of local

18. Buck Jones, quoted in Martha Kendrick Cobb, "The Legacy of a Trio of Justice Seekers," in *Witness for Justice*, May 20, 2002. Online: http://www.ucc.org/justice/witness/wfj052002.htm.

19. "'Toxic Tour' Marks 15th Anniversary," *United Church News*, June 2002. Online: http://www.ucc.org/ucnews/jun02/toxic.htm.

churches in key environmental decisions by the government.[20] These items suggested ways African Americans could influence government policy from a Christian perspective.

As a result of the NCC Summit, on March 13 and 14, 1998, approximately twelve African American church leaders toured toxic sites in Louisiana communities, including Convent, Oakville, and new Sarpy/Norco. The NCC Eco-Justice Working Group and Black Church Liaison Committee and the United States Conference of World Council of Churches sponsored the tours. The leaders traveled around communities polluted by PVC, a toxic dump, and "fumes, explosions, and fires" from twenty-seven oil refineries. They scheduled a meeting with Gore, which was ultimately canceled, to plead the case of the Louisiana communities.[21]

## AGENDA FOR ACTION

An agenda for action for environmental justice by the African American church is based on this theology and history of BELT. Dorceta Taylor outlines three options for environmental justice nonprofits: (a) join established mainstream organizations; (b) create their own organizations, rejecting any collaboration or coalitions with the mainstream; or (c) start new organizations, using the resources available from mainstream organizations.[22] Based on Taylor's recommendations, biblical mandates, and the realities of environmental racism, the third option best suits the African American church and the community. African Americans in the church are called to operate and serve in a multicultural world that includes whites. In addition, African Americans are not isolated and are part of a community that includes whites—some of whom are racist—that wield great economic, social, and political power. The African American church must be practical while resolving environmental racism, even when biblical beliefs including unconditional love and the realities of mainstream racism collide.

20. "National Black Church Environmental and Economic Justice Summit," 3.

21. "African American Denominational Leaders Pledge Their Support against Environmental Racism," *AME Christian Recorder*, May 18, 1998, 11.

22. Dorceta Taylor, "Can the Environmental Movement Attract and Maintain the Support of Minorities," in *Race and the Incidence of Environmental Hazards: A Time of Discourse*, ed. Bunyan Bryant and Paul Mohai (Boulder, CO: Westview, 1992) 28–54.

The following fifteen-point environmental justice agenda for action is based on a theology and history of social and environmental justice, grassroots activism, spirituality, and organization in the African American church:

1. Establish goals of self-sufficiency and autonomy in the African American community to eradicate environmental racism, applying the language, along with the theological and historical framework of BELT;

2. Teach the interrelated history of the African American church, civil rights, and environmental justice to the African American community as a foundation for meeting these goals;

3. Co-opt organizational, strategic planning, and management tools from mainstream or white environmentalists, including networking, tailoring them to the needs of the African American church and community;

4. Reverse the political apathy in the African community by modeling and combining historical civil rights activism—sit-ins and marches—with modern twenty-first-century lobbying, legislation, and law enforcement;

5. Focus narrowly on critical environmental problems, at least temporarily, that have threatened and diminished the health and longevity of African Americans, including solid waste management, incineration, pollution, and toxins, avoiding—for now—a drift toward the mainstream issues of wilderness and conservation, even if coalition-building remains limited among ethnic groups with conflicting agendas;

6. Create coalitions with other ethnic churches, including Native Americans and Latinos, without losing autonomy—in turn against power through increased numbers;

7. Acknowledge that coalitions with mainstream and other ethnic organizations are short- to midterm tools that ebb and flow depending on the needs of the African American church and the community, and on existing relationships with other ethnic groups;

8. Model and teach selfless Christian service for environmental justice in the African American community, as described in Galatians 5:13: "For you, brethren, have been called to liberty; only do not use

liberty as an opportunity for the flesh, but through love serve one
another";

9. Limit the role of mainstream environmentalists until they develop
a more holistic and equitable understanding of environmentalism
pertinent to the African American community;

10. Discard the historical model in which the African American
church relies on one or two charismatic religious leaders like King
to maintain a cohesive movement; instead train many new leaders
to develop management, coalition building, facilitation, and collaborative skills for environmental justice;

11. Organize church and community members, mixing traditional and
modern activism, including fliers, telephones, letters, e-mails, cel-
lular phones, and the Internet; and

12. Develop the growing national movement further, always remembering the importance of the first grassroots initiative, the foundation of environmental justice activism.

This agenda is the next step that can transform BELT, the genesis of
which was in Black liberation theology and a history of devil right activism by African Americans, into a theology that incorporates twenty-
first-century action.

Since the end of slavery, the vision for racial equality has been deferred in the United States. In 1865, Alexander Crummell, an African
American theologian, said, "The trials and suffering of this race have
been great for centuries. They have not yet ceased. They are not likely to
cease for along time. It may take two to three generations for the race to
get a firm and assured status in the land."[23] Crummell would be alarmed
at the tenuous standing of third-generation African Americans undermined by environmental racism in the twenty-first century. In response
to African Americans being inequitably exposed to toxic chemicals and
waste, the church is called to further expand grassroots and national
reform looking to BELT—justice, grassroots activism, spirituality, and
organization—based on the Bible. Combined, the history and theology
can be a "spearhead for reform" for African Americans embattled by environmental racism in the future.[24]

23. Alexander Crummell, "Incidents of Hope for the Negro Race in America: A
Thanksgiving Sermon, November 26 th, 1895." Online: http://memory.loc.gov.

24. Allen F. Davis, *Spearheads for Reform: The Social Settlements and the Progressive*

# PART SEVEN

# Global Future

# Anthropology, Mission, and the African Woman

LINDA E. THOMAS

I COME TO THE task of understanding and analyzing mission from a hermeneutic of plurality.[1] I work from my many contexts, and thus, I consider myself a multi-disciplined scholar. I approach this project first from my social location.

I work as a Black woman but with the juxtaposition of being an African American *Christian* woman, ordained in the United Methodist Church. I am called to the *missio Dei*, to evangelize, to witness to Christ's presence. I work necessarily from a place of tension and complexity: a hermeneutic of plurality.

Adding right on to our list, I approach the work as an African American Ordained Christian Theologian in the Womanist tradition. Enough said . . . almost. I am also an anthropologist.

In this paper, I use an ethnographic methodology to examine what second, third, fourth, and fifth generation African Christians have to say about mission on their continent. *Missio Dei* so often comes from what we know as the "Great Commission" (Matthew 28:16–20)—words, by the way, that do not appear in the passage itself. The Commission, as interpreted in the West, commands Christians to go all over the world telling people about their God and teaching western ways.

This approach to entering a new community, culture, or religion does not work with my approach to anthropology and mission. Rather, the method I use, both for understanding *missio Dei* and conducting re-

1. I want to express my thanks to my research assistant, Jamie Jazdzyk, for conceptualizing the notion of "plural" in our conversations about this lecture.

search, better fits with Luke's version of *missio Dei* (Luke 9:1–9; 10:1–10). Here, Jesus sends the disciples out not with an agenda of telling about Jesus. No, he sends his disciples with no bag, no food, not much at all. Jesus sends them out not to call people to receive Christ. Quite contrarily, Jesus sends them to stand at the door of the stranger both hungry and tired with the hope that the good people of the house or the street will *receive them*, feed them, and save the disciples from the elements.

This is the approach I take as a theologian trained in anthropology. In my work, I am missionized, a concept to which I will return later in this essay. I come to the persons and communities and diaries and songs of Africans in order to listen. As an anthropologist, I cannot be a community member; I am a guest, privileged to privilege the voices of Africans and their histories of Christian mission. I look not to the colonists or the European priests. I look to the people who did not need to file reports detailing how many persons they baptized. I listen closely for the voices that can save me and you from repeating the inexcusable violence that so dominates what we call *missio Dei*. Let us be missionized this day.

I rely on sources whose voice respects the pluralities and dynamism of African religiosity, culture, and philosophy. More specifically, I privilege those voices that for *far too long* have not and are not yet given the authority due them. We will be missionized today by the voices of African women.

Critical liberation theology, and may I dare say, Jesus, speak theological truth to power from the street, the AIDS clinic, the battle field— all those places we see on mission advertisements, on glossy fundraising posters, all those places we can pretend are "over there."

My training and my experience of the Spirit of God compel me to give authority to the voices and experiences of those trapped by structures that cause perpetual poverty and pervasive oppression. (Last time I checked, that's who Jesus was. He did not reach down to the poor; he was poor—a subtle difference overlooked for millennia). Today, the statisticians tell us that African women are at the top—the top of the list of the bottom, that is. Of the United Nations' list of most impoverished nations and people, women across the continent of Africa top the list of most poor, least educated, and those who have lowest access to power— political, domestic, economic, social, and simply the power to turn on a light bulb.

As Cameroonian theologian, Louise Tappa, puts it, [the African woman] "incarnates the mass of the poor and the oppressed."[2] How right she is: 58% of women living in Sub-Saharan Africa have HIV/AIDS. 40% of pregnant women in Botswana have been infected with HIV and/or are living with full-blown AIDS.[3] In some countries, the ratio of infection in girls and boys is as high as 6:1—six girls infected for every boy.

During the civil war in Liberia, men raped at least 40% of Liberian women. According to the UN, rape and sexual slavery have been one of the most common war crimes. Women who became pregnant as a result were frequently turned to the street, rejected by their husbands and ostracized by families.[4] The World Health Organization launched a major program to reach thousands of women in North Dafur in an effort to learn the extent of rape crimes. Every single girl or woman had been raped by a man—often men, or they knew someone who had been raped. The WHO reports rape as a crime of terror and states that no girl or woman is safe.

The WHO has named the rates of death while giving childbirth an "invisible epidemic." In Africa, and elsewhere, women are 100 times more likely to die in childbirth than in wealthy countries like the U.S. This startling number increases with the WHO report that only 50% of deaths during childbirth are reported.

Tappa recognizes the Jesus of the gospels not as a man reaching down to help "those poor people." Instead, she proclaims that *Jesus is one of "those poor people," one of "those African women."*

The same Spirit of Jesus is the same Spirit of African women. That is where God may be found, in most radical suffering. Tappa states, "I believe that when [the African] woman has really come to understand the message of liberation that Jesus bears, she will be able to take her brothers by the hand and lead them to the way of liberation that is ours."[5]

2. Louise Tappa, "The Christ-Event from the Viewpoint of African Women: A Protestant Perspective," in *With Passion and Compassion: Third World Women Doing Theology: Reflections from the Women's Commission of the Ecumenical Association of Third World Theologians*, ed. Virginia Fabella and Mercy Amba Oduyoye (Maryknoll, NY: Orbis, 1988) 33.

3. Jodi L. Jacobson, Executive Director, the Center for Health and Gender Equity, "Women, HIV, and the Global Gag Rule: The Dis-Integration of US Global Aids Funding," press release, February 25, 2003.

4. Afrol news report, March 3, 2004. Online: http://www.afrol.com.

5. Tappa, "The Christ-Event from the Viewpoint of African Women," 33.

To whom do we listen, to whom do we look to missionize us? Well, today, we listen to the women of Africa in order that we, too, might be liberated and saved from the historical malpractice of *missio Dei*.

## LIBERATION DEFINED

Christians—well-intended for the most part—have erred sometimes, to understand and devote their lives to the *missio Dei*. A close read of just about any classical theology, so-called "orthodox" theology, supports the notion of *missio Dei* as being one of telling, curing, saving, doing something to people who believe differently about the cosmos and all that is in it. At the end of the day, historical *missio Dei*—and, my colleagues, one trip to Google.com will indicate that historical includes yesterday and right now. At the end of the day, *missio Dei* has been about telling others that we have the keys to the *kin*dom. They have got to get on board with the program, and we can teach "them." All we need are a few Bibles, some guns, sexually transmitted diseases, western social structures, education, proper clothing, oppressive sexual mores, and patriarchal church structures.

When I listen to those whose continent has been cut up by well-intended Christian men, chopped apart in ways that cause famine, I hear movement. I hear the Spirit of African women—no less than the Spirit of God—moving out from under the systemic poverty, sexism and racism that were planted inside the missionizing churches. I hear a movement. I've witnessed it in South Africa—a movement of liberation.

Today, the only *missio Dei* must have liberation at its core. It is, of course, the message in which our Scriptures are soaked. Biblically, from Isaiah to Luke to Revelation, the history of the people of God is one of a God who liberates. In Trinitarian language, it is the work of the Spirit to liberate. The Spirit creates, liberates, and sustains. *Ruach* never stops making something new or making something happen. The question at hand is who among us will slow down enough to listen to this good news, or who among us will sit at the feet of the women of Sudan, of Chad or of Uganda or of Nigeria to hear their good news?

The good news must identify most plainly with liberation. The Spirit liberates; that's her vocation. She liberates from unjust situations and systems. Unjust situations and systems try to contain the unruly Spirit and her people. Such systems and structures erect barriers and perpetuate violence toward women. They deny that women's bodies reflect the image of God, that humanity's essential power is to create, to generate, to produce/reproduce. Unjust situations and systems cannot contain the Spirit indwelling.

In Hebrew, she is *Ruach*, the God who continually creates life anew. According to the Priestly tradition, all it took was her breath to call the cosmos into being. The creeds name her the Giver of Life, in Greek *Zoopoion*, the "Maker," the "Poet" of Life. In Greek, *pneuma*, spirit, is the source of Jesus's power to restore life; indeed, *pneuma* resurrected him. When he expired and breathed his last, the *Spiritus*, in Latin, inspired his dry bones by conspiring with him. This Spirit, the Liberator, has and does exterminate the situations and systems that fear new creation brought about by conspiracy. This Spirit of God "keeps going and going and going," overturning tables (often in the temples) and healing on the Sabbath (in spite of our erected churches). This is scary stuff for any neatly packaged evangelistic mission trip.

The Spirit demands liberation, and she lives in us. Ghanaian theologian Mercy Amba Odoyoye sees clearly and writes, "All limitations to the fullness of life envisaged in the Christ Event ought to be completely uprooted."[6] She appropriates to her context these words that Jesus appropriated from Isaiah. Let us receive, be missionized, by the African woman whose breath speaks these words of liberative *missio Dei:*

> The poor will hear good news.
> Those who are depressed will feel the comfort that stimulates
>     action;
> Those who are oppressed will be encouraged and enabled to free
>     themselves
> Abilities rather than disabilities will be what counts [sic].
> All who are blind to their own and others' oppression will come to
>     new insights
> And God will pardon all at the jubilee.
> It will be a new beginning for all.[7]

## THE CONCEPT OF THE AFRICAN WOMAN

The Spirit that is God is the same Spirit that blends herself within our tissues and tendons to wrap up her life with ours. The transcendent Spirit

---

6. Mercy Amba Oduyoye, *Daughters of Anowa: African Women and Patriarchy* (Maryknoll, NY: Orbis, 1997) 4.

7. Ibid.

that creates heaven and earth is also immanent, indwelling, and indivisible from our midst. The immanent Spirit is multicultural, multivalent, and multifaceted. This makes the Spirit allusive, hard to define, and very unconventional. Situations and systems that prefer restrictive order would do well to learn that the Spirit is not monomorphic. She moves from and in person to person, dwelling with the chaff and the wheat. The Spirit is not interested in monopoly, monotony, or monogamy—metaphorically speaking.

As a womanist anthropologist, I witness the plurality of the Spirit across vastly different social contexts. I witness the plurality of the Spirit in the grand variety of African women. There is no monolithic African woman. Kenyan ethicist Nyambura J. Njoroge writes, "African women theologians have acknowledged that there is nothing like 'the African Woman': rather there are broad influences in Africa that condition women's lives with varying degrees of success."[8] The Spirit dwells in African women but does not control or constrict the person or power of any African Woman. Indeed, Spirit and Body conspire to create diversity.

The *missio Dei* must not only understand but also honor the *imago Dei* made manifest across the diverse cultures of Africa. All African women are made in the image of God. In the words of the African women theologians and ethicists in the Circle of Concerned African Women, the *missio Dei* is best fulfilled when it examines "the socio-economic and political situation in Africa through women's experiences."[9] Thus, my approach to missiology recognizes that the transcendent Spirit finds expression, creatively and immanently, in the vast array of beliefs, customs and ways of living among African women. Likewise, the transcendent Spirit knows intimately that economic, political, and social systems and situations oppress African women and do violence to the *imago dei* that is each African woman. Oppression of African women is "transgeographical."[10] Oppression of African women is oppression of God's own image and energy.

8. Nyambura J. Njoroge, *Kiama Kia Ngo: An African Christian Feminist Ethic of Resistance and Transformation* (Legon, Ghana: Legon Theological Studies Series Project in collaboration with Asempa Publishers, 2000) 126.

9. Ibid.

10. Irma McClaurin, "Introduction: Forging a Theory, Politics, Praxis, and Poetics of Black Feminist Anthropology," in *Black Feminist Anthropology: Theory, Politics, Praxis, and Poetics*, ed. Irma McClaurin (New Brunswick, NJ: Rutgers University Press, 2001) 9.

## FASHIONING A THEORY FOR DOING A WOMANIST APPROACH TO MISSION

A womanist approach to mission employs Alice Walker's definition of "womanist" in her text *In Search of Our Mothers' Gardens*. That definition, laid out in four parts, suggests that a womanist is *both* "bold and audacious," as well as "courageous and willful." Womanists know what it takes to have their voices heard in a culture and religious environment that does not want to hear the truth a womanist has to tell. A womanist appreciates the variety of life in our world and also sees that "nature" is created. It is a construct with power. A womanist loves her whole body as it bears the image of God; she owns her sexuality. A womanist expresses freely a range of emotional feelings and chooses *intentionally* to live as a relational being. With all she has to do, a womanist loves herself enough to make it a priority to take care of herself. Finally, womanism is different from feminism. In the words of Walker, "womanist is to feminist as purple to lavender."[11] Theologian Dwight Hopkins claims that "Walker's four-part definition contains aspects of (1) tradition; (2) community; (3) self, nature, and the Spirit; and (4) criticism of white feminism."[12] In this sense, a womanist is one who recognizes that she is created in the image of God (i.e., the *imago Dei*). Once she is conscious of her positive relationship to the divine, she celebrates this by taking the good news of liberation to others (i.e., the *missio Dei*).

A womanist theologian, then, *privileges* the voices, gives *authority* to the perspective and experience, of women of African descent. In this lecture, the focus is on African women who are some of the most impoverished and powerful women in our world. The approach to mission is to be missionized, to listen to the testimony, to witness the Spirit of God in action, and to resist the desire to proclaim, tell or contest. We must be saved by these women and through their experience as the hands and feet of the Lord in whose name we have forcibly baptized. These women know a thing or two about insurrection, resurrection and life everlasting. They survive and subvert systems with wisdom and courage that "shock and awe." My role as a womanist theologian and anthropologist, then, is to release the voices of those whose stories are untold.

11. Alice Walker, *In Search of Our Mother's Gardens: Womanist Prose* (New York: Harcourt Brace Jovanovich, 1983) xi.

12. Dwight N. Hopkins, *Introducing Black Theology of Liberation* (Maryknoll, NY: Orbis, 1999) 130.

## THE SUPPRESSION OF AFRICAN WOMEN'S VOICES

Diverse African women denounce the daily experience of systematic oppression. Scholars in the Circle of Concerned African Women call for resistance and proclaim liberation. Musimbi R.A. Kanyoro and Nyambura J. Njoroge write in the introduction of their book, *Groaning in Faith: African Women in the Household of God*: "In the deep pain of exclusion, domination and marginalization, we have the voices of wise women urging us to speak out and tell our stories, for which we alone hold the copyright."[13]

Kanyoro and Njoroge's book brings the voices of African women in East and Southern Africa to the public sphere so that others will come to know the "double reality of pain and faith experienced on the African continent."[14] African culture and Christian religion live in relationship, often tenuous, sometimes salvific. Secular and sacred influence one another. On paper, that may sound like a positive movement toward syncretism in the best sense of the word. The authors expose the double edge of the culture/religion dynamic: like attracts like. "Non-liberating cultural values, which are oppressive to women . . ." meet "like" notions in religion to increase rhetoric that restricts, represses and reinforces systems that do violence to the *imago Dei* of African women.[15] Too often, the combined power structures preach and teach the historically entrenched notion that women's *imago Dei* is a bit dimmer than men's.

The *imago Dei* of African women will not allow such destructive teaching to remain. The Spirit, *imago Dei,* embodied in African women supplies the power to proclaim a different version of the Good News: that any oppressive religious and cultural system or situation is simply *wrong.*

As outlined earlier, this is where the Spirit transcendent and immanent does her work. African women gather to contest, conjure, *conspire,* and call on the Spirit of God who has already started the work. Kanyoro and Njoroge offer a collection of stories of African women acting to in-surrect, resurrect, in-spire in-spite of what missionaries in union with culture teach.

13. Musimbi R. A. Kanyoro and N. J. Njoroge, "Introduction," in *Groaning in Faith: African Women in the Household of God,* ed. Musimbi R. A. Kanyoro and Nyambura J. Njoroge (Kenya: Acton, 1996) xii.

14. Ibid., xiii.

15. Ibid.

Women can look elsewhere for the good news—to Isaiah, Jesus, and African Scholar Mercy Amba Odoyoye. There is power—the power that created the heavens and earth, the power of the spirit that dwells inextricably in her people in the prophecy. The Word promises that the poor will finally hear good news, that the oppressed will free themselves, that oppressors will find a new way, and that it is time for the jubilee. That is the kind of Good News that Kanyoro and Njoroge claim can inspire "new ways of relating," give power to refuse to accept "oppression and indignity," and give birth to faith communities, *koinonia—koinonia* African style.[16]

## AFRICAN SCHOLARS' REFLECTIONS ABOUT MISSIONARIES AND THE IMPACT OF CHRISTIAN MISSIONS ON AFRICA

Let us hear now some voices of African persons tell us the history and experience of Christian mission. We begin with a story I first heard from Archbishop Desmond Tutu, a third generation African Christian, and heard again recently from Randall Robinson, an African American lawyer, author, and former head of TransAfrica. Pay attention because it is a short story. "When the missionaries came to us, we had the land and they had the Bibles. We reverently bowed our heads to pray. When we concluded our prayer and looked up, we had the Bibles, and the missionaries had the land."

This parable tells the truth the way parables tend to do—by shocking listeners from their comfort zone and rousing the cozy out of tradition. I find myself amazed at the resistance toward listening to the truth in such narratives. In many Christian communities this parable would be considered exaggeration—created only for shock value, dismissed as angry hyperbole, and simply fictional. Last time I checked, the Jesus of parables and the parables of Jesus met more than a fair share of resistance. The power of narrative is the way the story speaks truth to power. In the rich tradition of African American literature, fiction most certainly tells the truth.

Our question, then, is what does the painful past reveal about the ecclesiastical tendency to systematically oppress the *imago Dei* expressed differently from the image/idol created in the minds and from the contexts of the missionaries? What would happen if we truly, truly listened

16. Ibid.

and considered the narrative and the authoritative word that trumps our own. As I suggested early on in this lecture, time has come for us to listen. Christian missionizers simply talk too much. For a decade or so, it has been in scholarly circles quite en vogue to talk (ironically) about the need to listen and to care about the voices of the other, in this case, African persons. How, though, do we actually listen, as happened that first Pentecost, when we come with the goal to tell, proclaim and call African persons to realize that our way is the only way? Ultimately, and this travels far beyond the field of mission, ultimately, we who wield Christian mission theories and practice do not listen with the intent of being transformed and changed ourselves by what the "other" has to say. The history of Christian mission provides vivid evidence of the way that listening rarely equals structural transformation. More plainly, the history of Christian mission provides vivid evidence that what we call listening is a way we talk a good story.

If we are listening with an agenda, with firm resolve and definite conviction, we cannot honestly call that listening, can we? Perhaps we need to listen in order to be missionized.

Let us listen to the words of the late Ogbu U. Kalu, a third generation Nigerian Christian, who is the Henry Winters Luce Professor of World Christianity and Mission at McCormick Theological Seminary in Chicago, IL. Kalu's seminal article, "Church Presence in Africa: A Historical Analysis of the Evangelization Process" clearly locates the problem in "missionary history." Kalu writes, "Missionary history was and still is being written by missionaries and their protégés who have swallowed missionary ideology hook, line, and sinker. Missionary history is propagandist and unanalytical."[17] Already we hear a harsh critique of one who received many benefits from the mission movement but who knows personally the costs exacted. Kalu argues that missionary history produced a literary genre that "focused on how the Gospel came" to different parts of Africa but "ignored the socio-economic and political background of the host communities."[18] Moreover, Kalu asserts that "the history of Christianity in Africa is not only what missionaries did or did

---

17. Ogbu U. Kalu, "Church Presence in Africa: A Historical Analysis of the Evangelization Process," in *African Theology En Route*, ed. Kofi Appiah-Kubi and Sergio Torres (Maryknoll, NY: Orbis, 1981) 13.

18. Ibid., 14.

not do but also what Africans thought about what was going on and how they responded."[19]

It is this second point that gives a concrete lesson for those doing a liberative mission approach. According to Kalu such an approach, "should analyze the inner dynamics of the evangelization process, perceiving that process as an encounter between viable cosmologies and cultures. This method rejects European Christianity as the starting point of African church history. On the contrary, Africa and its cultures constitute the starting point."[20]

A third lesson is to acknowledge and appreciate the "alive universe" of various African peoples. For example, anthropologist R. S. Rattray does a remarkable job in describing the Ghanaian Ashanti religion and culture depicted in Ashanti cosmology.[21] He presents a vibrant cosmology with an elaborate social order. When missionary history overlooks or discounts these worldviews and cosmologies, the history is misleading if not fictitious. Kalu also contends that "missionaries came not only with various European and American cultural values but with an identifiable ideology characteristic of their age."[22] While Beyerhaus and Lefever in *The Responsible Church and Foreign Mission* contend that missionary goals and aims differed, Kalu describes a unified ideology at the beginning of the missionary enterprise.[23] He writes, "Though the Portuguese pretended to be looking for a mythical kingdom of Prester John and were inspired by the scientific advances of the Renaissance, their main aim was economic, and their view of Africans was racist."[24]

Finally, Kalu advances a salient point which is especially noteworthy for those who desire to learn from past mistakes. He says, "missionaries came [to Africa] with an amazing degree of confidence in the supremacy of Christianity and the European social and economic order. They came with the certainty that they were obeying the Great Command to go into all the world, baptizing and making disciples of all nations. Such

19. Ibid.

20. Ibid.

21. Robert Sutherland Rattray, *Ashanti* (Oxford: Clarendon, 1923; reprint, Westport, CT: Greenwood/African Universities Press, 1969).

22. Kalu, "Church Presence in Africa," 17.

23. Peter Beyerhaus and Henry Lefever, *The Responsible Church and the Foreign Mission* (London: World Dominion, 1964).

24. Kalu, "Church Presence in Africa," 17.

a sense of certainty often produced hard-headed insensitivity toward indigenous cultures."[25] Is it possible to fulfill the Great Commission and have sensitivity toward and respect of indigenous cultures? Yes, it is if one loses his/her own cultural confidence and claims only the faithfulness to the Gospel. Now the question is, is this even possible?

Musa Dube of Botswana thinks not. She writes from her own hermeneutic of plurality. Dube is an African Christian woman, New Testament scholar, and identifies herself as postcolonial and feminist. Through these multiple dimensions, she finds clarity. She argues convincingly that imperialism is in play whenever a dominant nation imposes economic, political, and cultural institutions upon foreign ones. Dube contends that mission is an imported cultural institution and as such "it is important to determine whether its strategies advocate power relations that resonate with the model of liberating interdependence or embrace a model consistent with imperialistic impositions."[26] The bold and audacious character of Womanist theology and the critical eye of anthropology lead me to argue that mission cannot escape imperialist tendencies. In other words, mission as we know it bears a striking resemblance to imperialist imposition.

Mercy Amba Oduyoye examines missionaries' inability to understand that *only those who practice indigenous religions and rituals can make a judgment about their modification or their usefulness*. Africans themselves have the ultimate responsibility for evaluating their use.[27] As I hear this African woman scholar who trained at Cambridge University speak, I believe that perhaps we could come closer together if the missionizers would turn around their mission and listen to the breath, wind, and spirit that speaks through the language, culture, and religion of African persons—who, by the way, are created in the very image of what is most holy.

25. Ibid., 18.

26. Musa W. Dube, *Postcolonial Feminist Interpretation of the Bible* (St. Louis: Chalice, 2000) 128.

27. Mercy Amba Oduyoye, "Women and Ritual in Africa," in *The Will to Arise: Women, Tradition, and the Church in Africa*, ed. Mercy Amba Oduyoye and Musimbi R. A. Kanyoro (Maryknoll, NY: Orbis, 1992) 9–10.

## RETURNING TO THE LUCAN MODEL OF MISSION

If we listen to Jesus instruct his disciples, we do not even need to bring Jesus. In Luke's account, the disciples embark on a very radical—and far more Jesus-like mission. They go out as beggars; they have nothing to give. They are neither teachers nor proselytizers. They go out to encounter God's *kin*dom in ways quite unorthodox. The disciples can only hope that someone in the street or in a house will receive them in mercy and with grace. The disciples have to rely on others.

The disciples do not bring God to others; no introduction is necessary. God's image greets them at the door; the Word comes to them when a stranger outside the gate says, "I have some extra bread if you're hungry." The disciples' work has nothing to do with changing others and everything to do with changing themselves. We do not create the *kin*dom; we receive it when we are invited in just as we are, accepted by the *imago Dei* of a stranger who offers to wash our dirty feet.

We do not build the *kin*dom by convincing African women to give up honoring ancestors. We glimpse the *kin*dom when we listen to the Word spoken through and see the image of God in women living in Africa. The *missio Dei* is in our midst precisely when we forget our bag with Jesus in it.

In the parabolic way Jesus prefers to teach, the disciples go to new towns and meet new people not to change but to be changed, not to tell but to listen, not with power but helpless. Jesus's approach to *missio Dei* is far less complicated and far more demanding. We have to live an ethic of *koinonia*—welcoming, receiving, and experiencing the Word and cherishing the *imago Dei* in people with whom we do not particularly have anything in common.

We receive a glimpse of the very *missio Dei* from the pluralities of *imago Dei* and multiple expressions of Spirit offered by Women of African descent. We experience "mission possible."

## CONCLUSION

In this lecture I have examined mission from the hermeneutic of plurality. My social location as an African American womanist anthropologist informs my understanding of the *missio Dei*. Most importantly, my understanding of the gospel necessitates that I open myself to be missionized as I stand present with others, particularly African women, to understand the amazing way that God in Jesus Christ works in the world. My understanding of the gospel means that I bring a liberation approach to mission as structures impact negatively the lives of African women who are made in God's image. Second, third, fourth and fifth generation African scholars have raised their voices to say that mission has to take away its imperialism, and I submit that perhaps the best thing that *missio Dei* can do is to influence governments and churches in the first world to be missionized by the liberating work of Jesus Christ made known to us in the poor, particularly, African women.

## 25

# The Black Church and Its Mission for
# the Twenty-first Century

DWIGHT N. HOPKINS

A T THE DAWN OF the twenty-first century, one of the major challenges for the Black church in the United States is global mission.
However, the church needs to engage in a new form of mission. Rather
than follow a type of imperialistic missionary work that we see carried
out by Europe and the U.S.A. in the eighteenth and nineteenth centuries,
a different Black church missionary activity would focus on solidarity,
healing, and liberation for oppressed communities and nations globally.
In other words, the African American church would internationalize the
best of the Black church tradition in partnership with the darker skin
peoples of the world.

This suggestion might seem like an additional or diversionary call
to the Black church at this point in its history. Is not the pastoral practice and overwhelming demands of the chocolate inner cities and Black
professionals in suburban ghettoes already stretching churches to their
limit? Do not more immediate life and death issues face us here at home?
Look at the continuing HIV and AIDS crisis. How about housing for the
working poor and homeless given the decision of major real estate and
bank monopolies to flood cities with new expensive townhouses and
condominiums? And the job market downsizing and permanent layoffs
have wreaked havoc on Black congregations and throughout the entire
African American community. It is an old saying but one still bursting
with meaning: Black folk are the last hired and the first fired.

These days, Black youth seem to have more meaningful income and cohesive culture by joining gang life. If a young fourteen-year-old Black boy can earn $1,000 per day being a soldier in a ghetto gang operation, $4 an hour flipping hamburgers at the corner restaurant provides no appeal. Yet this immediate gratification and bling-bling lifestyle have shortened the life expectancy of African American gang members to about age twenty-four or twenty-five. When parents would hope their children would be graduating from the university, city morgues are filling up with young Black folk in their early to mid-20s. And the children of Black professional and upper income families are suffering as well. Private school and college costs are skyrocketing. In some places, the private school tuition at the kindergarten level is the same as some college tuition twenty years ago. If parents are paying that much for five-year-olds, we can imagine what the price of the ticket is for college and university admissions.

The youth are the future and the dream for the freedom of the Black community. Lack of legitimate opportunities and community nurture will stunt the growth of Black progress for generations to come. At the other age group, African American elders also feel the squeeze. Pension funds have been slashed; in some instances they have been raided by multi-millionaire capitalists. Medicaid and Medicare budgets have shrunk. The costs of prescription drugs never go down and cheaper generic brands are blocked from entering the United States.

Housing, health care, jobs, the survival of youth, and the plight of the elders have forced the Black church to take on a variety of ministries in addition to the usual boy scouts and girl scouts. And we have not even mentioned the threats to the spiritual viability of the Black family. The rate of divorce in the United States is over fifty percent. Suicide has increased among Black youth. Teenage pregnancy appears to have no limit. There has always been a practice of the extended family. But today, the grandmother and grandfather figures, the ones who anchored the extended family, might be less than thirty-years-old. Added to the pressing time constraints of creative and positive Black church ministries are the day-to-day running of the church building and bureaucracy. There are choir rehearsals and deacon board meetings. And we haven't touched on the patience and preparation needed to prepare Sunday sermons, the heart of spiritual uplift and prophetic vision.

Given these realities, why should mission come to the forefront of Black church practice in the twenty-first century? Why should the Black church internationalize the best of its tradition in partnership with the darker skin peoples of the world? I would argue at least three reasons. One creation: Black folk were created out of an international system filled with different language and ethnic groups, and today the definition of being African American means an international person. Our African identity and our Black identity already reveal us as international people similar to other darker skin peoples and African peoples worldwide. Two tradition: The Black church has a long tradition of linking the well being of the African American community with oppressed nations and darker skin peoples globally. And three Jesus mission: The gospel message revealed in the Bible urges all who claim good news for the broken hearted and the oppressed to pursue the *missio dei,* that is to say, to carry forth the mission of God to all far and distant lands on behalf of the liberation of the poor.

## CREATED AS AN INTERNATIONAL PEOPLE

In August 1619, seventeen African men and three African women were brought by force to Jamestown, Virginia. A Dutch war ship dropped them off after selling them for some food, clothes, and fresh water. This historic arrival points to the metaphorical grandparents of all African Americans up until today. These ancestors birthed Black people. Prior to August 1619, there was no such people called Black Americans or African Americans. Black folk were created beginning with the seventeenth century. African Americans are only 400 years old. What is important to note for our purposes is how African Americans were created. People from hundreds of different language and ethnic groups were enslaved on the west coast of Africa, taken against their will across the Atlantic Ocean, and whipped into the slavery system in the so-called New World. Some were stolen from the male and female societies of, what we today call, Sierra Leone and Liberia.[1] We have to remember that modern nation states did not exist in Africa during this time. Instead they had their own international or multi-regional communities and empires. Thousands of different language groups and ethnic peoples existed in all directions on

1. Martha Washington Creel, *A Peculiar People: Slave Religion and Community-Culture among the Gullahs,* American Social Experience Series 7 (New York: New York University Press, 1988) 2.

the African western coast. White businessmen and Christians took Black bodies from the Fulani, Mandinke, Wolof, Bambara, and Serer.[2] What we now call Ghana and Nigeria contributed the Akan, Ashanti, Yoruba, Ewe, Ibo, and Twi. Others were ripped from the Ibibio, Arada, Biafada, and Bakongo language groups.[3]

Not only did the African ancestors of Black Americans originate from distinct language and ethnic groups. They also built various extended families, villages, clans, confederations, kingdoms, and empires and diverse political states.[4] They were, in fact, an international people. The empire of Ghana, dating back to the beginning of the Christian era and lasting into the eleventh century, constituted a large body of land with provinces.[5] Starting in the early thirteenth century, the Mali empire rose and surpassed the rule of Ghana. And then the fifteenth century witnessed the Songhay empire come into full blossom. Besides these huge international bodies, there existed lesser groupings of states on the west coast of Africa. For instance, the Wagadugu states ruled in the eleventh century, the Kanem grouping in the thirteenth century, and a smaller Congo empire held sway in the fourteenth century. In fact, even into the nineteenth century, the Oyo empire ruled across vast land areas.[6]

Important to note about all of these political states and empires is their extensive ability to trade across territorial boundaries. Obviously, extensive commercial interaction took place among all of the states in the west and north west coasts of Africa. But, even more, many of the larger empires conducted trade with Egypt and Europe.[7]

2. Albert J. Raboteau, *Slave Religion: The "Invisible Institution" in the Antebellum South* (New York: Oxford University Press, 1978) 5.

3. John W. Blassingame, *The Slave Community: Plantation Life in the Antebellum South* (New York: Oxford University Press, 1972) 2.

4. Benjamin Quarles, *The Negro in the Making of America* (New York: Collier, 1969) 16. Also see G. T. Strice and Caroline Ifeka, *Peoples and Empires of West Africa: West Africa in History, 1000–1800* (Nairobi, Kenya: Nelson, 1971); Kevin Shillington, *History of Africa*, rev. ed. (New York: St. Martin's, 1995); Roland Oliver, ed., *The Dawn of African History*, 2nd ed. (London: Oxford University Press, 1968); and Walter Rodney, *How Europe Underdeveloped Africa* (Washington, DC: Howard University Press, 1974) chap. 2.

5. Lerone Benett Jr., *Before the Mayflower: A History of Black America*, 6th ed. (New York: Penguin, 1993) 13–22.

6. John Hope Franklin and Alfred A. Moss Jr., *From Slavery to Freedom: A History of Negro Americans*, 6th ed. (New York: Knopf, 1988) 1–11.

7. George P. Rawick, *From Sundown to Sunup: The Making of the Black Community,*

Again, we can see a couple of implications for who we are as Black people or African Americans. Prior to European Christian explorers and missionaries, our ancestors who lived with their faith and witness to the High God were already engaged in international communications up and down west Africa, across the Sahara Desert to northeast Africa, and even trading in Europe. These pre-colonial ancestors of enslaved African people in the United States were an international people who linked their domestic affairs and well being with the plight and hope of darker skin peoples across different borders. The tradition of ancient Africa is a global one.

In addition, the creation of African Americans, beginning in 1619 Jamestown, Virginia, reveals that our blood is constituted by a host of different African cultural, ethnic, linguistic, and regional groupings. The white Christian slave masters in colonial America and similarly in the new U.S.A. broke up African communities from the same families, empires, villages, and languages. When these Christian slave owners made decisions on which enslaved Africans would mate to produce more Black workers for the plantation, the masters simply mated who ever was on their farms or who ever they could get from a neighboring plantation. The very being of Black folk means a mixture of diverse ancestry from the African west coast. This creation out of a mixture of peoples has led to a tradition of solidarity with global dark skin peoples.

## TRADITION OF SOLIDARITY WITH GLOBAL DARK SKIN PEOPLES

Though the European Christian slave trade and the white American Christian slave trade in Black bodies made it clear that the majority of Africans never would see their homelands again, still Black people fought for their freedom in the so-called New World while also keeping their eyes globally. They understood that slavery did not create them. God had already breath life into them before they entered the chattel system; and God stayed with them even during the brutality of bondage. The seventeenth century saw Black folk running away from slavery to Canada, while others remained in Dixie, land of cotton, tobacco, and sugar cane. Those left behind kept their dreams on a better land; but for

---

The American Slave: A Composite Autobiography 1 (Westport, CT: Greenwood, 1972) 15.

many heaven was their home—a home where folk would one day reunite with family members, ancestors, and other dark skin peoples. Some even dreamed of flying their way back to their earthly home Africa.[8] Whether pursuing their Canaan land of Canada, imagining liberation in heaven, or fixating on returning to the Continent, all plans for freedom had a profound religious basis and motivation.

Perhaps the clearest relationship between religious identity and international connections is found in the eighteenth century birth of Black Christian churches. During the 1700s, enslaved Black preachers established several African Baptist churches. George Liele, a Black man freed by his master who was pro-British in the War of Independence, organized some African churches in Georgia before he emigrated to Jamaica. Though born in the U.S., he built the first Black Baptist church in the Caribbean (1782). Andrew Bryan, a slave ordained by Liele but one who decided to remain in bondage in the U.S.A., started the First African Baptist Church in Savannah. Eleven years later (1793), the First African Baptist Church of Augusta, Georgia, sprang up.[9] Clearly southern Black folk, bond and free, intentionally named their churches African because they linked their Christian identity in North America with their African identity globally.

Likewise northern African Americans separated from white Christian brethren to conduct Christian religious affairs among their own kind. Richard Allen and Absalom Jones departed from the white St. Georges Methodist Episcopal Church of Philadelphia in 1787 and organized an African religious association called the Free African Society. Yet 1816 marked the founding of the A.M.E. denomination when the Free African Society, the Baltimore African church, the Union Church of Africans in Wilmington, Delaware, and others merged.[10] And the year 1820 brought about the African Methodist Episcopal Zion denomination. Black working class women, likewise, engaged in tying their Black identity with their cultural identity in recognition of their original heri-

8. See Dwight N. Hopkins, *Down, Up and Over: Slave Religion and Black Theology* (Minneapolis, MN: Fortress Press, 1999) and Dwight N. Hopkins, *Shoes That Fit Our Feet: Sources for a Constructive Black Theology* (Maryknoll, NY: Orbis Books, 1993) chapter 3.

9. Robin D. G. Kelley and Earl Lewis, eds., *To Make Our World Anew: A History of African Americans* (New York: Oxford University Press, 2000) 149; and Gayraud S. Wilmore, *Black Religion and Black Radicalism* (Maryknoll, NY: Orbis, 1998) 132.

10. Wilmore, ibid., 108–9.

tage from the Continent. In the early 1800s, they organized mutual aid relief societies, pooling their meager pennies to pay for burials, children without fathers, invalid community members, and widows. Specifically, they named their organizations the Daughter of Africa Society or the African Female Benevolent Society. The latter self-help group consisted of African-born ex-slaves.[11]

Indeed, the nineteenth century revealed a major blossoming of religious longing on the part of African American denominations toward their distant cousins in Africa and the Caribbean. Moving beyond merely naming their churches African, Black Christians took the initiative in the missionary field. Though I will later critique the standard theological doctrine of missiology, that is, the orthodox notion of planting Christian churches on foreign lands, the spiritual impulse to look toward darker skin peoples beyond the North American shores concerns us at this point. The Baptist preacher Lott Carey made several trips to Liberia to share the good news of the gospel. His early leadership across the Atlantic made him, perhaps, the premier symbol of Black American outreach to their original homeland. In 1824, Richard Allen sent forth church representatives to establish Haiti as the first international mission station for the African Methodist Episcopal Church.[12] The AME denomination, lest than thirty years later, undertook successful campaigns to broaden church work to Cuba, Antiqua, Virgin Islands, Dutch Guiana, British Guiana, Bermuda, Barbados, and Tobago. And A.M.E. bishop Henry McNeal Turner planted churches from Liberia to Cape Town.[13]

Back at home under the white Christian slave system in southern U.S.A., some enslaved Black communities approached their relation to darker skin peoples internationally from a different perspective. Instead of undertaking journeys to Africa or the Caribbean, the reverse would be true. Specifically, Denmark Vesey of Charleston, South Carolina, planned a Christian rebellion in 1822 against the slave system partially based on his expectations of definite international solidarity. Vesey had already purchased his own freedom. Yet his Christian good news of liberation for the oppressed focused his witness on destroying chattel existence for

11. Dorothy Sterling, ed., *We Are Your Sisters: Black Women in the Nineteenth Century* (New York: Norton, 1984) chap. 9.

12. Both references to Cary and Haiti can be found in Wilmore, *Black Religion and Black Radicalism*, 132.

13. Ibid., 149–57.

the rest of his oppressed sisters and brothers still caught in the grip of slavery. Vesey and other members of the African Church of Charleston planned a massive armed insurrection that, once initiated, would receive additional troops from Haiti and West Africa. The co-conspirators conjured an elaborate scheme to overpower the local white population with expectations of solidarity and reinforcements from darker skin peoples globally. In fact, some evidence suggests that one of Veseys Christian comrades had communicated with the president of Haiti.[14]

The twentieth century African American struggle for full humanity continues this tradition of fighting for human dignity and justice locally while building networks with the world's darker skin populations.[15] The premier religious freedom movement of the twentieth century, the civil rights movement led by the Black church, actively stretched forth its hands in solidarity with other oppressed peoples. In 1957, a year after the successful Montgomery, Alabama, bus boycott, Martin Luther King Jr. attended the independence ceremonies of Ghana. In 1959, King spent a month showing compassion for and building solidarity with the people of India. Note that both trips did not perceive Christian global contact as planting a church or taking people out of their own indigenous religions and forcing or massaging them into or asking them to join Christianity. King, an ordained clergy of the gospel of Jesus Christ, understood mission as standing in solidarity, showing compassion, and aiding the struggle for justice and liberation wherever darker skin communities found themselves. And in a very direct way in his Nobel Peace Prize speech, he stressed this tie between the Black American effort toward civil rights and the world's people of color.[16]

Most theologically and most dangerously, his anti-Vietnam War speech of April 4, 1967 displays this drum major for Jesus Christ at his

14. Vincent Harding, *There Is a River: The Black Struggle for Freedom in America* (New York: Harcourt Brace, 1981) 65–72; and Dwight N. Hopkins, *Down, Up, and Over: Slave Religion and Black Theology* (Minneapolis: Fortress, 2000) 134.

15. America's main intellectual of the twentieth century, W. E. B. DuBois, waged a life-long campaign bringing Black Americans' issues in concert with the darker skin nations and peoples. One instance: DuBois, "Colonialism, Democracy, and Peace after the War (Summer 1944)," in *Against Racism: Unpublished Essays, Papers, Addresses, 1887–1961*, ed. Herbert Aptheker (Amherst, MA: University of Massachusetts Press, 1985) 229–44.

16. James H. Cone, *Martin & Malcolm & America: A Dream or a Nightmare?* (Maryknoll, NY: Orbis, 1991) 312.

best. That prophetic oration and visionary call for poor people of colors' human dignity reveals a progressive understanding of Christian mission. King declared that the poor and oppressed people of Vietnam, like others globally, were inextricably intertwined with the poor and Black folk of the U.S.A. And King spoke explicitly as a preacher of Christ. Again, the substance of his words drew on solidarity, compassion, the humanity and freedom for the worlds poor, regardless of their religious choices. For him, this was the good news of the Bible.[17]

Fannie Lou Hamer, another stalwart Christian leader of the civil rights movement, embraced the Slave Spiritual, "This Little Light of Mine," as her personal faith expression. Yet, the shining of that light helped move her from the life and death situations of southern struggle to the new republic of Guinea in West Africa. There in 1964 in her meetings with the country's president and other citizens, Mrs. Hamer received a profound affirmation of her sense of being a child of God. Moreover, her encounter with darker skin peoples abroad not only increased her knowledge and compassion for their struggles. It also deepened further her appreciation for her own challenges in Mississippi.[18] She knew that poor and working class people were not alone; they operated in a global sphere.

During that same year, 1964, when Mrs. Hamer, the Christian, visited the Continent, Malcolm X, the Muslim, undertook a major inter-cultural and inter-religious tour throughout Nigeria, Ghana, Liberia, Senegal, Morocco, Algiers, Lebanon, Egypt, and Arabia. His travels brought him in contact with leaders of liberation movements throughout Asia, the Caribbean, Latin America, and, of course, Africa.[19] These dark skin freedom fighters of diverse religious and cultural backgrounds shared their solidarity and support for the Black American plight. Malcolm, in turn, offered the same.[20] From his return home until his death in February

17. Martin Luther King Jr., "A Time to Break Silence," in *A Testament of Hope: The Essential Writings of Martin Luther King Jr.*, ed. James Melvin Washington (San Francisco: Harper & Row, 1986) 231–44; and Dwight N. Hopkins, *Shoes That Fit Our Feet: Sources for a Constructive Black Theology* (Maryknoll, NY: Orbis, 1993) 187–89.

18. See Stokely Carmichael, *Ready for Revolution: The Life and Struggles of Stokely Carmichael (Kwame Ture)* (New York: Scribner, 2003) 317–18; and Kay Mills, *This Little Light of Mine: The Life of Fannie Lou Hamer* (New York: Dutton, 1993) 134–40.

19. Malcolm X, *The Autobiography of Malcolm X*, with the assistance of Alex Haley (New York: Grove, 1965) chaps. 17, 18, 19.

20. Malcolm X, *Two Speeches of Malcolm X* (New York: Pioneer, 1965) 22–23.

1965, Malcolm continually linked full equality and full humanity of African Americans with the darker skin peoples and countries on earth. Malcolm highlighted Pan Africanism and, while maintaining it, moved to a broader extended family comprised of all darker skin countries and communities globally.[21] In addition to his political and cultural analysis, what held this majority of the world's population together was at root a spirituality of solidarity and justice.

Organized Black Christian leaders' networks, likewise, continued the tradition of African Americans holding hands with the worlds oppressed peoples. The Black Theology Project emerged in 1976 and continued into the early 1990s. This Christian grouping represented the progressive wing of Black male and female pastors and professors. It held dialogues between African American women and Black women in Honduras, South Africa, Nicaragua, El Salvador, Mozambique, and Costa Rica. Along with accompanying the All African Conference of Churches on various country visits, BTP members visited Blacks in Brazil. In the same vein, BTP began a program of church exchanges between Black American pastors and those in oppressed countries. Black Cuban Christians were among the first to come to the U.S.[22]

Perhaps a fitting place to end this part of our discussion on tracing the tradition of the progressive wing of Black church and Black community approaches to mission is with the practice and theology of the National Conference of Black Christians (NCBC). NCBC began as the ad hoc National Committee of Negro Churchmen when it published its

---

21. Cone, *Martin & Malcolm & America*, 312–14; and Hopkins, *Shoes That Fit Our Feet*, 189–91. Another leader of the 1960s–1970s Black consciousness and Black power efforts is the Black Panther Party. They advanced a theory of intercommunalism, underscoring the international nature of Black Americans' attempts to be human. See Huey P. Newton, *Revolutionary Suicide* (New York: Harcourt Brace Jovanovich, 1973), chap. 32; and Newton, *To Die for the People* (New York: Vintage, 1972).

Black auto workers in Detroit, Michigan, in addition, show us this global spirituality of solidarity and justice for poor people. In May 1968, African American workers at Ford auto plants formed DRUM: Dodge Revolutionary Union Movement. DRUM supported various international peoples' struggles for self-determination and full humanity: in Palestine, South Africa, Mexico, Guatemala, Vietnam, and Rhodesia (Zimbabwe). See Dan Georgakas and Marvin Surkin, *Detroit, I Do Mind Dying*, 2nd ed. (Boston: South End, 1998); and "Our Thing Is DRUM! The League of Revolutionary Black Workers," in *Let Nobody Turn Us Around: Voices of Resistance, Reform, and Renewal*, ed. Manning Marable and Leith Mullings (Boston: Rowman & Littlefield, 2000) 486–89.

22. *The Black Theology Project* newsletter (Fall 1987) 2–3; and newsletter (Winter 1988) 4–5.

theological interpretation of the Black power slogan on July 31, 1966.[23] This group of Black male pastors and church administrators, along with one woman, launched the contemporary Black theology movement, which rose, not from the academy, but from church sanctuaries and the streets of urban America.

An ecumenical gathering of Christian prophets, NCBC initially organized many progressive Black preachers to take stands against the structural sins of white supremacist America. It, too, followed that tradition of working locally while networking internationally. Several trips were taken to Africa in coordination with the All African Conference of Churches. Global mission work, in these instances, was not so much one of planting churches abroad and trying to convert people to Jesus. Rather, NCBC met with the AACC as partners in solidarity and as Black Americans seeking to learn about their former homeland. What were the commonalities and differences between African Americans and Africans? And how could Black people with abundant resources, living in a American superpower, assist the process of attaining full humanity begun by African sisters and brothers on the Continent—a continent intentionally underdeveloped by Europe and the U.S.A.?[24]

A 1976 statement of NCBC provides some insight on how the National Conference engaged in mission work globally. The document begins by situating Black theology as the theology of the Black church, Protestant and Roman Catholic. Then it carves out a specific bridge between Black theology as Black church ecumenism, on the one hand, and the definition of missions, on the other. Black theology, in the words of NCBC, asserts the operational unity of all Black Christians as the first step toward a wider unity in which the restructuring of power relations in church and society and the liberation of the poor and oppressed will be recognized as the first priority of mission. The next sentences describe Jesus Christ revealing the divine self to Black people as the liberator of Blacks in Africa, the Caribbean, Latin America, and in North America. In fact, the document claims, Africans knew of the gospel by the end of the second century.

---

23. The full statement can be found as "Black Power: Statement of the National Committee of Negro Churchmen, July 31, 1966," in *Black Theology: A Documentary History, 1966–1979*, ed. Gayraud S. Wilmore and James H. Cone (Maryknoll, NY: Orbis, 1979) 23–30.

24. See Rodney, *How Europe Underdeveloped Africa*.

But, after asserting this fact, NCBC offers a qualification. Even if the gospel had not penetrated indigenous African Traditional Religions, "God did not leave [Godself] without a witness in Africa before the arrival of Christian missionaries . . . [God's] eternal power and deity was shown to all [humankind] from the creation of the world . . ." The argument here seems to be that, before the message of Jesus reached darker skin peoples throughout the earth, God had already revealed Godself to them. Presumably this divine revelation came in the indigenous religions of Africa, Asia, the Caribbean, Latin America, and the Pacific Islands. If God's salvation and liberation precede Jesus, then why should white orthodox missionary theology define the goal of mission work to be converting people to Christianity and enrolling them in the Christian church? In other words, why do darker skin peoples globally have to surrender their own indigenous spiritualities and religions and adopt Christ if God is already with them, if God has been with them since the creation of all creation? Here we expect a revolutionary re-definition of white orthodox missions—one whose substance is solidarity with, affirmation, and liberation of the broken-hearted, the poor and the oppressed. We seem to be entering a new era of missiology—one where Black Christians recognize and accept the presence of God among other darker skin peoples' spiritualities throughout the world.

However, the document appears to veer back to a white imperialistic type of mission goals when it states: "This truth of God [in Jesus Christ] was hidden in the traditional religions of Africa which awaited their fulfillment in the revelation of Jesus, the Liberator."[25] Okay. Darker skin peoples globally did have God revealed to them, but that type of revelation only indicated a partial revelation. And, furthermore, this partial revelation was hidden from them. It is not until white missionaries from Europe and North America and nineteenth-century Black missionaries' arrival are the majority of the world's people (that is, darker skin people) saved fully by Jesus Christ. If this be the case, then the mission of the African American church and Black theology is the exact equivalent of white orthodox missiology. That is to say, to be a Christian is to go abroad, plant churches, and force or persuade darker skin peoples

25. All quotes come from "Black Theology in 1976: Statement by the Theological Commission of the National Conference of Black Churchmen," in *Black Theology: A Documentary History*, 342.

to surrender their indigenous spiritualities. Either the Black American Christians' way or there is no way.

## THE BIBLE'S *MISSIO DEI*

Part of this apparent double message if not out right contradiction is fostered and nurtured by certain biblical passages around the *missio dei* or mission of God. In Matthew 28:18–20, the writer of this book remembers the following words of Jesus:

> I have been given all authority in heaven and on earth! Go to the people of all nations and make them my disciples. Baptize them in the name of the Father, the Son, and the Holy Spirit, and teach them to do everything I have told you. I will be with you always, even until the end of the world.[26]

Historically, beginning in the eighteenth century and continuing until today, the majority of white orthodox missionaries interpret this passage as starting Christian churches among darker skin peoples globally, as well as tearing them away from the religions, spiritualities, clothing, lifestyles, culture, and language of their parents and their grandparents. Most disturbing today is the growing ultra-conservative, neo-charismatic, Black American preachers who have contracted with right-wing American white preachers on the international God Channel.[27] This international station leaves the United States, beams up into space into a satellite that is authorized by the White House, State Department and the C.I.A., and returns to earth to reach millions of oppressed people in Africa, Asia, the Caribbean, Latin America, and the Pacific Islands.

In other words, the God Channel is not an innocent medium of spreading the good news of Christ Jesus. Like any other radio or TV stations broadcasting from the United States, it has to have clearance from the federal government and its secret agencies. My point is that the practice of conservative white orthodox interpretations of Matthew

---

26. This quote is from the *Holy Bible: African American Jubilee Edition, Contemporary English Version* (New York: American Bible Society, 1999).

27. From February 2005 to January 2006, I traveled to Africa, Asia, the Caribbean, and Latin America and observed the presence of the God Channel and its pro-superpower theology. Oftentimes, the indigenous, local leaders who have purchased this neo-charismatic, white orthodox missionary posture are more fanatical than the white and Black American religious and political leaders who sold them this theology of the empire.

28 suggests Jesus is like an army officer commanding his troops to conquer the world. One obvious problem exists in falsely depicting Jesus as
a military ruler who, through pre-emptive strike, unleashed hoards of
followers on the world's darker skin peoples. More substantively, I would
argue, the primary purpose of the God Channel and the white and Black
American neo-charismatic missionaries is to dominate the world with
U.S. civilization and the world policies of the federal government. Here
Matthew 28 has become a subterfuge to make the world not in Jesus
image, but in the image of the negative politics and corporate elites who
run the U.S.A. Neo-charismatic leaders employ Christianity to spread
the political, economic, and cultural systems of the one global empire.
Wherever Black and white American neo-charismatics go in Africa,
Asia, the Caribbean, Latin America, and the Pacific Islands, they use the
God Channel and their deliverance crusades to accomplish at least two
things. They viciously attack peoples' indigenous religions and cultures.
And they spread American capitalism and culture. Missionary work is
not the theology of Jesus; it is the theology of a superpower.[28] Restated,
Christianity grows globally only when it is backed by an empire.

We could say that the atrocious and wicked practices symbolized by
the perpetrators of the God Channel only represent their false interpretation of the biblical call to missions. Because an imperialistic superpower
gives resources to false religious leaders to conquer the globe does not
indict Jesus words in Matthew 28. For example, verse 19 clearly states:
"Go to the people of all nations and make them my disciples. Baptize
them in the name of the Father, the Son, and the Holy Spirit." Orthodox
Christianity calls this the Great Commission. Yet, the words "Great
Commission" appear nowhere in the passage. "Great Commission" actually signifies a white orthodox understanding of Jesus. Furthermore,
the phrase "make them my disciples" goes against the entire ministry
of Jesus earthly witness. Why would a God of love have to make others
see the beauty of the good news that Jesus brings to poor and oppressed
people in order for them to have life and have it abundantly? Perhaps
the thrust of these words from Jesus, given only to his 11 disciples on a
mountain, need to be juxtaposed with other Jesus teachings.

---

28. For theological analysis of the religion of globalization, see Hopkins, "The
Religion of Globalization," in *Relgions/Globalizations: Theories and Cases*, ed. Dwight
N. Hopkins, Lois Ann Lorentzen, Eduardo Mendieta, and David Batstone (Durham:
Duke University Press, 2001) 7–32.

Specifically, when we go back to Matthew 25:31–46, we discover the final judgment; a scene where humankind has to collectively account for their practice on earth. We do not encounter questions about a prosperity gospel, or a God Channel, or a deliverance ministry, or support of the economics, culture, and politics of a super power empire. Nor is there a demand to add up and present the numbers of darker skin peoples whom Christians have removed from their indigenous cultures, religions, and spiritualities. Jesus doesn't ask about how many people in the world have been converted to Christianity or how many Word Churches and mega-churches have been built. If we look closely, it also appears as if Jesus does not judge individuals one-by-one, but, instead, he judges the practice of groups of people. And fundamentally, Jesus judges all nations, not just Christians, but all people. Here, Jesus is not concerned whether one is a Christian or not. What makes one a follower of Jesus is if groups of people become witnesses for Jesus. Put differently, we experience ultimate life when we feed the hungry, give drink to the thirsty, give welcome to the stranger, give clothing to the naked, give care to the sick, and visit poor and working class people in prison. Having ultimate life means collectively serving and being with the poor and working people—the unimportant people in society, the least of these. In the entire Bible, Matthew 25 is the only direct instructions and criteria for how to get into heaven.

It should not surprise us that Jesus ends his ministry with his commission in Matthew 25 about serving the poor and working people to have ultimate life. Why? Because, in his first public address where he tells the world what his one mission is, he says the same thing. We can easily see how Luke 4:18–21 stands as Jesus' inaugural address. The first public words that God gives to the world are not unimportant, insignificant, or off-the-cuff remarks. Christians believe that Jesus is the messiah. Now how does the messiah define his own understanding of mission? What is the theology of mission for Jesus? Luke 4:18-19 reads:

> The Spirit of the Lord is upon me, because [it] has anointed me to bring good news to the poor. [It] has sent me to proclaim release to the captives and recovery of sight to the blind, to let the oppressed go free, to proclaim the year of the Lords favor.

Now turning from this New Revised Standard Version translation to the Contemporary English Version, we find:

> The Lord's Spirit has come to me, because [it] has chosen me to tell the good news to the poor. The Lord has sent me to announce freedom for prisoners, to give sight to the blind, to free everyone who suffers, and to say, This is the year the Lord has chosen.

And the King James Version offers this translation:

> The Spirit of the Lord is upon me, because [it] hath anointed me to preach the gospel to the poor; [it] hath sent me to heal the brokenhearted, to preach deliverance to the captives, and recovering of sight to the blind, to set at liberty them that are bruised, to preach the acceptable year of the Lord.

The purpose of missionary work around the world does not concern spreading a prosperity gospel; or a God Channel; or a deliverance ministry; or support of the economics, culture, and politics of a superpower empire. Nor is the purpose of mission to add up the numbers of darker skin peoples whom Christians have removed from their indigenous cultures, religions, and spiritualities. Jesus doesn't ask about how many people in the world have been converted to Christianity or how many Word Churches and mega-churches have been built. Like the final judgment and great commission of Matthew 25, the purpose of mission underscores good news to poor people, healing broken hearts, releasing poor people from jail, curing blindness, and liberating the oppressed people of the world and bringing freedom for those who suffer. The purpose of mission globally focuses on the poor, by struggling together with them in a liberation, freedom, and healing movement and by letting them know that, in fact, right now is their year of liberation and freedom.

Based on Jesus final judgment and instructions for mission, we judge the words of every other human being in the Bible, including Paul.

## WALKING IN JESUS MISSION

If we walk in the mission of Jesus, we have to take seriously the three major points we have made so far in our conversation. One—*creation*: Black folk were created out of an international system filled with different language and ethnic groups; and today the definition of being African American means an international person. Our African identity and our Black identity already reveal us as international people similar to other darker skin peoples and African peoples worldwide. Two—*tradition*: The Black church has a long tradition of linking the well being of the African American community with oppressed nations and darker skin peoples globally. And three—*Jesus mission*: The gospel message revealed in the Bible urges all who claim good news for the broken hearted and the oppressed to pursue the *missio dei*, that is to say, to carry forth the mission of God to all far and distant lands on behalf of the liberation of the poor.

How does the African American church carry this out? I suggest forging global ties through an International Association of Black Religions and Spiritualities. Darker skin people worldwide would come together to learn about and support efforts on behalf of the poor; that is to say, transformation of individuals who suffer and changing systems that keep poor people poor and oppressed.

Today dark skin peoples or Black communities globally share some basic commonalities. First are the variety of expressions of spiritualities and religions. Whether Africa, Asia, the Caribbean, Latin America, the Pacific Islands, or Black people in Europe and the U.S.A., a sense of values glue our peoples, communities, and oppressed nations together. For us, spiritualities and religions unite the sacred and secular as one. This progressive worldview and practice exists in all forms of Black spiritualities and religions: such as indigenous, traditional, pre-colonial, post-colonial, Islamic, Santeria, Candomble, Christian, and other mainstream and non-mainstream types. The sacred covers all reality.

A major experience of spiritualities and religions or our sacred values is collective and individual human dignity. The necessity to have human dignity stands at the center of what it means to be a human being. Being human is dignity for the identity of oppressed peoples and of the individual self. And individual human dignity takes place within the context of community human dignity.

Human dignity is close to human rights. But dignity is different from rights. To have human rights assumes that an oppressed community or an individual already enjoys dignity. So human dignity comes before human rights.

What is human dignity? It is made up of at least three parts: self-love, self-esteem, and self-confidence. Self-love means an oppressed people loves their own identity—how the sacred has created them and how they are born beautiful and healthy and sacred as a people. Love of self accepts the self without wanting to be someone else. Self-love in an oppressed community embraces its culture (of course, while learning from other cultures), wisdom, languages, spiritualities, religions, ancestors, and ways of being, seeing, and acting in the world. And self-love includes a love of nature, animals, birds, plants, fish, air, water, earth, and the minerals of the earth.

Self-esteem happens when a people who love themselves put value on themselves. There is worth to our very being. We hold our selves in high regard. When an oppressed community loves itself, it values its history, ancestry, land, language, traditions, its unborn, its very existence, its right to live on earth, and its connections to the sacred and all of creation. What worth do we have for ourselves, our bodies, minds, and spirit? What worth do we put on our ancestors, the present, children, and the unborn? What worth do we have for nature and all of creation? What worth do we put on our families and our extended families?

If we love ourselves and hold ourselves in high esteem, we become more self-confident as an oppressed people. Self-confidence helps us to act out our love and esteem of self in the world around us, especially as a peoples' movement to change the world. With confidence we protect our being and creation. We move in the world to challenge those obstacles that prevent the health of human beings and creation. We have strong confidence in the future and the future of our unborn. We struggle for justice now. And we have a deep hope in a better society and better relations between humans and all of creation. We have hope that healthy societies will one day come on earth. Self-confidence encourages an oppressed people to define its own self and the space around it in such a way that we are in harmony and balance with our selves, neighbors, our ancestor, all of creation, and the sacred.

In addition to our spiritualities and religions, defined by collective and individual human dignity, we are all Black people. By Black we mean the darker skin communities of the world. Black is a broad umbrella word. It represents more than skin color. It stands for a tradition of struggle against colonialism caused by Europe and the U.S.A. It represents a history of being the objects of Christian missionary work. Today it indicates attacks on our culture by global propaganda that tries to define what beauty is and the effort to force the entire world to become like the culture of only one superpower. So from the negative side, to be Black is to be ugly, dirty, to lack leadership abilities, to be ignorant, uncivilized, backward, savage, volatile, overly sexed, of low morals, and criminals.

Blackness, in its negative sense, sometimes means passive consumers of products from the major monopoly capitalist corporations in the world. Not only are we seen as easy consumers of these products. Our communities are the ones who work and produce the wealth, products, and income for the small group of families, primarily from the U.S.A. and Europe, who own and control the majority of human beings and creation. These elite families and monopoly capitalist corporations have historically stolen and continue today to steal wealth, money, land, and resources from the Third World and from Black folk's labor in the U.S. The increasing monopolization of wealth and income taking place globally shows us that the key concern for the world's majority is the elimination of poverty and the establishment of justice.

But we also have to admit that just as Black spiritualities and religions have been positive by sustaining us, helping us to survive and thrive, and resisting negative forces outside of our communities, our own Black spiritualities and religions have a deep negative side This negative side comes from the unhealthy aspects of our traditions and from us accepting the negative influences of powers seeking to control us and our land. Not all parts of Black religions and spiritualities are positive. A key sign of our harmful spiritualities and religions is the extra oppression faced by women. We have to be aware of negative external and internal factors. But our main vision is to realize that Black religions and spiritualities mean that another world is possible.

## PROBLEMS

Various obstacles block the vision of another world. One of the major problems confronting oppressed Black communities or darker skin people globally is the lack of international connections. Too many of us are unaware of and not tied to each other. In many examples, we do not know of thousands of grassroots communities struggling for human dignity on a daily basis. If we can connect these life-and-death movements internationally, it will give us more solidarity, resources, and hope for our local efforts and our children's future. Too often lack of connection keeps our eyes looking at the demands and tasks of local experiences. Yet an international network can help turn our eyes to global friends dealing with similar challenges. Concrete support for the local can come from peoples' movements throughout the world. How can we also learn from all of our local victories? How can we exchange information about the similar ways the small group of major powers are affecting our peoples daily existence?

Many of the situations and histories of darker skin peoples around the world show some similarities: gender analysis and balanced gender participation in society, decrease and eventual elimination of poverty, inter-religious dialogue and cooperation, ecology, recovery of indigenous cultures, land dispossession, sexual violence against girls and women, economic fairness, religious freedom, HIV and AIDS, blockades against our countries by a major superpower, youth crime and disillusionment, artistic and material culture, our ability to create new knowledge, democracy defined by our own local cultures and traditions. How can ordinary people have ownership of the resources and governing structures in their own country? What does equality look like if it is defined by the bottom of our societies, and the need to educate our youth?

Other parallel concerns include: the increased presence of transnational businesses, the growth of evangelical Christian missionaries (mainly from the economically developed countries), loss of land, structural adjustment programs demanded by international financial organizations, disruption of cultures due to movements from rural to urban areas, the extra pressures and burdens on women, and centralization of a global mono-culture (through television, movies, music, food tastes, and clothing styles) make critical differences in peoples everyday lives. All of these things greatly impact religion and spirituality, especially for poor people who don't have access to wealth, media, and other resources to put their voices into global discussions.

## OBJECTIVES

An attempt to build an international network of Black religions and spiritualities is one movement to help put oppressed peoples and poor peoples voices into international conversations. We think that Black religions and spiritualities throughout the world provide strong, positive resources. Black peoples' countries, communities, and local networks offer unlimited examples of how to work for a better world. An international association can offer another way for progressive religious and spiritual people to show that the dominant, negative religions and spiritualities spreading globally are just one way. Unfortunately the international media, missionaries, and money have come together on a global scale to serve the cultural, political, and economic interests of only a small sector of the earth's six billion people. A Black religions and spiritualities association can try to show a more healthy way in the interests of the world's majority. And important lessons and leadership come from darker peoples who occupy every land base and body of water on earth.

The network can link the local to the global. At the same time, the network can encourage its member countries to make alliances with more groups and organizations inside of each country. As people of faith, all of us are working very hard on important issues facing our communities. Because of the demands of our tasks, sometimes we do not have the time or energy to link hands with groups in our own countries. One objective of the international association is to help broaden ties within each nation.

In addition to creating a global network of progressive peoples and encouraging each country to reach out to other groups in their own contexts, an international association on Black religions and spiritualities can help the development of human dignity for oppressed peoples and communities. We all can become more hopeful to know that solidarity exists across the waters and among continents. The local victories and setbacks are not only part of a larger connection, but they are important. This sense of belonging to a larger relationship and this sense of being important can increase human dignity: self-love, self-esteem, and self-confidence within each of our own unique movements. And so a global association builds human dignity for the local. The lessons and leadership from the local further strengthens the international association. Human dignity of love, esteem, and confidence focuses on working toward a better possible world. The international network can act on issues that all countries have in common. The global association can also agree on a critical issue affecting only one or two countries.

A fourth objective of an international network on Black religions and spiritualities is to practice a new model for women and men working together. Structurally it could always have a fifty percent male and fifty percent female representation. Obviously this structure works against those negative parts of our traditions and current practices that put women in the role of followers. But more importantly, a structure of gender equality offers a way to always draw on the rich wisdom, experience, and intellect that women bring to Black spiritualities and religions.

The point is to use all resources we bring from our local contexts into an international network.

Another important objective is the survival, thriving, and future of our youth. History teaches us and common sense tells us that the future of any people or society is in the hands of young people. For instance, Jesus was only 33 years old when he was lynched. The international association can have a special focus on building the human dignity of our youth (girls and boys, and young men and women) by putting youth in contact with youth in other countries. In fact, in each local context, we have at least one thing that ties us together. Some part of our work deals with educating young people and young adults. Perhaps young people and young adults could be one of the major objectives of the network.

Let us conclude by simply stating the following. History, our ancestors, our children, and the gospel itself will judge us. I believe that another world is possible for the least of these.[29]

29. The International Association of Black Religions and Spiritualities was formed in January of 2006 in Cape Town, South Africa and continues to be active today. It includes delegates from the following 14 countries: Dalits from India, Burakumin in Japan, Aboriginals from Australia, Fiji, Native Hawaiians (Hawaii), Black Americans (USA), Blacks British (from England), South Africa, Botswana, Zimbabwe, Ghana, Jamaica, Blacks in Brazil, and Blacks in Cuba. Its website: www.iabrs.org The two International Communications Coordinators are Dwight N. Hopkins (USA) and Marjorie Lewis (Jamaica).

# Contributors

Michael Joseph Brown
Emory University, Candler School of Theology
Atlanta, GA

D. Darius Butler
graduate student
Vanderbilt University Divinity School
Nashville, TN

Iva E. Carruthers
Samuel DeWitt Proctor Conference

James H. Cone
Union Theological Seminary
New York, NY

Keri Harrison Day
Brite Divinity School
Fort Worth, TX

Kelly Brown Douglas
Goucher College
Baltimore, MD

Sharon Watson Fluker
The Fund for Theological Education
Atlanta, Georgia

Dianne D. Glave
Center for Bioenvironmental Research
Tulane and Xavier Universities
New Orleans, LA

Jacquelyn Grant
The Interdenominational Theological Center
Atlanta, GA

Horace L. Griffin
The General Theological Seminary of the Episcopal Church
New York, NY

Forrest E. Harris
Director, Kelly Miller Smith Institute on Black Church Studies
The Divinity School, Vanderbilt University
President, American Baptist College
Nashville, TN

James H. Harris
Second Baptist Church and
Virginia Union University
Richmond, VA

Diana L. Hayes
Georgetown University
Washington, DC

Renee L. Hill
Lambda Legal Defense and Educational Fund
New York, NY

Dwight N. Hopkins
University of Chicago Divinity School
Chicago, IL

Brandee Jasmine Mimitzraiem
graduate student
Garrett-Evangelical Theological Seminary
Evanston, IL

Jamie T. Phelps, OP
Xavier University
New Orleans, LA

Alton B. Pollard III
Howard University Divinity School
Washington, DC

Patricia A. Reeberg
Saint Paul Baptist Church
Bronx, NY

J. Alfred Smith Sr.
Allen Temple Baptist Church, Oakland, CA
American Baptist Seminary of the West
and the Graduate Theological Union, Berkeley, CA

Linda E. Thomas
Lutheran School of Theology at Chicago
Chicago, IL

Emilie M. Townes
Yale Divinity School
New Haven, CT

Dennis W. Wiley
Covenant Baptist Church
Washington, DC

Jeremiah A. Wright Jr.
Pastor Emeritus
Trinity United Church of Christ
Chicago, IL

Josiah U. Young
Wesley Theological Seminary
Washington, DC

# Scripture Index